models *of* counseling

gifted children, adolescents,
and young adults

models *of* counseling
counseling
gifted children, adolescents, and young adults

edited by

Sal **Mendaglio**, Ph.D.

& Jean Sunde **Peterson**, Ph.D.

PRUFROCK PRESS INC.
WACO, TX

Library of Congress Cataloging-in-Publication Data

Models of counseling gifted children, adolescents, and young adults / edited by Sal Mendaglio &
Jean Sunde Peterson.
    p. cm.
  Includes bibliographical references.
  ISBN-13: 978-1-59363-206-9 (pbk.)
  ISBN-10: 1-59363-206-1
  1. Gifted children—Education. 2. Gifted children—Counseling of. 3. Educational counseling. I.
Mendaglio, Sal, 1946– II. Peterson, Jean Sunde, 1941–
  LC3993.2.M595 2007
  371.95—dc22
                                              2006020737

Prufrock Press Inc.
P.O. Box 8813
Waco, TX 76714-8813
Phone: (800) 998-2208
Fax: (800) 240-0333
http://www.prufrock.com

To our spouses—our partners and best friends,
Barbara and Reuben

Contents

Part III: Conclusion

chapter 11

PART I
Introduction

chapter 1

Introduction

by Sal Mendaglio

A few years ago, I was counseling a family of a gifted child named Johnny (a pseudonym), who was displaying a variety of behaviors that were disturbing to both his teachers and parents. Johnny had seen a number of helping professionals, both school-based and independent. The most recent professional that his parents had consulted was a child psychiatrist who suspected that Johnny had Asperger's syndrome. At the parents' request, I met with the psychiatrist a number of times to provide input into her treatment plan for Johnny. During those meetings, with parents present, I suggested alternate explanations for some of Johnny's behaviors, based on my model of counseling gifted individuals. Rather than interpreting the behaviors as symptoms, I proposed that they be seen as manifestations of giftedness. In one of the meetings, the mother asked the psychiatrist whether she had any knowledge of giftedness, to which the psychiatrist responded that she did not. When Johnny's mother asked why that was the case, the psychiatrist replied, "Because Sal has been stingy with his knowledge." All present laughed at the remark, but it left an indelible impression on me. Prior to that remark, I had been generally aware that giftedness was not a topic covered by programs preparing counselors and psychologists because I was teaching in a graduate program for such professionals. However, that child psychiatrist's remark emphasized the need for providing resources for helping professionals regarding counseling gifted individuals. Helping professionals do indeed encounter gifted individuals of all ages as clients or patients.

At the time of that seminal incident, I was well aware of the dearth of publications on counseling gifted individuals. Literature searches revealed a multitude of citations using the keywords *counseling* and *gifted*; however, very few related directly to conducting counseling with clients who are gifted. This state of affairs is reflected in the current literature in the field of gifted education. Though the psychological study of giftedness in North America had its origins in the early part of last century with the work of Terman (1925), some 80 years later there are still precious few book titles on counseling gifted individuals. The few available include Ziv (1977), Colangelo and Zaffrann (1979), and Silverman (1993). These provide useful insights for counseling professionals, but the content of these books does not provide theoretical approaches to counseling that practitioners can use to guide their practice or develop their own approaches to counseling gifted individuals. In contrast, this book is designed to provide practitioners and students in the helping professions (i.e., counselors, social workers, psychologists, and psychiatrists) models of counseling, developed by experienced counselors of gifted individuals.

Readers will discover that this book, although focused on clients who are gifted, represents a microcosm of the field of counseling and psychotherapy. The eight models presented in this book are diverse approaches to counseling gifted individuals. The variety of the models reflects, on a small scale, the diversity seen in the field of counseling and psychotherapy, which is said to contain about 300 approaches (Cormier & Cormier, 1998). Readers familiar with the field of counseling and psychotherapy will see references to familiar theories in many of the models, though some models represent unique perspectives.

Another similarity to the field of counseling and psychotherapy is the use of the term *counseling* in the title. Texts dealing with approaches to psychological interventions have used *psychotherapy* (e.g., Corsini & Wedding, 1989), *counseling* (e.g., Gladding, 1996), and both *counseling* and *psychotherapy* (e.g., Corey, 2005) in their titles to refer to the same theories. For example, in some texts, Rogers' person-centered therapy is a theory of psychotherapy (Corsini & Wedding), but in another text, it is presented as a theory of counseling (Gladding). In this book, *counseling* and *therapy* (the abbreviated form of psychotherapy) are synonymous, as they also are in the field.

A final similarity between this book and the field of counseling is the presentation of the models. A chapter outline was developed and distributed to all contributors. The outline was based on the organizational structure of established texts in the field of counseling. To construct the outline, I perused popular counseling and psychotherapy textbooks (e.g., Corey, 1996; Corsini & Wedding, 1989). A primary motivation for the final form of the chapter outline was to make the information accessible to the intended audiences (i.e.,

TABLE 1.1

Models Chapter Outline

Conception of Giftedness	Model of Counseling	Application
Influences	Influences	Presenting Problems
Definition	Definition of counseling	Case Illustration
Characteristics	Role of counselor	
Assumptions	Role of Client	
Conception of Personality	Goals	
Personality	Relationship	
Personality of gifted individuals	Assessment	
	Process	

students and practitioners in the field of counseling and psychotherapy) by using a format familiar to them. Each chapter includes headings that relate to both counseling and giftedness.

The chapter outline was created for three additional reasons. First, the outline was intended to facilitate contributors' articulation of their models. All lead contributors had experience in counseling gifted individuals, but none had an explicit, comprehensive version of their models, at least not in the form needed for the present volume. Given the uniqueness of the undertaking, the chapter outline was designed to help contributors formally communicate approaches that they developed in the course of counseling gifted individuals. Second, the outline was developed to ensure that contributors would present their views on topics deemed relevant to the theme of the book. In my vision of this text, contributors needed to include their conceptions of giftedness and personality, key elements of the counseling process, and a case illustration. (See Table 1.1 for the outline used by the authors of the models chapters.) Third, the outline was intended to produce a consistency in the contributors' discussion of their models, which should help facilitate readers' comparison of the various approaches.

Models of Counseling the Gifted

There are three parts to the present volume. *Part 1: Introduction* includes two chapters. In this chapter, I have discussed the inspiration for embarking on the production of this book. I have briefly described how this volume reflects some of the characteristics of the field of counseling, as well as the development and rationale for a chapter outline for presenting the models.

In Chapter 2, Sidney Moon provides an overview of conceptions and issues related to counseling gifted individuals. She presents a detailed analysis of historical and current conceptions of giftedness, which will enable readers to fully appreciate the diverse conceptions of giftedness evident in the chapters in Part II. Moon's critical evaluation of the empirical and nonempirical literature related to counseling gifted individuals presents the state of the field of gifted education with respect to counseling. In addition to providing useful information, Moon's chapter serves as an expanded rationale for this book.

Part II: The Models contains eight models that are presented here, in this format, for the first time by our contributors. In general, the models are systematic eclectic approaches to counseling in which contributors have combined a variety of theoretical strands and their own conceptions of giftedness.

In Chapter 3, Sal Mendaglio describes his affective-cognitive therapy model that is used in his work with gifted individuals. Mendaglio's model infuses his conception of giftedness into an eclectic blend of humanistic and cognitive-behavioral theoretical approaches.

In Chapter 4, Volker Thomas, Karen Ray, and Sidney Moon describe their approach to counseling gifted individuals—a largely family-systems approach. Their model has also been influenced by humanistic and cognitive-behavioral counseling.

In Chapter 5, Jean Peterson describes her developmental approach—one that is used when counseling gifted youth. Based on humanistic and family-systems theories, Peterson's model is applicable to both remedial and preventive work with gifted youth.

In Chapter 6, Caryln Saunders presents a model forged from an array of sources. Influences for her approach are theorists in the humanistic tradition, theoretical perspectives on academic underachievement, and various researchers in gifted education.

In Chapter 7, Catherine Boland and Miraca Gross describe a model used in counseling highly gifted children and adolescents. Their model concerns itself with evidence-based practices for the treatment of psychological distress.

In Chapter 8, Andrew Mahoney, Don Martin, and Magy Martin describe a gifted-identity-formation model developed specifically for application with gifted children and adolescents. Similar to some of the other models, the Gifted Identity Formation model draws upon various theories of counseling, including systems, humanistic, cognitive-behavioral, solution-focused, and narrative.

In Chapter 9, Barbara Kerr describes her model of counseling gifted individuals, which focuses on talent development. Kerr's model is an intriguing blend of research-based strategies and shamanic creativity.

In Chapter 10, Albert Ziegler and Heidrun Stoeger describe an 11-step counseling-cycle model developed specifically for use with gifted students. Rooted in concepts derived from biology and sociology, the model also draws from learning theory, biographical research, and systems theory.

Part III: Conclusion contains the conclusion chapter. In Chapter 11, Jean Peterson provides a summary of the eight models. Using the headings found in the outline for the chapters on models, Peterson compares and contrasts the models and also includes a complex grid to facilitate comparing and contrasting.

References

Colangelo, N., & Zaffrann, R. T. (1979). *New voices in counseling the gifted*. Dubuque, IA: Kendall Hunt.

Corey, G. (1996). *Theory and practice of counseling and psychotherapy* (4th ed.). Pacific Grove, CA: Brooks/Cole.

Corey, G. (2005). *Theory and practice of counseling and psychotherapy* (6th ed.). Pacific Grove, CA: Brooks/Cole.

Cormier, S., & Cormier, B. (1998). *Interview strategies for helpers*. Pacific Grove, CA: Brooks/Cole.

Corsini, R., & Wedding, D. (1989). *Current psychotherapies* (4th ed.). Itasca, IL: F. E. Peacock.

Gladding, S. T. (1996). *Counseling a comprehensive profession*. Englewood Cliffs, NJ: Merrill.

Silverman, L. K. (Ed.). (1993). *Counseling the gifted and talented*. Denver: Love.

Terman, L. M. (1925). *Genetic studies of genius: Vol. 1. Mental and physical traits of a thousand gifted children*. Stanford, CA: Stanford University Press.

Ziv, A. (1977). *Counseling the intellectually gifted child*. Toronto, Ontario, Canada: Guidance Centre University of Toronto.

chapter 2

Counseling Issues
and Research

by Sidney M. Moon

By definition, gifted children and adolescents are different from the norm. Their differences create both resilience and stress for them and their families (Neihart, Reis, Robinson, & Moon, 2002). In order to work effectively with gifted children and their families, counselors need to have a basic understanding of the unique characteristics and needs of gifted and talented youth. Understanding is a prerequisite to the creation of a positive therapeutic relationship. The therapeutic relationship, in turn, is one of the most important common factors underlying successful therapy (Sprenkle & Blow, 2004). The purposes of this chapter are (a) to give counselors and psychologists an overview of current conceptions of giftedness, (b) to help counselors and psychologists understand the characteristics and adjustment issues of gifted youth, and (c) to provide an overview of the existing research on counseling interventions designed specifically for gifted and talented children.

What Is Giftedness?

Easy to pose and hard to answer, the question of what constitutes giftedness is one that all professionals who work with gifted and talented youth need to consider. The question has been answered differently in various historical periods and by various scholars. Controversy continues to exist over the definition of *giftedness*. There is no clear consensus about giftedness even in the field of gifted and talented studies. The question tends to be answered differently by researchers, parents, and school personnel. Researchers often rely on psychometric definitions because such definitions are easy to operationalize with existing measurement instruments like intelligence tests or off-grade-level aptitude tests. Parents, on the other hand, tend to place more weight on behavioral characteristics that they can observe, especially with very young children. For example, they begin wondering if their 3-year-old child might be gifted when they see that the child can recognize colors and shapes and write all of the letters of the alphabet. School personnel who define giftedness are usually doing so to decide which children need, and would benefit from, gifted and talented programming. Hence, they are making high-stakes decisions that affect children's lives. Like researchers, they lean toward easily measured characteristics, but, unlike researchers, they may use a committee to make the final decision about giftedness using multiple sources of evidence, some formal, such as achievement tests, and some informal, such as teacher or peer nominations. As these examples demonstrate, there are a wide range of conceptions of giftedness and a wide variety of ways to operationalize it. Counselors who work with gifted children can benefit from knowledge of the historical development and current conceptions of giftedness. With this knowledge, they have a conceptual schema to understand why particular individuals with whom they are working might be called gifted and how their giftedness might influence their psychosocial development and the counseling process.

A Brief History of Conceptions of Giftedness

Although unusual abilities have been noted anecdotally for many centuries, the scientific study of giftedness is a fairly recent phenomenon. Early research on giftedness focused on general intelligence. Galton (1822–1911) was one of the first scientists to become interested in measuring attributes of human beings, including intelligence (Galton, 1869, 1883). A cousin of Charles Darwin, Galton is widely considered to be the first to study individual differences in intelligence. Based on his belief that "genius" had a strong hereditary component, he developed the notion that most individual-difference traits, including intelligence, were distributed according to a bell-curve pattern with most individuals falling in the average range and a few falling at the extremes. He called those in the upper extremes of intelligence "geniuses."

Binet, a French psychologist, built on these ideas by developing the first individual intelligence test to measure what average children ages 3–11 could be expected to do so that it would be easier to determine which children might struggle with the academic tasks of typical elementary schools. Further test development followed, essentially operationalizing *intelligence* as the ability to do the tasks on the tests. In other words, psychological measurement drove early conceptualizations of intelligence and giftedness.

In the 1920s, Lewis Terman, a precocious scholar from rural Indiana who worked at Stanford University in California, developed the Stanford-Binet Intelligence test (Terman, 1916). Terman (1925) used his new test to find elementary school children who had a measured IQ more than two standard deviations above the mean on the test. This work represented the first attempt to identify gifted children through a psychological test and is considered by many to be the beginning of the field of gifted education. Terman then followed the identified students for many years, in the process revealing a great deal about the unique needs and characteristics of these such individuals (Terman & Oden, 1959).

A different way of looking at abilities began with the work of Charles Spearman. Spearman (1904) was the first psychologist to develop a theory of individual differences in intelligence. He was also the inventor of a technique called factor analysis that has been used to identify abilities. Spearman theorized that intelligence was a general capacity to process information, a capacity he called *g*, or general intelligence.

Thurstone (1931, 1947), a psychologist from the Carnegie Institute of Technology, built on Spearman's work to create more sophisticated methods of factor analysis. He then applied his factor-analytic methods to the study of cognitive abilities. Whereas Spearman had identified a single general factor of intelligence, Thurstone's methods identified seven specific abilities, which he called Primary Mental Abilities (Thurstone, 1938). The abilities he identified were word fluency, verbal comprehension, number facility, memory, induction, spatial perception, and perceptual speed.

More recently, John Carroll (1993) conducted a massive survey of a large volume of factor-analytic studies of cognitive abilities. Carroll's results synthesized the work of Spearman and Thurstone, creating a model of cognitive abilities that was organized hierarchically with the general *g* factor identified by Spearman at the top of the hierarchy and a smaller subset of more specific cognitive abilities, like those identified by Thurstone, in the next tier of the hierarchy. The specific abilities Carroll identified in the second tier of the hierarchy included language, reasoning, memory, visual perception, idea production, and knowledge. Each of these broad areas of specific abilities was composed of many discrete skills and abilities, creating a three-tiered model of human ability. In the factor-analytic tradition, gifted individuals are those who have high levels of general intelligence in combination with high ability in one or more of the specific areas in the second tier of the model. However, gifted individuals usually are not equally gifted in *all* of the second-tier-level abilities.

As a result, these approaches suggest that there are large individual differences within the gifted population.

Current Conceptions of Giftedness

Conceptions of giftedness have changed over time (Tannenbaum, 2000). Notions of giftedness are influenced by culture, politics, and research findings (Moon & Rosselli, 2000). Historically, the trend has been from narrow, intellectual conceptions of giftedness, like the one proposed by Terman, to broader, more inclusive definitions, like the one embedded in Carroll's model of human cognitive abilities. For example, Gardner (1983, 1999) speaks of multiple intelligences, only three of which are measured on traditional intelligence tests. Sternberg (2000) conceptualizes giftedness as developing expertise, a more dynamic way of conceptualizing advanced abilities than that proposed by either Carroll or Gardner. Renzulli (1978, 1986) focuses on the development of gifted behaviors, another dynamic view of giftedness. He believes that gifted performances require average ability, not exceptional IQ, in combination with creativity and task commitment.

Gagné (1985, 1999, 2000) combines many of these more current conceptions into a complex theory that suggests that raw abilities (gifts) of many kinds are converted into demonstrated talents through a long-term process that involves intrapersonal and environmental catalysts. Gagné (1998) has also presented a proposal for considering subcategories, or levels of giftedness, within any particular talent domain. Gagné's theory is considered by many to be the most comprehensive and valid of the current theories of giftedness. A graphic description of his theory is reproduced in Figure 2.1.

The various types of conceptual definitions of giftedness have been summarized by Moon (2006) in five categories: psychometric, neurobiological/cognitive, creative-productive, psychosocial, and composite. Definitions in each of these categories have been used to operationalize conceptions of giftedness and create very specific procedures for identifying gifted children in school settings (see Table 2.1).

Sternberg and Davidson have developed a framework for categorizing conceptions of giftedness for research purposes (Sternberg, 1985; Sternberg & Davidson, 1986). They categorize conceptions into two broad categories: implicit and explicit theories. Implicit approaches are primarily theoretical. They cannot be empirically tested except by showing that other people have similar implicit theories. Explicit theories, on the other hand, are testable. According to Sternberg and Davidson, explicit theorists "presuppose definitions, and seek to interrelate such definitions to a network of psychological or educational theory and data" (p. 3). Explicit theories, in turn, can be subdivided into three research traditions or approaches: cognitive, developmental, and domain-specific.

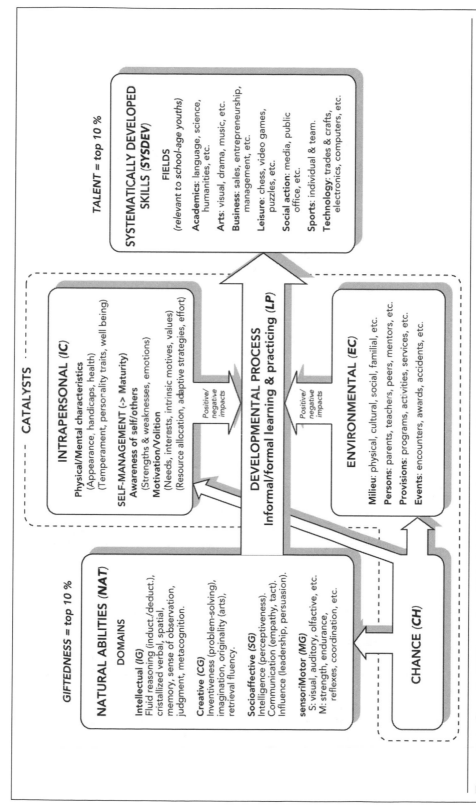

Figure 2.1. Gagné's Differentiated Model of Giftedness and Talent

Note. From "Talent Development in Sports," by J. H. A. Van Rossum and F. Gagné in F. A. Dixon and S. M. Moon (Eds.), *The Handbook of Secondary Gifted Education* (p. 283), 2006, Waco, TX: Prufrock Press. Copyright ©2006 by Prufrock Press. Reprinted with permission.

TABLE 2.1

Current Conceptions of Giftedness and Their Operationalization in School Settings

1. *Psychometric*—definitions based on test scores. Examples: Terman (Terman, 1925) defined giftedness as a score over 140 on the Stanford-Binet IQ test and Stanley and his colleagues (Benbow & Stanley, 1983; Stanley, 1996) defined giftedness as a high score on an off-grade-level test of mathematical or verbal reasoning ability. These definitions are very easy to operationalize; in fact, they are examples of situations where conceptual and operational definitions merge. Some states have adopted psychometric definitions of giftedness.

2. *Neurobiological/Cognitive*—definitions based on findings from neuroscience and/or cognitive science. Carroll's model of human cognitive abilities is a good example of this approach (Carroll, 1993). Gardner's multiple intelligences and Sternberg's analytical, creative, and practical intelligences are additional examples (Gardner, 1999; Sternberg, 1985; Sternberg & Clinkenbeard, 1995). These definitions are somewhat harder to operationalize through standardized tests than those that are psychometric and generally are operationalized with multiple measures, including both tests, when available, and performance-based assessments.

3. *Creative-Productive*—definitions based on examining the life histories of creative-productive adults. Renzulli's three-ring conception of giftedness is an example (Renzulli, 1978). These definitions are usually operationalized with multiple measures, including standardized tests of intellectual ability and academic achievement in combination with authentic assessments, interviews, teacher/peer/self nominations, and other subjective measures of talent potential.

4. *Psychosocial*—definitions that emphasize the role of both the individual and his/her environment in the development of giftedness. Tannenbaum (Tannenbaum, 1986) and and Gagné (2000) are examples of scholars who have developed psychosocial conceptions of giftedness. These definitions provide the broadest possible framework for giftedness and, as a result, provide the least guidance for creating operational definitions for specific programming options.

5. *Composite*—definitions that borrow from multiple theoretical perspectives. The 1972 Marland Report (Marland, 1972) and the 1993 *National Excellence* report (U.S. Department of Education, 1993) promote composite definitions of giftedness for school settings. Legal definitions are often composite definitions modeled after the original Marland Report definition. The Jacob Javits Act includes a composite definition of giftedness, and many state definitions are composite definitions. Composite definitions are generally operationalized with separate multiple-assessment identification procedures for each of the talent areas addressed (e.g., intellectual, academic, creative, visual and performing arts, leadership).

Note. Adapted from "Developing a Definition of Giftedness," by S. M. Moon, in J. H. Purcell and R. D. Eckert (Eds.), *A Guidebook for Developing Educational Services and Programs* (pp. 23–31), 2006, Thousand Oaks, CA: Corwin Press.

In spite of the rich fabric of current theoretical definitions of giftedness, most of the research literature on gifted children tends to define giftedness either by scores on standardized tests or by participation in school or university programming for academically gifted students. In public school settings, the most common ways to operationalize giftedness are (a) IQ test scores one or more standard deviations above the norm, (b) achievement test scores in a specific academic area, or (c) selection by an identification committee based on assessment data that is both quantitative and qualitative (e.g., test scores, student portfolios, interviews, rating scales, etc.; Johnsen, 2004). The latter method is considered best practice because it uses multiple measures to create a profile of each child's strengths and weaknesses and is more likely to be culture-fair and bias-free.

Behavioral Characteristics

Often giftedness is initially identified through astute observation of the behaviors of a gifted child, especially when children are very young. Parents and other adults who interact with a 3-year-old child who has a large vocabulary and can write her name can see the child's intellectual ability demonstrated in the things that she can do. Giftedness can be identified through behavioral checklists of typical behaviors that can be observed in children who have high cognitive ability. Such checklists are generally included in textbooks on how to identify and work with gifted, creative, and talented children. An example of a typical checklist of the characteristics of gifted learners is given in Table 2.2.

One problem with many of these informal behavioral checklists is that they mix cognitive, affective, and conative items on the same scale. For example, the checklist shown in Table 2.2 includes several conative items such as "is an independent worker," "has lots of initiative," and "has a long attention span." While these may be characteristic of many gifted individuals, they often are not characteristic of the gifted persons who seek the services of professional psychologists and counselors. These individuals are more likely to be bright individuals who are underachieving due to problems such as depression, Attention Deficit/Hyperactivity Disorder (ADHD), family conflicts, and/or anxiety. Such individuals often have difficulties sustaining attention, taking initiative, and working independently. Hence, such mixed behavioral checklists should be used with caution by psychologists.

Psychologists who want to use behavioral checklists to screen for giftedness in their practice should use ones that include only cognitive items and/or create their own by lifting the purely cognitive items from existing checklists. For the checklist in Table 2.2 these would be items like "has a large vocabulary," "has a good memory for things heard or read," and "understands relationships and comprehends meanings." Cultural issues need to be taken into consideration when clinicians use behavioral checklists to identify giftedness. For example, it is hard to assess intelligence through behavior if the child is

T A B L E   2 . 2

Characteristics of Gifted Learners and Curriculum Implications

Characteristics of the Gifted Learner	Curriculum Implications
Reads well and widely	Individualize a reading program that diagnoses reading level and prescribes reading material based on that level Form a literary group of similar students for discussions Develop critical reading skills Focus on analysis and interpretation in reading material
Has a large vocabulary	Introduce a foreign language Focus on vocabulary building Develop word relationship skills (antonyms, homonyms, and so on)
Has a good memory for things heard or read	Have student present ideas on a topic to the class Have student prepare a skit or play for production Build in Trivial Pursuit activities
Is curious and asks probing questions	Develop an understanding of the scientific method Focus on observation skills
Is an independent worker and has lots of initiative	Focus on independent project work Teach organizational skills and study skills
Has a long attention span	Assign work that is long-term Introduce complex topics for reading, discussion, and project work
Has complex thoughts and ideas	Work on critical thinking skills (analysis, synthesis, evaluation) Develop writing skills
Is widely informed about many topics	Stimulate broad reading patterns Develop special units of study that address current interests
Shows good judgment and logic	Organize a field trip for the class Prepare a parent night Teach formal logic
Understands relationships and comprehends meanings	Provide multidisciplinary experiences Structure activities that require students to work across fields on special group/individual projects Organize curriculum by issues and examine those issues from different perspectives (e.g., poverty—economic, social, personal, education views)
Produces original or unusual products or ideas	Practice skills of fluency, flexibility, elaboration, and originality Work on specific product development

Note. From *Comprehensive Curriculum for Gifted Learners* (2nd ed., pp. 158–159), by J. VanTassel-Baska, 1994, Boston: Allyn & Bacon. Copyright ©1994 by Allyn & Bacon. Reprinted with permission.

not fluent in English. In addition, children generally do not exhibit behaviors that are not valued in their culture, and some cultures do not value all of the traits that are commonly included on behavioral checklists to identify giftedness (Peterson, 1999).

A few more formal checklists have been developed and validated for educational purposes. These checklists are generally used to identify gifted and talented children for enriched and accelerated school programs in one or more academic areas. It would be helpful for measurement specialists to design a short screening instrument for giftedness that could be used by psychologists to assess whether a particular client should be referred for a more comprehensive psychological assessment of intelligence. If such an instrument were based on one of the modern theoretical conceptions of giftedness and included only cognitive items, it could be used by psychologists to determine if giftedness was affecting their client's experiences and should be taken into account during the counseling process. Even with such an instrument, however, cultural issues would need to be considered, as the instrument might not be equally effective in identifying talented children in all cultures.

Affective and Conative Issues

Most adults who work with gifted children believe these children experience unique affective (social/emotional) and conative (motivational) issues throughout their development (Moon, 2003b; Moon, Kelly, & Feldhusen, 1997). This is true even though group comparison research consistently finds that gifted children are as well adjusted or even better adjusted than comparison groups of average-ability children (Neihart et al., 2002). These unique issues include being different from their chronological age peers and having career goals that require extended schooling.

There is little evidence, however, that gifted children have unique temperaments. Instead, there are large within-group differences in temperament in the gifted population that give rise to even larger differences in affective, conative, and personality characteristics. It is important for psychologists to understand that the gifted population is far from homogenous, especially with respect to their psychological and social characteristics. Hence, counseling with gifted individuals needs to be sufficiently individualized to take these differences into account.

At the same time, there is some research that suggests that groups of gifted individuals possess some social, emotional, and personality traits in greater abundance than the norm. For example, Silverman (1998) reports that research done with Dabrowski's concept of overexcitabilities (see Table 2.3) suggests that gifted persons have higher than average levels of intellectual and emotional overexcitability (Gallagher, 1985; Piechowski & Colangelo, 1984; Piechowski & Cunningham, 1985; Schiever, 1985; Silverman, 1998). Emotional overexcitability includes intensity of feelings and emotions, strong somatic and affective

TABLE 2.3

Forms and Expressions of Psychic Overexcitability

Psychomotor
  Surplus of energy
  Psychomotor expression of emotional tension

Sensual
  Enhanced sensory and aesthetic pleasure
  Sensual expression of emotional tension

Intellectual
  Intensified activity of the mind
  Penchant for probing questions
  Interest in solving problems

Imaginational
  Free play of the imagination
  Capacity for fantasy
  Spontaneous imagery as an expression of emotional tension
  Low tolerance for boredom

Emotional
  Intensified feelings and emotions
  Strong somatic expressions
  Strong affective expressions
  Capacity for strong attachments, deep relationships
  Well-differentiated feelings toward self

Note. Adapted from *Criteria for Rating the Intensity of Overexcitabilities* by R. F. Falk, M. Piechowski, and S. Lind, 1994, unpublished manuscript, University of Akron, Department of Sociology, and from "Developmental Potential" by M. M. Piechowski, in N. Colangelo and R. T. Zaffran (Eds.), *New Voices in Counseling the Gifted* (pp. 25–57), 1979, Dubuque, IA: Kendall/Hunt.

expressions, capacity for deep relationships, and well-differentiated feelings toward the self. All of these characteristics are relevant to social/emotional adjustment and may affect the course of therapy with gifted and talented persons. In addition, gifted adolescents have been found to have elevated levels of imaginational overexcitability (Gallagher; Schiever), and gifted artists tend to have higher emotional and imaginational overexcitabilities than intellectually gifted persons who are not artists (Piechowski, Silverman, & Falk, 1985). Among gifted students, family membership and gender account for most of the variation in overexcitability scores (Tieso, 2004). Tieso found that mothers' imaginational and emotional overexcitability scores had significant positive effects on their gifted children's scores, while fathers' imaginational overexcitability had a negative effect on their children's imaginational scores. Tieso also found that gifted females tend to score higher on emotional excitability and gifted males score higher on intellectual excitability.

Similarly, personality research conducted with the Myers-Briggs Type Inventory suggests that gifted individuals come in all 16 MBTI types, but are not equally distributed among the types. The primary type found among gifted elementary-aged children is INFP, and the primary type found among gifted adolescents is INTP (Silverman, 1998). In general, gifted persons are much more likely to be intuitive types and introverts than typical individuals (Silverman). There is also evidence in the clinical literature that gifted persons are more sensitive than typical children (Mendaglio, 1995). Mendaglio defines *sensitivity* as having four components: self-awareness, perspective-taking, empathy, and emotional experience (i.e., awareness of one's own emotional states). Counselors need to understand these characteristics of gifted persons and use strategies that capitalize on their strengths and preferences.

The affective and conative development of gifted individuals is strongly influenced by their contexts and environments. As with other children, families, schools, and social systems all influence whether an individual child's characteristics lead to resilience or dysfunction. Environments that provide an appropriate balance of challenge and support are most likely to facilitate positive development in gifted children and adolescents (Csikszentmihalyi, Rathunde, & Whalen, 1993). As with other children, family dysfunction can derail the social/emotional development of gifted youth (Frey & Wendorf, 1985; Sowa & May, 1997; Wendorf & Frey, 1985).

A far more common negative influence on the social, emotional, and motivational development of gifted children, however, is an inappropriate school environment. An undifferentiated, on-grade-level school placement usually provides insufficient challenge for gifted students and/or leads to rejection by chronological age peers that do not understand or relate to the gifted children (Gross, 1993; Robinson, Reis, Neihart, & Moon, 2002). Hence, it is vitally important for counselors and psychologists to assess school situations when working with gifted children and adolescents. If gifted children are experiencing inappropriate school programming, the highest intervention priority may be to advocate for changes in the school setting that will enable the child to experience more appropriate levels of challenge and have opportunities to interact with cognitive peers in addition to, or instead of, chronological age peers. The higher the child's level of giftedness, the more important it becomes to pay attention to educational issues. If counselors do not have the expertise to assess the appropriateness of the school environment and advocate for appropriate changes, they should team with experts in gifted education for this aspect of their work with gifted children and adolescents.

Different issues tend to be salient for specific subpopulations of gifted and talented youth such as females, minorities, and the twice-exceptional. For example, African American students tend to experience peer cultures that do not support or are hostile to academic achievement (Ford, 1996; Steinberg, 1996). Gifted females face strong conflicts between affiliation and achievement, especially at the middle-school level (Clasen & Clasen, 1995; Reis, 1998). Gifted persons who have co-occurring Attention Deficit Disorder are at high risk for anxiety and depression because of the internal dyssynchrony they feel between their areas of ability and disability (Kaufmann, Kalbfleisch, & Castellanos, 2000; Moon, Zentall, Grskovic, Hall, & Stormont, 2001; Zentall, Moon, Hall, & Grskovic, 2001). Counselors who are aware of the typical issues affecting specific subpopulations of gifted students will be able to normalize their client's struggles and gather targeted resources to assist them in addressing their concerns. Some counselors choose to specialize in treating specific subpopulations of gifted students. For example, Linda Silverman, founder of the Gifted Development Center in Denver, CO, has developed a specialization in working with spatially gifted learners and, as a result, has become one of the leading national experts on the needs and characteristics of this subgroup of gifted students (Silverman, 2002).

More attention has been paid to the unique social/emotional adjustment issues facing gifted and talented children than to their unique conative, or motivational, issues. There are many reasons for this neglect of motivational issues in the field of gifted education. One is that giftedness and motivation are often blended or confused, as noted above in the section on behavioral characteristics. Such blending of motivational and cognitive characteristics creates the erroneous belief that all gifted students are highly motivated, especially for academic tasks. Another reason for the neglect can be framed in terms of Dweck's (1999) distinction between entity and incremental beliefs. Entity theorists believe, often unconsciously, that a trait is something one is born with, something one either has or does not have, and therefore cannot do much about; incremental theorists, on the other hand, believe that the same trait is a set of skills that can be developed. In the 20th century, the field of gifted education, like much of psychology, has tended to hold an entity view of motivation. One result of this entity orientation has been to divide gifted students into two categories: those with motivation (achievers) and those without it (underachievers). Motivation then becomes an issue only for the small subpopulation of gifted children and adolescents who are not doing well in school. Indeed, much of the research on motivation in the field of gifted education focuses on underachievers. Even theorists who feature motivation as an essential component of gifted performances have tended to see motivation through an entity lens (i.e., as something that either is or is not present in specific gifted persons at specific times). Only recently have scholars proposed that it is important to develop incremental theories of motivation that see motivation as a set of skills and dispositions that can be developed (Gottfried, Gottfried, Cook, & Morris, 2005; Moon, 2003b). These newer incremental theories are laying a necessary foundation for the development of counseling interventions focused on the development of specific motivational skills, and so they will be of strong interest to those in the counseling professions.

Counseling Interventions

Many scholars have written about how to differentiate educational environments for gifted and talented students (Maker & Nielson, 1996; Schiever & Maker, 2003; Tomlinson, 1995; VanTassel-Baska, 1994; VanTassel-Baska & Little, 2003; VanTassel-Baska, Zuo, Avery, & Little, 2002). Unfortunately, much less attention has been paid to how to differentiate counseling for gifted and talented students (Colangelo, 2003; Moon & Hall, 1998), in spite of the fact that the need for differentiated counseling for gifted students has been supported by survey research and the work of a few specialized clinics worldwide (Moon et al., 1997; Rimm, 2003; Silverman, 1993b; Wieczerkowski & Prado, 1991). A recent search of Psych Info yielded only 296 published papers using the search terms "gifted and counseling," 80 papers using the search terms "gifted and therapy," and 58 with the search terms "gifted and psychotherapy." There was some overlap in the papers found, and many dealt with giftedness only tangentially. Very few of the papers reported empirical studies; most of the literature on counseling gifted students is either theoretical or clinical.

However, some clinicians have developed models for counseling gifted students, and these models can provide provisional guidance for clinicians working with this population (Moon, 2003a; Reis & Moon, 2002; Rimm, 1995). One of the purposes of this chapter is to provide a schematic overview of the existing counseling models and to indicate which models are supported by empirical research. The models reviewed have been divided into two broad categories: guidance models and therapy models. The guidance models are brief, preventative models for guiding gifted children and their parents that can be implemented by school counselors in school settings. The therapy models are both brief and long-term intervention models that are best implemented by licensed psychologists, family therapists, social workers, and mental health counselors in private practice.

Guidance Models

Because the field of gifted education is dominated by educators, most of the counseling models that have been developed in the field are guidance models, rather than therapy models. Guidance models are appropriate for implementation in school settings. These models tend to focus on assessment and/or psychoeducation. Psychoeducational interventions recommended by the models include addressing typical affective issues affecting the gifted population, such as introversion, and/or typical issues facing parents who are raising a gifted child, such as how to encourage talent development. A few of the models focus on a specific subpopulation of gifted children. For example, Rimm's (1995, 2003) trifocal model focuses on underachievers. Some guidance models are implemented as a component of a gifted program. For example, the Autonomous Learner program model includes several components that address the affective needs of identified, gifted secondary students (Betts & Kercher, 1999). Sample individual, group, and family guidance models are discussed in more detail below.

Individual Guidance Models

One of the best-elaborated individual guidance models for working with gifted clients has been Silverman's (1993c) developmental model. This comprehensive model was based on Silverman's extensive clinical work specializing in assessing and guiding gifted persons. The model has three components: characteristics, interventions, and goals. The characteristics component suggests that counselors who work with gifted students need to take into account their unique intellectual characteristics, such as rapid learning rate, analytical and divergent thinking ability, and capacity for reflection, as well as their unique personality characteristics, such as intensity, sensitivity/empathy, and tendency toward introversion. Recommended interventions are broadly stated and address multiple spheres of influence, including the self, home, school, peers, and community. For example, grouping with peers is a recommended school/peer intervention, bibliotherapy a recommended self-intervention, and working with mentors a recommended community intervention. Silverman also recommended a wide array of counseling interventions including peer, family, individual, and support groups on an as-needed basis. The goals of counseling in Silverman's model were to create autonomous, ethical, altruistic, and self-actualizing individuals.

Silverman (1993d) believed that individual counseling could be valuable for gifted persons for two reasons: self-development and healing. Therapy for self-development is guidance work and will be discussed in this section. Therapy for healing will be discussed in the next section, as it is more similar to traditional psychotherapy. Silverman's self-development model suggested providing gifted clients with assistance with issues like career development, preparation for marriage, learning conflict-resolution skills, and actualizing talent potential. Career counseling has been recommended by several other psychologists and counselors who have experience in working with gifted students (Greene, 2002; Kelly, 1991; Kerr & Cheryl, 1991; Kerr, 1993). There is some empirical evidence that such counseling needs to be differentiated for gifted students because they have advanced career maturity (Kelly).

Developmental approaches to counseling have also been recommended by several other experts in gifted education (Colangelo, 2003; Colangelo & Assouline, 2000; Mahoney, 1997; VanTassel-Baska, 1998). For example, VanTassel-Baska recommends three types of school-based counseling provisions: academic program planning, life/career planning, and psychosocial counseling that focuses on the preservation of affective differences. VanTassel-Baska also recommends a number of specific strategies that teachers can use to promote the affective development of gifted students in the classroom. Each recommended strategy is linked to the social/emotional needs it addresses. To help gifted students gain realistic assessments of their abilities, she recommends regular assessment and homogeneous grouping. To develop social skills, she recommends teaching creative problem-solving skills, creating role-playing scenarios, and devising simulations.

Group Guidance Models

Two types of group models have been developed. One type provides guidance for working with gifted adolescents. For example, Colangelo and Peterson (1993) recommend working with voluntary groups of gifted students at the secondary level who want to explore questions such as "What does it mean to be gifted?" and "Have you ever deliberately hidden your giftedness? If so, why?" The objectives of this type of group counseling include helping gifted students understand what it means to be gifted; dealing with issues that are sometimes associated with giftedness, such as multipotentiality, perfectionism, and procrastination; coaching them on effective strategies for dealing with systems that are not adapted to their needs; and addressing gender issues. Group counseling models for gifted students can also focus on more general developmental concerns. Such groups are totally preventative in purpose. Guidance for this type of group can be found in the *Talk with Teens* series (Peterson, 1993, 1995). Peterson developed these two books for gifted adolescents, so the discussions suggested are appropriate for them.

Group counseling models have also been developed to guide parents of gifted children. For example, SENG, a national organization whose purpose is to support the social/emotional needs of gifted students, has developed a parent group model and published a guide for SENG facilitators to use when facilitating parent-guidance groups (Webb & DeVries, 1993).

Unfortunately, there is no empirical research supporting the efficacy of guidance groups for gifted students and/or their parents. Such research is needed before guidance groups can be unequivocally recommended. However, anecdotal and clinical evidence do support the value of such groups. The fact that both gifted individuals and their parents choose to participate in such groups voluntarily also suggests they are needed. Both types of guidance groups could be sponsored in an evening format by psychologists in private practice or community agency settings. Facilitators of guidance groups for gifted youth and their parents should be knowledgeable about giftedness, have positive attitudes toward gifted individuals and their families, and have good group counseling skills.

Family Guidance Models

Counselors from the guidance tradition often work with parents of gifted students, especially when they practice outside of school settings in university or community clinics. The presenting problems most often addressed with parents at family guidance clinics specializing in working with gifted students include school issues, parenting concerns, and social/emotional development (Moon, 2003a). Silverman's developmental model, which is discussed above as an individual model, includes work with parents of gifted children. For example, Silverman works with parents of gifted children on issues such as parental perceptions of competence, family relationships, provision of stimulation outside of school, strategies to foster self-discipline, and the need for helping parents understand their own giftedness and further their own development (Silverman, 1991, 1993a).

Most clinics that provide guidance for parents of gifted students also provide comprehensive assessment services (Moon, 2003a). If the assessment suggests that the child is gifted, guidance work begins with the parents to provide them with information about gifted children, help the parents learn strategies for supporting their child's development, and advocate for specialized school services (B. Gridley, personal communication, May 24, 2001; Wendorf & Frey, 1985; Wieczerkowski & Prado, 1991). Such clinics may also offer group counseling for parents following a model like the SENG parent group model discussed above. The primary strategy used for counseling is psychoeducation. The published literature on parent guidance is dominated by clinicians trained in individual therapy traditions, such as educational psychologists, counseling psychologists, school counselors, school psychologists, and clinical psychologists. Perhaps as a result, most of the models proposed are not fully systemic. They tend to deal separately with the parent and child subsystems and to focus the family component of their models on parental guidance rather than on interactions in the family system. Systemic family models are discussed in the family section of the therapy models below.

Therapy Models

As noted above, little attention has been paid to developing differentiated psychotherapy models for working with gifted persons. Indeed, this volume includes some of the first published reports from clinicians who have developed models for differentiating individual and family psychotherapy when working with gifted persons. In the review of prior literature, no published papers were found reporting on models for group therapy with gifted students or on strategies for differentiating other types of group therapy, such as substance-abuse recovery groups, for gifted participants. Therefore, group therapy models are not discussed here. There were a few reports of differentiated individual and family psychotherapy, and, therefore, this section focuses on those two areas. As with the guidance models, however, there is little empirical support for effectiveness of the therapy models reviewed.

Individual

Silverman (1993d) believed that individual psychotherapy is warranted when gifted students make suicidal statements, experience intense isolation or alienation, have difficulty expressing or controlling anger, act out sexually, give evidence of any kind of abuse, chronically underachieve, seem depressed, and/ or experience trauma or loss. These issues are similar to the issues that bring other children and adolescents into individual psychotherapy. When engaging in individual therapy with gifted students, Silverman suggested using play-therapy techniques for gifted children under the age of 10 and more adult techniques for older children. Specific therapeutic techniques recommended by Silverman for individual counseling included inviting the client to share feelings; using active listening; exploring positive aspects of the problem; helping clients analyze, clarify, and prioritize issues; using bibliotherapy to help students understand and solve personal problems; determining what can be changed; examining basic assumptions; reflecting discrepancies; assisting with goal setting; teaching stress-reduction techniques; asking clients to observe before attempting to change; recognizing and acknowledging progress; and knowing when to refer. Silverman also recommended family therapy for gifted clients with family issues. Experience working with gifted children is important in Silverman's model so that therapists do not misinterpret typical aspects of giftedness or allow themselves to be manipulated by their clients. Unfortunately, there are no empirical studies of Silverman's approach, and her model rests on a foundation of extensive experience with gifted and talented persons. Her model may not be effective when used by novice therapists who lack her experience and understanding of gifted individuals. There is, however, some research to support the use of some of the interventions recommended by Silverman. For example, there is empirical support for the effectiveness of bibliotherapy when working with gifted clients (Hébert, 1991, 2000).

Family

Family counseling has been recommended for gifted students with the following presenting problems: underachievement, dual exceptionalities, family conflict and/or transitions, and child internalizing or externalizing disorders (Moon, 2003a; Moon & Hall, 1998). Moon reviewed four types of systemic approaches to family therapy with families of gifted children: the Family FIRO Model (Colangelo & Assouline, 1993); structural-strategic approaches (Frey & Wendorf, 1985; Moon, Nelson, & Piercy, 1993; Wendorf & Frey, 1985); imaginative, postmodern approaches (Bourdeau & Thomas, 2003; Moon & Thomas, 2003; Thomas, 1995, 1999); and integrated approaches (Moon et al., 1993). All of these approaches have been utilized with reported success by university-based clinicians who specialize in working with gifted children. Detailed descriptions of the use of these approaches are available in the literature, but, as is so often the case, there is little research supporting the efficacy of the recommended interventions, and no studies have compared the models to each other.

Models for Specific Subpopulations

Twice-Exceptional

Assessment is an important issue in counseling any gifted student, and it is especially important for effectively counseling twice-exceptional students

(Colangelo, 2003; Moon & Hall, 1998; Webb et al., 2005). Unfortunately, assessment errors are common in the area of dual exceptionality. Two types of errors occur: (a) gifted students are misdiagnosed as having a disability that they do not actually have because their giftedness is misinterpreted; and (b) gifted students with co-occurring disabilities are not identified as either gifted or disabled because their giftedness masks their disability and their disability masks their giftedness. To prevent diagnostic errors, all assessments of gifted students for dual exceptionalities should be conducted by specialists with training in individualized assessment of gifted students and in the disorder being assessed. Detailed guidance for effective diagnostic work with gifted and talented children is provided in the book *Misdiagnosis and Dual Diagnoses of Gifted Children and Adults* (Webb et al.). This helpful volume covers assessment for many disorders, including ADHD, Oppositional Defiant Disorder, Narcissistic Personality Disorder, Obsessive-Compulsive Disorder, mood disorders, learning disabilities, and Asperger's syndrome.

Once gifted students are accurately assessed as having a co-occurring disorder, counseling can be helpful. Individual, family, and group counseling have been recommended for twice-exceptional students (Mendaglio, 1993; Moon & Hall, 1998). Mendaglio recommends individual or group therapy for twice-exceptional students. Techniques recommended for both individual and group therapy with twice-exceptional students include structuring, checking perceptions, and asking open questions. Individual therapy is recommended for twice-exceptional students who have experienced emotional trauma and/or who have severe behavior problems. Group therapy is recommended for addressing typical issues facing twice-exceptional students, such as frustration with the internal discrepancies they experience between areas of ability and disability or peer rejection. Mendaglio likes using group counseling with these students because of the therapeutic value of students learning that others share similar problems. In addition, small groups are an ideal vehicle for learning social skills, which are often deficient in twice-exceptional students. Peer feedback may be more effective in stimulating positive changes in the behavior of twice-exceptional students than adult feedback, and groups provide a good setting for constructive feedback from peers. Mendaglio also stresses that it is essential that counselors who work with these students, whether individually or in groups, have dispositions that facilitate counseling, such as patience, tolerance, and understanding of the unique issues facing twice-exceptional individuals. Finally, Mendaglio recommends that interventions for twice-exceptional students focus on the affective domain and take a multidimensional approach, addressing the entire student system by viewing parents and teachers as clients along with the student. Moon and Hall also recommend a systemic approach when working with twice-exceptional students, although they promote family therapy as the primary modality. Moon and Hall recommend family therapy for these students because it ensures that the parents see themselves as clients and enables the therapist to work with parents to de-pathologize the behaviors of the twice-exceptional child, advocate for appropriate school services, and create a supportive emotional system at home.

Underachievers

The current state of research on underachievement was summarized in a review published in *Gifted Child Quarterly* (Reis & McCoach, 2000). Reis and McCoach summarized the various ways that *underachievement* has been defined in the literature and the intrapersonal and interpersonal factors that have been found to be associated with underachievement. They also noted that research on interventions to reverse underachievement is scarce and that the research that has been done on interventions tends to yield mixed or inconclusive results.

Underachievement has been cited as the most frequent presenting problem for counseling clinics specializing in work with gifted children and their families (Colangelo, 2003). Clinical recommendations for working with underachievers have been developed (Colangelo; Rimm, 2003; Weiner, 1992). Colangelo recommended viewing underachievement as a relationship between the gifted student and his or her teachers, parents, or peers, rather than as a psychometric event, and recommends focusing on breaking the attention-getting cycle by ignoring the underachieving behavior and positively reinforcing achievement behaviors. Weiner recommended differentiating interventions for various types of underachievers based on whether their primary issue is deficient reward systems, cognitive or emotional handicaps, passive-aggressive tendencies, or educational gaps. He recommends counseling interventions for the first three types and educational interventions for the last type. For underachievers with deficient reward systems, his recommendations parallel those of Colangelo. For students with cognitive or emotional handicaps, his recommendations are similar to those noted above for working with twice-exceptional students. For underachievers with passive-aggressive tendencies, he recommended family therapy, noting that the therapy is more likely to be successful if the student is a willing participant in therapy. Other clinicians have supported the value of family therapy as an effective treatment modality for underachievement, especially for students in elementary or middle school (Moon & Hall, 1998).

Rimm has developed an elaborate, systemic model for intervention to reverse underachievement among gifted students that she calls the Trifocal Model (Rimm, 1995, 2003). Although there have not been any independent, scientific studies of the Trifocal Model, Rimm (1995) has stated that the approach has been successful in reversing underachievement in 4 out of 5 students who come to her Family Achievement Clinic for assistance with underachieving behaviors. The Trifocal Model focuses simultaneously on the individual, the home system, and the school system. The model has six steps, beginning with an extensive assessment to determine the extent and direction of the child's underachievement. The assessment is followed by (a) communication with parents and teachers via conferences; (b) interventions to change expectations of students, peers, siblings, parents, and teachers; (c) encouragement of underachiever identification with positive role models; and (d) correction of specific skill deficits. These initial five steps are then followed by more targeted interventions, which are differentiated for various types of underachievers. Rimm's assessment model categorizes underachievers into three types: dependent, dominant conforming, and dominant nonconforming. The model specifies different interventions for each of the three types to conclude the intervention process.

Other Individual Differences

Although gender and ethnicity do not usually bring gifted persons to counseling, these individual differences can affect gifted students' identity and development. Therefore, it is important for counselors who work with gifted and talented persons to be aware of ways in which gender and ethnicity affect the identify development of gifted persons, peer relationships, achievement, and the counseling process (Ford, Harris, & Schuerger, 1993; Plucker, 1996, 1998; Reis, 1998). For example, gifted females face both internal and external barriers to talent development because of stereotyping and sociocultural conditioning (Reis, 2002). Achievement-affiliation conflicts can develop among African Americans when, as is often the case, their peer culture is not supportive of academic achievement (Clasen & Clasen, 1995; Ford, 1996; Steinberg, 1996). Other individual differences that can affect counseling include sexual orientation (Cohn, 2002; Peterson & Rischar, 2000), creativity (Fishkin, Cramond, & Olszewski-Kubilius, 1999), and, as noted earlier, disabilities. Hence, psychologists who work with gifted students need to be knowledgeable about both giftedness and individual differences in the gifted population.

Conclusion

In summary, although it is clear that gifted and talented youth have unique social and emotional issues that warrant differentiated counseling intervention, most psychologists are not trained to address these issues, and very little empirical research exists to guide counseling practice with gifted individuals. The current volume makes a major contribution to the literature by summarizing a wide variety of counseling models that have been utilized by clinicians who are working with gifted youth.

As shown in Table 11.1 on pp. 295–299, the models vary greatly in their theoretical underpinnings, conceptions of giftedness, and assumptions. The approaches they take to the counseling process, however, are remarkably similar. All of the approaches take a positive psychology perspective and emphasize interactive techniques that facilitate optimal development, rather than a pathology-oriented approach based on the medical model of therapy. The approaches described here were co-created with high-potential individuals. They stress the development of human potential, convey respect for the client, and create a sense of partnership in the therapeutic process. Underlying all the approaches is a belief that clients have the solutions to their problems within them. The role of the counselor in the models discussed is fluid and ambiguous, rather than clearly defined by a detailed treatment manual. The counselor is seen as a change agent who works with the client in a process that cannot be completely predicted, but emerges creatively from therapeutic dialogue.

Although it was not the original intent of this volume to blaze new trails in psychotherapy, it seems quite possible that the innovative work reported here can inform psychotherapy in general. Perhaps psychologists can learn from their work with talented youth how to assist all of their clients in playing an active part in the counseling process. Counseling with the gifted is strength based. It is focused on full development of potential, in addition to remediating problems. It builds on strengths and encourages self-reflection, goal setting, and autonomy. Although this type of counseling seems particularly well-suited to gifted and talented clients, it may be beneficial in preventative counseling with a wide range of youth.

In the language of theory, the counseling models reported in this volume encourage gifted students to increase personal talent (Moon, 2003b)—that is, the ability to both set and achieve difficult goals and create a satisfying life. This volume provides several well-defined models for counseling procedures that build personal talent in gifted youth. Most are brief therapy models limited to 1–10 sessions. All are specified in sufficient detail for replication. It is hoped that the clear presentation of the practice-validated models in this volume will stimulate the research community to engage in sustained empirical research on the models to assist in evaluating their effectiveness in helping gifted students develop personal talent.

References

Benbow, C. P., & Stanley, J. C. (Eds.). (1983). *Academic precocity: Aspects of its development.* Baltimore: Johns Hopkins University Press.

Betts, G., & Kercher, J. (1999). *Autonomous learner model: Optimizing ability.* Greeley, CO: ALPS.

Bourdeau, B., & Thomas, V. (2003). Counseling gifted clients and their families: Comparing clients' and counselors' perspectives. *Journal of Secondary Gifted Education, 14,* 114–126.

Carroll, J. B. (1993). *Human cognitive abilities.* Cambridge, England: Cambridge University Press.

Clasen, D. R., & Clasen, R. E. (1995). Underachievement of highly able students and the peer society. *Gifted and Talented International, 10,* 67–76.

Cohn, S. J. (2002). Gifted students who are gay, lesbian, or bisexual. In M. Neihart, S. M. Reis, N. M. Robinson, & S. M. Moon (Eds.), *The social and emotional development of gifted children: What do we know?* (pp. 145–154). Waco, TX: Prufrock Press.

Colangelo, N. (2003). Counseling gifted students. In N. Colangelo & G. A. Davis (Eds.), *Handbook of gifted education* (pp. 373–387). Boston: Allyn & Bacon.

Colangelo, N., & Assouline, A. (1993). Families of gifted children: A research agenda. *Quest, 4*(1), 1–4.

Colangelo, N., & Assouline, S. G. (2000). Counseling gifted students. In K. A. Heller, F. J. Mönks, & R. J. Sternberg (Eds.), *International handbook of giftedness and talent* (pp. 595–607). Amsterdam: Elsevier.

Colangelo, N., & Peterson, J. S. (1993). Group counseling with gifted students. In L. K. Silverman (Ed.), *Counseling the gifted and talented* (pp. 111–129). Denver, CO: Love.

Csikszentmihalyi, M., Rathunde, K., & Whalen, S. (1993). *Talented teenagers: The roots of success and failure.* Cambridge, England: Cambridge University Press.

Dweck, C. S. (1999). *Self-theories: Their role in motivation, personality, and development.* Philadelphia: Psychology Press.

Falk, R. F., Piechowski, M., & Lind, S. (1994). *Criteria for rating the intensity of over-excitabilities.* Unpublished manuscript, University of Akron, Department of Sociology, OH.

Fishkin, A. S., Cramond, B., & Olszewski-Kubilius, P. (Eds.). (1999). *Investigating creativity in youth: Research and methods.* Cresskill, NJ: Hampton Press.

Ford, D. Y. (1996). *Reversing underachievement among gifted Black students: Promising practices and programs.* New York: Teachers College Press.

Ford, D. Y., Harris, J., & Schuerger, J. M. (1993). Racial identity development among gifted Black students: Counseling issues and concerns. *Journal of Counseling and Development, 71,* 409–417.

Frey, J., & Wendorf, D. J. (1985). Families of gifted children. In L. L'Abate (Ed.), *Handbook of family psychology and therapy* (Vol. 2, pp. 781–809). Homewood, IL: Dorsey Press.

Gagné, F. (1985). Giftedness and talent: Reexamining a reexamination of the definitions. *Gifted Child Quarterly, 29*(3), 103–119.

Gagné, F. (1998). A proposal for subcategories within gifted or talented populations. *Gifted Child Quarterly, 42,* 87–95.

Gagné, F. (1999). My convictions about the nature of abilities, gifts, and talents. *Journal for the Education of the Gifted, 22,* 109–136.

Gagné, F. (2000). Understanding the complex choreography of talent development. In K. A. Heller, F. J. Mönks, R. J. Sternberg, & R. F. Subotnik (Eds.), *International handbook of giftedness and talent* (pp. 67–79). Amsterdam: Elsevier.

Gallagher, S. A. (1985). A comparison of the concept of overexcitabilities with measures of creativity and school achievement in sixth grade students. *Roeper Review, 8,* 115–119.

Galton, F. (1869). *Hereditary genius: An inquiry into its laws and consequences.* London: Collins.

Galton, F. (1883). *Inquiries into human faculty and development.* London: Macmillan.

Gardner, H. (1983). *Frames of mind: The theory of multiple intelligences.* New York: Basic Books.

Gardner, H. (1999). *Intelligence reframed: Multiple intelligences for the 21st century.* New York: Basic Books.

Gottfried, A. W., Gottfried, A. E., Cook, C. R., & Morris, P. E. (2005). Educational characteristics of adolescents with gifted academic intrinsic motivation: A longitudinal investigation of school entry through early adulthood. *Gifted Child Quarterly, 49,* 172–186

Greene, M. J. (2002). Career counseling for gifted and talented students. In M. Neihart, S. M. Reis, N. M. Robinson, & S. M. Moon (Eds.), *The social and emotional devel-*

opment of gifted children: What do we know? (pp. 223–236). Waco, TX: Prufrock Press.

Gross, M. U. M. (1993). *Exceptionally gifted children.* London: Routledge.

Hébert, T. P. (1991). Meeting the affective needs of bright boys through bibliotherapy. *Roeper Review, 13,* 207–212.

Hébert, T. P. (2000). Helping high ability students overcome math anxiety through bibliotherapy. *Journal of Secondary Gifted Education, 8,* 164–178.

Johnsen, S. K. (Ed.). (2004). *Identifying gifted students: A practical guide.* Waco, TX: Prufrock Press.

Kaufmann, F., Kalbfleisch, M. L., & Castellanos, F. X. (2000). *Attention deficit disorders and gifted students: What do we really know?* Storrs: National Research Center on the Gifted and Talented, University of Connecticut.

Kelly, K. R. (1991). A profile of the career development characteristics of young gifted adolescents: Examining gender and multicultural differences. *Roeper Review, 13,* 202–206.

Kerr, B., & Cheryl, E. (1991). Career counseling with academically talented students: Effects of a value-based intervention. *Journal of Counseling Psychology, 38,* 309–314.

Kerr, K. B. (1993). Career assessment for gifted girls and women. *Journal of Career Assessment, 1,* 258–266.

Mahoney, A. S. (1997). In search of gifted identity: From abstract concept to workable counseling constructs. *Roeper Review, 20,* 222–227.

Maker, C. J., & Nielson, A. B. (1996). *Curriculum development and teaching: Strategies for gifted learners.* Austin, TX: ProEd.

Marland, S. P., Jr. (1972). *Education of the gifted and talented: Report to the Congress of the United States by the U.S. Commissioner of Education and background papers submitted to the U.S. Office of Education,* 2 vols. Washington, DC: U.S. Government Printing Office. (Government Documents, Y4.L 11/2: G36)

Mendaglio, S. (1993). Counseling gifted learning disabled: Individual and group counseling techniques. In L. K. Silverman (Ed.), *Counseling the gifted and talented* (pp. 131–149). Denver, CO: Love.

Mendaglio, S. (1995). Sensitivity among gifted persons: A multi-faceted perspective. *Roeper Review, 17,* 169–172.

Moon, S. M. (2003a). Counseling families. In N. Colangelo & G. A. Davis (Eds.), *Handbook of gifted education* (pp. 388–402). Boston: Allyn & Bacon.

Moon, S. M. (2003b). Personal talent. *High Ability Studies, 14*(1), 5–21.

Moon, S. M. (2006). Developing a definition of giftedness. In J. H. Purcell & R. D. Eckert (Eds.), *Designing services and programs for high-ability learners* (pp. 23–31). Thousand Oaks, CA: Corwin Press.

Moon, S. M., & Hall, A. S. (1998). Family therapy with intellectually and creatively gifted children. *Journal of Marital and Family Therapy, 24,* 59–80.

Moon, S. M., Kelly, K. R., & Feldhusen, J. F. (1997). Specialized counseling services for gifted youth and their families: A needs assessment. *Gifted Child Quarterly, 41,* 16–25.

Moon, S. M., Nelson, T. S., & Piercy, F. P. (1993). Family therapy with a highly gifted adolescent. *Journal of Family Psychotherapy, 4,* 1–16.

Moon, S. M., & Rosselli, H. C. (2000). Developing gifted programs. In K. Heller, F. Mönks, R. Sternberg, & R. Subotnik (Eds.), *International handbook of giftedness and talent* (pp. 499–521). Amsterdam: Elsevier.

Moon, S. M., & Thomas, V. (2003). Family therapy with gifted and talented adolescents. *Journal of Secondary Gifted Education, 14*, 107–113.

Moon, S. M., Zentall, S. S., Grskovic, J. A., Hall, A., & Stormont, M. (2001). Emotional and social characteristics of boys with AD/HD and/or giftedness: A comparative case study. *Journal for the Education of the Gifted, 24*, 207–247.

Neihart, M., Reis, S., Robinson, N., & Moon, S. M. (Eds.). (2002). *The social and emotional development of gifted children: What do we know?* Waco, TX: Prufrock Press.

Peterson, J., & Rischar, H. (2000). Gifted and gay: A study of the adolescent experience. *Gifted Child Quarterly, 44*, 231–246.

Peterson, J. S. (1993). *Talk with teens about self and stress: 50 guided discussions for school and counseling groups.* Minneapolis, MN: Free Spirit.

Peterson, J. S. (1995). *Talk with teens about feelings, family, relationships, and the future: 50 guided discussions for school and counseling groups.* Minneapolis, MN: Free Spirit.

Peterson, J. S. (1999). Gifted—through whose cultural lens? An application of the postpositivistic mode of inquiry. *Journal for the Education of the Gifted, 22*, 354–383.

Piechowski, M. M. (1979). Developmental potential. In N. Colangelo & R. T. Zaffran (Eds.), *New voices in counseling the gifted* (pp. 25–57). Dubuque, IA: Kendall/Hunt.

Piechowski, M. M., & Colangelo, N. (1984). Developmental potential of the gifted. *Gifted Child Quarterly, 8*, 80–88.

Piechowski, M. M., & Cunningham, K. (1985). Patterns of overexcitability in a group of artists. *Journal of Creative Behavior, 19*, 153–174.

Piechowski, M. M., Silverman, L. K., & Falk, R. F. (1985). Comparison of intellectually and artistically gifted on five dimensions of mental functioning. *Perceptual and Motor Skills, 60*, 539–545.

Plucker, J. A. (1996). Gifted Asian-American students: Identification, curricular, and counseling concerns. *Journal for the Education of the Gifted, 19*, 314–343.

Plucker, J. A. (1998). Gender, race, and grade differences in gifted adolescents' coping strategies. *Journal for the Education of the Gifted, 21*, 423–436.

Reis, S. M. (1998). *Work left undone: Choices and compromises of talented females.* Mansfield Center, CT: Creative Learning Press.

Reis, S. M. (2002). Gifted females in elementary and secondary school. In M. Neihart, S. M. Reis, N. M. Robinson, & S. M. Moon (Eds.), *The social and emotional development of gifted children: What do we know?* (pp. 125–135). Waco, TX: Prufrock Press.

Reis, S. M., & McCoach, D. B. (2000). The underachievement of gifted students: What do we know and where do we go? *Gifted Child Quarterly, 44*, 152–170.

Reis, S. M., & Moon, S. M. (2002). Models and strategies for counseling, guidance, and social and emotional support of gifted and talented students. In M. Neihart, S. M. Reis, N. M. Robinson, & S. M. Moon (Eds.), *The social and emotional development of gifted children: What do we know?* (pp. 251–265). Waco, TX: Prufrock Press.

Renzulli, J. S. (1978). What makes giftedness? Re-examining a definition. *Phi Delta Kappan, 60*, 180–184, 261.

Renzulli, J. S. (1986). The three-ring conception of giftedness: A developmental model for creative productivity. In R. J. Sternberg & J. E. Davidson (Eds.), *Conceptions of giftedness* (pp. 53–92). Cambridge, England: Cambridge University Press.

Rimm, S. (1995). *Why bright kids get poor grades and what you can do about it.* New York: Crown.

Rimm, S. B. (2003). Underachievement: A national epidemic. In N. Colangelo & G. A. Davis (Eds.), *Handbook of gifted education* (pp. 424–443). Boston: Allyn & Bacon.

Robinson, N. M., Reis, S. M., Neihart, M., & Moon, S. M. (2002). Social and emotional issues: What have we learned and what should we do now? In M. Neihart, S. M. Reis, N. Robinson, & S. M. Moon (Eds.), *The social and emotional development of gifted children: What do we know?* (pp. 267–288). Waco, TX: Prufrock Press.

Schiever, S. W. (1985). Creative personality characteristics and dimensions of mental functioning in gifted adolescents. *Roeper Review, 7*, 223–226.

Schiever, S. W., & Maker, C. J. (2003). New directions in enrichment and acceleration. In N. Colangelo & G. A. Davis (Eds.), *Handbook of gifted education* (pp. 163–173). Boston: Allyn & Bacon.

Silverman, L. K. (1991). Family counseling. In N. Colangelo & G. A. Davis (Eds.), *Handbook of gifted education.* Boston: Allyn & Bacon.

Silverman, L. K. (1993a). Counseling families. In L. K. Silverman (Ed.), *Counseling the gifted and talented* (pp. 151–178). Denver, CO: Love.

Silverman, L. K. (1993b). *Counseling the gifted and talented.* Denver, CO: Love.

Silverman, L. K. (1993c). A developmental model for counseling the gifted. In L. K. Silverman (Ed.), *Counseling the gifted and talented* (pp. 51–78). Denver, CO: Love.

Silverman, L. K. (1993d). Techniques for preventive counseling. In L. K. Silverman (Ed.), *Counseling the gifted and talented* (pp. 81–109). Denver, CO: Love.

Silverman, L. K. (1998). Personality and learning styles of gifted children. In J. VanTassel-Baska (Ed.), *Excellence in educating gifted and talented learners* (pp. 29–65). Denver, CO: Love.

Silverman, L. K. (2002). *Upside-down brilliance: The visual spatial learner.* Denver, CO: DeLeon Publishing.

Sowa, C. J., & May, K. M. (1997). Expanding Lazarus and Folkman's paradigm to the social and emotional adjustment of gifted children. *Gifted Child Quarterly, 41*, 36–43.

Spearman, C. (1904). "General intelligence," objectively determined and measured. *American Journal of Psychology, 15*, 201–293.

Sprenkle, D. H., & Blow, A. H. (2004). Common factors and our sacred models. *Journal of Marital and Family Therapy, 30*, 113–130.

Stanley, J. C. (1996). In the beginning: The study of mathematically precocious youth. In C. P. Benbow & D. Lubinski (Eds.), *Intellectual talent: Psychometric and social issues* (pp. 225–235). Baltimore: Johns Hopkins University Press.

Steinberg, L. (1996). *Beyond the classroom.* New York: Simon & Schuster.

Sternberg, R. J. (1985). *Beyond IQ: A triarchic theory of human intelligence.* Cambridge, England: Cambridge University Press.

Sternberg, R. J. (2000). Giftedness as developing expertise. In K. A. Heller, F. J. Mönks, R. J. Sternberg, & R. F. Subotnik (Eds.), *International handbook of giftedness and talent* (pp. 55–66). Amsterdam: Elsevier.

Sternberg, R. J., & Clinkenbeard, P. R. (1995). The triarchic model applied to identifying, teaching, and assessing gifted children. *Roeper Review, 17*, 274–280.

Sternberg, R. J., & Davidson, J. E. (Eds.). (1986). *Conceptions of giftedness.* Cambridge, England: Cambridge University Press.

Tannenbaum, A. J. (1986). Giftedness: A psychological approach. In R. J. Sternberg & J. E. Davidson (Eds.), *Conceptions of giftedness* (pp. 21–52). New York: Cambridge University Press.

Tannenbaum, A. J. (2000). A history of giftedness in school and society. In K. A. Heller, F. J. Mönks, R. J. Sternberg, & R. F. Subotnik (Eds.), *International handbook of giftedness and talent* (pp. 23–54). Amsterdam: Elsevier.

Terman, L. M. (1916). *The measurement of intelligence: An explanation of and a complete scale for the use of the Stanford revision and extension of the Binet–Simon intelligence scale.* Boston: Houghton-Mifflin.

Terman, L. M. (1925). *Genetic studies of genius: Vol. 1. Mental and physical traits of a thousand gifted children.* Stanford, CA: Stanford University Press.

Terman, L. M., & Oden, M. H. (1959). *Genetic studies of genius: Vol. 5. The gifted group at mid-life: Thirty-five years' follow-up of the superior child.* Stanford, CA: Stanford University Press.

Thomas, V. (1995). Of thorns and roses: The use of the "Brier Rose" fairy tale in therapy with families of gifted children. *Contemporary Family Therapy, 17*(1), 83–91.

Thomas, V. (1999). David and the Family Bane: Therapy with a gifted child and his family. *Journal of Family Psychology, 10,* 15–24.

Thurstone, L. L. (1931). Multiple factor analysis. *Psychological Review, 38,* 406–427.

Thurstone, L. L. (1938). *Primary mental abilities.* Chicago: University of Chicago Press.

Thurstone, L. L. (1947). *Multiple factor analysis: A development and expansion of the vectors of mind.* Chicago: University of Chicago Press.

Tieso, C. (2004). Patterns of overexcitabilities in identified gifted students: A hierarchical model. Unpublished manuscript.

Tomlinson, C. (1995). *How to differentiate instruction in mixed ability classrooms.* Alexandria, VA: Association for Supervision and Curriculum Development.

U.S. Department of Education, Office of Educational Research and Improvement. (1993). *National excellence: A case for developing America's talent.* Washington, DC: U.S. Government Printing Office.

Van Rossum, J. H. A., & Gagné, F. (2006). Talent development in sports. In F. A. Dixon & S. M. Moon (Eds.), *The handbook of secondary gifted education* (pp. 281–316). Waco, TX: Prufrock Press.

VanTassel-Baska, J. (1994). *Comprehensive curriculum for gifted learners* (2nd ed.). Boston: Allyn & Bacon.

VanTassel-Baska, J. (1998). Counseling talented learners. In J. VanTassel-Baska (Ed.), *Excellence in educating gifted and talented learners* (pp. 498–510). Denver, CO: Love.

VanTassel-Baska, J., & Little, C. A. (Eds.). (2003). *Content-based curriculum for high-ability learners.* Waco, TX: Prufrock Press.

VanTassel-Baska, J., Zuo, L., Avery, L. D., & Little, C. A. (2002). Curriculum study of gifted-student learning in the language arts. *Gifted Child Quarterly, 46,* 30–44.

Webb, J. T., Amend, E. R., Webb, N. E., Goerss, J., Beljan, P., & Olenchak, F. R. (2005). *Misdiagnosis and dual diagnoses of gifted children and adults.* Scottsdale, AZ: Great Potential Press.

Webb, J. T., & DeVries, A. R. (1993). *Training manual for facilitators of SENG model guided discussion groups.* Dayton, OH: Ohio Psychology Press.

Wendorf, D. J., & Frey, J. (1985). Family therapy with the intellectually gifted. *The American Journal of Family Therapy, 13,* 31–38.

Wieczerkowski, W., & Prado, T. M. (1991). Parental fears and expectations from the point of view of a counseling centre for the gifted. *European Journal for High Ability, 2,* 56–72.

Weiner, I. B. (1992). *Psychological disturbance in adolescence.* New York: John Wiley & Sons.

Zentall, S. S., Moon, S. M., Hall, A. M., & Grskovic, J. A. (2001). Learning and motivational characteristics of boys with AD/HD and/or giftedness: A multiple case study. *Exceptional Children, 67,* 499–519.

PART II
The Models

chapter 3

Affective-Cognitive Therapy for Counseling Gifted Individuals

by Sal Mendaglio

Conception of Giftedness

Influences

The works of Terman (1926), Marland (1972), Renzulli (1978, 2002), and Gardner (1993) have influenced my definition of *giftedness*. Each of these authors proposes a unique perspective on giftedness. Their definitions range from a one-dimensional view, to a multidimensional view; from a focus on intelligence alone, to the inclusion of personality dimensions; from potential, to production. My definition is an attempt to resolve the tensions I experienced in considering the conceptions of these four individuals.

In Terman's definition, gifted individuals are those whose scores fall in the top 1% on the Stanford-Binet or similar measures of intelligence (Terman, 1926). Terman's approach led me to believe that giftedness is intellectual prowess. This view of giftedness is in stark contrast to current approaches that see his approach as narrow in scope.

Marland (1972) provided a multidimensional conception of giftedness, suggesting that students may be identified as gifted (and therefore eligible for American federal government funding) in several areas: intellect, creativity, art, leadership, and specific academic subjects. Giftedness was associated with students' exceptional potential for performing at levels significantly higher than the levels of performance of their agemates. While the multifaceted approach had an initial intuitive appeal, it was difficult for me to accept that a student who could excel in mathematics did not have potential to excel in other academic areas. However, the distinction between potential and performance made sense to me because it allowed for the phenomenon of academic underachievement of gifted students. Without the potential-performance distinction, giftedness would have to be defined as exceptional performance exclusively.

Renzulli's (1978) three-ring conception uses *gifted* to describe behavior, rather than individuals. Gifted behavior occurs when there is an interaction among three traits (i.e., three rings): above-average ability, high levels of task commitment, and high levels of creativity. Above-average ability refers to cognitive ability such as abstract thought, adaptation, and rapid information processing. Task commitment refers to motivational characteristics such as effort, determination, focus, self-confidence, high standards, and a drive to achieve. Creativity refers to such characteristics as flexibility, openness to experiences, curiosity, and risk-taking. Becoming familiar with Renzulli's conception of gifted behavior challenged me to crystallize my own view. Conceiving giftedness as gifted behavior, which I equated with exceptional achievement, was in stark contrast with the Marlandian focus on exceptional potential. Marland and Renzulli facilitated my commitment to a critical element of my definition of giftedness: the potential-performance distinction.

Gardner's (1993) theory of multiple intelligences (MI) has also influenced my definition of giftedness. Gardner initially listed seven intelligences: logical-mathematical, linguistic, bodily-kinesthetic, musical, spatial, interpersonal, and intrapersonal. To this list he later added naturalistic and spiritual intelligences (Gardner, 1999). Gardner (1993) defined *intelligence* as "the ability to solve problems, or create products, that are valued within one or more cultural settings" (p. X)

There are several themes that emerged from the perspectives discussed above. All approaches implicated intelligence in giftedness. The level of intelligence, however, varied. Terman and Marland seemed to agree on superior intelligence, and Renzulli proposed above-average ability. I believed that Gardner was unclear in this point (e.g., Does giftedness mean the possession of all intelligences? Is there a cut-off score for each intelligence?). Terman had a unitary approach, while Marland, Renzulli, and Gardner had a multidimensional perspective. Marland's multidimensional approach focused on the areas in which giftedness could be exhibited by students—for example, a particular academic domain. Multidimensionality in Renzulli's definition is seen in the inputs creating gifted behavior—that is, the three rings. For Gardner, the MIs themselves represented the multidimensionality. Marland referred to both potential and performance in his definition. Terman's approach, with its exclusive focus on intelligence, could be seen as emphasizing potential, as well. On the other hand, Renzulli and Gardner emphasized production. They seemed to emphasize a certain type of production, namely, the socially valued type. Renzulli equated gifted behavior with creative products, whereas Gardner made creative products explicit in his definition of intelligence.

Three difficulties arose from these themes: intelligence as multiple, giftedness as production, and giftedness as value laden. While MI was an intriguing theory of intelligence, it is simply that. In addition, it was not satisfying methodologically to have an increasing number of intelligences proclaimed from time to time. Underachievement contradicted the association of giftedness with production. Teachers and parents are all too familiar with the differentiation between potential and performance. The view of giftedness as socially valued could not account for historical figures, as well as contemporaries, who have wreaked havoc on society.

Definition

The following definition underlies my model of counseling gifted individuals: Giftedness is superior intellectual potential with many possible manifestations, some of which are socially acceptable.

Superior Intellectual Potential

At the core of giftedness is superior intellectual potential. I equate this with general intelligence, g (Spearman, 1927), and consider it innate. My use of the word *superior* is as a descriptor of intelligence only, not human worth: All individuals are of equal value. There is evidence that the Wechsler scales (e.g., Wechsler, 2003) are good estimates of g, so I support the use of these tests to identify gifted individuals. I am not convinced that there is sufficient empirical support for adopting an MI approach to intelligence. *Potential* is used to distinguish giftedness from achievement or production.

Many Possible Manifestations

There are a myriad of ways that giftedness may be manifested. I prefer the term *manifestations* to *intelligences*. What we see in extraordinary human achievement is the application of superior intellectual potential in a particular domain. When a student excels in mathematics, it is the result of the focusing of giftedness in that subject. The reason for its manifestation in that academic subject, and not another, lies in environmental influences. That is, extraordinary achievement in mathematics is not due to a mathematics intelligence, but rather to social environmental influences. Excellence in music or athletics results from environmental influences, such as parental expectations and encouragement.

The implication of this definition of giftedness is that the potential is inherent in the individual, but how it is expressed is the result of the individual's interaction with his environment, particularly the social environment. This extends to the possibility that giftedness is not manifested because of lack of educational and other opportunities or poor socialization practices. In my view, giftedness still exists, regardless of its lack of actualization or manifestation in excellence.

Social Acceptability

When giftedness is manifested, its forms may be socially acceptable, unacceptable, or prized. In short, giftedness is superior intellectual potential that may be used for good or evil purposes. Equating giftedness with socially valued products restricts the applicability of the concept. Giftedness, then, becomes associated with goodness or virtue. The products or manifestations of giftedness may contribute to the betterment of society or wreak havoc on it.

Contrast With Current Conceptions

Current conceptions are typically liberal and broad (Renzulli, 2002). In contrast, my definition is conservative and narrow, which is terminology that also is used to refer to Terman's approach to giftedness. Focusing on superior, rather than above-average, ability, has the effect of reducing the pool of individuals who fall in the gifted category. However, my definition is similar to elements of current broad conceptions. The notion of superior intelligence is seen in Marland's (1972) continuing popular definition (Stephens & Karnes, 2000), which uses exceptional cognitive ability. The potential-production distinction is seen in Marland and in Gagné's (2003) definitions. Exceptional potential or achievement is a critical part of Marland's definition. Gagné's use of the terms *gifted* and *talented* illustrates this dichotomy. Gifted refers to raw ability, whereas talented refers to demonstration or manifestation of gifts. In a general sense, Gagné's *gift* is analogous with my *giftedness*; the difference lies in his multiple versus my singular conception.

Defining giftedness based on intelligence or cognitive ability is seen in research in the field and in identification practices in gifted education. Researchers who study gifted individuals typically use the scores on tests of cognitive ability. Similarly, school districts that offer gifted education programs often use scores on intelligence tests to select students. For example, an IQ score of 130 or higher on the Wechsler Intelligence Scale for Children (Wechsler, 2003) is often used to select students for gifted programs in Canada and the United States.

Characteristics

My conception of giftedness consists of two types of characteristics: cognitive and affective. Cognitive characteristics include advanced comprehension, efficient information processing, and excellent memory. There are numerous

T A B L E   3 . 1

**Facets and Dimensions
of Heightened Multifaceted Sensitivity**

Dimension / Orientation	Cognitive	Affective
Self-oriented	Self-awareness	Emotional experience
Other-oriented	Perspective-taking	Empathy

other cognitive characteristics that I could mention, but I selected these three as particularly useful for my counseling.

I selected affective characteristics from extensive lists of differentiating characteristics (e.g., Clark, 1997) by using two criteria. The characteristics needed to be logically connected with my definition of giftedness, with its focus on superior general intelligence. Because there is virtually no empirical basis for the characteristics attributed to gifted individuals, it seemed necessary to anchor traits to my conception of giftedness. The characteristics also needed to relate to the affective or emotional domain of client functioning. A theme emerged in my work with clients who were gifted: intense emotionality. I needed a way of understanding this emotionality. Three characteristics met the criteria: heightened sensitivity, heightened self-criticism, and emotional intensity.

Intense Emotionality

Heightened Sensitivity. Heightened sensitivity is a characteristic commonly ascribed to gifted individuals (e.g., Clark, 1997; Lovecky, 1992; Roeper, 1982; Silverman, 1993), and awareness is a common theme in the depiction of sensitivity (Mendaglio, 1995). Using awareness as a foundational concept, I developed a model of sensitivity called heightened multifaceted sensitivity (HMS; Mendaglio, 2003). HMS is enhanced awareness of behavior, emotions, and cognitions pertaining to self and others. I assume that awareness is related to intelligence, with awareness increasing as the level of intelligence increases. From this perspective, all people are sensitive, and gifted people, *because* of their giftedness, are highly aware: HMS is part of giftedness. HMS is shaped by the social environment, particularly by the socialization process, but not created by it.

HMS includes four facets, two that represent sensitivity directed at self and two directed at other people. Both self- and other-oriented heightened sensitivity have cognitive and affective dimensions (see Table 3.1).

Self-oriented HMS consists of heightened self-awareness (cognitive dimension), whereby gifted persons are greatly cognizant of their own behaviors, thoughts, and feelings. In self-awareness, the intellectual understanding of these aspects is the focus. In the affective dimension of self-oriented HMS (i.e., emotional experience), gifted individuals are presumed to have a strong awareness of their emotionality. In a sense, emotional experience is a special case of self-awareness—that is, self-awareness of one's emotional states. *Emotional experience*, as used here, is in line with Lewis and Michaelson's (1983) use of the phrase. In Lewis's model of emotions, emotional experience is enacted when we say, "I am happy/sad," (i.e., when we become aware of our emotional states and label them). It is important to note that in this usage, emotional experience is by no means automatic, as are emotional states, but rather a product of learning. According to Lewis, we need to learn to attend to our emotional states, develop an emotion lexicon, and "connect the dots" between and among various aspects of situations we are in, detect the emotion states, and identify the emotion label that best suits the experience. Such is emotional experience. Psychologists tend to assume that the emotional experience is innate. When psychologists ask the question, "How did you feel when . . ." and a reply is not forthcoming, there is a tendency to view this as client resistance. In some cases, a lack of response may stem from a lack of opportunity to learn emotional experience. The view that emotional experience is learned is particularly useful in understanding young children's "I don't know" responses to emotion-eliciting questions.

Other-oriented HMS consists of perspective-taking (cognitive dimension) and empathy (affective dimension). Perspective-taking refers to the understanding of the behaviors, emotions, and thoughts of others. Other than what is available through direct observation (i.e., other people's behaviors), perspective-taking relies on inferential processes. Others' emotions and thoughts are not directly available to us. We infer others' emotional states and thoughts based on, among other things, prior knowledge and our observations of them. It is important to note that HMS suggests that gifted persons engage in a heightened form of perspective-taking, but it does not imply that the products of inferential processes are accurate depictions of others' internal states. While enhanced perspective-taking does not guarantee accuracy, accuracy can be increased with practice.

Empathy is the final facet of HMS. In its usage here, empathy is akin to the approach taken in developmental psychology, rather than in counseling and psychotherapy (Mendaglio, 2005). In HMS, empathy is used to refer to emotional contagion or vicarious experiencing of other people's emotions. This form of empathy does occur in counseling and psychotherapy, but the goal is not necessarily to experience what clients feel. As a facet of HMS, gifted individuals have a tendency to experience the emotions of others, this being particularly evident in young gifted children. Counselors and psychotherapists from time to time experience what their clients feel, but that is not the objective of empathy in clinical practice. Empathy, especially in the Rogerian context, is a two-fold process of approximating clients' internal states (i.e., thoughts and emotions) and communicating our inferences to them. In this sense, empathy in counseling is more a blend of perspective-taking and effective interpersonal communication. Heightened empathy, in HMS, is associated with gifted individuals, who, because of their giftedness, tend to take on the emotions of others as if they were their own.

I must hasten to add some clarification of HMS, lest readers view it as value laden. First, heightened sensitivity is a cognitive, neutral term. It is conceived as being part of giftedness. Sensitivity conceptualized as "awareness," a cognitive process, can be logically connected to intelligence. All facets of HMS, including empathy, may have positive and negative outcomes for individuals. Self-awareness and emotional experience may be beneficial, because knowledge of oneself and attunement to one's emotions may spur persons on to personal growth. On the other hand, self-oriented HMS may be of such intensity that it stifles growth: Painful self-consciousness and preoccupation with one's emotions may become impediments to development. Similarly, other-oriented HMS may lead to either growth or distress. Keen understanding of others' perspectives and attunement to their emotions may lead to reduced egocentric thought processes and altruistic behavior. On the other hand, these facets of HMS may result in a loss of self and being overwhelmed by others' distress.

An additional characteristic of HMS is reflected in the experience-expression dimension. HMS as a cognitive process is, by definition, covert. Implicit in my view of HMS is that it is a trait experienced by gifted individuals, but its products are not necessarily expressed. In short, the presence of HMS—the experience of it—is conceived as part of giftedness; whether it is expressed, or to what degree, is a function of gifted individuals' socialization. For example, whether gifted individuals express the products of their emotional experience or empathy will depend on the rules of emotion expression that they learned in the process of their socialization. An important implication of the experience-expression dimension is this: not seeing it does not mean it is not there.

Heightened Self-Criticism. Heightened self-criticism is a second characteristic I associate with giftedness. Unlike heightened sensitivity, heightened self-criticism (HSC) as a characteristic of gifted individuals is encountered only occasionally in scholarly literature (e.g., Clark, 1997). Self-criticism is an analytic approach to self. It is premised on the notion that with intellectual prowess comes spontaneous attention to detail in the environment with a tendency to place everything "under the microscope." HSC means placing aspects of oneself under scrutiny. *Criticism*, with its negative implication, is used because I believe that the products of this introspective evaluative process are generally negative. Having said that, I believe that a result of this self-analysis is the motivation toward personal growth. On the other hand, it may have negative outcomes such as anxiety, depression, and despair. Though HSC may lead to low self-esteem, the terms *HSC* and *low self-esteem* are not synonymous.

Emotional Intensity. Emotional intensity (EI) is a third characteristic that I believe is part of giftedness. This concept can be summed up by this state-

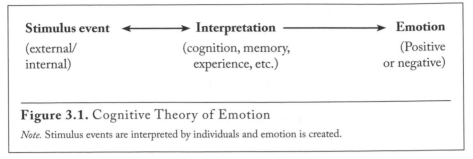

Figure 3.1. Cognitive Theory of Emotion

Note. Stimulus events are interpreted by individuals and emotion is created.

ment: Gifted persons feel more because they see more. In effect, I believe that gifted persons have the potential for experiencing a complex and intense emotional life. As with the general population, though, the eventual experience and expression of emotions are dependent on cultural and socialization factors.

The three characteristics that I associate with giftedness share several themes. First, they are considered part of giftedness, shaped by the social environment. Second, as cognitive processes, I presume that they are experienced, but not necessarily expressed. Third, these characteristics are neutral, leading to diverse outcomes for the individual. Fourth, these characteristics are evident in the general population; they vary according to level of intelligence.

Cognitive Theory of Emotion

My conception of gifted individuals' emotionality rests on a cognitive theory of emotion (Lewis & Michaelson, 1983). In this approach to emotions, we literally create our emotions. As such, statements such as "You make me so angry!" are inaccurate. The essence of my cognitive theory is presented in Figure 3.1.

In my cognitive theory of emotion, emotions are created by our interpretation of stimulus events in their contexts of occurrence. Interpretation is used to denote a variety of cognitive processes, such as information processing; memory, especially affective; and level of self-esteem associated with the event and context. Stimulus events may be either real or imaginary: an actual event or a product of the imagination. Interpretation is at the heart of this approach to emotion generation. As a cognitive process, interpretation is presumed to be heavily influenced by level of intelligence. A high level of intelligence is associated with rapid information processing and accessing short- and long-term memory. From this perspective, greater intelligence is associated with more and intense emotions. Further, with rapid processing comes rapid rise and fall of emotions as new information is accessed. As with heightened sensitivity and self-criticism, emotional intensity is perceived as a neutral process. The outcomes of emotional intensity are both positive and negative.

In my theorizing about emotion, I, like others (e.g., Greenberg, 2002), refer to primary and secondary emotions. My conception of these terms is grounded in the cognitive theory of emotions. Primary emotions are those produced by a first interpretation of a stimulus event, as in Figure 3.1. Secondary emotions result from an individual's additional interpretation, of any or all

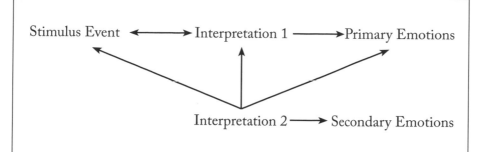

Figure 3.2. Primary and secondary emotions

Note. Primary emotions result from interpretation 1 of a stimulus event. Secondary emotions are created by a second interpretation of any or all of the components in the primary emotion process.

of the components in Figure 3.1. The additional interpretation, or secondary interpretation, leads to the creation of new emotions (see Figure 3.2). In primary emotions, interpretation may be seen as answering this question: What does this event have to do with my well-being? If the interpretation is that it enhances my well-being, positive emotions occur. On the other hand, if the event is seen as detrimental, negative emotions result. In secondary emotions, an individual's interpretation may pose various questions: Why did I perceive the situation the way I did? Why do I take things so personally? Why can't I handle my emotions better? What's wrong with me? Secondary emotions are created by people's "second guessing" themselves. While primary emotions are the results of an evaluation of an event, secondary emotions are the results of an evaluation of the self.

The regular occurrence of secondary emotions motivates individuals to seek help. When emotional experience remains at the primary level, emotions are short-term disruptions, arising and flowing out of individuals' experience. Secondary emotions, however, are more problematic. There is a significant increase in the emotional burden experienced. Secondary interpretation interferes with the release of primary emotions. Emotions arising out of the second evaluation are added to the original emotions. Because of their self-referent nature, secondary emotions are more difficult to release. Using common techniques for emotional discharge such as distraction and expression becomes more challenging when the emotions are related to self. It is likely more difficult for individuals to distract themselves from their thoughts about self than from events. Expression of self-referent emotions seems generally more difficult than those bound to events.

Assumptions

I do use the phrase *gifted individuals*, but my thinking about giftedness is better captured in the phrase *individuals who are gifted*. Using *child who is gifted* emphasizes that gifted children share a great deal in common with other children, while simultaneously acknowledging that they have characteristics that differentiate gifted children from other children. To work effectively with gifted individuals, both general knowledge and knowledge relating to giftedness are needed. For effective teaching, parenting, or counseling of gifted individuals, in addition to sound general principles associated with each realm, gifted individuals' differentiating characteristics need to be taken into account.

The characteristics that accompany giftedness are an intensified form of human traits. Intelligence, sensitivity, self-criticism, and emotionality occur in heightened forms in gifted individuals. The effect of the interaction of these characteristics leads to gifted individuals' different experiences of reality—to a general intensification of reality. Although there are common characteristics that affect gifted individuals' experiences, this population is not a homogenous group. Gifted individuals are unique as a result of innate and environmental differences. For example, the social environment, with particular emphasis on socialization practices, is a significant force contributing to the uniqueness.

A final assumption relates to my work in counseling children and their parents. I assume that young gifted individuals know and understand the expectations of their parents and teachers because of their cognitive characteristics. Their advanced comprehension and excellent memories suggest that gifted children understand and remember significant adults' expectations. In addition, by the time parents seek counseling, they have typically repeated their requests and expectations to their children. The adjustment difficulties of children that lead to seeking psychological consultation are rarely the result of gifted children's lack of knowledge or understanding of expectations.

Conception of Personality

Personality

Personality is the product of an interaction between an individual's temperament and a social environment. Temperament is innate and forms the raw material from which personality is forged. The socialization process that an individual experiences is the most important influence on personality development. Parents or other caregivers are primary shapers of temperament, both in terms of occurrence and duration of influence. It is through their day-to-day interaction with children that temperamental tendencies become personality traits. I believe that the early patterns of parent-child interactions leave indelible marks, which influence individuals for a lifetime.

Self-concept is a central component of personality that I use in my model of counseling. Self-concept is multidimensional in nature and multitheoretical in conception. Dimensions of self-concepts include academic, social, physical, and moral/ethical. My conception of self-concept is grounded on three theoretical orientations: reflected appraisals, social comparison, and attribution (Pyryt & Mendaglio, 1994; Mendaglio & Pyryt, 1995).

There appears to be a consensus on the multidimensional nature of self-concept (e.g., Harter, 1999; Marsh, 1990). Therefore, I will not discuss this aspect of self-concept. My focus instead is the multitheoretical conception.

The reflected-appraisals orientation emphasizes the contribution of the social environment to creating and maintaining self-concept. From this vantage point, self-concept is a social product arising out of daily interactions with significant others, primarily parents. An individual constructs a conception of self using self-referent feedback from caregivers and other family members. As the sphere of interaction widens, others, such as teachers and peers, are included as significant others. Significant others, in this approach, have a direct contribution to the creation of self-concept.

Social comparison emphasizes individuals' own contributions to self-concept development. Social comparison is a self-evaluative process by which we compare our standing with that of others on various areas of human functioning. Students, for example, commonly compare their performance on tests and assignments with fellow students. The product of such interpersonal comparisons (i.e., whether the marks received are higher or lower than others) has concomitant influences on students' academic self-concepts.

Attribution also focuses on individuals' contributions to self-concept development. Attribution refers to the meaning individuals give to events they experience. A critical element in attribution processes is self-observation, whereby individuals respond to themselves as if they were other people. The meanings attributed to what is observed both influences and is influenced by self-concept. A common application of this process is in the arena of academic achievement. How students explain to themselves the cause of their successes and failures reflects and influences self-concept. Causal attributions of success to chance, ability, or effort are associated with differential effects on self-concept development.

Dabrowski's theory of positive disintegration (TPD; Dabrowski, 1964, 1967) is a theory of personality that underlies my work with some clients who are gifted. TPD is a complex theory, in the tradition of comprehensive theories such as Freud's (1949), Adler's (1954), and Sullivan's (1953), which reframes familiar psychological constructs, including personality. In contrast to a generally accepted view that personality is a construct that is attributed to all individuals, for Dabrowski (1973), personality is the pinnacle of human development. Personality is achieved by those individuals who have undergone a particular process of psychological growth and development. The process of positive disintegration is essential to personality development. Through positive disintegration, instincts and drives leading to egocentric gratification are replaced with values and morals leading to altruistic behavior. The experience of intense negative emotions such as anxiety, guilt, and shame is an essential ingredient of the disintegration process. Positive disintegration shapes personality. Unlike the valence-free use of the term in psychology, *personality* in TPD is a positive moral term. Personality includes notions of self-awareness, self-directedness, and congruence. Dabrowski (1973) used personality to refer to those who have become truly human. Those who have attained personality are not seen in counselors' offices; those with intense emotional experiences on the developmental path are the ones we are likely to encounter in counseling.

Personality of Gifted Students/Persons

Three characteristics discussed previously—heightened sensitivity, heightened self-criticism, and emotional intensity—are part of the personality (the term is used here in its general psychological sense) of gifted individuals. I believe that their greater awareness, which is the core of heightened sensitivity, affects the quality of their experience. Greater awareness associated with superior intelligence affects personality development including self-concept. From a reflected-appraisals perspective, gifted children are particularly aware of the verbal and nonverbal communication of significant others. As a result, gifted children may detect negative emotions that parents are trying to mask in themselves. When using social-comparison processes, gifted students may select inappropriate referent persons (e.g., eminent historical figures rather than classmates) with whom to compare accomplishments. From an attribution perspective, gifted individuals may be very aware of self to the point of debilitating self-consciousness.

A tendency to question authority is another personality dimension I attribute to giftedness. I see this tendency as a neutral by-product of superior intelligence that is initially spontaneously expressed by children. In time, however, questioning of authority may be used by some gifted individuals to intentionally frustrate or manipulate others. Questioning of authority influences the socialization process. Socialization of children requires their acceptance of parental authority. In fact, the acceptance of parental authority is a cornerstone of socialization. Challenging authority interferes with parental attempts to teach gifted children the behaviors needed to function in the particular society they are in, such as personal hygiene and food etiquette. Questioning of authority may extend to other legitimate authority figures, such as teachers. This tendency to challenge authority poses a unique challenge to adults who parent or teach gifted children. When *questioning* authority becomes *challenging* authority, gifted children are likely to be identified as maladjusted.

Some gifted individuals manifest characteristics associated with Dabrowski's theory of personality. Specifically, some gifted individuals manifest the potential for advanced development, which is associated with positive disintegration. A hallmark of these clients is intense negative emotions motivated by caring for others and/or experiencing a real-ideal self-discrepancy. These are the individuals who are intensely saddened by the plight of others or are anguished by the realization that they are not living up to their ideals. While virtually all clients seek counseling because of intense negative emotions, the reasons for these emotions vary. Not all emotional experiences meet the Dabrowskian criteria.

Model of Counseling

Influences

Several theorists who have made contributions to the field of counseling and psychotherapy and other areas of psychology have influenced the evolution of my approach to counseling. From the field of counseling and psychotherapy, I have relied heavily on Rogers' (1980) person-centered therapy, Perls' (Perls, Hefferline, & Goodman, 1951) Gestalt therapy, Ellis' (Ellis, 2000) rational emotive behavioral therapy, and Sullivan's (1953) interpersonal theory. I have used these theorists to both guide the counseling process and to help me conceptualize clients' experiences. To further this conceptualizing, I also have drawn on Piaget's (Piaget & Inhelder, 1969) cognitive developmental theory, Lewis' (2000) cognitive theory of emotion, and Dabrowski's (1964, 1967) theory of positive disintegration. I have interwoven selected components of these theoretical strands to create my systematic eclectic model of counseling.

Rogers' (1980) contribution to my approach is seen in the importance I place on the counseling relationship. The core conditions that he identified are particularly important for establishing a relationship, but also are important in maintaining it. Providing the conditions of acceptance, empathy, and congruence (Rogers, 1951) throughout the counseling process is an essential context for effective counseling.

Perls' (Perls et al., 1951) concepts of awareness and confrontation are important elements in my approach. Similar to Gestalt therapists (Jacobs, 1989), I include self-awareness and self-acceptance in my use of *awareness*. I believe that enhancing client awareness has significant therapeutic value; therefore, it is a fundamental objective in my approach. Confrontation is also incorporated into my approach. However, it is not the Perlsian type, which is likely too threatening for many clients. The confrontation that I use is, in essence, an invitation to clients to further their awareness by gently pointing out discrepancies in their communication.

Ellis' (2000) notions of personality and homework are embedded in my model. Didactically, I use his ABC description of personality, whereby people interpret an activating event (A) by using their belief system (B) to produce a consequence (C). I also use homework assignments that flow from the concepts used in sessions with clients. This aspect of my work was influenced by Ellis' emphasis on the need for counselors to bridge what goes on in sessions and the real world of the client.

Sullivan's (1953) perspective emphasizes the central influence of social interaction in human development. In my use of his theory, I have focused on conceptualizing presenting problems as the product of clients' interactions with significant others. Unless there is some physical evidence to the contrary, client issues are not resident within the client, but instead are created as the result of feedback received from significant others. This conception extends to my approach to emotions such as anxiety, which Sullivan viewed as interpersonal in origin.

The other theorists have influenced my understanding of client experiences. Piaget's (Piaget & Inhelder, 1969) cognitive developmental theory is useful in understanding parents' descriptions of their children's behaviors and thinking. I use Lewis' (2000) cognitive theory of emotions, discussed previously, to teach clients how their interpretations cause emotions. I also use his descriptions of emotional experience and emotional expression to educate clients regarding emotions. Finally, I use concepts drawn from Dabrowski's (1964, 1967) theory of positive disintegration to understand some clients whose experience includes intense negative emotions driven by inner conflict.

Definition of Counseling

Counseling is an interactive process directed by a counselor to provide psychological assistance to clients in areas that they present. Counseling is rooted in a relationship between the counselor and the client. The counseling relationship is established solely to meet the needs of the client. Once goals have been met, the process of counseling is terminated. Each of the parties in counseling brings expertise to the encounter.

The counselor brings expertise in counseling theory, techniques, and knowledge of various specific presenting problems and also general knowledge in areas such as human development. The counselor is the expert on the process of counseling. The client brings expertise on his or her own life experience and knowledge of the situation. The client is the expert on him- or herself. Counselor expertise should always take into account and adapt to client expertise.

I arrived at this definition of counseling in the course of teaching graduate students in a counseling psychology program. Teaching demands that professors take a stand on what they teach. During my discussion of the various definitions of counseling, students typically inquired about my view of counseling. In articulating my definition for them, I believed that it needed to reflect not only my view of the nature of counseling, but what I actually did in practice.

Adding the descriptor *psychological* to *assistance* is necessary because *counselor*, unlike *psychologist*, is an uncontrolled word. There are many uses of counselor and counseling: financial, fitness, and dietary are some examples. Anyone can use the word *counselor* to refer to him- or herself.

Implicit in my definition is the ethical responsibility of counselors. The counseling relationship is created to meet clients' needs. Counselors cannot use the process to meet their own personal/social needs. Counseling processes need to be terminated once the objectives are met.

An interactive process is used to capture two aspects of my approach. Counseling occurs in the ongoing conversation between counselor and client. *Process* is a term that refers to a gradual, rather than rapid, procedure. The counselor and the client engage at the request of the client, who determines the initial focus of counseling by articulating a presenting problem. Where the process actually finishes may change as a result of the interaction between client and counselor. The counselor has the responsibility to direct the process by using her or his professional skills and knowledge and taking into account clients' uniqueness and perspectives. Although the definition places the responsibility for the process on the counselor, clients must never be left behind: Diversion from presenting problems to other areas uncovered by the counselor occurs only with client agreement.

Role of Counselor

My function in counseling is to direct the counseling process by using the model that I have developed. This direction is done in a flexible way, analogous to a teacher who has constructed a lesson plan but is prepared to adapt it to his or her students' needs. The direction is done in a manner that is sensitive to clients, but I believe that directing the process is my responsibility, not the client's.

In my model, I enact the roles of facilitator, problem solver, and educator, as needed, throughout the counseling process. Generally, the facilitative role is most visible at the beginning of counseling, where the focus is in relationship building. I adopt a facilitative role in any stage of counseling when, for example, clients' emotions are apparent or when an impasse is reached. As counseling progresses, I adopt the roles of problem solver and teacher.

At the outset of counseling and often in the first telephone contact, I explain my approach. In the initial stage of counseling, I adopt a facilitative role, encouraging clients to tell their stories. In subsequent counseling sessions, I introduce concepts to clients, asking them to what degree, if any, the concepts help them understand their experience. Essentially, I take a didactic approach, presenting a concept in the context of a session and requesting feedback from clients regarding the appropriateness of the concept in capturing their experiences. My focus at this stage of counseling is to create a conceptual framework by which my clients and I can make sense of their experiences.

There is an intentional progression from a nondirective role to a directive and didactic role. Initially the client determines the content of the sessions. As I develop a deeper understanding of my clients' situations, I become more active in suggesting topics of conversation and proposing ways of interpreting clients' analyses of their situations. This transformation of roles is implemented with careful attention to clients' level of acceptance of the appropriateness of the procedure.

Role of Client

Clients need to be motivated and active in the counseling process. I believe that counseling can work only with motivated clients, given my definition that counseling is an interactive process between a counselor and client. I actively encourage clients to provide me with honest answers to my questions and to alert me should they take issue with something I say in the sessions. With clients who are gifted, I have learned that their giftedness is active in the counseling sessions regardless of their presenting problems. I believe it is their natural inclination to question authority, and so I make it explicit from the outset that I need them to feel free to voice their opinions and feelings about the process and me. Specifically, I encourage clients to provide feedback on the conceptual framework and the homework I assign. Client input in these areas is key to a successful counseling outcome.

Goals

The primary goal of counseling is to use psychological expertise to help clients deal with challenges they encounter. In this sense, counseling is a form of applied psychology. Many times counseling involves helping clients solve problems; at other times it necessitates helping them accept situations that cannot be changed. A subgoal, particularly when working with clients who are gifted, is helping clients to understand their current situation. In my experience, gifted individuals have a greater need than do other clients to understand the experiences that led them to seek counseling. An important part of helping them resolve their presenting problems is creating a framework for them to use to understand their experiences. Whatever conceptualization is created, however, needs to pass their scrutiny; otherwise it is of no value.

Relationship

Relationship is a critical ingredient in counseling effectiveness. A strong counseling relationship is required for two related reasons. First, it provides a safe environment for clients. By using empathy, congruence, and acceptance I become a nonthreatening stimulus to my clients. This posture enhances their level of comfort in a situation in which they have made themselves vulnerable. Second, the better the counseling relationship, the more valid the information revealed by clients. While client comfort is an important matter, more important is the accuracy of data that I have available for my continuous analysis of client information.

The counseling relationship is unique in the realm of relationships. It is created to meet the needs of only one party, namely, the client. Unlike other relationships that are characterized (or should be characterized) by mutuality, the counseling relationship is exclusively unidirectional in terms of need fulfillment. Once the goals of counseling have been met, the relationship is terminated.

Assessment

When counseling gifted individuals, I prefer not to engage in traditional formal psychological assessment to determine the presence of giftedness or disorder. In the case of adults, their giftedness is preestablished by their being graduates of gifted education programs or by their occupational status, such as medicine, law, and engineering. This rough gauge of giftedness is sufficient for my counseling purposes. In the case of young clients, they are typically identified prior to being referred to me. Typically, gifted students are referred after a psychological assessment sparked by school-related difficulties (e.g., academic underachievement, behavior problems). Because my clientele are usually pre-identified as gifted, I rarely administer tests of cognitive abilities.

In a similar vein, I do not formally assess for such disorders as Attention Deficit/Hyperactivity Disorder (ADHD) or Asperger's syndrome. Parents or teachers of gifted students with dual or multiple exceptionalities refer such clients, but only after diagnoses have been completed. Whereas I administer a cognitive abilities test if necessary, I do not formally identify for such *Diagnostic and Statistical Manual* (4th ed.; DSM-IV; American Psychiatric Association, 1994) disorders as ADHD. Such disorders are psychiatric conditions rooted in a medical model. Although I find having knowledge of these disorders necessary, I find little in a diagnosis that is useful in guiding my counseling process. A diagnosis of a psychiatric/medical condition logically leads to a medical intervention, namely, medication, rather than a particular counseling approach. In my model, I encourage descriptive accounts of the behaviors associated with the disorder. Specifically, I ask parents or adult clients to set the disorder aside and to describe what behaviors they associate with the disorder.

My assessment of clients is conducted through an analysis of their descriptions of their presenting problems. While I facilitate their elaboration of their issues, I use an array of concepts to assess their situation. I first focus on their presenting problem and begin my assessment at that point, using my general knowledge of the issue. For example, if it is depression, I tend to view descriptions of their situation through a learned-helplessness lens (Abramson, Seligman, & Teasdale, 1978). I encourage clients to apply that conception to confirm or disconfirm its applicability to their situations. With clients who are gifted, I look for manifestations of their cognitive characteristics, such as their use of language and analytic abilities. If they appear to possess superior intellectual potential, I look for evidence of the affective characteristics of heightened sensitivity, self-criticism, and emotional intensity. I also listen for references to anxiety. My assessment is conducted using concepts fundamental to my model, and the goal is to create a psychological portrait of clients so that I can incorporate it into the counseling process.

Process

In the initial session, I try to accomplish several objectives: obtain a general idea of the presenting problem, explain my approach, and "think out loud." I encourage clients to elaborate on their presenting problem. I explain my model, and I illustrate how I process information as I think out loud, using my concepts to interpret what they say. Homework assignments are part of my model, and I typically assign a homework assignment at the end of the first session.

Subsequent sessions are normally a combination of activities. Clients are encouraged to explore their situation with particular emphasis on the emotionality associated with their experiences. There are several important concepts that I introduce in a predetermined sequence. These are used to construct a framework within which clients may view their experiences. Conceptual frameworks are co-constructed with clients and refined until clients feel that these "theories" account for the "data" of their experience. Homework assignments are used to assess these hypothetical structures.

I am not committed to short-term counseling found in various forms of brief therapy. On the other hand, my model does not reflect the duration that insight or dynamic approaches to therapy do. Philosophically, I approach duration of counseling with a pragmatic attitude: I make a commitment to clients that I will work with them until we achieve their objectives or until they find that the process is not helpful. In the latter case, termination after referral is warranted. Given my problem-solving approach, the duration of counseling tends to be relatively brief. Based on experience, counseling duration is between 6 and 12 sessions held weekly. Where client situations are particularly complex, the process may be rather protracted at times, spanning a year to 18 months.

The stages in my model of counseling, represented in Table 3.2, are a combination of Meichenbaum's (1985) Conceptual phase and a generally accepted model (Cormier & Cormier, 1998). My Conceptual stage is designed to accomplish several objectives: exploration of a presenting problem, development of a counseling relationship, creation of a conceptual framework, and specification of goals.

Similar to the work of Meichenbaum (1985), a conceptual framework is co-constructed with clients. I draw from a standard conceptual pool: my definition of giftedness and associated characteristics, cognitive theory of emotion,

TABLE 3.2

Stages of Counseling

Stage	Objective	Counselor Activity
Conceptual	Developing relationship Exploring presenting problem	Use of core conditions (empathy, congruence, nonjudgmental attitude)
	Co-creating a conceptual framework Setting goals	Didactic application of conceptions of giftedness (definition and characteristics) and emotion (cognitive theory; primary and secondary emotions)
	Homework	Awareness exercises
Action	Implementing conceptual framework to accomplish goals	Confrontation Cognitive restructuring Empirical attitude Emotion awareness exercises Emotion experience exercises Other (created to address presenting problems)
Evaluation	Assessing client progress	Decision to proceed to Termination or return to previous stage
Termination	Reinforcing a sense of agency in clients	Emphasis on clients' implementation of concepts in daily life as the critical element in success of counseling
	Temporal comparison	Guidance of client to contrast current functioning to that at initiation of counseling
	Easing clients out of the process	Scheduling of follow-up sessions

interpersonal theory of anxiety, cognitive development, and positive disintegration. Clients contribute by providing detailed self-disclosure regarding their situation. In addition, clients also contribute their own notions of giftedness and additional characteristics of giftedness. Clients' views of giftedness are added to the pool of ideas that is used to create the framework. Those concepts that resonate with clients are kept; those that do not are rejected. It is important to note that clients are the judge of whether a specific concept is useful to enhancing their understanding of their issues.

An important didactic element in the co-creation of a conceptual framework is increasing clients' awareness of their underlying assumptions. Similar to rational emotive behavioral therapists (Ellis, 2000), I aim to make clients' implicit assumptions explicit. My objective is two-fold: to teach clients that their assumptions drive their behaviors and emotions and to help them reformulate their assumptions as needed. With gifted individuals, increasing their awareness regarding their assumptions is usually sufficient to trigger a spontaneous self-correction process.

Emotionality is a central theme in my approach. Conceptual frameworks are primarily concerned with helping clients who are gifted understand their intense emotions. To accomplish this, I use the cognitive theory of emotion and the characteristics of giftedness. My aim is to help clients understand emotions so that they can develop greater self-regulation of emotions.

The emotion of anxiety receives special attention in discussions of emotions in the Conceptual stage of the model. I describe anxiety as the distress arising out of our expectations of negative outcomes with which we are convinced that we cannot cope. Further, I believe that anxiety underlies virtually all forms of psychological difficulties. Such notions about anxiety are used to help clients conceptualize their distressing situations.

In the Conceptual stage, the focus on emotions extends to homework assignments, which are aimed at increasing awareness of emotionality in daily life. One assignment is designed to increase awareness of negative emotions during emotion-eliciting situations. In addition, homework is aimed at enhancing clients' awareness of assumptions underlying their behaviors and emotions in daily living.

Homework assignments are used to begin subsequent sessions. If homework was not completed, reasons for this are analyzed; if completed, clients are positively reinforced. Discussion of homework assignments is also used to teach clients the nature of change used in my model. During discussions of completed homework, clients' attention is focused on indications of improvement, no matter how small. In this way, I educate clients to view change as occurring incrementally.

While establishing a relationship and working toward a common interpretation of the issues, I engage clients in a discussion to determine what they hope to achieve in counseling—that is, the objectives that will guide our work together. At times clients need assistance in articulating specific, concrete objectives from their initially vague general statements. Clients are also helped to state these in positive rather than negative terms. Because clients who are gifted learn quickly, we can complete the Conceptual stage fairly quickly and then progress to the next stage.

Action is the second stage. In this phase, two types of techniques aimed at promoting client change are used. One type consists of established techniques drawn from other approaches and techniques that I derive from the conceptual framework developed with clients. My approach to techniques is analogous to the Gestalt therapists' approach, in which techniques are classified as exercises and experiments. Exercises are ready-made techniques that a therapist selects from a menu; experiments are techniques that a therapist creates from interactions with clients (Zinker, 1978). In the "Techniques" section on page 56, both types of techniques that I use will be discussed.

Whether the techniques are established or created, I make explicit the connection between a technique and the conceptual framework developed in the first stage. My experience with clients who are gifted suggests that it is paramount that these clients see the connection between any strategy that I suggest and our previous discussions. Without this explicit connection, I would anticipate resistance to the suggestions.

Analogous to cognitive behavioral therapists, homework is assigned to facilitate the transfer of learning from the counseling session to clients' daily lives (Ellis, 2000; Meichenbaum, 1985). When debriefing regarding homework, I continue my education on the topic of change as a process. I ask for a detailed account of their experiences with homework. In the process, I help them see the gains they have made. Further, I help them make the connection between the changes and their actions. Typically, at this juncture, clients rarely include minor gains when they report on the homework. A common initial response is that there was no change. However, as they provide the details, change, though minor, is often visible. I find that it is important to help clients see these "glimmers"; otherwise they may become discouraged. With gifted individuals, I have found that this is best accomplished by identifying the small changes inherent in their descriptions of events rather than through leading questions. Another way of identifying minor changes is through temporal comparison. I ask clients to compare how they handled target situations before counseling and how they did in the course of doing their homework. My objective is to increase clients' awareness of the gains, albeit small initially, they are making. Further, I reinforce a sense of agency: The gains they are making are the result of their replacing old, ineffective patterns with new ones.

Evaluation is the third stage of the model. The purpose of this stage is to assess clients' progress, for the purposes of deciding whether to recycle through earlier stages or proceed to the Termination stage. If significant progress has not been accomplished, we return to a previous stage. This may require, for example, a reconsideration of the conceptual framework or implementation of other techniques. If clients and I agree on the achievement of significant progress, I introduce the possibility of ending the counseling process.

Termination is the fourth and final stage. In my model, Termination is a *stage* and not simply one session. I have two objectives for this stage. First, I want to reinforce a sense of agency in clients. Clients are engaged in a comprehensive temporal comparison: They are asked to recall in detail their situation at the start of counseling and contrast it with their current situation. The counseling process is reviewed with particular emphasis on emotions. During this discussion, I convey to the clients that, even though I provided concepts, it was their effort at implementing them in their daily lives that was the critical element in creating improvements. Second, I want to ease clients out of the counseling process while ensuring that the changes persist. This involves scheduling a number of follow-up sessions. I use the following rule of thumb: The longer the counseling process, the greater the number of follow-up sessions needed. Typically, one session scheduled one month after termination has been initiated suffices.

Techniques

I use two types of techniques: established and created. The established techniques are drawn from humanistic and cognitive-behavioral approaches to counseling and psychotherapy. Created techniques flow from the common components of conceptual frameworks developed with clients.

The following are established techniques:

- *Counselor conditions.* Throughout my contact with clients, empathy, non-judgmental attitude, and congruence (Rogers, 1951) are used to maintain a helping relationship and to enhance openness in communication.

- *Confrontation.* One of the ways I enhance clients' awareness is through confronting them when their communication is characterized by discrepancy. I view confrontation as an important vehicle for increasing clients' self-knowledge. When clients present verbal-nonverbal or talk-behavior discrepancy, they are confronted. Confrontation is used only when a relationship has been established. The implementation of this technique rests on a description of the discrepant elements. Analogous to contemporary use of confrontation in Gestalt therapy, contrasted with Perls' aggressive style (Yontef, 1995), I use confrontation to invite clients to engage in further self-exploration.

- *Cognitive restructuring.* My use of cognitive restructuring focuses on clients' assumptions and reflects the Gestalt view of awareness. While some cognitive-behavior therapists have focused on distorted inferences or irrational beliefs (Cormier & Cormier, 1998), I have focused on clients' assumptions underlying their interpretation of situations that lead to intense negative emotions. In my application of this technique with clients who are gifted, I have noticed that the simple awareness of their assumptions is often sufficient to result in a replacement of faulty assumptions with ones that are more logical or rational. Based on experience applying this form of cognitive restructuring, I believe that the Gestalt view of awareness is particularly applicable to clients who are gifted; that is, awareness in itself is curative (Jacobs, 1989).

- *Homework.* Another cognitive behavioral technique (Ellis, 2000; Meichenbaum, 1985), the homework assignment, is an integral part of my model. Homework is used for two purposes: to convey the action-oriented quality of my approach and to bridge counseling sessions and daily living. Assigning homework at the first session reinforces in clients' minds that my approach is problem solving and not an insight-oriented talk therapy. In addition, homework is used to convey that understanding one's situation is not sufficient; new assumptions must be implemented in daily life before change can occur. Cognitive restructuring helps clients replace their faulty assumptions; homework incorporates new assumptions. A common response during the construction of a conceptual framework is "I already know that about me." Homework assignments are aimed at communicating that their understanding, whether it stems from them or from a counseling session, is useful only when it is applied in their daily lives.

Created techniques include the following:

- *Empirical attitude.* Clients are taught to employ an empirical attitude toward the application of the concepts used in sessions. Homework assignments, flowing from a conceptual framework, are analogous to experiments. As the clients implement homework (treatment), they are asked to observe the effects on their thinking, emotions, and, where appropriate, others' responses. Consistent with the action orientation of my model, for a concept to be deemed effective, clients need to see the positive effects of its application to daily living.
- *Emotion awareness.* Clients are taught that emotion awareness is a prerequisite for emotion regulation. In addition to obtaining descriptions of emotions in areas related to presenting problems, I focus their attention on emotion experience during the session. I use this particularly when there are only nonverbal cues indicating *potential* emotional experiencing. This work is reinforced by homework assignments of self-monitoring of emotional experiences in daily life. At times, clients are instructed to keep a log that will be discussed in subsequent sessions.
- *Emotion expression.* Clients are taught the importance of expressing their emotions, where possible. The objective is emotion release, rather than an attempt to change others' behaviors. Targets of emotion-expression exercises are clients' significant others. With some clients, the task is to change the pattern of emotion suppression they have developed. With other clients, the task is to teach them appropriate modes of expression.
- *Other.* Other techniques aimed at improving clients' presenting issues are created in cooperation with clients. These may include developing action plans to deal with study habits and organizational skills with academic underachievers or parent strategies for effective handling of gifted children's behavior problems.

Application

Presenting Problems

I use the model described in this chapter to deal with a variety of social/emotional adjustment problems of gifted individuals of all ages. Gifted adults seek counseling for parenting concerns, relationship issues, and existential crises. For parent and relationship counseling, I apply the model as presented. In the case of crises of meaning, the focus is on matters such as clients' aware-ness and acceptance rather than on behavior-change techniques. Gifted youth are typically referred for academic underachievement, at times associated with other exceptionalities such as ADHD, learning disabilities (LD), or Asperger's syndrome. In addition, gifted students are referred for social difficulties, behav-ioral disorders, and emotional disturbances often manifested in school settings. The model is not designed to work with clients manifesting psychoses; when these are apparent, I make referrals to other helping professionals.

Case Illustration

The creation of a conceptual framework is foundational to my approach. To illustrate this component of my model, I have chosen my work with a gifted student whose presenting problem is academic underachievement. The client is a 16-year-old female high school student in a gifted and talented education program. The transcript that follows contains segments of my first two inter-views with the client.

First Interview

Counselor (Co): In the first session, one of my objectives is to get an idea of what your concerns are. As you talk about them, I will think out loud with you so that you can see how I think about things. I think that before we can decide what to do, we need to come up with a way of understanding what you are experiencing that makes sense to both of us. So, please begin and tell me why you wanted to see me.

Client (Cl): OK. I go to high school. I'm in grade 11. I was talking to one of my teachers and I mentioned to her that I thought I had ADD because I have trouble concentrating on things. Like, I read something six times and I can't remember what's happening. She said that I may not have the typical symp-toms of ADD. She said that I may be one of those introverted ADD people, not like the ones who have to get up and walk and talk.

Co: [*Provides information about ADHD and its subtypes*] Your teacher was probably referring to the primarily inattentive type of ADHD . . .

Cl: OK.

Co: . . . which does not have the hyperactivity component. She was prob-ably saying that your issues are with attention, not the behavioral part. You identified this problem this year?

Cl: I was in GATE [Gifted and Talented Education] for junior high, so I don't think I have severe ADHD by any means. Compared to other kids in my class, who had severe problems, mine wasn't noticed because it is so mild, if it's there at all.

Co: OK.

Cl: And then last year in grade 10 . . . I had done Math 10 and Science 10 in grade 9 so I took three courses online and the only course I had in class was Sports Medicine and I ended up getting 95% in that. The previous term,

I had Social Studies 10AP [Advanced Placement], English 10AP, Spanish 10, and Gym, and my marks took a real nose dive. In social [studies], I ended with 60% and English, about the same.

Co: You must have been shocked!

Cl: I was but I wasn't. At the first part of the year, I thought things were going OK, and then the first thing I got back in the term was 60 in social [studies].

Co: You probably thought, "This can't be right."

Cl: Yeah, and all my marks were on that scale, regardless of whether I tried or not. So, I just stopped doing work. And, my work ethic slacked off.

Co: What was your work ethic like up to that point?

Cl: You didn't have to do any work in the GATE program I was in.

Co: What about earlier on?

Cl: Elementary school? It was easy.

Co: Little effort, great marks?

Cl: Yeah.

Co: You mentioned ADD, and we've talked a little about your school experiences, can you tell me what you'd like to work on with me?

Cl: What I want is ways to cope with things. When I sit down for a big project, like, I'll work really hard for 20 minutes; and, then I won't be able to do any work for 15; and, usually it's all at the last minute because I don't want to do it until then. I can't sit down and force myself to work.

Co: OK. I want you to know how I am thinking about what you've been telling me. Rather than looking at your situation as ADHD, I'd rather begin by seeing it as academic underachievement. When I work with gifted persons, I first try to understand their concerns by using characteristics that I attribute to giftedness. If that doesn't work, then I look for other explanations, such as ADHD.

Cl: Well, I don't want to say that there is something wrong with me [ADHD], but I don't want to believe that I'm a bad person with my work ethic problem. I truly think that I am a better person than that.

Co: Well, I really don't think that you are a bad person. In fact, the way I am thinking about your situation, as academic underachievement, is in line with what some people have written about. Some writers call underachievement a "predictable crisis" for gifted students. My version of it is this: Basically you were coasting along. Then you "hit the wall." If you hadn't taken the AP courses, you may have delayed this, but I think it would have happened eventually.

Cl: Yeah, I guess.

Co: Let's see if my thinking about this applies to you. Because of your giftedness, in your early school years, learning seemed effortless and you were getting great marks. Then, when you began taking courses that required more effort, like the AP courses, you hit the wall, meaning that your school marks began to decline sharply.

Cl: Yeah, I get it. I think it does apply. Last year, there were kids who did lots of homework every night, but I didn't even open my textbook at home. I still got 69%. It's not good at all, but I still passed it.

Co: Yes, and if someone else with less ability did what you did, she would have gotten failing marks.

Cl: Yeah.

After a while she talks about how challenging the task of changing patterns appears to her. I continue with developing a conceptual framework by introducing characteristics of giftedness.

Cl: I know that I need to change things, and it's not so bad. Changing your work ethic is a big thing. It is really broad.

Co: We will work on your work ethic. But, because of how I work, we first need to come to a mutual understanding of what may be causing the work ethic issue. Then, we can figure out what to do about it. Is that OK with you?

Cl:: Yeah, that's fine.

Co: Let me suggest something to you and you'll have to tell me honestly whether this applies to you.

Cl: OK.

Co: I want to use giftedness and the characteristics that I associate with it to understand your situation. I think that gifted people evaluate and analyze every thing. Let's apply it to you. When you are given a task by your teachers, you don't simply say, "OK, I'll go ahead and do it," do you?

Cl: Of course not, and my teachers hate it. Sometimes, I look at an assignment and I think of a better way of doing it. Other times, I think an assignment is silly and it's not worth my time doing it. Once, my science teacher gave us an assignment to write a textbook on globalization. Talk about ambiguity! I thought that the assignment was so bad that I didn't do it. And, I hate doing essays and reflections. . . . I can't write things I feel; I can write things I think.

Co: Now, there's a whole area that we haven't touched on yet, the emotional side of you.

Cl: Have you ever done the true colors?

Co: What about them?

Cl: You see, I'm blue, I'm supposed to be one of those people who feel this or that, not think it.

Co: I don't know about true colors. It may be that you feel things but you don't express them.

Cl: Yes.

Co: Now, we are talking about a core element in my view of giftedness, and that is heightened sensitivity. I think that you, because you are a gifted person, are very sensitive.

Cl: OK.

Co: I have drawn this conclusion: The more intelligent a person is, the more sensitive she is; because I define sensitivity in terms of awareness. When I think of sensitivity, I make a distinction between experience and expression. Being very sensitive doesn't mean that you go around expressing your feelings.

Cl: [*attentive*] OK.

Co: You are very aware of others' feelings and your own feelings. So, you feel deeply, but the people around you may never know it.

Cl: Yeah, people think I'm cold hearted.

Co: But, that's not what you're really like, is it?

Cl: No. Would being sensitive prompt me to overreactions?

Co: In my theorizing? Absolutely.

Cl: This makes a lot of sense. You know, that's why I went into the GATE program. Because of my hypersensitivity to other kids' reactions to me. I was tall, I was smart, and so kids thought, "Let's single her out."

Co: So, because of your giftedness, you were the target of a lot of teasing and it was very hard on you.

Cl: Yeah.

Co: Heightened sensitivity also works in other ways that can add to our stress, by sensing and taking on the emotional burdens of others.

Cl: Yeah, I have a friend who was talking to me the other day about the problems she is having at home. I felt really bad for her. Sometimes I have to tell people that I can't listen to them because it makes me feel really, really sad. I'll start feeling really bad. I'll start feeling their feelings myself.

[*Client returns to exploration of academic underachievement.*]

Co: There is another part of my thinking that relates to this. Over the years you probably received a lot of positive feedback about your intelligence and being told you were gifted.

Cl: Yes, I remember that happening.

Co: And so, you likely associated effortless learning with being gifted. After a while you may have incorporated that thinking into your identity or self-concept. Let's see if all of this theorizing applies to you. When did you begin noticing the slide in your grades?

Cl: It probably started in grade 9 math and science.

Co: In my experience, the decline usually starts in those subjects because in math and science you either know the material or you don't. You can't fake it. You can't draw as much on your general knowledge as you can with other school subjects.

Cl: In math and science I just stopped doing the work. Social [studies] and English through junior high were excellent. My teachers would say that they were really impressed with my work. So, I didn't have to do certain projects and I would still go out with an 85% [*laughing*].

Co: So, it seems that my theorizing may apply to you. Can you relate to the part about associating giftedness with effortless learning?

Cl: Yes.

Co: Let me tell you what this also means to me and see if this applies to you, too. You may think, "If I have to put effort into my school work, I can't be gifted." This may have become part of your identify.

Cl: [sounds surprised] Yeah, I do think that I can't be gifted if I have to work at something.

As the session ends, I summarize our discussion.

Second Interview

Co: Did our session last week spark any thoughts?

Cl: Yes, we were talking about identity. I kind of thought about that. It's weird what makes up your identity and what doesn't. Yet, you still think it does. So, I thought about that a lot. That was interesting.

Co: Would you mind elaborating?

Cl: I never really thought that being called gifted was part of my identity. It's really important for me that people think I'm smart, and I like having the upper hand in day-to-day conversations. It's interesting to realize that about yourself after 16 years.

Co: So, that's what stood out for you? Was there anything else?

Cl: No, that was it.

Co: Well, let's talk about identity in the sense of how you view your self and what is important to you.

Cl: Material things are not that big of a deal for me. It's nice to have them, but they don't affect who I am.

Co: Um-hm.

Cl: Like, clothing is not really an issue. I can dress one way or the other, and it doesn't bother me. My horse would probably be the only thing . . .

Co: Part of your identity? "I'm a person who has a horse."

Cl: Yeah. My family is very athletic, something that I did not inherit. So, the fact that I have a sport that I can excel at is very important. And, in my sport, presentation is everything, and that suits me because I'm such a perfectionist.

Co: I wonder what perfectionism means to you.

Cl: I get frustrated when it's not right. To me that's what it is. To other people, I can watch them and I can say they're perfectionists because they do something over and over again. I get so frustrated that I can't get past the first roadblock. I'll just throw up my hands in the air; I just walk away.

Co: Does that apply in all areas of your life?

Cl: School especially, because that's always supposed to have been easy for me. Riding not so much, because I knew from the beginning that I had to work at it. No one is naturally gifted at riding . . .

Co: Hmm.

Cl: . . . and so I got used to working at it.

Co: It seems to me that you selected that area. It wasn't imposed on you.

Cl: And it was one of those things that my parents weren't too excited about. And so, I had to . . . I was 10 years old; I called every single horse barn in the phone book and found out who had the best prices, and we went from there.

Co: Talk about determination!

Cl: [*laughs*] Yeah, well, I wanted to do it.

Co: If you want to do something, you really get into it.

Cl: Yeah, and ultimately my parents saw that I was going to spend my own money to buy the horse, and so they bought it for me, and they still pay the monthly bills [*chuckling*].

Co: They saw your determination.

Cl: Yeah, I guess it was rewarded.

Co: Yeah . . . I'd like to go back to perfectionism. How is that manifested in your school work?

Cl: Frustration!

Co: Would you elaborate?

Cl: If I do an assignment and I don't think it's good enough, I just won't hand it in.

Co: You need to meet your expectations.

Cl: Yes, I have had teachers tell me that I have very high expectations. And sometimes I don't get around to finishing a project because I keep forgetting about it until the day it's due, and then I say, "Oh my God!"

Co: And so, you experience anxiety?

Cl: Yeah.

Co: I wonder if you use rationalization to deal with the anxiety around assignments. For example, do you say to yourself, "It's not worth that much anyway or it's a stupid assignment . . . "

Cl: That one! I like that one.

Co: "It's dumb—why would I do this?"

Cl: I know. It's redundant, not covering the curriculum like it's supposed to. It's laziness on his [teacher's] part; why should I do his work for him? Yeah, there are some pretty good rationalizations that I use.

Co: Are there times when you complete assignments and then you look at them and you say, "This is garbage. I'm not going to hand this in."?

Cl: Yep!

Co: You have a variety of ways of dealing with the anxiety around assignments, some of which . . .

Cl: If nothing else I am creative. I do have expectations, and if I don't meet them, I shut down. I think of ways of getting around it. I'm not the kind of person who keeps trying and trying because all my life I've been able to do things the first time. So, if I can't do it the first time, what makes me think that I can do it the second, third, or fourth?

Co: It's really that history of being able to do things very quickly and doing them well the first time that influenced how you approach assignments.

Cl: Yeah.

[*Introduction of the heightened self-criticism characteristic*]

Co: I wonder if this process is perfectionism. I see it more as self-criticism. You reflect on your assignment and you think, "I'm not doing this as well as I should." So, you are criticizing your performance. And you criticize yourself for not meeting your expectations instead of someone else's.

Cl: Yeah, and it's funny because my parents have always been really OK with my school marks. I think it's because they realized that, if they put any extra pressure on me, that would be it. I'd be done. I would do less work.

Co: Uhm.

Cl: I'll get 60s in school. If my friends got 60s, they'd be grounded. Sometimes, I wish that they [her parents] had put that extra pressure on me when I was younger.

Co: Uhm.

Cl: But, then I take a step back from the situation, and I think, "OK, if I had somebody else's expectations to consider, what would happen?" That would be too much because I am very hard on myself.

Co: You'd likely shut down completely, if you had to meet yours and somebody else's expectations.

Cl: Yeah, like, if people start criticizing me, I just attack . . . because I'll hear it but I won't be listening, because I don't want to, because of that oversensitivity thing.

Co: I see.

Cl: It's kind of a defense mechanism.

Co: What may be going on there is the result of both sensitivity and self-criticism.

Cl: Yeah.

Co: I'd like to understand further how self-criticism works in you. Let me give you a scenario. Suppose your mother says to you something like, "I noticed how you are doing your assignment, why don't you do it this other way?" What would you do?

Cl: I'd say, "Fine! Do you want to do it?" And, I would go on being very, very defensive. I hear a kind of superiority in her voice. I don't deal well with that.

Co: What does that superiority mean to you?

Cl: It means that . . . it's not so much that they think they're better than me but that they think I'm worse than they are.

Co: Is it possible that they think that they know what to do better than you do? That they know what you should be doing?

Cl: Yeah.

Co: Which is a little different than what you were saying. I'm just trying to⁷ figure this out.

Cl: It's not that they think that they know better. They think that I know worse. I've been thinking this way for a very long time. I can't think of a time when I wasn't interpreting people's comments about me in this way.

Co: So, whenever there was commentary directed at you or what you were doing, that would be your typical response. You thought that they were putting you down. Would the phrase "implied criticism of you" capture this?

Cl: Yes!

Co: So, you take commentary on you as implied criticism.

Cl: Yeah.

Co: And, you likely perceive the criticism as threatening. Then, you become defensive and go on the attack.

Cl: Yeah. My dad is really bad for that. He says, "Are you doing your home-work?" I'm sitting there and I get so frustrated. He sees me sitting there, and he can tell if I am or I'm not. I get really abrupt with him. He is quite a bit like me personality-wise, so he gets abrupt and it's not really a good encounter.

Co: OK, I'll be Dad. "So, are you doing your homework?"

Cl: [*laughs*] He doesn't say it like that.

Co: You mean he says it with an edge in his voice?

Cl: Yeah. He says, "SO, are you DOING your homework?" He knows that I'm not, implying that I should be. Then I say, "Daaaad!"

Co: There's a lot going on in that brief encounter.

Cl: Yeah.

[*Discussion of conception of giftedness, sensitivity, emotional experience, and emotional expression*]

Cl: My brother and sister are both very intelligent, but emotionally they are not at the same level as me. For me, there's intelligent and gifted. Intelligent means that you are just as smart as the gifted person, but the gifted person has more emotional baggage. All my friends are very smart, and they all get high marks. My best friend, in particular, the one who is stressed, she doesn't seem like the friends that I had in GATE, but she's very smart.

Co: It's interesting to hear your comments about intelligence and giftedness. Let's compare our views on this. I don't distinguish between being very smart and being gifted. To me being gifted means being very smart. I think that sensitivity is related to intelligence so that the greater the intelligence, the greater the sensitivity. The interpretation that I give to the difference in emotions is that there is a difference between experience and expression of emotions. So, if you have two people with the same intelligence, they should have the same level of sensitivity, which means that they have the potential to be very emotional.

Cl: Yeah?

Co: The source of any difference in emotional expression is in the social environment.

Cl: Oh, OK.

Co: One way to look at it is that sensitivity creates emotion. Whether they are expressed or not is another matter.

Cl: That's where the emotional issues come into play?

Co: In a way. There's a difference between emotional experience and emotional expression. Emotional experience is part of sensitivity. Emotional expression depends on the environment.

Cl: Oh, OK.

Co: If you are in an environment that doesn't encourage expression, then you will learn not to express your emotions. We learn rules about expressing our feelings as we get feedback from others, especially from parents. It's our parents' and others' responses to our emotional expression that initially teaches us whether and how we should express our emotions. The experience part is there. Whether we express our sensitivity depends on the environment that we were raised in.

Cl: Yeah, I can see that. Girls are told that it's OK to cry, and then they are looked down upon for being emotional. I didn't want that. So, I said, "No." I have the emotional expression of a 16-year-old guy.

Co: You put effort into suppressing the expression of your emotions.

Cl: Yes, and now I am feeling the repercussions

Co: What are some of the repercussions?

Cl: The fact that everything is bottled up. My one friend is a good comparison for me because it gives me something tangible to look at. She is so different. She's very needy. She always needs affection. She always needs a boyfriend. She always needs to tell you what's wrong with her, and she's super moody. I'm sitting here thinking, "OK, it's not like you are the only person feeling this way. Trust me." I just have enough sense to keep it inside, so that makes it tougher for me because I don't want to act like her, and I need to keep it all inside.

Co: But, at the same time, you have the need to express it . . .

Cl: [*simultaneously*] Express it.

Co: . . . and emotions need to be expressed.

Cl: Yes, but there are very few people I trust with any little amount, let alone the entire thing. Just because of what happened in elementary school. I've learned my lesson there. Knowledge is power.

Co: Yeah.

Cl: If I tell somebody something . . .

Co: "They'll use it against me."

Cl: Exactly!

Co: If there's that chance, I'm not going to risk revealing my feelings.

Cl: Yeah, that's a heck of a lot of trust to be put onto someone.

Co: You know, going back to identity and self-concept, I think that emotions are at the core of our self-concept. A person has to feel very safe to reveal feelings that are part of her innermost sense of self. Unless you feel safe, you're not going to risk it. What if you are rejected?

Cl: It's not even that. Many, many people are not as secretive as me. If people tell others things about themselves, it's not a big deal for them. But, if someone tells other people things that I've told them about me, that's it. I'm done! It's not for any other reason than I have worked so hard to keep it all inside. If more than three people know some personal thing about me, I get anxious.

Co: What we are talking about now is a good example of what I was saying earlier about emotional expression. If you did not have those very bad experiences in elementary school, you probably would not have come up with your way of coping with emotions.

Cl: Yeah, and probably it's also because my parents treated me like a little adult.

Co: Right. Yeah.

Cl: I was treated emotionally like an adult. Like, when I was 6 years old and I would say "I hate" something or someone, they would say do not say *hate*; it's such a strong word. Well, when you are 6 years old you do hate! I was also told that I had to let things out in little spurts.

Co: So, it started with your being treated like an adult, and those experiences in school were added. I think there were other things that contributed to your style of emotional expression, but these are two significant events [that] stand out for you.

Cl: Yeah.

Co: But, we're talking about the *expression* of your emotions.

Cl: Yeah.

Co: Not the experience.

Cl: Yeah, there's lots of experience!

Co: And that's how I see sensitivity operating. Sensitivity generates emotions. Whether they are expressed or not is determined by the environment and the rules of emotion expression we have learned.

Cl: And, if my mother were here she would say that there are plenty of opportunities for her [the client] to express her emotions at home. There is. But, when I do, I feel guilty. Guilt is right there with my concept of self. I feel very guilty.

Co: So, what causes all that guilt?

Cl: I don't know. I'm well off, and my parents are always saying, "You're well off so you have to help others." Well, yeah, so I feel guilty because I'm not doing enough to help others. I can't watch the news or certain movies because I sympathize too much with the people. That's probably why I could never be a doctor or a psychologist. During the summer we put on a riding camp for the women at the women's shelter, and that is the most stressful time for me. It's hard. I have been physically sick during that time. It is so heartbreaking. I have cried every day after being with the women and their children. And when I try to talk to others about my feelings about this, they say, "Oh well, you just have to try to give them as good an experience as possible."

Co: When you try to express your feelings, others just don't understand.

Cl: No, they don't.

Co: I understand your experience from the point of view of heightened sensitivity. You are deeply affected by the plight of others because of your attunement to others' feelings and awareness of their predicaments.

This continues until the conceptual framework is fully developed. In subsequent sessions, the framework was used to understand her academic underachievement.

References

Abramson, L.Y., Seligman, M. E. P., & Teasdale, J. D. (1978). Learned helplessness in humans: Critique and reformulation. *Journal of Abnormal Psychology, 87*, 49–74.

Adler, A. (1954). *Understanding human nature.* New York: Fawcett.

American Psychiatric Association. (1994). *Diagnostic and statistical manual of mental disorders* (4th ed.). Washington, DC: American Psychiatric Association.

Clark, B. (1997). *Growing up gifted: Developing the potential of children at home and at school.* Upper Saddle River, NJ: Merrill.

Cormier, S., & Cormier, B. (1998). *Interview strategies for helpers.* Pacific Grove, CA: Brooks/Cole.

Dabrowski, K. (1964). *Positive disintegration.* Boston: Little, Brown.

Dabrowski, K. (1967). *Personality-shaping through disintegration.* Boston: Little, Brown.

Dabrowski, K. (1973). *The dynamics of concepts.* London: Gryf.

Ellis, A. (2000). Rational emotive behavior therapy. In R. Corsini & D. Wedding (Eds.), *Current psychotherapies* (6th ed., pp. 168–204). Itasca, IL: F. E. Peacock.

Freud, S. (1949). *An outline of psychoanalysis.* New York: Norton.

Gagné, F. (2003). Transforming gifts into talents: The DMGT as a developmental theory. In N. Colangelo & G. A. Davis (Eds.), *Handbook of gifted education* (3rd ed., pp. 60–74). Boston: Allyn & Bacon.

Gardner, H. (1993). *Frames of mind: The theory of multiple intelligences.* New York: Basic Books.

Gardner, H. (1999). *Intelligence reframed: Multiple intelligences for the 21st century.* New York: Basic Books.

Greenberg, L. S. (2002). *Emotion-focused therapy: Coaching clients to work through their feelings.* Washington, DC: American Psychological Association.

Harter, S. (1999). *Developmental approaches to self-processes.* New York: Guilford Press.

Jacobs, L. (1989). Dialogue in Gestalt theory and therapy. *The Gestalt Journal, 12*, 25–67.

Lewis, M. (2000). The emergence of human emotions. In M. Lewis & J. M. Haviland-Jones (Eds.), *Handbook of emotions* (2nd ed., pp. 265–280). New York: Guilford Press.

Lewis, M., & Michaelson, L. (1983). *Children's emotions and moods: Developmental theory and measurement.* New York: Plenum Press.

Lovecky, D. V. (1992). Exploring social and emotional aspects of giftedness in children. *Roeper Review, 15,* 18–25.

Marland, S. P., Jr. (1972). *Education of the gifted and talented: Report to the Congress of the United States by the U.S. Commissioner of Education.* Washington, DC: U.S. Government Printing Office.

Marsh, H. W. (1990). *Self-Description II manual.* Macarthur, Australia: Publication Unit, Faculty of Education, University of Western Sydney (Macarthur).

Meichenbaum, D. (1985). *Stress inoculation training.* New York: Pergamon Press.

Mendaglio, S. (1995). Sensitivity among gifted persons: A multi-faceted perspective. *Roeper Review, 17,* 169–172.

Mendaglio, S. (2003). Heightened multifaceted sensitivity of gifted students: Implications for counseling. *Journal of Secondary Gifted Education, 14,* 72–82.

Mendaglio, S. (2005). Counseling gifted persons: Taking giftedness into account. *Gifted Education International, 9,* 204–212.

Mendaglio, S., & Pyryt, M. C. (1995). Self-concepts of gifted students: Assessment-based intervention. *Teaching Exceptional Children, 27*(3), 40–45.

Perls, F., Hefferline, R., & Goodman, R. (1951). *Gestalt therapy integrated: Excitement and growth in the human personality.* New York: Dell.

Piaget, J., & Inhelder, B. (1969). *The psychology of the child.* New York: Basic Books.

Pyryt, M. C., & Mendaglio, S. (1994). The multidimensional self-concept: A comparison of gifted and average-ability adolescents. *Journal for the Education of the Gifted, 17,* 299–305.

Renzulli, J. S. (1978). What makes giftedness? Reexamining a definition. *Phi Delta Kappan, 63,* 619–620.

Renzulli, J. S. (2002). Emerging conceptions of giftedness: Building a bridge to the new century, *Exceptionality, 10*(2), 67–75.

Roeper, A. (1982). How the gifted cope with their emotions. *Roeper Review, 5*(2), 21–24.

Rogers, C. (1951). *Client-centered therapy.* Boston: Houghton Mifflin.

Rogers, C. R. (1980). *A way of being.* Boston: Houghton Mifflin.

Silverman, L. K. (Ed.). (1993). *Counseling the gifted and talented.* Denver, CO: Love.

Spearman, C. E. (1927). *The abilities of man.* New York: Macmillan.

Stephens, K. R., & Karnes, F. A. (2000). State definitions for the gifted and talented revisited. *Exceptional Children, 66,* 219–238.

Sullivan, H. S. (1953). *Interpersonal theory of psychiatry.* New York: Norton.

Terman, L. M. (1926). *Genius studies of genius: Vol. 1. Mental and physical traits of a thousand gifted children.* Stanford, CA: Stanford University Press.

Wechsler, D. (2003). *Wechsler Intelligence Scale for Children—Fourth Edition: Technical and interpretive manual.* San Antonio, TX: Psychological Corporation.

Yontef, G. (1995). Gestalt therapy. In A. S. Gurman & S. B. Messer (Eds.), *Essential psychotherapies: Theory and practice* (pp. 261–303). New York: Guilford Press.

Zinker, J. (1978). *Creative processes in Gestalt therapy.* New York: Random House.

chapter 4

A Systems Approach to Counseling Gifted Individuals and Their Families

*by Volker Thomas, Karen E. Ray,
and Sidney M. Moon*

Introduction

*I*n this chapter we integrate our perspectives, Thomas bringing a family therapy background, with its emphasis on systemic thinking and interventions, and Ray bringing experience with families in the education system. We are in accord that it is crucial to think broadly and beyond an individual point of view. Our framework is clearly systemic, including that the family itself is also affected by larger systems. Ray views systemic thinking as being mindful of the context of clients' lives, including influences on the family, as well as family members' influences on each other. She brings expertise in individual differences and how they affect counseling concerns. Thomas would describe those differences as relating to the family's interactional patterns and their emotional reactions to giftedness. Moon's influence on this chapter was indirect, through formulating two of the three models to be described and providing insights regarding using all with gifted students.

We will use concepts and terms from both of our orientations here, and they may be synonymous. *Therapist* and *counselor* refer to the clinician who is working with the family; *therapy* and *counseling* refer to the process of working with the family. The goal when working with family members includes affecting all family members, not just the gifted child, because all family members are affected by the identified child's giftedness, and all family members implicitly or explicitly influence the gifted child. This work can be done in sessions with individuals, parents, or all family members.

Conception of Giftedness

Influences

We both were drawn to the arena of counseling the gifted by a concatenation of events and location. Thomas was a family therapist working at the University of Iowa when the Belin-Blank Center for Gifted Education was interested in developing family counseling approaches for gifted students. He and center director Nick Colangelo developed a model that was clearly defined and could be evaluated. During the past 12 years, as a Purdue University faculty member, Thomas has collaborated with Sidney Moon, director of the Purdue Gifted Education Resource Institute (GERI). Ray's son was found eligible for an outreach program at the University of Minnesota, affiliated with the Study of Mathematically Precocious Youth (SMPY; Stanley, 1996). It took her some time to discover what her son's eligibility meant. When she did have some understanding, she looked for programs for gifted students and found GERI. Her first influences were Julian Stanley and John Feldhusen, in that they created the summer residential program that provided a much-needed service for her son. She has also been influenced by the gifted students she has counseled and the families of gifted students with whom she has worked, either in counseling or consultation. However, Barbara Kerr, Susan Jackson, Jean Peterson, Linda Silverman, and Nick Colangelo have also been strong influences.

Definition

Giftedness is like a geode with multifaceted crystals inside. The exterior is ordinary, not greatly distinguishable from other rocks. We are aware, of course, that a geologist might find a geode easily distinguishable. Inside are a multitude of crystals, varying in color, size, composition, and complexity. Nothing is in straight rows or neat columns. If a crystal is removed from the geode, it can be examined in some depth: weighing it, measuring it, analyzing its crystalline structure, bombarding it with X-rays. However, removing a crystal changes the geode's character, and then it is no longer a geode. Giftedness is similar in that it is a holistic concept that cannot easily be separated into component parts.

A commonly used definition of *giftedness* comes from Marland (1971) and describes various aspects of giftedness:

> Gifted and talented children are those identified by professionally qualified persons who, by virtue of outstanding abilities, are capable of high performance. These children require differentiated educational programs and/or services beyond those normally provided by the regular school program in order to realize their (potential) contribution to self and society. Children capable of high performance include those who have demonstrated any of the following abilities or aptitudes, singly or in combination: (a) general intellectual ability, (b) specific academic aptitude, (c) creative or productive thinking, (d) leadership ability, (e) visual and performing arts aptitude, and (f) psychomotor ability. (pp. I-3 to I-4)

This definition focuses attention on discrete abilities, and that aspect has proven important for identifying children for special programs. Furthermore, problems in educational systems may bring families of gifted children to therapy (Moon & Hall, 1998; Wierczerkowski & Prado, 1991). Even when the giftedness is apparent in only one area, it is still part of a whole entity and needs to be addressed in a holistic manner.

The definition from the Columbus Group (1991) emphasizes the uneven development that is often found in gifted individuals during their early life:

> Giftedness is asynchronous development in which advanced cognitive abilities and heightened intensity combine to create inner experiences and awareness that are qualitatively different from the norm. This asynchrony increases with higher intellectual capacity. The uniqueness of the gifted renders them particularly vulnerable and requires modifications in parenting, teaching and counseling in order for them to develop optimally. (n.p.)

Asynchronous development (Silverman, 1997) refers to development that is uneven: advanced in some domains, age appropriate in others, and slow in others. It is sometimes a source of frustration to the gifted person and is confounding to adults who expect social skills or fine motor skills to be on par with cognitive ability. This is seen most vividly in individuals who are gifted and have a concomitant exceptionality that is disabling in some way (e.g., learning disability, ADHD, emotional disorder, Asperger's syndrome). Although other manifestations of asynchronous development may not be as dramatic, the counselor nevertheless needs to have expertise in family approaches, giftedness, normal and abnormal development, and any specific presenting problems to be effective. It is important to understand whether concerns related to asynchrony are normal developmental events, a manifestation of the giftedness, or indicative of some process gone awry (e.g., a child who is in a parentified role; Bowen, 1978).

Other definitions of giftedness rely on biological, psychosocial, or cognitive perspectives (Moon & Hall, 1998). The biological approach draws from genetic and neurological studies and points to the genetic factors that are implicated in the inheritance of giftedness. Understanding the biological perspective is important because it is likely that, if one person in the family is gifted, others are likely to be as well. Counselors operating from the kind of systemic approach that we are advocating need to be aware of that. However, it is also possible that a child in a family is much more intelligent than the parents and may even be leading and managing the family covertly or overtly. This role reversal is a significant consideration in most family systems approaches.

Psychosocial definitions abound in education and involve intellectual ability and other factors, such as motivation, self-concept, supports and barriers to achievement, and task commitment (Moon & Hall, 1998). Because a number of the issues that bring gifted individuals to therapy stem from their being mismatched with the educational system (Webb, 1993), it is crucial to understand the manner in which the family meshes with education. It is also important to understand the perspective of the school in these cases, knowing what is important to teachers and administrators. Cognitive approaches to identification are often used in education, but are perhaps the most unfamiliar to family therapists. These approaches rely on a score, often on intelligence or aptitude tests, to determine a level of ability. Despite noteworthy problems with intelligence tests, they are used frequently to identify students as gifted (Sternberg, 1990).

All of these approaches have some merit and can inform the family therapist, deepening our understanding of the complexity of the family. However, it is important to work with the definition of giftedness that the family accepts and to examine the effect of that definition on family functioning. Is the giftedness seen as an advantage? Does it come with attendant stresses? How do various members of the family describe it and react to it? Is the family organized around the giftedness (Moon, Jurich, & Feldhusen, 1998)? Are they oblivious to it? What function does focusing on the giftedness fulfill for the family? What conflicts does it allow them to avoid? If a family does not realize that some or several of its members are gifted, what problems might be alleviated by attention to the giftedness and related academic needs? Finally, we understand that different levels of giftedness (e.g., mild, moderate, profound) may need interventions tailored to the ability levels of individuals and their families.

Characteristics

Authors writing about giftedness often include lists of characteristics of gifted people such as overexcitabilities, perfectionism, or sensitivity (e.g.,

Lovecky, 2000). These conceptual pieces, often originating in the observations of professionals working with gifted youth, provide an excellent starting point for thinking about giftedness. However, we believe that there is not sufficient research evidence to establish that these are either consistent characteristics of gifted individuals or are seen more often in gifted individuals than in others. We have certainly seen gifted people with these characteristics, but we have also seen gifted individuals without them. Likewise, we have seen nongifted people with and without these characteristics. On the other hand, some characteristics related to cognitive functioning have been researched, such as the need for complexity and precision; early abstract reasoning; the ability to understand complex patterns rapidly (Lovecky, 1994); better memory systems; larger and complex knowledge bases; the use of different processing strategies (Butterfield & Feretti, 1987); the tendency to rely on idiosyncratic patterns of abilities to shape their environment and find problems to solve; and the ability to conceptualize higher order relationships (Sternberg & Davidson, 1985). However, even when certain characteristics do exist, their expression may vary, depending on racial-ethnic group membership (Robinson & Clinkenbeard, 1998). Some of them are germane to a systems approach to counseling. For example, if one individual has a tendency to shape the family environment and is the problem-finder in the family, that individual may be bearing an inordinate share of the responsibility for family functioning.

The differences between gifted and nongifted individuals may be a matter of degree rather than of type of characteristics (Rogers, 1986). That is a helpful position for the family counselor to take. Although it is still important to have knowledge of the commonalities related to giftedness, our perspective focuses more on how those characteristics interact within the family system and then with larger systems (e.g., school, community) in which the family is embedded. The family counselor may also capitalize on the cognitive strengths as an asset in family counseling. This focus allows the counselor to address individual differences (e.g., level of giftedness, racial-ethnic background, adjustment) while maintaining an overall focus on the system.

Assumptions

Our primary assumption about giftedness is that it is embedded in a system: first within the family system, then within the school, and then within society. People are born with unique characteristics and, because their experiences and positions are different, they actually grow up in different environments even within the same family. Certainly there are significant differences in the personalities of gifted individuals, as well as in gender, race and ethnicity, socioeconomic status, and any concomitant disabilities. The problem does not lie in the difference itself, but in the adjustment to that difference within the individual, family, school, and society. We see giftedness from a dialectical perspective. There are often benefits that accompany giftedness, but there are also costs. A person can find great joy in thinking or creating, but experience anomie and unintentional alienation from others because the area of giftedness may be unusual and thus difficult for others to cope with. Privileges are the front side of giftedness, and discrimination is the back side. Although there does appear to be a genetic, brain-based foundation for giftedness, the development and expression of giftedness are strongly influenced by the person's environment.

Conception of Personality

Personality

Personality is a strange concept for family therapists to apply to therapy. Thomas does not deal with it often in marriage and family therapy, focusing instead on relationships. On the other hand, personality is a bedrock in the individual differences approach in psychology, which is Ray's background. Broadly defined as the pervasive and enduring patterns of perceiving, relating to, and thinking about self and the environment, personality is seen as being exhibited in a broad range of contexts (American Psychiatric Association [APA], 2000). Personality traits are adaptive or maladaptive. If an individual's personality is inflexible and causes distress, it may be called a personality disorder (APA). There is increasing evidence that personality is strongly influenced by genetic contributions (McCrae, 2000), even though the expression of personality may be affected by the environment. *Temperament* is traditionally used to describe children's approach to the world and is thought of as innate. *Personality* is more often used to refer to adult's pattern of perception, behavior, and interaction (Diener, 2000). However, there are people who see that temperament and personality are the same construct (T. Berndt, personal communication, April, 2005). When Ray uses the term *personality*, she applies it to both children and adults, being mindful of the genetic and environmental influences on the development of personality.

We might look at one person's personality as causing problems for a family, but even then, we look at that person's perceptions, behavior, and interactions in light of the perceptions, behavior, and interactions of the entire group. It is possible, perhaps even common, to operate from a family systems perspective without using any kind of specific personality assessment. However, we pay attention to the pervasive and enduring patterns of interaction that are present, and in that sense, it might be said that we deal with the personality of the family as a whole. Our therapeutic goal with the family often involves changing some of the existing patterns of interaction that are causing difficulties for the family.

Personality of Gifted Individuals

We simply do not believe that there is a distinct personality pattern associated with giftedness. Using the terminology of the NEO Personality Inventory-R (NEO PI-R; Costa & McCrae, 1992) we have seen gifted individuals who were neurotic or healthy, extroverted or introverted, open to experience or inflexible, agreeable or not, and conscientious or not. We have found similar results with the Myers-Briggs Type Indicator (Myers & Myers, 1980): Gifted people can be introverted or extroverted, use sensing or intuition, use thinking or feeling, and use judgment or perception. In working with the family, we seek to develop a deep understanding of the contributions of each member to the group. As such, we pay attention to the variations in perceptions, behavior, and interactions of each person. However, we do not see gifted individuals as having any personality factors that are specific to the person's giftedness.

Model of Counseling

Influences

Education and Professional Training

Thomas's primary influence stems from family systems approaches. After training in Germany at the University of Göttingen for his initial degree in economics, he next studied social work at the University of Kassel. He moved to the United States to complete his Ph.D. in family social science, with a specialization in marriage and family therapy, at the University of Minnesota. There he trained with David Olsen, Pauline Boss, and William Doherty, who had worked with Nicholas Colangelo at the University of Iowa. Colangelo, Sidney Moon, and John Feldhusen have all been influential in adapting family systems thinking for conceptualizing and working with gifted students.

Ray obtained her bachelor's degree in American studies with a secondary education endorsement at Western Michigan University. After working as a teacher, she pursued her master's degree in community counseling at Winona State University and is currently a doctoral candidate at Purdue University in counseling psychology. Her insights about normative development vis-à-vis exceptionalities related to giftedness reflect her background in education. Her graduate work has focused on a counseling psychology perspective, with its emphasis on person-environment interactions, people's assets and strengths, intact personalities, brief interventions, and vocational development (Gelso & Fretz, 1992). Client-centered counseling, systems approaches, prevention, cognitive-behavioral, humanistic, solution-focused, narrative, and Gestalt approaches have all influenced her work. While working as a master's-level counselor, she found that she often worked with families and began learning about structural and Bowenian interventions.

Models of Counseling Using Systemic Approaches

Models of counseling using systemic approaches have also influenced us. To this point, we have been writing as though we were using one model of counseling—a systemic model. In actuality, we try to match models to clients and their needs. Thus, we draw from or use a variety of models within the systems perspective. When counseling gifted individuals from a systems perspective, we propose using one of three models (Thomas & Moon, 2004): the Belin-Blank Center model (Colangelo & Davis, 1997), a combined structural-strategic approach (Haley, 1976; Minuchin, 1974), or an imaginative-postmodern approach (Freeman, Epston, & Lobovits, 1997; White & Epston, 1990) that relies on narrative and solution-focused thinking. The Belin-Blank Center model was developed specifically for use with gifted students and their families, and the other two approaches dovetail well with the strengths common in gifted families. The structural-strategic approach combines two influential movements from family systems work. The imaginative-postmodern approach takes advantage of the verbal and imaginational strengths of gifted people. As we continue in this chapter, some sections will be essentially the same across all three approaches, and these will be described in a single section: our definition of counseling, the goals of counseling, the relationship between counselor and client, and the process of counseling. Other topics have much in common across models, but with certain details specific to one model: the role of the counselor, the role of the client, and assessment. There will be an overall section for each of those and more specific information within the section for each approach.

Definition of Counseling

Counseling is a dynamic process. People who are experts about their life, strengths, and problems ask for help from a counselor who has expertise in system (e.g., self, family, school, or society) processes and dynamics, human development, wellness, pathology, diversity, and therapeutic techniques. Through this process, counselors and clients identify goals and strategies and resources to achieve those goals. We often see our first task in family systems work as convincing the family that they have expertise that is needed in our sessions. A corollary of that is that we tend not to give advice or provide guidance. We are interested in promoting the family's ability to discover solutions within and around themselves rather than seek us out each time there are recalcitrant problems. Our rationale for this definition is that it is respectful to all parties concerned, it works for us, the synergy of this approach makes our interventions more powerful and more long lasting, and responsibility for the success of our sessions is shared.

Ray began developing this point of view about 6 months into her professional counseling career. She was meeting with a 15-year-old drug dealer for counseling, enjoying her professional role as someone who could give guidance and advice to this troubled young man. The consensus of the community was that this young man was too far gone to be helped, but still the kind of person who needed crucial guidance and advice. After taking his history and becoming acquainted with him and his family, Ray concluded that she could not do as well in his situation as he was doing, and she could offer no advice or guidance. She quickly became client-centered and worked with the family to improve matters. Considerably chastened, she rethought her professional role and through the years developed the concept of a system of experts, varying in area of expertise.

Thomas realized when first working with gifted children and their families that they had many resources, but could not see or realize them for numerous reasons that worked at intrafamilial (e.g., family of origin) and extrafamilial (e.g., school, peers) levels. Helping families to tap into these resources and reflect on their context was frequently all that was needed for these families to become "unstuck" (Thomas, 1995).

Goals

Overall, our goal is to improve relationships among family members and between the family and other systems the family interacts with (Robbins & Szapocznik, 2000). Our plan is not to change the problem that is presented, but to change the context of the problem. This difference is subtle, but critical. In other therapeutic frameworks, the goal may relate to an accomplishment or resolution of an issue. We focus on the processes that occur within the family system, and between the family and its context, confident that, as we affect those processes, the family will be more able to solve problems themselves. Because we are presenting three models of counseling, our terminology may differ somewhat from time to time (see Table 4.1). If we are using the Belin-Blank model, we may talk about reducing enmeshment. In the structural-strategic model, we may suggest that patterns of interaction need to be changed and relationships within the family and between the family and other systems improved (Robbins & Szapocznik). If we are using a postmodern therapy approach, we might talk about externalizing the problem or reauthoring the story the family tells. The most important concept is that we are consistently thinking in terms of changing the entire system. Family systems experts (Hoffman, 2001) have noted that change may trigger anxiety for some family members, and we are alert for that.

Relationship

Our relationship with the client is the crucial component of family treatment. We build relationships with each individual in the family, we enter the

TABLE 4.1

Comparison of Three Systems Models for Counseling Gifted Individuals and Their Families

	Belin–Blank Model	Structural–Strategic	Imaginative–Postmodern
Influences	Family systems approaches; gifted education concepts	Structural family therapy (Minuchin, 1974); Strategic family therapy (Haley, 1976)	Postmodern philosophers (Wittgenstein, Foucault, Derrida); narrative therapy; solution-focused therapy (White & Epston, 1990)
Focus of Counseling	Family's emotional and relational dynamics, especially related to inclusion, control, and intimacy; cohesion and adaptability	Mitigate risk factors; enhance protective factors; interaction patterns among family members and between family and other systems	Promote thick description of the existing situation to open up unconsidered possibilities; find exceptions and unique outcomes
Goals	Improve relationships between family members; improve relationship between family and other systems	Improve relationships among family members; improve relationship between family and other systems	Improve relationships among family members; improve relationships between the family and other systems
Role of Counselor	Provider of expertise and direction; consultant; temporary member of the family system; ally	Provide expertise and direction; observe and participate in family's interaction; actively change interactional patterns	Facilitator, co-creator, cheerleader; empowerer of family members; challenger of oppressive practices
Role of Client	Conceptualize and problem solve; implement suggestions	Family open to change interactional patterns; use intellectual ability to learn to think systemically	Reauthor life; rediscover strengths; act on strengths

Relationship	Relationship as a crucial component to counseling; counselor as temporary consultant for the family system, in turn functioning within multiple systems; therapeutic alliance enabling change	Relationship as a crucial component to counseling; counselor as temporary member of the family system, in turn functioning within multiple systems; therapeutic alliance enables change	Relationship as a crucial component to counseling; temporary consultants in the family's reauthoring process; therapeutic alliance enables change
Assessment	Family Adaptability and Cohesion Scale III (Olson, Portner, & Lavee; 1985); Family Environment Scale (Moos & Moos, 1986)	Gather information from school records; observe family in session on an ongoing basis	Consult with the family to obtain their assessment
Techniques	Reduce enmeshment; increase intimacy; increase inclusion	Join; provide information and coaching; work in the present; reframe; work with alliances and boundaries; generate enactments; mitigate risk factors; enhance protective factors; restructure interactional patterns	Use scaling, miracle question, thick description; identify unique outcomes; reauthor problem-saturated stories
Personality in Counseling	Not particularly relevant	Provide information about each individual's approach	Imagination, creativity, and verbal strengths are helpful, although not necessary
Process	Business-like; information-based	Sessions reflect family's typical functioning and therefore may sometimes be intense	Creative, unpredictable, energetic

family system temporarily, and we maintain awareness of, and sometimes engage in, the systems outside of the family that affect family functioning. For instance, the giftedness of one child may create tensions within the family (cf. Silverman, 2000). We understand that our entry into individual and multiple relationships with family members is, in itself, apt to trigger some changes. The relationship is the foundation for our work, providing the bedrock that makes our interventions safe and available to the family.

We begin our relationship during the first contact with the family, whether that is by phone or in person, during which we listen empathically. Our sincere interest in each member of the family and about each system affecting family interactions continues to build the relationship during our meetings with them. We use empathy and active listening and pay attention to how the processes happen within the family and between the family and its context, asking questions and sharing information as needed. The alliance is founded on our practice of identifying strengths and processes that are going well (Lopez, Snyder, & Rasmussen, 2003), although we are candid in speaking about difficult processes, interactions, and issues, demonstrating that it is safe to address the painful side of family life. Through all of this, we maintain awareness that the forces that maintain equilibrium in a family are powerful and may have a tendency to draw us into the melee. Therefore, it is important for us to be alert and avoid joining in such a way that we maintain the existing dysfunctional interactional patterns within the family system.

Techniques

Techniques used in all three models with clinical families to help the family change its interactional patterns include working in the present, reframing, and working with boundaries and alliances (Minuchin & Fishman, 1981). The specific techniques used within each model are described below. When working in the present, the counselor encourages the family members to behave in their typical manner while with the counselor. We should mention that this takes a significant amount of trust on the part of family members and can be frightening for them. When they reach a point where they are less guarded, this enactment (Minuchin & Fishman) of the way they usually behave allows the family to *show* the counselor their interaction, thus making it available for intervention and suggestions about possible changes. This enactment also avoids having the family talk *about* the content of their interaction, which leads to intellectualizing and stagnation rather than change. A counselor who can successfully encourage family members to enact their usual patterns of interaction in session is doing well because individuals and families usually do not report their interactions as accurately as an observer would, and family members often behave differently when with a counselor than they do normally.

Reframing (Haley, 1976; Minuchin & Fishman, 1981) is a useful technique that allows family members to experiment with a different perspective related to issues that have been troubling them. A classic reframe is describing a glass of water as half full instead of half empty. We use reframing to help the family see actions and events in a more complex manner, noting their positive, as well as their troublesome, aspects. For example, if a family complains about a teacher who insults gifted students in general and also about their vocal and sometimes rude 15-year-old daughter, we probably join with the family and commiserate about the tactlessness and ignorance of the teacher and also point out that this is an opportunity for the 15-year-old to observe, analyze, and evaluate rude behavior.

We also share with them our belief about how much the parents care about their daughter. In families experiencing problems, alliances of individual family members are often organized around people outside of the family rather than people inside the family. For example, teenagers may ally with a friend's family instead of their own. The boundaries among family members or between the family and other systems may be too rigid or too flexible, instead of strong enough to hold the family together and flexible enough to give breathing room. Working with boundaries and alliances involves changing alliances in order to support appropriate behavior. For example, we encourage gifted teenagers to bring a gifted friend along to family sessions, if the rest of the family members do not object.

Belin-Blank Center Model

Phase One: Assessment. The Belin–Blank Center model (Colangelo & Davis, 1997) is brief, usually five to six sessions, and strength based, focusing on the family's emotional and relational dynamics especially related to inclusion, control, and intimacy (Doherty, Colangelo, & Hovander, 1991). Of the three approaches, this model relies the most on the counselor's expertise and direction. Families who work well in this model have a specific problem and are in need of specific information to solve the problem. We begin phase one with an assessment based on the Family Adaptability and Cohesion Scales III (FACES III; Olson et al., 1985) and the Family Environment Scale (FES; Moos & Moos, 1986). The FACES III is used to assess the adaptation and cohesion of the family, while the FES measures 10 dimensions of a family's social environment to derive an identification of the type of family environment present: expression oriented, structure oriented, independence oriented, achievement oriented, moral/religious oriented, and conflict oriented. These two instruments used together provide a rich source of information. Once we have come to an agreement with the family on the therapeutic goal, we move to phase two. This is a brief-therapy model and capitalizes on the conceptual and problem-solving strengths of gifted families (Thomas & Moon, 2004). Although the interventions may include providing information and problem solving, this approach avoids intellectualizing about the therapeutic goal by focusing on the process among family members and between the family and other systems.

Phase Two: Techniques. During phase two, we might use any of a number of techniques, depending on the issue being addressed. If the family is enmeshed, we provide support for the development of more appropriate levels of closeness. If the issue is school related, we provide information for the family to use in contacts with the school. For example, Thomas once worked with a family of a 7-year-old girl who underachieved in a gifted elementary program and was afraid of going to school. During the assessment phase the FACES III and FES results indicated an enmeshed relationship between mom and daughter, while dad was disengaged from both of them. At the same time, the family was highly achievement oriented and conflict avoidant. Based on these findings, Thomas suggested as goals for therapy that the father become a team with his wife to develop strategies for confronting and working through potential conflicts with a teacher at school who was highly critical of their daughter. Thomas did role-plays with the parents and then attended their meeting with the teacher, during which the issues with the daughter were addressed constructively. The parents got along better, the girl's fear of going to school decreased, the teacher became more supportive, and the girl's achievement improved.

Structural-Strategic Model

Phase One: Assessment. The structural-strategic model both capitalizes on the family's intellectual ability by teaching them how to see relational issues systematically (Thomas & Moon, 2004) and circumvents intellectualizing through enactments and paradoxical interventions (Minuchin, 1974). When using this approach, phase one consists of gathering information. We gather information about achievement in school from school testing and grade reports. The interaction in sessions and the family's input provide information about family dynamics. Based on this assessment, the counselor classifies families into problem or clinical categories for treatment. The problem-category families with gifted individuals need guidance and information, usually related to home and school interaction. Because of this likelihood, it is important for the counselor to have a good working knowledge of school systems and gifted education. Families in the clinical category have issues that are most suitable for structural-strategic interventions. At both levels of intervention, the counselor focuses on mitigating risk factors that contribute to the problem, enhancing protective factors that ameliorate the problem, and creating interventions that are practical and attainable, problem focused, and well planned (Robbins & Szapocznik, 2000). Once the dysfunctional interactional patterns have been identified, during phase two the counselor works with the family to change these to more functional patterns.

Phase Two: Techniques. Minuchin and Fishman (1981) suggested the following techniques during phase two. Problem families benefit from information and coaching about interaction with the systems in which the family is involved. Joining is the first technique used and remains an important technique throughout treatment. The counselor needs to engage the family by maintaining the existing family structure rules whenever possible (especially important when there are diversity issues), tracking how the family talks about issues and how they interact around those issues, and mimesis (i.e., matching) the family's style, pace, and mood (Robbins & Szapocznik, 2000).

Imaginative-Postmodern Model

Our imaginative-postmodern model (de Shazer, 1985; Freeman et al., 1997; White & Epston, 1990) incorporates thinking from narrative and solution-focused therapies. This meshes well with imagination, and the resulting creativity can be life-changing. Gifted families often have exceptional creative and verbal strengths, as well as areas of their lives that are going well; in these cases, we see the solution as already being in place. Combining imagination, verbal strengths, and existing solutions provides ample tools to use in this approach.

Phase One: Assessment. Phase one is assessment, but it is the most informal of the assessments used in the three approaches. We use information from clinical interviews and pay attention to the stories each family member brings to the session. We do not need corroborating evidence when working in this model because the change agent already exists and the specific problem becomes irrelevant.

Phase Two: Techniques. If we approach the presenting problem from a narrative point of view, we seek to help people restructure their stories, because we have found that changing the story people tell about themselves and others changes the situation. We help people move from "thin descriptions" of their lives, which prevent movement and change, to complex, "thick descriptions" that allow for movement (Geertz, 1973; White & Epston, 1990). Stories described in thin terms are rigid and stereotypical, while those with thick descriptions allow multiple perspectives. It is rather like the change of perspective that comes with standing on a ladder or taking a different route to work or even something as simple as tying your shoes differently. We might tell a fairy tale that reminds us of the family's story but with an ending that promotes courage and energy and connection (Thomas, 1995). Or, the family can create their own fairy tale with the ending they want. In some ways, this looks like a lazy approach to counseling, but "anything that allows people to participate in their lives in ways they couldn't before" (J. Diamond, personal communication, 2002) is useful for growth.

With a solution-focused frame (de Shazer, 1985), we listen to the story of the problem and then ask the family members what they each want to happen. Then we look for those times when that solution already has existed: the exceptions to the rule of the problem. The key point with solution-focused therapy is to pay attention to the times when the family is successful and to replicate those times by paying attention to the differences that precede them. It may be that the differences appear small, but that is not a problem. A key concept is that people have good reasons for doing what they do, and exploring the benefits of behavior that is troubling them may reveal avenues to change (Berg, n.d.).

As we work with people, we may ask them to scale their solutions, that is, periodically assess how they are doing. Scaling is helpful in the initial stages of therapy when people tend to pay more attention to the work left to do rather than to the progress they have already made. We simply ask them to rate their situation on a 10-point scale. Their point of reference is when they decided to come in for counseling (i.e., 1), with 10 being how they will feel when they no longer need therapy. Almost always, there has been some improvement during the time between deciding to seek counseling and our first session with them, and we begin asking what contributed to the improvement, helping the family to discover what they are already doing that is helpful. Then, instead of asking about what it would take to get to their goal, we ask what it would take to move one point up on the scale. This is an increment that is possible and leads to small but consistent change.

In phase two, scaling questions can be used to track the improvement the family has experienced while in counseling. For example, a dad suggests that between the second and third session he moved from a 4 to a 5 on a 10-point scale. Then the counselor asks what happened to help the family members move up 1 point on the scale and how a 5 is different from a 4.

Role of the Counselor

We see the role of the counselor as changing throughout the process of counseling. Initially, people often come to family therapy expecting answers and direction, operating in a medical model of expert and patient (Bordeaux, 2001). Our first role in these cases is educator and persuader, offering a different approach to helping. Next, we often function as a negotiator, sorting out which problem we will work on together, that problem often being different from the presenting problem (Moon & Thomas, 2003). Then we are allies and cheerleaders, joining the client or family to help pick out their strengths and marshal their resources. Once we have focused on an area to work on and have identified the family's strengths and resources, we become the chairperson of a crucial committee made up of the entire family, all with particular expertise relevant to this issue. Because our committee has connections with other entities such as school, work, and community, we are occasionally liaisons to those groups or advisors as the family interacts with the groups. From time to time we switch and act as a forward observer, calling in the coordinates for the troops with the weapons. Please note that we do not intend to offend the sensibilities of people who support war or oppose it; we merely offer a metaphor for our work. Our point is that we sometimes give some direction or some pointers, but it is the family that is actually doing the work. We may also act like a guide on an Outward Bound trek, offering some instruction and pointers, but leaving the work up to the hikers. At the end of our sessions, we become a concierge, coordinating a celebration with the family to celebrate its journey and growth.

Role of the Client

We see the client, whether it is an individual, family, or school, as being active, oriented to a goal, and capable of using his or her own expertise in service of his or her own goals. Thus the client is not the passive recipient of our ideas and advice. This perspective leads to some tension initially because families often come to counseling with an expectation that it will be similar to a visit to the doctor's office: They will describe the symptoms, and the counselor will identify the problem and prescribe a solution, which the family will go home and implement. This is a relatively passive role and the antithesis of a family systems approach. Fortunately for us when working with this population, gifted people gravitate toward an active role. They seem to be relieved to have more input than expected.

Assessment

Assessment is an essential piece in our work with gifted individuals and their families, and what kind of assessment we do depends on the model of intervention we will be using. The assessments that are specific to each approach were detailed in preceding sections here. However, for any approach, we use a clinical interview, gathering information from the family and observing what is said and what is not said, ascertaining what the patterns of interaction are between family members, and examining other sources of data. Assessment in the postmodern approach is similar to the structural-strategic model in that the counselor relies heavily on clinical interviews to gather information, whereas the Belin-Blank model relies more on sources of information outside of the family. Another tool that we use across these models is the family genogram (McGoldrick, Gerson, & Shellenberger, 1999). This is a graphical method of eliciting a family history that provides a visual description of the physical composition of the family, as well as information about interaction patterns, family history, and patterns of problems. We have found that families with gifted members can provide considerable input for the genogram and quickly grasp the systemic influences on each member and on the family as a whole.

We concur with the importance of assessing the family system, but our training and experience point to the utility of certain types of individual assessment even when using a systems approach. Although we do not see a need for an extensive testing battery in routine family systems approaches, there are some times when selected instruments are helpful. Especially with gifted individuals, some reliable assessment of intelligence or aptitude is indicated. However, intelligence tests that are administered in groups are not as reliable as individually administered tests (Schecter, 1992) and often have ceilings that are too low to be useful with gifted populations. Many current individual instruments share the problem of low ceilings (Feldhusen, 1991; Feldhusen & Jarwan, 1993), making them less than useful, because it is important to know how much and what kinds of giftedness we are working with. Varying levels affect family dynamics differently.

Additionally, it is important to consider the possibility that the identified patient may be twice exceptional, meaning that, in addition to giftedness, there may be a learning, emotional, or physical disability (Olenchak & Reis, 2002). Learning disabilities in particular may be masked to both the individual and the family by compensating strategies or apparent underachievement.

Furthermore, counseling psychologists have particular expertise in educational and vocational counseling. Because the worlds of school and work are systems with which the family regularly interacts and by which they are affected, information about adjustment in those areas may provide important sources of information about external factors affecting the family.

There are a number of instruments that can be used to assess the vocational realm, but there are several that we use routinely: the NEO PI-R (Costa & McCrae, 1992); the Myers-Briggs Type Indicator ([MBTI]; Myers, McCaulley, Quenk, & Hammer, 1998); and the Career Key Indicator (Jones, 1990). These are not interchangeable, and it is possible to use each instrument independently. The NEO PI-R provides information about personality, which leads to greater understanding of people's interactions; the MBTI uses an exceptionally user-friendly format to examine modes of interaction; and the Career Key provides information about career interests that is useful in looking at person-environment fit. The choice to use any of these instruments should be made after the counselor has a working knowledge of the family. Indicators of a need for more assessment of this kind include identifying problems with educational and work systems; finding no apparent deficits in interactions among the family members (admittedly a rare occurrence); and when working with the family, not producing results commensurate with the investment and effort of counselor and family.

Process

We would have to say, with Hamlet, "There are more things in heaven and earth, Horatio, Than are dreamt of in your philosophy" (Hamlet, Act I, Scene 5), because we have experienced more varieties of counseling sessions than we had ever dreamed of. Given that our perception of clients is that they are experts in their systems and direct much of the process, we never know what to expect. The first few sessions tend to be similar across clients, but after that, each situation is dramatically different. In those early sessions, we gather information, but we also start to work at identifying the underlying processes. If the entire family comes in for sessions, there is usually a lot of talking, except when there is not. If we are seeing individual clients, it is apt to be quieter, except when it is not. We want to note that, even when we see clients individually, we use a systems perspective.

Perhaps the best way to describe our counseling sessions with gifted children and their families is that they include sharing perspectives, analyzing situations, and being open to what grows out of our relationship. Of course, this approach capitalizes on the strengths of many gifted families, and while we are happy to rely on those strengths, it is important not to fall into the trap of allowing anyone to begin intellectualizing about what is happening. Because of this, we pay attention to feelings, as most counselors do.

We adjust our work in sessions to accommodate cultural differences. Sue and Sue (1999) have presented issues related to a number of racial-ethnic groups. For instance, with an Asian family we may be more restrained about gathering information and more directive in our methods, and with an African American family we may respond with more self-disclosure to establish an egalitarian relationship based on our commonalities. With Native American families, we may pay attention to including relatives from outside of the nuclear family because those collateral contacts are significant in many of these cultures. Having mentioned these interventions, we want to point out that therapy for gifted individuals and their families has many of the problems that education for gifted students does: There is an overrepresentation of Caucasian, middle-class clients and an underrepresentation from ethnic-racial minorities and people from poverty.

The process of counseling is heady work and often emotionally charged. We see rhythms of interaction as people approach each other and then back away—and approach us and back away. We see growth and changes with some regression at times. People are often rigid at first, but almost always eventually relax in sessions. Even though people see us about problems and there may be some tears, we frequently share moments of joy with them.

The image of a river may be an appropriate metaphor for viewing the process of therapy. Imagine a river, beautiful to be sure, but turbulent, with a swift current. The surface is rough and choppy. The river's banks are forested, leaving this section in privacy. As we wade into the river, we realize that it is cold, an autumn cold, and even on the edges the current tugs at our feet. Walking to the center of the river we become aware of the mossy rocks, slippery and hard, on the river bed. We also notice that the current is carrying all kinds of debris—branches, boxes, and some rocks that mysteriously float in the current. *Float* is not quite an accurate word because they are moving with the speed of the current and have become dangerous missiles. We notice a family in the river, too, churning and struggling, bumping each other and bumping us, too, now that we are in the river. Everything is chaotic and confusing and seems to repeat itself over and over. (This detail indicates that the river contains some kind of circling, which is improbable, but nevertheless, please imagine it, for the sake of the image.) Everyone is in danger of drowning, and finally, it is too much, and we become *determined*. We face upstream, plant our feet shoulder-width apart, pushing through the moss to the solid rocks to gain secure footing, hold out our arms, and begin to catch people as they buffet us. As we hold on to the people, they all begin to allow the garbage to pass by and draw together.

While they do that, the current slows, the turbulence is reduced, and the water becomes warmer. In this scenario, they never get out of the river, which after all these years is getting a bit crowded, but we hope you see the point. Entering into people's lives is often a rough experience, and our expertise provides an anchor and point of stability for them to start reworking their lives.

Our counseling process is relatively short, usually no more than 6–10 sessions. We find that duration fits with what gifted families can absorb and fit into their extremely busy lives. If we use an exercise metaphor, with counseling sessions as the repetitions and sets of exercises, some clients come in for one set with five reps and others come in for multiple sets over extended time periods. The initial stages involve assessment and may take one to two sessions, perhaps even a bit longer in complicated situations. The working stage varies in length, depending on the problem, the system, and schedules. We do our best to have a final session to celebrate gains, review what we have all learned (we likely have learned something, too), and provide a formal ending. When we have been successful while working with the family, this closure is usually something the family readily agrees with. If not, progress halts sometime during the working phase without as much closure.

Application

Presenting Problems

Because we have worked in different settings, we have tended to see different presenting problems. Thomas has worked in marriage and family clinics. In those settings, parents often bring in children for school-related problems. He conceptualizes those systemically and works with the entire family, considering what function the symptom might have for the family. For instance, if a student is in repeated fights at school and the family is focusing their attention on the student, what is the family not paying attention to? Marital distress? Previous deaths in the family? There are also families who come in for services related to family problems such as discord or rebelliousness. Other families come in for services related to one member's depression or anxiety.

Ray has worked as a generalist in community mental health centers and school settings. In these contexts, she has seen a variety of problems over a wide range of ages. With gifted individuals, the problems are most often related to depression, anxiety, and school although there are also relationship issues (usually romantic), abuse problems, and chemical dependency concerns. She sees a physical or genetic component to many of these problems in addition to learned patterns of interaction that influence them. This perspective leads to a systemic approach that is not only cognizant of the person and his or her current situation but also conscious of the dynamics among and between history, physiology, personality, and environment. Almost every problem appears to be multifaceted and requires complex thinking to understand and remedy. The interventions Ray uses may not appear to be complex, but the thinking behind them is multilayered and occasionally chaotic. One difficulty associated with thinking about problems in this manner is the resulting confusion that sometimes occurs. The positive aspect of this approach is that there are multiple points of entry into the problem and potentially multiple angles of intervention.

Both of us are willing to use collateral resources. For instance, we make referrals for medication for depression or anxiety if counseling alone does not provide enough relief. If the client or a family member presents us with issues related to chemical abuse or dependency, we suggest attending a 12-step program. We encourage people to use meditation, exercise, involvement in service activities, journaling, pampering themselves, and social contacts in addition to our work in counseling, because various clients we have worked with have found these to be therapeutic. Anything that is a constructive part of the client's system can contribute to therapeutic change.

Case Illustration: An Imaginative-Postmodern Approach

Sam came to counseling with Ray as a 17-year-old, high school junior from a small, rural district. His grades and behavior at school were exemplary. He had a variety of interests and had set up and moderated a computer bulletin board in addition to participating in school activities such as band, Quiz Bowl, and debate. These activities were supported by his parents, who were both employed as teachers in the district he and his 12-year-old brother attended. Sam's presenting problem was described as his feeling unhappy at school. The assessment phase involved three individual sessions with Sam and two telephone consultations with his mother. Neither of them reported anything that sounded problematic in the family; in fact, they described a number of positive experiences. Both believed that Sam had a comfortable and active group of friends. There was no report of other symptoms to suggest mental illness or chemical dependency.

The unhappiness at school did not seem related to anything that happened while Sam was at school, but rather to his desire to graduate from high school at the end of his junior year. He had enough credits to graduate already in the fall of that year and would finish almost all of his required classes by the end of it. The one exception to that desire was government class, required for graduation and traditionally taken as a senior. Sam wanted to take it in the second semester of his junior year when he was scheduled for a study hall—and then graduate a year early. The school allowed students to take government in their junior year but also had a "seat time" requirement, calling for 4 years of attendance in classes prior to earning a diploma. Sam explained that he had already taken all of the high-level courses offered by the school, including Advanced Placement courses. He described himself as feeling out of place academically in a high school setting and dreaded taking low-level classes for a year in order to finish one semester-long requirement. While he acknowledged that the social situation was comfortable for him, he said that he could also have a positive social situation in other settings and needed to go to college to have an appropriate academic situation. His goal for counseling was to find some way out of his current situation.

Ray provided ideas related to possible solutions: obtain a General Education Diploma (GED), appeal the principal's decision, or use the district's dual-enrollment option. They explored options, seeking out risk factors and protective factors. His parents were supportive of his desire to graduate early, but even with insider knowledge, they could not see a way to accomplish his goal. They objected to using the GED system on principle, stating that Sam could earn a regular diploma and deserved to be able to do that. They reported being apprehensive about the effects to their jobs if they challenged the high school principal's decision. In addition, there had been other appeals related to the seat-time requirement over the previous 3 years, and the board of education had supported the policy in each case. Although Sam's case was probably the strongest academically, the administration did not see significant differences between his request and those that had been denied. Dual enrollment was a stronger possibility, but as this option was studied, it became evident that it would be prohibitively expensive for the family because, even though tuition would be paid by the school district, related expenses, particularly travel expenses to the nearest college, would be prohibitive. This choice would also involve Sam taking unnecessary and undesired high school courses because he would still need to be on the high school campus for a half day during both semesters. Ray and Sam worked at developing a thick description of the situation in order to unearth unrecognized possibilities. However, the family had already pondered all of the possibilities that were generated.

Identification of solutions to the problem indicated that Sam and his family really were doing well in all areas of their lives. They simply wanted to be able to apply their existing solution behavior to a new situation.

The influence of larger systems on the family system is apparent in this case. The family is essentially stable and supportive of each other, they are engaged with and include each other, they have appropriate levels of intimacy, and their interaction is positive. Ray focused on defining the desired situation and creating the story of how they would like events to transpire. The story that Sam and his family wanted was clear: He was done with high school even if high school personnel did not believe it. He was moving on and needed help to do that.

At this point, Ray began contacting college admission officers and her peers (consultants and counselors of gifted and talented) to obtain information, believing that they had probably faced similar situations in the past and might have ideas. She quickly found that it is relatively common for admissions departments at universities to field these inquiries, and therefore they had developed policies to guide their responses. They had discovered that students in Sam's position were exceptionally able, highly motivated, and could easily adapt to the social setting of college. Further, and most importantly, they were willing to accept students without a high school diploma and without requiring recommendations from high school personnel. They needed transcripts of Sam's high school grades, results of standardized college admission testing (which Sam already had), and his college application. When Ray presented this option to Sam and his family, they were energized. This was a story they could believe in. Sam applied to several elite colleges and was accepted by many of them. He chose to matriculate the next fall, sans high school diploma. He continued to see Ray for support through the rest of his junior year of high school. They talked about his ability to create his own story and approach in spite of the obstacles he had encountered, the uniqueness of his family's ability to support him, and how they were all unique in their small town. In some ways, this was an unusual counseling situation because the presenting problem was solved. However, one of the strengths of an imaginative-postmodern approach is its creativity and openness to looking at problems from unusual perspectives. Ray decided that although the presenting problem had been solved, the system features that created it still existed and remained problematic.

After his first year, Sam's mother called Ray when his grade reports arrived. He had been incredibly successful in the cauldron of an elite school. He appeared to her to have adjusted well to academic and social demands and reported that he was satisfied with the outcome of his decision.

This counseling situation turned out to be somewhat unusual in that there were no internal problems with the family's communication and problem-solving ability. Nonetheless, Sam was in considerable distress due to the policies and decisions of the larger system that affected him, as well as his family. In turn, a system at an even higher level provided the eventual solution.

Elsewhere Thomas (1995, 1999) reported about two gifted children and their families with whom he used an imaginative-postmodern approach. The first family (Thomas, 1995) had a 7-year-old girl who was highly gifted creatively and was afraid to go to school. When Thomas told the family the Grimm's fairy tale of "Brier Rose," the girl identified so much with the imaginative character in the fairy tale that they were able to generate creative solutions for the school problem. The second family (Thomas, 1999) had an academically highly gifted 12-year-old boy who fought in school with children who called him "weirdo" and provoked him on a regular basis. The mother identified the boy as a "bane" because of his behavior at school and at home, where he would become defensive about his parents' request to behave more appropriately at school. The boy said it was the *family* bane, which led Thomas to use that metaphor. He gave the boy a plastic Dr. Seuss figure to represent the bane and asked the boy to consult with the family bane when he felt angry. The boy finally had an ally who would listen to him and help him generate behaviorally appropriate alternatives for fighting the injustices done to him at school and at home. Once the parents understood that this was an issue of fairness and justice for their son, they began to support him, which decreased the tension at home. A parent-teacher conference at school yielded more protection for the boy at school, and he was given more challenging, individualized assignments. As a consequence, the boy ceased being the bane of the family and could behave like a smart 12-year-old boy.

Conclusion

Our approaches to counseling gifted individuals and their families are based on an amalgamation of clinical experience and systems approaches to counseling. Because there is little empirical evidence related to counseling gifted individuals (Moon, 2002), we continue to experiment and evaluate our work. We believe that those who choose to work with gifted clients need a solid knowledge of the issues and contextual factors that affect gifted individuals in addition to typical counseling skills. However, we have found this population rewarding to work with and hope to see more counselors undertake counseling with gifted individuals and their families, perhaps taking advantage of information available in journals and at conferences specifically geared to giftedness.

References

American Psychiatric Association. (2000). *Diagnostic and statistical manual of mental disorders* (4th ed., Text Rev.). Washington, DC: Author.

Berg, I. K. (n.d.). *Hot tips.* Retrieved February 20, 2006, from http://www.brief-therapy.org/insoo_essays.htm

Bordeaux, B. (2001). *Therapy with gifted clients: Honest disagreement is often a good sign of progress.* Unpublished manuscript.

Bowen, M. (1978). *Family therapy in clinical practice.* New York: Aronson.

Butterfield, E. C., & Feretti, R. P. (1987). Toward a theoretical integration of cognitive hypotheses about intellectual differences among children. In J. G. Borkowski & J. D. Day (Eds.), *Cognition in special children: Comparative approaches to retardation, learning disabilities, and giftedness* (pp. 195–233). Norwood, NJ: Ablex.

Colangelo, N., & Davis, G. A. (Eds.). (1997). *Handbook of gifted education* (2nd ed.). Boston: Allyn & Bacon.

Columbus Group. (1991, July). *Unpublished transcript of the meeting of the Columbus Group.* Columbus, OH.

Costa, P. T., Jr., & McCrae, R. R. (1992). *Revised NEO personality inventory (NEO-PI-R) and NEO five-factor inventory (NEO-FFI) professional manual.* Odessa, FL: Psychological Assessment Resources.

Diener, E. (2000). Subjective well being: The science of happiness and a proposal for a national index. *American Psychologist, 55,* 24–43.

de Shazer, S. (1985). *Keys to solution in brief therapy.* New York: W. W. Norton.

Doherty, W. L., Colangelo, N., & Hovander, D. (1991). Priority setting in family change and clinical practice: The family FIRO model. *Family Process, 30,* 227–240.

Feldhusen, J. F. (1991). Identification of gifted and talented youth. In M. C. Wang, M. C. Reynolds, & H. J. Walberg (Eds.), *Handbook of special education: Research and practice.* New York: Pergamon Press.

Feldhusen, J. F., & Jarwan, F. A. (1993). Identification of gifted and talented youth for educational programs. In K. A. Heller, F. J. Mönks, & A. H. Passow (Eds.), *International handbook of research on giftedness and talent* (pp. 223–252). New York: Pergamon Press.

Freeman, J., Epston, D., & Lobovits, D. (1997). *Playful approaches to serious problems: Narrative therapy with children and their families.* New York: W. W. Norton.

Geertz, C. (1973). Thick description: Toward an interpretive theory of cultures. In C. Geertz, *The interpretation of cultures* (pp. 3–32). New York: HarperCollins.

Gelso, D. J., & Fretz, B. R. (1992). *Counseling psychology.* Fort Worth, TX: Harcourt, Brace, Jovanovich.

Haley, J. (1976). *Problem-solving therapy.* San Francisco: Jossey-Bass.

Hoffman, L. (2001). *Family therapy: An intimate history.* New York: W. W. Norton and Company.

Jones, L. K. (1990). The Career Key: An investigation of the reliability and validity of its scales and its helpfulness to college students. *Measurement and evaluation in counseling and development, 23,* 67–76.

Lopez, S. J., Snyder, C. R., & Rasmussen, H. N. (2003). Striking a vital balance: Developing a complementary focus on human weakness and strength through positive psychological assessment. In S. J. Lopez & C. R. Snyder (Eds.), *Positive psychological assessment* (pp. 3–20). Washington, DC: American Psychological Association.

Lovecky, D. V. (1994). Exceptionally gifted children: Different minds. *Roeper Review, 17,* 116–122.

Lovecky, D. V. (2000). The quest for meaning: Counseling issues with gifted children and adolescents. In L. Silverman (Ed.), *Counseling the gifted and talented* (pp. 29–50). Denver, CO: Love.

Marland, S. P. (1971). *Education of the gifted and talented* (Report No. 72–5020). Washington, DC: U.S. Office of Education.

McCrae, R. R. (2000). Emotional intelligence from the perspective of the Five-Factor Model. In R. Bar-On & J. D. A. Parker (Eds.), *The handbook of emotional intelligence* (pp. 263–276). San Francisco: Jossey-Bass.

McGoldrick, M., Gerson, R., & Shellenberger, S. (1999). *Genograms: Assessment and interventions.* New York: W. W. Norton and Company.

Minuchin, S. (1974). *Families and family therapy.* Cambridge, MA: Harvard University Press.

Minuchin, S., & Fishman, H. C. (1981). *Family therapy techniques.* Cambridge, MA: Harvard University Press.

Moon, S. M. (2002). Counseling needs and strategies. In M. Neihart, S. M. Reis, N. M. Robinson, & S. M. Moon (Eds.), *The social and emotional development of gifted children: What do we know?* (pp. 213–222). Waco, TX: Prufrock Press.

Moon, S. M., & Hall A. S. (1998). Family therapy with intellectually and creatively gifted children. *Journal of Marital and Family Therapy, 24,* 59–80.

Moon, S. M., Jurich, J. A., & Feldhusen, J. F. (1998). Families of gifted children: Cradles of development. In R. C. Friedman & K. B. Rogers (Eds.), *Talent in context: Historical and social perspectives on giftedness* (pp. 81–99). Washington, DC: American Psychological Association.

Moon, S. M., & Thomas, V. (2003). Family therapy with gifted and talented adolescents. *Journal of Secondary Gifted Education, 14*, 107–113.

Moos, R., & Moos, B. (1986). *Family environment scale manual* (2nd ed.). Palo Alto, CA: Consulting Psychologists Press.

Myers, I. B., McCaulley, M. H., Quenk, N. L., & Hammer, A. L. (1998). *MBTI manual: A guide to the development and use of the Myers-Briggs Type Indicator* (3rd ed.). Mountain View, CA: Consulting Psychologists Press.

Myers, I. B., & Myers, P. (1980). *Gifts differing.* Palo Alto, CA: Consulting Psychologists Press.

Olenchak, F. R., & Reis, S. M. (2002). Gifted students with learning disabilities. In M. Neihart, S. M. Reis, N. M. Robinson, & S. M. Moon (Eds.), *The social and emotional development of gifted children: What do we know?* (pp. 177–192). Waco, TX: Prufrock Press.

Olson, D., Portner, J., & Lavee, Y. (1985). *FACES III Manual.* St. Paul, MN: Family Social Science.

Robbins, M. S., & Szapocznik, J. (2000, April). *Brief strategic family therapy* (NCJ 179825). Washington, DC: U.S. Department of Justice, Office of Justice Programs, Office of Juvenile Justice and Delinquency Prevention.

Robinson, A., & Clinkenbeard, P. R. (1998). Giftedness: An exceptionality examined. *Annual Review of Psychology, 49*, 117–139.

Rogers, K. B. (1986). Do the gifted think and learn differently? A review of recent research and its implications for instruction. *Journal for the Education of the Gifted, 10*, 17–39.

Schecter, J. (1992). Comparing different measures of intelligence. *Understanding Our Gifted, 4*, 14–15.

Silverman, L. (1997). The construct of asynchronous development. *Peabody Journal of Education, 72*, 36–58.

Silverman, L. (2000). Counseling families. In L. Silverman (Ed.), *Counseling the gifted and talented* (pp. 151–178). Denver, CO: Love.

Stanley, J. C. (1996). In the beginning: The study of mathematically precocious youth. In C. P. Benbow & D. Lubinski (Eds.), *Intellectual talent: Psychometric and social issues* (pp. 225–235). Baltimore: Johns Hopkins University Press.

Sternberg, R. J. (1990). *Metaphors of mind: Conceptions of the nature of intelligence.* New York: Cambridge University Press.

Sternberg, R. J., & Davidson, J. E. (1985). Cognitive development in the gifted and talented. In F. D. Horowitz & M. O'Brien (Eds.), *The gifted and talented: Developmental perspectives* (pp. 37–74). Washington, DC: American Psychological Association.

Sue, D. W., & Sue, D. (1999). *Counseling the culturally different: Theory and practice.* New York: John Wiley & Sons.

Thomas, V. (1995). Of thorns and roses: The use of the "Brier Rose" fairy tale in therapy with families of gifted children. *Contemporary Family Therapy, 17*, 83–91.

Thomas, V. (1999). David and the family bane: Therapy with a gifted child and his family. *Journal of Family Psychotherapy, 10*, 15–24

Thomas, V., & Moon, S. (2004, September). *Therapy with gifted children and their families.* Workshop presented at the 62nd Annual Conference of the American Association for Marriage and Family Therapy, Atlanta, GA.

Webb, J. T. (1993). Nurturing social-emotional development of gifted children. In K. A. Heller, F. J. Mönks, & A. H. Passow (Eds.), *International handbook of research and development of giftedness and talent* (pp. 525–538). New York: Pergamon Press.

White, D., & Epston, D. (1990). *Narrative means to therapeutic ends.* New York: W. W. Norton.

Wierczerkowski, W., & Prado, T. M. (1991). Parental fears and expectations from the point of view of a counseling centre for the gifted. *European Journal for High Ability, 2,* 56–73.

chapter 5

A Developmental Perspective

by Jean Sunde Peterson

Conception of Giftedness

Influences

During my 19 years as a teacher of English at various school levels, I did not resonate with the idea of "gifted education" or "needs of gifted children." I generally taught literature and writing with a constructivist approach, and the experiential emphasis of my courses and the open-endedness of my assignments seemed to provide highly able students with challenge, autonomy, and opportunities to be creative. I naïvely assumed my teaching peers were providing the same. I was not excited by the push for special programs for gifted students when it occurred in the early 1980s in my school context.

However, like many who are belatedly converted, I eventually invested heavily in efforts to improve the school experience for gifted students. I coordinated a complex, multifaceted high school program for gifted students during the last 5 of my 24 years in K–12 education and, as one element of the program, actually facilitated 10 noon-hour discussion groups per week (Peterson, 1990), geared to affective concerns. Those groups taught me about the social and emotional concerns of gifted adolescents and helped me establish research direction prior to counselor-education doctoral work, which my work with gifted adolescents had inspired.

My graduate assistantship at the Belin-Blank Center for Gifted Education at The University of Iowa provided me with opportunities to work with gifted children and adolescents, including work in a counseling clinic for gifted children and their families. Later, I did small-group work with gifted students in a middle school. In the next few years, as I began my second career as a counselor educator, I served as a part-time counselor in two substance abuse treatment centers and in two schools for troubled adolescents. In these venues, I sometimes encountered individuals with remarkable abilities. At the same time, more than half of my clients in a small private practice were highly able. These individuals all taught me about affective concerns related to giftedness. My conceptualization of "affective curriculum" (Peterson, 2003) in gifted education resulted from these experiences.

During these years various individuals also had an impact on my perspectives. In the early 1980s, Roger Taylor conducted a district-wide in-service program on meeting the needs of gifted students. His passion about the social and emotional development of gifted youth challenged my skepticism and piqued my interest. The gifted education coordinator in the district where I created the high school program, Penny Oldfather, now at the University of Georgia, supported my then-unusual idea of weekly discussion groups focusing on social and emotional development. Volker Thomas at The University of Iowa, now at Purdue University, taught and supervised me in marriage and family therapy and helped me frame my perspectives on giftedness within various systems. Dierdre Lovecky (1992) authored one of the first articles in the professional literature that resonated with my professional experiences, especially with its discussion of sensitivity and intensity. When I began attending National Association for Gifted Children (NAGC) conventions, I met Tracy Cross (Ball State University) and Lawrence Coleman (now at the University of Toledo), both of whom were interested in nonacademic concerns of gifted kids. Through NAGC, I also became personally acquainted with Michael Piechowski (1999), who had brought Dabrowski's (1967) concept of overexcitabilities and advanced emotional development to gifted education and continues to excite the field with insights related to emotional intelligence and giftedness.

Most of my research employs qualitative methods, and the individuals mentioned above had much to do with my interest in exploring the subjective experience of various phenomena. In regard to research, I should note here that I studied the language of mainstream teachers and individuals from five nonmainstream communities as they discussed the term *giftedness*. Not only did I find that the dominant-culture teachers conceptualized the phenomenon idiosyncratically among themselves (more than 40 different "definitions"), but also that their ad-hoc criteria, as reflected in the themes that emerged, differed considerably from those that emerged in each nonmainstream community. Obviously, giftedness is a context-bound, problematic construct, not universally agreed upon. Nevertheless, in terms of extraordinary abilities in the school context, I argue that individuals at the upper tail of the bell curve of intellectual giftedness (and also of other talent domains) have special needs, and that it is inevitable that some term will be applied to them in professional and lay contexts, regardless of culture. In my discussion here, I usually use the term to reflect a high level of intellectual nimbleness.

Definition

I view giftedness both narrowly and broadly—perhaps more extremely, in both cases, than do many in the field. I will limit my comments here to gifted individuals during their school years, because that is the population I have worked with most. School experiences have great impact on present and future life, of course. I will explain here the narrowness and broadness of my view as these relate to what I believe programs for gifted students should attend to in the interest of nurturing high-ability children.

My definition of *giftedness* reflects a fairly narrow view, regarding who should be served in special school programs, in the sense that if education for gifted students is to meet critical educational needs that general education does not or cannot, it needs to focus on students whose needs are not met in heterogeneous, inclusive classrooms without highly differentiated instruction. Therefore, I define giftedness to be an ability level located in the top 2–3%, by some formal or informal measure, in some area—for example, general intellectual ability or a domain-specific ability or talent, which can include areas valued in nonmainstream cultures and not valued in the dominant culture. High academic *achievement* is not required. In fact, this definition does not necessarily include students who earn high grades in classroom work. I believe that the academic needs of many conscientious, above-average students with high academic performance may indeed be met sufficiently in the classroom, even without greatly differentiated curriculum. They may be sufficiently challenged and satisfied. Of course, teachers should differentiate classroom instruction and teaching approaches for these and all other students, and I am not opposed to programs for gifted students that target a higher percentage of students. However, if meeting critical *needs* (i.e., beyond enrichment) is the goal, those at the extreme generally or in specific domains should be the focus of special programs, just as in special education programs. Such a needs-based criterion also helps advocates to defend programs when necessary.

My view is broad not only in terms of conceptualizing giftedness, but also in providing services. If identification of "the gifted" is to be inclusive of a broad range of high abilities, and if gifted education programs are intended to find and serve students from nonmainstream groups, programs need to be created accordingly. All gifted kids do not relish or need more-and-faster components, which are common in special programs, and which reflect the dominant U.S. culture's valuing of individual, conspicuous, and competitive achievement (Peterson, 1999). Programs should fit children, not vice versa. Therefore, programs need also to attend to gifts valued in minority cultures. In general, there is a lack of programming for nonmainstream gifted children (cf. Peterson), including those with hidden or obvious disabilities and those from nonmainstream cultural and ethnic groups who may not promote the *kinds* of productivity, work ethic, and motivation that are familiar to dominant-culture teachers. My own research (Peterson & Margolin, 1997) underscored that mainstream teachers (including those who direct and teach in gifted programs) look for "demonstrated giftedness" in behaviors that reflect dominant-culture values, especially verbal ability and assertiveness, social ease, competitive academic performance, and involvement in school activities (i.e., familiar and valued qualities in U.S. schools). Clearly, gifted students with low English proficiency or from cultures that value gifts other than these (e.g., listening, nurturing, selfless service, stoicism, making something out of nothing, artistic expression, respect for elders) and do *not* value "standing out," may not be identified (Peterson). I believe that programs should offer academic remediation especially tailored to the needs of bright, talented students who have language and/or education deficiencies. These and others clearly *need* special programming, arguably more so than high-average students who are functioning well in school.

My view is likewise broad in focusing more on the affective than on the cognitive, although I recognize that it is important that schools and programs address both in order to meet critical needs. The affective is the foundation for school and future success, and if affective needs are not addressed, gifted children may not have sufficient comfort in school, at home, and within themselves to learn and function effectively, both academically *and* interpersonally. Therefore, my counseling usually does not make performance the primary concern or goal, even with academic underachievers. My interest is in whether individuals are functioning effectively in their worlds, comfortable with themselves and successfully meeting developmental challenges.

I believe that programs that identify only those children who are stellar performers academically do not affirm the many bright, talented, and intellectually nimble children who, for a wide range of reasons, episodically or chronically, cannot or will not perform in the achievement-driven school environment. In fact, my earlier classroom teaching always kept gifted underachievers in mind, and my research has focused on them as well. I have concluded that underachievement is often related to development challenges, regardless of family (high or low functioning) or social (smooth or rough) contexts. Unfortunately, many of the oft-cited findings about "gifted children" have been based on samples that are not inclusive enough, potentially generating assumptions that do not embrace those who do not fit the high-achieving, academically motivated stereotype.

I believe that education for the gifted should serve highly able students who do not achieve well academically or who have problems with behavior. I certainly recognize that programs are woefully understaffed, often leading to one-size-fits-all curricula, secondary-level programs comprised solely of advanced courses, and little time for gifted education teachers/coordinators to help classroom teachers meet gifted students' needs in the classroom. Regardless, I believe that programs need to be sensitive to nonstereotypical gifted students, including those who are "troubled." The sensitivity and intensity mentioned earlier may put them at special risk in difficult circumstances. Programs can, most importantly, meet a critical *need* by affirming their potential and offering support during the school years. Their gifts may not be affirmed elsewhere.

In addition, some highly able children have academic gaps because their lives lack stability. More-and-faster programs may not appeal to them and, in fact, may not be appropriate. A poor fit in such programs may send only negative messages to them and reinforce teachers' negative perceptions. Other kinds of programs are then in order—to affirm ability; bring them together with other highly able students to discuss developmental concerns; fill socialization gaps; provide a low-stress, nonevaluative environment; and bridge cross-cultural chasms. Differentiating curriculum becomes less of a concern at the secondary level, when advanced-level courses are available. However, even in classes where students are homogeneous regarding ability, teachers need to pay attention to differences between teaching and learning styles, stress levels, and difficulties related to the teacher-student relationship.

Characteristics

Lovecky's (1992) discussion of giftedness continues to be useful to me. She describes five characteristics of gifted individuals: divergent thinking, excitability, sensitivity, perceptiveness, and entelechy (drivenness). When I was an English teacher, divergent thinkers (in contrast with convergent thinkers, who fit well with structured, sequential teaching styles) were my best writers and thinkers. They were able to synthesize disparate strands in the literature and were open to multiple perspectives. I appreciated the excitabilities that sometimes wreaked havoc in their academic, cocurricular, and personal lives. I observed hypersensitive responses, not only to literature, but also to romantic relationships, peers in general, joys and disappointments related to school activities, and transitions in their families, such as separation and divorce, death losses, relocation, parental unemployment, serious illness, accidents, and parents' marital tensions. These students expressed insights uniquely and sometimes poetically in their essays. I also witnessed a drivenness that propelled some to be involved and excel in a broad array of endeavors.

I concluded that these five elements, though usually advantageous for students of language and literature, were also potentially problematic, affecting relationships with teachers, peers, and family and unsettling students internally as well. These characteristics could also contribute to problems with classroom learning. Divergent thinking may interfere with concentration and may rankle some teachers—by challenging "right" answers, for example. Such thinking can also contribute to insomnia (a problem frequently reported by discussion group members), when the multiplicity of mental strands prevents closing the curtain on the day's stage. Divergent thinking might even be confused with Attention Deficit/Hyperactivity Disorder (ADHD; American Psychiatric Association, 2000). Excitability may interfere with relationships, classroom conduct, and concentration, with the mind dancing in response to multiple pieces of classroom and social information. It might also be pathologized by professionals (Webb et al., 2005).

Sensitivity may have an impact on normal developmental transitions, contributing to fears, discomfort, and grief over associated losses. Sensitivity may also affect peer relationships. Sensitivity to internal and external messages of high expectation can contribute to perfectionism, leaving gifted individuals unable to take appropriate social and academic risks, set reasonable standards, enjoy the *process* of learning, start or stop projects, relax, play, or affirm self and others. Sensitivity to justice and fairness, a clear vision of what *ought* to be, and extreme moral values may make living in the world (and in their particular world) extremely difficult. Depression, obsessive-compulsive behaviors, and eating disorders may eventually be manifested in highly sensitive individuals in response to fear, anger, environmental "bombardment," and need for control, especially if predisposed (cf. American Psychiatric Association, 2000).

In addition, sensitive gifted individuals may find it difficult to "small-talk"; may quickly doubt their ability and feel unarmed and vulnerable when facing new intellectual challenges without prior knowledge; may be preoccupied with feeling "different"; may be vulnerable to direct or indirect bullying; and may have difficulty differentiating themselves from high-functioning parents. Gifted individuals may be precociously preoccupied with existential concerns, even as young children, but may not be able to verbalize them. They may also not feel known and appreciated for anything other than their performance in school. They may deny emotions or keep a tight lid on them in order to protect an image of invulnerability (Peterson, 1998). Homosexual individuals have particular challenges in this regard, and one study (Peterson & Rischar, 2000) found that some became "hyper-involved" to have balance and outlet, to have a structured, safe place at school (p. 238), and to compensate for the realization that they would not be accepted by significant people in their lives if they were "out" (p. 239).

Gifted individuals' perceptiveness may mean that nuances of relationships, including their parents' and their own with family, peers, and teachers, are sensed intensely, with potential negative impact on daily functioning. Entelechy may serve some individuals well, especially if enjoyment and satisfaction accompany the drivenness. However, it can also leave little time for self-reflection, rest, and repair.

Assumptions

The following assumptions, based on clinical experience, guide me when I counsel gifted students:

- Gifted students are socially and emotionally complex.
- Hypersensitivities or overexcitabilities, as well as other characteristics associated with giftedness, may play a role in personal and interpersonal difficulties.
- Gifted students may believe, accurately, that they are seen mostly as performers who can and should "make people proud."
- Image control, with much to protect, is often a priority for gifted students and may hinder their asking for help.
- Gifted children and adolescents are faced with the same developmental tasks as their less-able age peers, but the former have particular challenges that are associated with giftedness, and their *experience* of development is qualitatively different.
- Each individual is part of several systems—for example, family, school, peers, religious group, cocurricular activity, individual classrooms, class cohort—and counselors can help them to negotiate those systems.
- School counselors can play important roles in the lives of gifted students.
- School counselors, as well as other school personnel, may have attitudes about gifted kids that potentially interfere with the helping relationship— for example, that giftedness means goodness, ease, no problems, unfair advantages, arrogance, or elitism.
- Most gifted students are reluctant to pursue counseling, either in school or elsewhere (cf. Peterson, 1990)

Recognizing that gifted children and adolescents are not exempt from distressing life events and concerns related to simply "growing up," I also make additional general assumptions:

- All need to be taken seriously and be heard.
- Both shy individuals and outgoing individuals want to be recognized and "known."
- All need support, no matter how strong and successful they might seem.
- All feel stressed at times.
- All are sensitive to family tension.
- All feel angry at times.
- All feel socially inept and uncomfortable at times.
- All worry about the future at times.
- All, no matter how smooth and self-confident they may appear, need practice talking honestly about social and emotional concerns.
- All wear a façade at times.

Conception of Personality

Personality

I find interesting Costa and McCrae's (1994) attempt to integrate various approaches to personality development. They found six interrelated elements in diverse theories of personality: basic tendencies, external influences, characteristic adaptations, self-concept, objective biography, and dynamic processes. As a systems-oriented counselor, I believe that tendencies interact with external influences, such as cohort, culture, family dynamics, socioeconomic status, and objective "events," to produce adaptations, which in turn affect self-concept—and therefore personality—complexly. Personality is dynamic, and external influences on a person's life potentially shape personality significantly, although basic tendencies may make even middle-age changes somewhat predictable (cf. Helson & Moane, 1987). Costa and McCrae noted that personality appears to stabilize during the 20s, and that view reflects my clinical observations that significant fluctuations during adolescence often give way to stability later. It is important to remain open, in clinical work, to the possibility that personality can change both dramatically and positively.

Personality of Gifted Individuals

Giftedness is an overlay on basic temperament (e.g., extraversion, risk-taking, conscientiousness, shyness), with intellectual ability, performance talent, hypersensitivity, perfectionism, and drivenness, for example, potentially exacerbating or exerting constraints on basic tendencies. Level of school performance, an adaptation to an external influence, and amount of education, related to biographical benchmarks, undoubtedly play roles in the development of self-concept in gifted individuals. However, regardless of which trait or domain a bell curve of ability reflects, giftedness represents a differentness that gifted individuals must incorporate into their identity (Mahoney, 1998). At various points in their development, they may not be comfortable with their abilities, and their discomfort may affect their ability to adapt to one or more of their various environments (e.g., home, school, community, friendship groups) and contribute to alterations in personality. Their various environments also influence whether they become arrogant, withdrawn, assertive, or confident, for instance. "Habits" of achievement and underachievement, established early in life (cf. Peterson, 2000; Santiago-Rivera, Bernstein, & Gard, 1995), may affect how their personality develops as well.

Model of Counseling

Influences

Several theorists contributed to how I conceptualize client issues. Adler's (1927/1954; Gilliland & James, 1998) views were important early influences: that the important problems in life are social problems and that social interest, including the need to belong and contribute, is related to productivity and happiness. In addition, my becoming aware of Erikson's (1968) view of human development led to awareness of developmental stuckness and developmental transitions, helpful both when working with individuals and families and when doing psychoeducational work with youth.

I often use a family-systems framework for conceptualizing individual clients' presenting problems, including those of young clients in schools. Here, a primary influence was Minuchin's (1974) structural systems framework, including attention to subsystems, roles, family homeostasis, and individual and family boundaries. The metaframeworks of Breunlin, Schwartz, and MacKune-Karrer (1992) also provided me with a tool for assessing families and providing points of access, and from it I created techniques for working with individual clients, as well, including young children. One of these techniques was used in the case presented at the end of this chapter. In general, I like the fact that a family-systems approach does not focus on blame, does not focus on one individual, can involve everyone in a family, and can have positive outcomes for individual family members and also for the family collectively. School counselors with family-systems training can sometimes arrange a flexible schedule for the purpose of counseling families at school after regular work hours in regard to achievement or behavior problems. They can also apply a systems perspective to work with individual students.

The techniques I use also reflect other influences. I quickly embraced Rogers' (1951) faith in a person's ability to self-actualize, which makes easy the focus on strengths in counseling. Satir (1988) also influenced me with her emphasis on clear, direct communication in families; hearing everyone in the system; flexibility and variability in therapy; and being willing to have intimate contact with a family in order to have positive behavioral outcomes. I enjoy writing and am quite conscious of, and interested in, language in my work, in line with my interest in qualitative research. Reflecting that, I sometimes use White and Epston's (1990) technique of writing a letter to private-practice clients between sessions in order to provide support and reinforce session gains. Clients willingly give me permission to take notes during sessions "so that I can remember accurately what we say," and gifted individuals, particularly, seem intrigued by the patterns and themes that I can reflect back to them, based on my notes. Finally, my friend and frequent coauthor John Littrell (1998) continually increased my awareness of brief, solution-focused counseling, and slowly I became a believer. I like the forward movement and positive vision of solution-focused work. I now incorporate it regularly in skills-training as a counselor educator.

Finally, I am rarely confrontational in my work, because I believe, especially when working with children and adolescents, that counseling should feel safe and generate willingness to continue working, regardless of whether the venue is a school or a treatment center. In general, I believe it is more difficult to gain the trust of young clients than of adults, and I certainly do not want to behave like significant adults who have been heavy-handed and critical with them. Instead, I use subtle, interpersonally engaging approaches, including gentle humor, for illuminating discrepancies or faulty thinking.

Definition of Counseling

I ask my graduate students to figure out ways to describe their work to first-time clients, regardless of age, ability, and context. We have found the following statements to be appropriate and effective, depending on age and developmental level:

- Counseling is for normal people who have something to work on in their lives.
- Counselors listen carefully in order to learn what people feel, think about, enjoy and dislike, and are confused about.
- Counselors can help people to feel better and live more effectively.
- Counselors can help people not to feel stuck anymore about something.
- Counselors can help people make changes.
- Counseling can help to prevent problems in living and to prevent problems from becoming worse.
- Counselors can help people discover and affirm their strengths.
- Counselors look for good things in people and do not judge or criticize.
- Rather than giving advice, counselors try to help people solve their own problems.
- Counselors can help people make sense of things that seem confusing or complicated.
- Counselors can provide, or direct someone to, a safe harbor of support during crises.
- Counselors believe that, with a little help, people can figure out how to move ahead.

Counseling is distinguished from other helping professions, at least to some extent, in its focus on developmental problems of normal people of all ages and on helping them deal with stressors and complex emotions related to everyday living. The focus on personal strengths and personal growth, rather than on pathology, also distinguishes counseling from some other fields. Not preoccupied with the past, but respecting it, counseling also emphasizes short-term processes in the present, related to rational planning, decision-making, relational difficulties, or situational pressures, for example. Counselors may work with several formats (e.g., individual, small group, large group, family) in a wide variety of venues, perhaps more so than other helping professionals.

Role of Counselor

Self-Reflection

It is important for counselors of gifted individuals to self-reflect about their own feelings about achievement, underachievement, giftedness, arrogance, the school years, teachers, extroversion, and introversion—in order to be able to be fully present for a gifted client of any age. Counselors should also avoid a simplistic, linear view of complex and idiosyncratic phenomena, such as achievement or underachievement. In addition, it is important that counselors avoid engaging in competitive one-upmanship in sessions in order to demonstrate their own ability. Counselors should also avoid rescuing gifted individuals, often a temptation when gifted clients are nice, compliant, needy, feeling victimized, or feeling paralyzed by expectations. Gifted individuals can be especially engaging, and counselors need to avoid becoming overly invested in them emotionally to the extent that ability to help is compromised. Especially when dealing with children of highly invested parents, it may be important to assist the children in developing boundaries and appropriate self-sufficiency so that they can eventually achieve a healthy level of differentiation.

Entering Their World

It is easy for counselors to view seemingly competent gifted individuals as stronger, more confident, and more capable than they really are, socially and emotionally. Regardless of school success level, it is important to avoid becoming overly interested in their achievement or underachievement, because such preoccupation of significant adults elsewhere in their lives may be a problem. Gifted individuals can become highly invested clients, a delight to work with, with brilliant insights and the ability to articulate complex phenomena. However, some, accustomed to impressing others, may *need* to be impressive. They may also test counselors with strong, unsettling verbal assertions, including criticism. In addition, a facade of invulnerability may mask horrendous circumstances and experiences. With that in mind, counselors need to stay poised and nonjudgmental, regardless of what is presented. Counselors need to enter the world of gifted clients, no less so than when working with others, and learn about the intersection of giftedness with development in particular contexts.

A Developmental Focus

In fact, I believe that development should be the initial focus—and sometimes the sole focus—of counseling. Giftedness may contribute to difficulties with developmental transitions because of the overlay of hypersensitivity and intensity when facing unsettling life events, such as puberty, leaving home, changing schools, losing friends, and moving to new locations. Change means loss, and loss means grief, and gifted youth may be no more consciously aware of those phenomena than are those with lesser ability. In fact, psychoeducational information may help gifted clients at any age to gain cognitive control in difficult situations.

In my experience, when offered proactively or as a backdrop for presenting problems, gifted clients find information about development helpful, interesting, and reassuring. Normalizing developmental anxieties is particularly important, because many gifted children and adolescents do not share concerns with their peers or family readily, believing that they should "figure it out" by themselves and perhaps fearing a loss of image if they reveal fears and doubts. I frequently remark that their concerns "make sense." Counselors can indeed help complex gifted individuals make sense of themselves, their behavior, their situation, or their own or their family's stage of development. Counselors can help gifted individuals become developmentally "unstuck."

Validation

Gifted individuals are no different from anyone else in terms of needing to be heard and validated as a child, adolescent, adult, son, daughter, friend—certainly more than just an achiever, underachiever, delinquent, or star performer. They may even need to have their intelligence validated, because academic self-confidence in underachieving individuals, for instance, may have been eroded over time. They need to hear that they are not "defective" if they are gay (Peterson & Rischar, 2000), underachieving, or perfectionistic. They may continually have heard messages that they can and should *be* better, *do* better, and focus on the future, not on the present. Counselors can affirm them as they *are*, in the present, and validate their concerns, especially important if clients appear to fear revealing vulnerabilities and anxieties. Counselors can also give them permission to change—from underachievement, perfectionism, being a bully, or being a victim. In fact, underachievers may need to be encouraged to get what they *need* from their family or institution, instead of sacrificing themselves to it. Understandably, underachieving young clients from difficult environments may not spontaneously mention academic concerns, because other aspects of their lives may be much more salient. Focusing on school may be quite difficult for them. In such cases, reframing negatives to positives can be especially effective when working with gifted kids (e.g., "You had to work pretty hard to get your parents' attention so that you could get some help." "I can see your leadership in how your friends pay attention to what you say and do.")

Role of Client

The client should work harder than I do. However, I accept responsibility for being a keen observer, being responsive, and ascertaining client readiness for various stages of our work together. Any behaviors that might be deemed "resistant" are seen instead as reflecting a lack of readiness or capability for what I have incorporated into a session. It is my responsibility to make appropriate adjustments. However, in general, I expect the young client to engage in collaborative work in sessions; complete "homework" that I assign and we agree on; reflect and apply insights and new skills outside of sessions; allow me to nudge him or her to new awareness; and take initiative to move toward more effective living, which is a fundamental tenet of counseling.

Goals

The goals of counseling in my approach are increased self-awareness, enhanced skills, and personal growth, all of which should foster healthy social and emotional development. I do not begin with the goal of clinical diagnosis, although I am certainly alert to symptoms of pathology. In fact, my basic approach probably does not vary much between working with identified pathology and working with problems in living and normal developmental challenges. Regardless of circumstances, I keep development in mind. On the other hand, even though profound giftedness, for example, is not a diagnostic category in the *Diagnostic and Statistical Manual* (4th ed.; American Psychiatric Association, 2000), I treat such extreme differentness as something that individuals and families must "deal with," like any significant aberration that affects family and other systems. I focus on the impact of profound giftedness on the social, emotional, and cognitive development of the individual—and probably on family development, as well, if I am working with the family.

Relationship

A collaborative, comfortable working relationship is basic to effective counseling. Gifted individuals need this as much as anyone else. However, a trusting relationship may be especially difficult to establish with gifted clients because of hypersensitive antennae, an assumption that "no one understands because I'm so different," and extra layers of mistrust if there has been trauma.

I build relationship through focusing on development first and then on normalizing feelings and behaviors in the context of "normal development" and giftedness (e.g., "That makes sense that you'd respond that way."). I also build relationship by offering pertinent information related to giftedness, particularly about hypersensitive responses to developmental challenges and life events. I give undivided attention and employ microcounseling skills, but also use small talk at the outset of sessions and respectful humor, when appropriate.

Assessment

I typically conduct a complex informal assessment of underachievement when that is the presenting problem. I assume that underachievement may be within the gifted individual's control if there are no intellectual, neurological, or physical constraints and if the environment is generally conducive to achievement. I keep potential contributing factors, mentioned earlier, in mind as I explore the complexity of the phenomenon. However, fundamentally, I keep development in mind. Challenges related to development can have an impact on school achievement, and developmental gains also have the potential to resolve underachievement.

My own development-oriented research found that 20% of gifted underachievers became achievers before high school graduation (Peterson & Colangelo, 1996), and 41% achieved better in college than in high school (Peterson, 2000). Underachievers took *fewer* courses than did achievers during high school, but did not take more "easy" courses, a phenomenon that might have resulted in their having only slightly lower college entrance test scores than did achievers (Peterson & Colangelo). However, regardless of course selection, 87% of underachievers did attend college, and, just as in another study (Peterson, 2002), some extreme high school underachievers did indeed graduate from college in 4 years.

Another study (Peterson, 2001) found that successful females who were once adolescent underachievers were "feisty" during high school. In that qualitative study, teacher and/or parent indifference was a major theme, but having an achieving mentor during adolescence and being in an achievement-oriented milieu were associated with reversing underachievement later. Career direction often came during the 20s, and some males did not begin to achieve academically until their mid-30s. In that study, and in one longitudinal study (Peterson, 2002), a convergence of various developmental task accomplishments coincided with increased academic motivation in young adulthood or adulthood. Distancing from troubled or overfunctioning (i.e., parents doing things for children that children should be doing for themselves) families was associated with positive development, and individuals who accomplished that were eventually able to come home again comfortably.

I sometimes use the following questions for informal assessment (not in a solution-focused mode) and to provoke thought about achievement in both individual and small-group work:

- How much do adults "make a fuss" about your achievement or underachievement?
- What do they say (or what are their attitudes) about school achievement?
- Who is most concerned about your achievement or underachievement?
- What would be different if you suddenly (or gradually) became an (the opposite)?
- What would you gain? Lose?
- Who would notice?
- How would you feel?

Process

During the years I was in significant practice, whether with individuals, couples, or families, I worked mostly short term, often fewer than 5 sessions and rarely more than 10. Now, as then, after I elicit just enough details and emotion to acquaint me with relevant issues and concerns, the individual or family and I establish a problem that can be addressed. I do not hurry this accounting, because the details often illuminate important aspects, and I can take advantage of opportunities to reflect feeling and meaning and build the relationship. However, I intentionally punctuate any client narrative frequently in order to maintain some level of intentionality and to avoid extended problem-oriented language. If I am working with more than one person in the session, I make sure that each person is invited to speak, starting with the youngest, if able to talk. I want everyone to be heard.

Depending on presenting issues, I might then move into a somewhat solution-focused mode for all or most of the remaining sessions, processing the session regularly at the end in order to help clients self-reflect about the experience of counseling and develop skills in articulating feelings and thoughts. I make sure that I deal with termination appropriately, usually mentioning two sessions in advance of the end of a series of sessions that I have confidence we will be able to come to some sort of closure by then. I am sensitive to the complexities of termination and intentionally process the feelings of loss and change that may accompany it. I keep the idea of hypersensitivity in mind as we carefully process the upcoming transition.

I have found that gifted clients appreciate and respond well to collaborative work. They appreciate credible feedback about themselves, and accurate reflections help to build crucial trust. High-ability clients also generally respond well to having their increasing skills affirmed. It is important for counselors to understand that the highly able need this validation as much as anyone else does.

Techniques

Brief Work

When using a brief, solution-focused approach, not only in schools, where usually only brief work is possible, but also in other clinical contexts when there appears to be a problem to be solved, I might ask some of the following, which reflect directions encouraged by various advocates of brief approaches (e.g., de Shazer, 1985; Littrell, 1998; Watzlawick, Weakland, & Fisch, 1974):

- What has brought you to counseling?
- How is it a problem for you?
- How have you tried to solve the problem so far?
- How do you think you could make the problem bigger?
- How could you make the problem smaller?

- Tell me about a time when this isn't/wasn't a problem.
- What were you doing differently at that time so that it wasn't a problem?
- How were you able to accomplish that?
- What is one thing, even a small thing, that you would be willing to do to begin to solve the problem?
- When do you think you would be able to do that?
- How will your life be different when the problem is solved? How might you be different?
- Who will notice first when you change? Who next? What will they notice?

Externalizing the Problem With "Parts Talk"

In order to counter a client's feeling that he or she is "totally bad," perhaps starting with the second session, I might attempt to externalize the problem (White & Epston, 1990), perhaps by graphically applying the "internal family systems" aspects of metaframeworks, mentioned earlier (Breunlin et al., 1992). I sometimes draw multiple (perhaps 20 to 30) adjacent circles on tagboard around a center point to represent what either the client or I deem to be his or her "parts" (e.g., a good son part, a worried part, a confident part, an unconfident part, an angry part, a good friend part, a perfectionist part, an underachieving part, a sensitive part, an embarrassed part). I ask which parts are relied on most, and which parts cause problems. We color those parts according to whether they are reliable or problematic. Certainly clients are, as I say to them, "not just a big blob of temper," for example. We might talk about how one activated part interferes with, or diminishes, another part. During subsequent sessions I might ask, "How big was your temper part this past week? On a scale of 1 to 10, how much were you able to keep it in line?" "How were your other parts affected when the temper part got big?" In short, we establish that the client is made up of many parts, only some of which are problematic. The client can externalize the problem by holding it at arm's length, be somewhat objective, and feel agency for controlling its size. This technique is effective across a wide age range, from children in brief work in schools to adults in agencies. It can also be effective in deconstructing troublesome developmental transitions and family communication problems. I incorporated this technique into my work with the client in the case presented at the conclusion of this chapter.

As soon as I can be credible, I try to point out client strengths, perhaps reframing what has been viewed only negatively by the client and others. If nothing else, I can say, "You were gutsy enough to come to counseling. Many people can't do that." I might observe, "You seem pretty sensitive to your mother's needs during this tense time" or "You're a survivor" or "You had the courage not to achieve—in a family that values achievement highly." If adolescents are fighting "the system," I encourage them to "be selfish" and to get what they need from it, instead of sacrificing themselves to it.

Calling Attention to Resilience

The resilience literature is helpful for identifying strengths. The following list is a compilation of factors of resilience often discussed (Higgins, 1994; Rak & Patterson, 1996; Werner, 1986). Reference to these has the potential to provide hope in difficult situations, including for young children (e.g., "Even in your very difficult life, you've got some things in your favor. Researchers have found that these things help kids to have a better life in the future, and you've got several of them."):

- problem-solving skills;
- ability to engage others;
- optimistic view of circumstances;
- positive vision of a meaningful life;
- ability to be alert, spontaneous;
- desire for novel experiences;
- sustained primary caretaker early in life;
- structure at home;
- role models outside of the home, caretakers, a confidante;
- proactive perspective;
- self-understanding; and
- intelligence.

The fact that intelligence appears on most lists of factors of resilience can be offered as hope for gifted individuals. The hypersensitivity associated with intelligence can exacerbate some difficulties, as noted earlier, but, in general, intellectual nimbleness can help to "figure things out," establish helpful cognitive structure, and make sense of confusing situations (cf. Peterson & Ray, 2006b). Counselors can note the factors that apply to their clients' situations and express confidence in their ability to survive—and be even stronger and wiser as life continues (e.g., "You'll figure out how to get what you need. I don't know when that will happen, but I am confident that you will." Or, "You'll do what you need to do when you're ready."). My own study of a gifted survivor of multiple traumas (Peterson, 2006b) underscored the importance of her intuitive intelligence, proactive perspective, and ability to engage others, among several factors that helped her to survive and repair.

Activities

Sometimes, for variety, especially for helping shy, anxious, and/or untrusting individuals become comfortable with counseling, or helping the counseling process to move out of impasse, I employ pencil-and-paper activities from my own books (Peterson, 1993, 1995, 2006a) with high-ability individuals. They seem to appreciate being able to work thoughtfully in a new way and having the activity provide new, expressive vocabulary for them. The activity sheets usually take no more than 3–5 minutes to complete, but can help to generate conversation even over several sessions. Activities include checklists, sentence stems, or scaling exercises, such as the following:

- I Would Like to Give Myself Permission to . . . ;
- Three Selves;
- Family Roles (a list of 30);
- Family Values (a scaling exercise, with 25 values expressed in lay language);
- Gifts from People Who Matter; and
- Learning Styles (a scaling exercise, with 25 statements reflecting preferences).

These activities typically move young clients quickly into self-reflection. The Family Roles exercise is an effective catalyst for family discussion, because family members often differ in whom they list for various roles. An individual client can also benefit from pondering family roles with this activity. Because of their abilities, gifted children and adolescents sometimes inappropriately have adult-level responsibilities at home and/or are given inordinate deference. The activity provides a chance to express feelings about those roles and explore strategies for being more in the "child" role.

Regardless of presenting issues, I am always alert to the possibility of depression, suicidal ideation, and thoughts of violence. My own research (Peterson, 1997, 2002) has found not only that gifted students often do not trust that school counselors can relate to them and understand their concerns (Peterson, 1990), but also that they tend not to communicate their distress to teachers or parents (Peterson, 2002; Peterson & Rischar, 2000). A national study of bullying (Peterson & Ray, 2006a, 2006b) found that victims tended not to tell adults about being victimized, that many felt despair over not being able to stop the bullying, and that 29% of gifted eighth graders (37% of gifted males) had violent thoughts. Counselors therefore need to observe young gifted clients carefully.

Small-Group Work

I have a strong bias in favor of semistructured, focused-but-flexible, development-oriented small-group work with gifted children and adolescents. Such groups provide opportunities for inclusion, support, and comfort in school and also help students increase self-awareness, gain insights, explore identity issues, enhance self-esteem, and break down cross-cultural and peer-culture stereotypes. Groups move them momentarily out of a competitive, evaluative environment to a safe place where, ideally, no one dominates, no grades are given, and no one judges. Groups offer a safe, affirming place to learn skills for relating to peers, employers, future partners, and their future offspring, such as giving and receiving feedback, self-advocacy, asking for help, coping with stressful situations, and regulating intense emotions. Groups can also provide helpful psychoeducational information related to development. Grouping gifted students homogeneously by ability and age enhances the possibility that trust will be established and that group members will find commonalities as they discuss developmental transitions. Group size should be relatively small, so that members can feel heard, but large enough to increase social information. Facilitators can create a group culture that celebrates expression of affective concerns by complimenting members when they have "put words on something very complicated."

These techniques notwithstanding, I want to add that, especially with adolescents, and especially with those who have been traumatized and/or are bereaved, my main function may be simply to be a safe harbor, help them survive a difficult and frightening time in their lives, or help them navigate a developmental stage, during which they are struggling to forge an identity, find direction, establish a mature relationship, or leave home, for example. I have assumed that posture many times and have not doubted myself in doing that. Young clients typically have limited autonomy and must go home at the end of the school day. Counselors can alert community support services to neglect or abuse, but, even then, helping professionals may be limited to figuratively standing beside children and adolescents and exploring coping strategies. I avoid criticizing parents, because parents remain parents, regardless of circumstances or interventions, and strident criticism of parents may negatively affect a child's sense of self. When home situations are significantly dysfunctional, I might comment that parents may not know how to do things differently, but generally I try to focus on what the child can do to stay safe and survive.

Graphic Illustration

My model of counseling gifted individuals includes both proactive and reactive elements (see Figure 5.1). In order to prevent problems from developing or developing further, counselors can focus on building skills related to articulating affective concerns, providing psychoeducational information about various developmental challenges, offering assistance prior to and during developmental transitions, and being a supportive presence when challenging life events occur. These strategies and postures are especially appropriate for school counselors, but may be employed in other venues as well. These modes are also usually more feasible in schools than in other contexts. Ideally, the result is social and emotional health.

When counseling is sought or required, presenting issues, which may intersect and overlap, are likely to fall into the categories of developmental concerns, classroom issues, social concerns, environmental factors, stress from self-expectations and expectations from others, and hypersensitivity, the last frequently associated with giftedness in the scholarly literature. In response, counselors conceptualize issues from developmental and systems perspectives, and, when appropriate, use a brief, solution-focused approach.

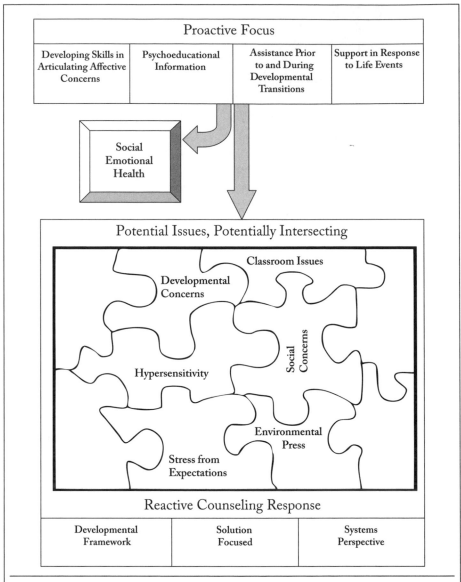

Figure 5.1. Conceptualizing counseling for gifted children and adolescents

Application

Presenting Problems

I have not worked with many involuntary children or adolescents. Gifted clients are typically high achieving or significantly underachieving. Presenting problems are usually related in some way to development. Some of the adolescents who were in the prevention-oriented discussion groups mentioned earlier sought individual counseling at school or elsewhere after gaining comfort and trust in their group.

Issues of High-Achievers

Memorable high-achieving adolescents were dealing with issues related to identity, autonomy, differentiating from family, finding direction, sexual orientation, extricating from a cult-leader-type talent mentor in the community, earlier sexual abuse, boyfriend abuse, stress from internal and external pressures, explosive anger, anxiety, an eating disorder, parental divorce, a sibling's ADHD, a terminally ill family member, feeling overscheduled, substance abuse, family chaos, parental substance abuse, depression, or suicidal ideation.

Issues of Underachievers

Memorable gifted underachievers were in significant conflict with parents or other family members, struggled to differentiate themselves from their family, were frustrated with school, or abused substances. Some were painfully shy, worried about not getting into college, lacked direction, or lacked academic success in college. While some had strong social skills, others were lonely, reclusive, discouraged, frustrated, depressed, and suicidal. Many learned differently, thought complexly, or were highly creative. Some struggled with perfectionism. Noncompliant, angry underachievers challenged authority.

Some underachievers seemed to be a poor fit in both home and school contexts. In other cases, underachievers were apparently responding to difficult life events and family stress. Some had experienced parental unemployment, were caught between acrimonious parents after a divorce, were ignored by divorcing parents, had difficulty adjusting to a blended family, had no quiet place to do homework, or had adult-like responsibilities at home. For still others, developmental transitions seemed to be problematic. Some underachievers were paralyzed by their own or others' high expectations.

Regardless of what issues are brought to counseling, I typically begin with a developmental framework (i.e., where the individual is developmentally, and what developmental tasks might be causing problems). Simultaneously I look for strengths that I can affirm credibly.

Underachievement is a common presenting problem. I believe many situations and characteristics can contribute to it. Gifted underachievers have often been the most articulate and interesting members of the small groups I have facilitated. Their behaviors and their perspectives about school usually "make sense." I recognize that underachievers may have a poor fit in the competitive school environment (Rimm, 1995). I do not believe that the individual, competitive, conspicuous achievement orientation of the dominant culture (and therefore of U.S. schools) is the standard against which all other values should be measured. I have learned to associate some underachievers' idealism and sensitivity to justice with the notion that competition and "standing out" are uncomfortable for some highly capable individuals. In addition, students from some nonmainstream cultures may value nonbookish learning, wisdom instead of knowledge, practical application of knowledge, and service to others, all of which are usually not on the lists of behaviors teachers view as reflecting motivation or giftedness (Peterson, 1999). Motivation is in the eye of the beholder, of course, and teachers and parents may miss underachievers' intense motivation to invest in nonacademic, noncompetitive enterprises, where they function well.

Other factors may also play a role. Underachievers may have a learning disability or experience a poor match of teaching style and learning style (Neihart & Olenchak, 2002). Dependence or dominance, either one assuaging anxiety and providing a momentary sense of control, may negatively affect school success (Rimm, 1995). Underachievers may have difficulty with developmental challenges or may experience arrested development or developmental asynchrony (Silverman, 1997), the latter with social or emotional development lagging far behind cognitive development.

In addition, from a systems perspective, underachievement might be an expression of loyalty to family values that do not support academic achievement, including anti-school, anti-education, or anti-authority attitudes. Simply "not doing" may also represent passive resistance: Perhaps achievement is the only thing the child or adolescent can control in an environment perceived to be highly controlling. Underachievement might also have a function, such as forcing parents to work together—or stay together (cf. Minuchin & Fishman, 1981). It might even be a way to connect with a parent who is uncomfortable with anything related to school.

Issues of Families or Individual Issues Related to Family

Besides underachievement, gifted families have presented with a child or adolescent with issues related to profound giftedness, insomnia, grade acceleration, dual exceptionalities (giftedness and a disability), early entrance into college, loneliness or other friendship issues, depression, suicidal ideation, oppositional defiance, extreme perfectionism, symptoms of autism, substance abuse, criminal behavior, or extreme temper outbursts. Gifted children have also presented problems related to parents' marital stress, parental anxiety, lack of family structure (e.g., no reasonable bedtime or time and space to do homework), family focus on a "problem child" or on a sibling with a disability, or parentification (a child who has assumed the role of parent).

Problems Not Dealt With

Though I have indeed counseled individuals with significant pathology, I typically refer them to other professionals with expertise in that pathology. On a few occasions I have worked in tandem with psychiatrists and psychologists on complex issues. I typically work mostly in the mode of primary (proactively helping individuals cope with developmental tasks, as with small groups), secondary (preventing small or potential problems from becoming serious), and tertiary (preventing current problems from becoming worse, preventing relapses, resolving problems) prevention (Baker & Gerler, 2004, pp. 43–44).

Case Illustration

The following excerpts from the second of two sessions with a gifted underachiever illustrate a systems perspective; use of psychoeducational information; focus on developmental tasks (identity, differentiation, direction); affirmation of ability; application of the concept of internal family system (Breunlin et al., 1992); and externalization of the problem (White & Epston, 1990). I have used variations of this approach with both young children and adolescents and adults as well.

Rob (not his actual name) is laconic and serious, highly focused on the interaction. Even though the many short lines in the excerpts here might be imagined as "rapid," we do not speak quickly. He typically pauses thoughtfully before responding. At the end of his first year in college, he now has to do well on final exams or leave college. During the first session, he reveals severe academic underachievement and a long-standing lack of discipline ("playing the time away"). I learn that his parents divorced before he entered kindergarten, and his mother remarried. It is clear that his academic situation and the final exams feel huge, and I use a "Mt. Everest" metaphor.

At the second session, we discuss "work," and I ask about his parents' attitudes about their work. He says he does not know his stepfather's attitude about work, but his biological father enjoys his work at a mental health agency, and his mother finds her work as a teacher satisfying. Rob finds interesting my reference to school as his work and indicates that his attitude toward his work is more "down" than theirs. He is able to list similarities between school and work. We explore the idea of finding meaning in work and talk about his perceptions of his parents in that regard. I compliment him for the specificity of his comments. He listens carefully to brief psychoeducational information about Gardner's (1983) multiple intelligences and indicates that his verbal intelligence is stronger than his logical/mathematical, that he "did OK" in high school athletics, and that he has a good sense of music. I affirm those strengths and frame his ability to "figure out engines and machines" as "another good strength that he can rely on." He does not think he is intrapersonally intelligent, and I make a mental note of that.

I then assess his high school achievement milieu, because I view that as potentially significant not only to self-assessment, but also to whether an underachiever can make positive academic adjustments later (cf. Peterson, 2001). When I ask him to tell me about someone who was always an academic achiever, he describes his good friend Richard ("He has a personality like mine."). I ask if he thinks they are similar in intelligence—in "raw material."

> **Cl:** No, he's a little beyond me.
> **Co:** How do you know that?
> **Cl:** I don't know. He got a 35 on his ACT.
> **Co:** How do you think he did that—got a 35?

Cl: What do you mean?

Co: How do people do that? [*Rob shrugs.*] What did *you* get?

Cl: A couple of 30s.

Co: Very high, you know. So what do you think the difference was—between your "very high" and his "very high"?

Cl: I don't know.

Co: My hunch is that you and Richard hung around together because you are pretty equal, pretty alike in raw material—in mental nimbleness. Do you compare yourself to Richard a lot? [*I am affirming his ability.*]

Cl: No.

Co: You just relaxed and got along OK.

Cl: Yeah.

Co: Makes sense. I'll bet you were a lot alike. He got a 35, and you got 30s. Both of you in those high percentiles—of all those kids that took the ACT. Not bad at all. Both of you. The ACT is pretty much built on what you've learned in school, and if you weren't a super-charged academic student during high school . . .

Cl: No.

Co: So, that might have been a difference. Richard was really motivated. He did what he needed to do to get A's. Maybe he took the hardest math and science courses, paid attention to the details.

Cl: Yeah.

Co: That might have been the difference between your high scores. Any doubt about your ability—the raw material you have to work with? The raw material that probably helped you and Richard be kindred spirits?

Cl: No.

Co: I assume everybody doubts that once in a while. I was just curious if you have any times in your life when you sort of doubt your ability.

Cl: After I do poorly.

Rob describes other high achievers.

Co: What made you different from those guys—along the way?

Cl: Maybe it was something about the way they were brought up.

Co: What would be the difference?

Cl: I don't know. My parents are more . . . they just sort of let me handle it until things went wrong, and then they'd jump in and I'd get back to par, and then they'd just leave it alone.

Co: That's interesting. So, they'd let you be until you'd sink a little bit, and then they'd get on you. And if they didn't keep bringing it up, you'd start going down again.

Cl: Yeah. After they backed off a bit.

Co: Hmmm. What do you think of that?

Cl: I don't know. It kind of annoyed me.

Co: Their getting involved or not getting involved?

Cl: Their not being involved. I just thought that they should've been involved all the time.

Co: So, maybe your underachievement part, if we want to put a word on it, had a function.

I introduce the "parts" language of the internal family system of metaframe-works (Breunlin et al., 1992).

Cl: Maybe.

Co: And if it had a function? Put words on that for me. What function would it have had?

Cl: Detrimental.

Co: To you.

Cl: To me.

Co: What else might it have accomplished?

Cl: Independence, maybe. It taught me how to take more responsibility for myself.

Co: I'll bet it did. And, you did take responsibility. That's a nice flipside—independence and taking responsibility for yourself. [*As soon as I believe I have credibility, I focus on strengths. I am also affirming agency.*]

Cl: Yeah.

Co: You were calling some shots, learning how to call shots. Possibly even more than Richard, in a sense?

Cl: Yeah. It's . . . his mom is, well, she's not a teacher, but she works at a college, and his dad's a CEO of a big deal. They're really. . . she's really on their backs all the time.

Co: So, there was pressure—and some payoff for Richard for achieving, probably. What you've described suggests that he might have influences from the outside that provide some motivation. You were left to find it from inside. Maybe Richard appreciated and respected your having to find that independently.

Cl: Mm-hmm. Maybe—yeah.

Co: It strikes me that maybe you won't find it someplace else. You're finding it inside. That's a strength. Maybe Richard is even starting to find it inside more as a young adult. You're doing that. Maybe still a bit angry at having to do that. [*Focusing on strengths*]

Cl: Maybe.

[. . .]

Co: Back to the function. When you were sinking, and they'd get involved, and you'd go up, underachievement had sort of a function. It got them involved. Sort of an accomplishment. [*I employ general, extended reframing here.*] Problem solving. Short term, it had a benefit. That's just a thought—like a hypothesis. Stuff we do—probably has a function. [*I continue an emphasis on the function of a symptom.*]

Cl: Hmm. Yeah.

Co: It sounds like you got them to pay attention—got them involved.

Cl: Quite a few times.

Co: You needed something. Got something to happen. It makes sense to me, looking in from the outside. Now you're wrestling alone with it in college, wondering whether you should even continue with academic life right now.

Cl: [*Nods.*]

I begin to externalize the problem.

Co: This may seem silly to you, but I keep this little guy [plastic figure, 4 inches high] handy when we need a symbol of some kind. He's actually a German cartoon character, not familiar here, and that makes him a good symbol. Let's just say he represents underachievement—like "playing away the time," or whatever it means when you don't do what you need to do for classes. This guy keeps you from doing that good stuff that would get you A's and B's. There's an underachieving part of you, among many, many parts of you. You're a complex, interesting, multitextured person with an interesting story and an interesting life. I find that underachievers usually are interesting people, by the way. Not typical, rubber-stamp types [*again, a reframe*]. Right now, though, whatever you are, you've been having a hard time with this underachiever part. It's sort of governed your life. I'd like to learn how this part of you has been affecting you.

Cl: It makes me more laid back.

Co: OK. . . .

Cl: Maybe more open-minded. More frustrated.

Co: So—two positives and then a negative. Interesting that even a part like this can have two sides.

Cl: I'm not sure what else.

Co: OK. Well, it got your parents' attention along the way, frustrated you, made you laid back and open-minded. Who was affected by this underachievement part besides you?

Cl: My parents, I think.

Co: Are they affected now?

Cl: I don't know.

Co: I wonder if they're affected. You're not there with them anymore.

Cl: I'm not sure.

Co: Would you like them to be affected?

Cl: I'm not sure. No. It's just—maybe that's not the right word—*affected*.

Co: What would be the word?

Cl: They know, you know, about me—and that there. [*He is looking at the figure. At this point, he has externalized the problem.*]

Co: Your dad is aware of this? [*I am pointing at the figure*]

Cl: My dad? Yeah, sure.

Co: How does he react to that? [*I am pointing at the figure*]

Cl: He doesn't—not that I know of.

Co: Would you like him to?

Cl: Not anymore.

Co: You used to—but don't want that anymore?

Cl: No.

Co: You're paying for it yourself at this point?

Cl: It's mine now. [*This is a significant statement of ownership.*]

Co: Does your mom talk about it?

Cl: No.

Co: That's OK?

Cl: Yeah.

Co: OK. I'm going to put him way over there. [*I move the figure to the edge of the table.*] In fact, let's get rid of him. [*I move the figure behind a stack of books.*]

Cl: Right.

Co: What would be different? [*Here I move into a solution focus.*]

Cl: Ummm. I probably wouldn't have questions about the next couple of years.

Co: OK—there's the Mt. Everest idea from last time. You could see farther into the future because Mt. Everest wouldn't be in the way. OK. What else if that guy weren't there, messing things up? If that part of you were in sync somehow?

Cl: A little more self-confidence, maybe.

Co: Keep going. That part has been pretty important. If you could shape up that part, get your leader part to be in charge of that guy, what would be different? Take a peek around Mt. Everest.

Cl: [*Leaning forward, looking intense*] I'm not sure.

Co: Let's bring him back, then. He's pretty strong. OK. What does he represent, this part of you?

Cl: I don't know.

Co: Hmmm. Last time we talked about being stuck.

Cl: Yeah—maybe that.

Co: OK. If you weren't stuck, what would be going on in your life? I don't know your life.

Cl: I'd be happy—happier. Wouldn't be stuck. I don't know.

Co: You can't see past this person very easily.

Cl: I guess not.

Co: A pretty powerful, controlling part right now. Would you behave differently if he didn't control you?

Cl: Yeah. I'm sure I would. I'd definitely be more focused.

Co: How about socially—if this guy weren't exerting so much control over you? Any changes?

Cl: Maybe not be so laid back or casual about things.

Co: And if you weren't so laid back and casual, what would your life be like?

Cl: More boring.

Co: So, being casual and laid back is not boring. Am I reading that right?

Cl: Yeah, for me.

Co: So, if this guy weren't there, putting up a block, interfering or whatever he does, your life might be more boring.

Cl: No, I mean, I'm not saying that that would be a big problem.

Co: That's an interesting thought. When you said "laid back," I was thinking you meant carefree.

Cl: Yeah, but not *lazy*.

Co: OK. You clarified something for me. Thanks. So you're not sure you want to get rid of him completely.

Cl: Yeah, you know . . . not get rid of him. Maybe just calm him down or hide him in a closet or something.

Co: OK. Tame him down or put him in a closet, so you know he'd still be there, but you'd be in charge. If you toned him down, how much achievement do you think you could crank out?

Cl: More than now. I can't tell for sure.

Co: Would there be a scared part—if he got tucked away? Would another part of you get scared?

Cl: What do you mean?

Co: I'm just wondering. It sounds to me like there might be a little concern about life being a little bit boring and not so carefree. Maybe there's another part that doesn't even know how achievement would feel, and it might be sort of scary.

Cl: Yeah.

Co: What might be scary about achieving?

Cl: Scary—I don't know. [*He appears to be in deep thought.*]

Co: Can you imagine yourself getting maybe a 2.0, or 3.0, and your mom and friends would know about it?

Cl: I guess I'd still be able to say I was underachieving.

Co: Relatively speaking, you'd be up a notch in the grade book. People usually improve in small increments—hard to leap from one place to another all at once—but it's possible to take one test at a time now and make some progress over several months to a respectable grade point. Let's imagine that. Does anything feel sort of scary about that?

Cl: I'd have to keep it up. I'd have to.

Co: A scary thought—to think about keeping it up?

Cl: Be fun trying, I guess.

Co: Fun trying [*I smile.*].

Cl: Yeah.

Co: You never know. You've got the brains. Something is keeping you from leaping into academic success—has done that for quite a while. We're not sure why this guy has so much influence on you, but whenever this part is doing its stuff, the other parts get mowed down. But I sense that there's a part of you that would like to turn it around, at least to some extent. That part would like to be happier and would like to get unstuck. That's going to be the job of your leader part—to shake this guy up, be feisty with him, harness him in honor of the exams.

Cl: Mm-hmm. Yeah.

Near the end of the session, I connect the idea of stuckness to not being able to move ahead to the next stage of life—in his case, being launched into adulthood. I speculate that "that guy" might be keeping him stuck. I suggest that most of his other parts are probably eager to move on. We process the session. He has come to counseling only because of the crisis related to the exams and concludes his counseling at the end of this session.

References

Adler, A. (1954). *Understanding human nature* (W. B. Wolf, trans.). New York: Fawcett Premier. (Original work published 1927)

American Psychiatric Association. (2000). *Diagnostic and statistical manual of mental disorders* (4th ed., Text Rev.). Washington, DC: Author.

Baker, S. B., & Gerler, E. R., Jr. (2004). *School counseling for the twenty-first century*. Upper Saddle River, NJ: Pearson/Merrill/Prentice Hall.

Breunlin, D. C., Schwartz, R. C., & MacKune-Karrer, B. (1992). *Metaframeworks: Transcending the models of family therapy*. San Francisco: Jossey-Bass.

Costa, P. T., Jr., & McCrae, R. R. (1994). Set like plaster? Evidence for the stability of adult personality. In T. F. Heatherton & J. L. Weinberger (Eds.), *Can personality change?* (pp. 21–41). Washington, DC: American Psychological Association.

Dabrowski, K. (1967). *Personality shaping through positive disintegration*. New York: Little, Brown.

de Shazer, S. (1985). *Keys to solution in brief therapy*. New York: Norton.

Erikson, E. H. (1968). *Identity: Youth and crisis*. New York: Norton.

Gardner, H. (1983). *Frames of mind: The theory of multiple intelligences*. New York: Basic Books.

Gilliland, B. E., & James, R. K. (1998). *Theories and strategies in counseling and psychotherapy*. Boston: Allyn & Bacon.

Helson, R., & Moane, G. (1987). Personality change in women from college to midlife. *Journal of Personality and Social Psychology, 53*, 176–186.

Higgins, G. O. (1994). *Resilient adults overcoming a cruel past*. San Francisco: Jossey-Bass.

Littrell, J. M. (1998). *Brief counseling in action*. New York: Norton.

Lovecky, D. (1992). Exploring social and emotional aspects of giftedness in children. *Roeper Review, 15*, 18–25.

Mahoney, A. S. (1998). In search of the gifted identity: From abstract concept to workable counseling constructs. *Roeper Review, 20*, 222–226.

Minuchin, S. (1974). *Families and family therapy*. Cambridge, MA: Harvard University Press.

Minuchin, S., & Fishman, H. C. (1981). *Family therapy techniques*. Cambridge, MA: Harvard University Press.

Neihart, M., & Olenchak, F. R. (2002). Creatively gifted children. In M. Neihart, S. M. Reis, N. M. Robinson, & S. M. Moon (Eds.), *The social and emotional development of gifted children: What do we know?* (pp. 165–175). Waco, TX: Prufrock Press.

Peterson, J. S. (1990). Noon-hour discussion groups: Dealing with the burdens of capability. *Gifted Child Today, 13*(4), 17–22.

Peterson, J. S. (1993). *Talk with teens about self and stress: 50 guided discussions for school and counseling groups*. Minneapolis, MN: Free Spirit.

Peterson, J. S. (1995). *Talk with teens about feelings, family, relationships, and the future: 50 guided discussions for school and counseling groups*. Minneapolis, MN: Free Spirit.

Peterson, J. S. (1997). Bright, troubled, and resilient, and not in a gifted program. *Journal of Secondary Gifted Education, 8*, 121–136.

Peterson, J. S. (1998). The burdens of capability. *Reclaiming Children and Youth, 6*, 194–198.

Peterson, J. S. (1999). Gifted—through whose cultural lens? An application of the postpositivistic mode of inquiry. *Journal for the Education of the Gifted, 22*, 354–383.

Peterson, J. S. (2000). A follow-up study of one group of achievers and underachievers four years after high school graduation. *Roeper Review, 22*, 217–224.

Peterson, J. S. (2001). Successful adults who were once adolescent underachievers. *Gifted Child Quarterly, 45*, 236–249.

Peterson, J. S. (2002). A longitudinal study of post-high-school development in gifted individuals at risk for poor educational outcomes. *Journal of Secondary Gifted Education, 14,* 6–18.

Peterson, J. S. (2003). An argument for proactive attention to affective concerns of gifted adolescents. *Journal of Secondary Gifted Education, 14,* 62–71.

Peterson, J. S. (2006a). *The essential guide to talking with teens: Ready-to-use discussions for school and youth groups.* Minneapolis, MN: Free Spirit.

Peterson, J. S. (2006b). *Gifted and traumatized: A study of adolescent development.* Manuscript in preparation.

Peterson, J. S., & Colangelo, N. (1996). Gifted achievers and underachievers: A comparison of patterns found in school files. *Journal of Counseling and Development, 74,* 399–407.

Peterson, J. S., & Margolin, L. (1997). Naming gifted children: An example of unintended "reproduction." *Journal for the Education of the Gifted, 21,* 82–100.

Peterson, J. S., & Ray, K. E. (2006a). Bullying among the gifted: The subjective experience. *Gifted Child Quarterly, 50,* 252–269.

Peterson, J. S., & Ray, K. E. (2006b). Bullying and the gifted: Victims, perpetrators, prevalence, and effects. *Gifted Child Quarterly, 50,* 148–168.

Peterson, J. S., & Rischar, H. (2000). Gifted and gay: A study of the adolescent experience. *Gifted Child Quarterly, 44,* 149–164.

Piechowski, M. M. (1999). Overexcitabilities. In M. A. Runco & S. R. Pritzker (Eds.), *Encyclopedia of creativity* (Vol. 2, pp. 325–334). San Diego, CA: Academic Press.

Rak, C., & Patterson, L. E. (1996). Promoting resilience in at-risk children. *Journal of Counseling & Development, 74,* 368–373.

Rimm, S. (1995). *Why bright kids get poor grades and what you can do about it.* New York: Three Rivers Press.

Rogers, C. (1951). *Client-centered therapy.* Boston: Houghton Mifflin.

Santiago-Rivera, A. L., Bernstein, B. L., & Gard, T. L. (1995). The importance of achievement and the appraisal of stressful events as predictors of coping. *Journal of College Student Development, 36,* 374–383.

Satir, V. (1988). *The new peoplemaking.* Palo Alto, CA: Science and Behavior Books.

Silverman, L. K. (1997). The construct of asynchronous development. *Peabody Journal of Education, 72*(3/4), 36–58.

Watzlawick, P., Weakland, J. H., & Fisch, R. (1974). *Change: Principles of problem formulation and problem resolution.* New York: Norton.

Webb, J. R., Amend, E. R., Webb, N. E., Goerss, J., Beljan, P., & Olenchak, F. R. (2005). *Misdiagnosis and dual diagnosis of gifted children and adults: ADHD, Bipolar, OCD, Asperger's, Depression, and other disorders.* Scottsdale, AZ: Great Potential Press.

Werner, E. (1986). Resilient children. *Young Children, 40,* 68–72.

White, M., & Epston, D. (1990). *Narrative means to therapeutic ends.* New York: Norton.

chapter 6

Counseling Underachieving Students and Their Parents

by Caryln L. Saunders

Conception of Giftedness

Influences

Influences on my approach to giftedness range from a strict statistical definition (the top 2% of the population on a standardized test of intelligence), to the lay definition of early precocious behavior in a particular area. (I have a granddaughter who at 18 months of age likes to eat an enormous variety of food, including kiwifruit and still-frozen strawberries. Is she gifted?)

Definitions are only a small part of the picture. I am most influenced by theories that are fairly inclusive and leave room for development, such as Maria Montessori's (1964) assumption of the educability of intelligence and therefore the inconstancy of IQ. Barbara Clark (1983) also speaks of the interaction between genetic capacity and environmental influences.

Defining a concept of giftedness rests on the concept of intelligence. Thus, a brief review of the common approaches to the understanding of intelligence might prove useful. Complexity is a given: When two dozen prominent theorists were asked to define intelligence, they gave two dozen different definitions (Sternberg & Detterman, 1986).

One influential approach is a psychometric one (American Psychological Association Task Force, 1995); that is, the result of measurement by what are commonly referred to as IQ tests or achievement tests. Although originally devised by Alfred Binet to distinguish mentally retarded children from those with behavior problems, these tests now are used for selection purposes: admission to special programs and services in elementary and secondary school. Julian Stanley (1979) emphasized the importance of paying more attention to scores on advanced tests during selection for high-level programs than to school grades or recommendations. In fact, these tests are reasonably accurate in predicting academic success.

Critics of this unitary approach propose theories of multiple intelligences. Gardner (1983) included musical, bodily-kinesthetic, and various forms of personal intelligences, as well as the more commonly referred to (and tested) abilities such as verbal, logical, mathematical, and spatial. Also in the realm of multiple intelligence theories is Sternberg's (1985) triarchic theory, which includes three basic aspects of intelligence: analytic, creative, and practical. Only analytic skills are measured by mainstream tests.

Definition

Although a simple definition of giftedness is elusive, I believe a gifted person is one who demonstrates a persistently precocious understanding of concepts and an application of those concepts in original and creative ways. Gifted kids learn more quickly than average kids. They also demonstrate greater creativity in expression. Indeed, the reality is that gifted children can be as different from each other as they are alike, which makes defining giftedness a problem. From an emotional standpoint, I believe that giftedness contributes to more intensity in reactions to events, depth of feeling, acute observations, and perfectionism. For purposes of counseling, I am more interested in the emotional and personality traits of gifted children than in the intellectual, and I keep in mind that the more extreme the giftedness, the more extreme may be some of the personality attributes.

Because tests for many of the attributes associated with an inclusive view of giftedness do not yet exist, a definition from my perspective would be qualitative rather than quantitative. When considering all of the factors that can affect a student's intellectual capacity, not to mention his or her IQ score, it is not difficult to see why a definition that includes multiple intelligences is appealing, especially from a counseling standpoint.

The demands of the marketplace (educational systems) seem to favor a unilateral approach to defining giftedness, namely recognizing attainment of a score deemed sufficient to qualify someone as "gifted" in a given school district. A child is either gifted or not. Thus, in practical reality for education, giftedness depends on a solitary IQ number, with statistical error not considered, and with the number varying from one school district to the next. This number may be determined by the quantity of children a district can afford to serve, with economics driving the cut-off score. This IQ score may be 125 in one school district or 135 in an adjoining district, depending on the local criterion. By this application, the same child could be deemed gifted in one district with an IQ of 130 and not gifted if his or her family later moved across town to a new home in another district with a higher qualifying score.

This approach to identification for special programs leaves much out of the equation when considering any particular child and certainly may exclude many students who need the services. From my perspective, this approach is too narrow even from an educational position—and much more so from a counseling position, which considers emotional, physical, family, and social, as well as cognitive, factors.

My position regarding school programs is that the best gifted program would be no gifted program, but rather an individual educational plan for every student, regardless of IQ. In my opinion, the definition of *gifted* is too complex and varied to limit services to those achieving a certain score on a test. Furthermore, being identified as gifted does not simplify the task of designing services to meet a child's needs, it does not make one more deserving of special attention, and it does not guarantee that a student's individual needs will be addressed. A plan for each student would avoid the dichotomy of "Is she?" or "Is she not?" The goal of the plan would be to look at many factors, both internal and external, in order to pinpoint both opportunities and barriers to learning and development without undue attention to a particular score on a test.

Because I often deal with underachieving gifted students, defining *academic underachievement* is in order. In general terms, it means that a child is not working up to his or her capacity. Instantly we run into a problem: Is a child who is getting poor grades but is grasping the content, as demonstrated on tests, underachieving? Delisle (1992) differentiates between *underachieving* and *nonproductive* by pointing out that nonproducers are at risk academically, but not psychologically, because they have confidence in their abilities, whereas underachievers are at risk both academically and psychologically because of their low self-esteem and dependent style of learning.

The issue of defining underachievement is important because acceptance into a gifted learning program often rests not only on IQ scores but also on achievement test scores and grades. Thus, if children are not producing, the unspoken message is that they do not *deserve* to be in a gifted program. A more helpful approach would be to view the gifted program as a means to reduce and remove impediments to productivity. Indeed, this issue of productivity means that often teachers are not typically good at identifying gifted children, although they can become more accurate with in-service training (Gear, 1978).

Assumptions

My assumptions regarding the gifted children I work with include their basic need for a relationship that they can rely on to support their emotional development. I assume, because they are gifted, that their feelings of being different from their peers serve to isolate them. Thus, they often need someone to help them accept themselves and to communicate their needs and feelings to their parents and teachers. I assume that achievement and self-esteem are closely linked, and that being gifted complicates the picture. If students are not exposed to new and challenging material, they do not learn; therefore they miss the experience of mastery and accomplishment. I assume that most kids would rather be making good grades, even if they initially profess otherwise. I assume that the underlying causes of underachievement are rooted in family dynamics rather than simply in a lack of study skills. I also assume that parents genuinely care about their children's well-being and overall success.

Conception of Personality

Personality

Maslow's (1970) hierarchy of needs holds that in order for an individual to progress to a higher level of psychological development, the needs at the lower level have to be met. Developmental theories rest on the idea that there is a sequential order of stages of development that all progress through physically, emotionally, socially, and intellectually. Webb, Meckstroth, and Tolan (1982) pointed out that gifted children are often *asynchronous* (i.e., they may be 7 years old chronologically, 12 years old intellectually, and 5 years old emotionally) in their development across different areas, thus complicating assessment and treatment. Transactional analysis (Berne, 1964; Harris, 1969) focuses on the emotional development of individuals from infancy, to adulthood, to parenthood. As a person matures, these stages become less actual and more behavioral. Transactional analysis also supplies a usable vocabulary to teach the family about their interactions and their effect on each other. In a family systems approach, the impact of life events on the entire family must be considered. If a parent loses his or her job, children may become anxious. Geographical moves, the loss of a grandparent, or a marital split between the parents all affect how a child learns. More important, events such as these affect the routine and structure of the family, with that alteration potentially upsetting study habits.

In addition, the systemic emotional reactions accompanying major changes in the family have a profound impact on the child, often without the parents realizing it.

Personality of Gifted Individuals

I do not think that there is a distinct personality associated with being gifted. I do think that gifted people possess some traits to a greater degree than others. However, these traits vary from one individual to another. Some display a sense of humor; some are very detail oriented; some are very quick and active. Nevertheless, some traits seem to appear with greater frequency in gifted individuals, such as an ability to grasp concepts quickly, an excellent memory, and novel problem-solving ability.

Model of Counseling

Influences

Counseling gifted children has suffered from the same stereotypes that educating them has: Because they are smart, they will do fine without special help. Thus, few clear models exist for counseling this population. Is giftedness a diagnosis to be "treated"? I would hope not. I would rather work from a model that considers giftedness an attribute that is a very important part of what the child brings to the counseling situation. A mental health professional, even one who does not utilize a medical model in treatment, must be aware of issues beyond giftedness, such as depression, anxiety, Attention Deficit/Hyperactivity Disorder, and vision problems, that may need medical intervention. Here I want to mention some authors who have written about underachievement because it is such a large part of my work as a counselor of gifted children.

Mandel and Marcus (1988) offered a comprehensive summary of what they labeled a voluminous and often contradictory literature on the psychology of underachievement. They cited Pirozzo (1982), who concluded that underachievement in gifted students can be related to personal adjustment difficulties, as well as limited academic programming in school, and that both sets of variables must be considered in remediation. Mandel and Marcus focused on differential diagnosis and treatment of underachievement, emphasizing that previous studies had usually assumed that underachievers were a homogeneous group to be treated with one approach. They identified five types of underachievers: Overanxious Disorder, Conduct Disorder, Academic, Identity Disorder, and Oppositional Defiant Disorder.

Rimm (1986) designed a Trifocal Approach, in which psychologists focus on the student, the parents, and the school, although she stated that many problems can be corrected without a psychologist. She presented a two-by-two grid to describe underachievers, with Dominant vs. Dependent characteristics on one side, and Conforming vs. Nonconforming on the adjacent side. She not only provided clear examples of types of underachievers, but she also spelled out many family-relationship patterns that foster underachievement behaviors. Giftedness adds a significant dimension to the mix of family factors.

Baker, Bridger, and Evans (1998) similarly explored three models of underachievement involving individual, family, and school issues. Each model revealed variables that were predictive of underachievement. The combined model was the strongest in predictive value, suggesting that the phenomenon is complex.

Kanevsky and Keighley (2003) found in a study based on individual interviews that their gifted subjects often felt boredom and a sense of moral indignation toward the activities they were offered as "education." Their disengagement from the curriculum was their "honorable" reaction to experiences they saw as inappropriate.

Three important factors that characterize achievers emerge, according to Siegle and McCoach (2003). Achievers (1) find value in their school experience, (2) believe they have the skills to be successful, and (3) trust their environment and believe they can succeed in it. Thus, they are more likely to produce self-regulated behavior.

Students underachieve (i.e., perform noticeably below their ability level) for a number of reasons. Being gifted compounds the number of reasons for underachievement. Studies of underachievers do not necessarily answer why underachievement occurs, but they shed light on various contributing factors. Addressing these factors comprehensively can yield positive results in reversing underachievement. However, as Pecaut (1979) and Mandel and Marcus (1988) emphasized, differential treatment, depending on the personality type of the student, yields the best results. Peterson and Colangelo (1996) concluded that attention to underachievement needs to occur before high school and probably before junior high.

The authors referred to in this section noted the importance of a careful assessment of the child, the family, and the school situation. They also viewed underachievement and the need for counseling from a developmental perspective, and this orientation guides the therapeutic process. Another common component is the importance of a comprehensive approach to the problems to be solved, which may involve practitioners from various fields, such as psychiatrists, nutritionists, eye specialists, social workers, psychologists, and educators, as well as counselors.

My counseling frame of reference reflects several basic influences: core conditions for counseling (Carkhuff, 1984); self-disclosure in therapy (Jourard, 1964); Maslow's (1970) hierarchy of needs; and transactional analysis (Berne, 1964, Harris, 1969). A hierarchy of needs theory is the underpinning for a developmental approach to differential diagnosis, as well as a gauge of growth in the therapeutic process. Core conditions refer to empathy, genuineness, and positive regard, which encourage openness and self-exploration on the part of the client. Mutual self-disclosure by both therapist and client furthers the process of trust, self-acceptance, and intimacy within the relationship. Transactional analysis provides an understanding of the dynamics of parent-child relationships, which may underlie underachievement issues.

I see these approaches as commonly used and trustworthy. Over the course of my career, I have come to think that one's theory is less important than knowing enough to apply theory in therapeutic settings. A theory gives one a rationale for prescriptions for change and a way to present that rationale to clients. It provides a language in which to communicate the recommendations to clients and a framework for them to understand new concepts.

Definition of Counseling

Counseling is a unique relationship in which the counselor creates an atmosphere for the client to explore thoughts, feelings, reactions, and motivations. This atmosphere is characterized by counselor empathy and acceptance so as to promote openness and honesty in the client, which in turn allows the client to experiment with changes in behavior. Self-exploration is facilitated by self-disclosure, which, according to Jourard (1971) is the key to a healthy personality. People who reveal themselves to others experience acceptance, which allows self-confidence to grow. Of course, they also risk criticism, which is why they tend to avoid it.

The counselor encourages self-disclosure with open-ended questions, with appropriate disclosures of his or her own, and by refraining from negative reactions to client disclosure. When a client discloses behavior that others might judge as negative, helpful responses might include the following: "I see. How did that turn out for you?" Or "Did that get the result that you wanted?" These types of responses allow clients to evaluate and change behaviors on their own, in contrast to being told what to do by someone in authority.

Role of Counselor

The counselor's roles are those of researcher, reflector, relater, model for parents, and supporter for personal exploration. I intend for us to walk down a path together.

Role of Client

The role of the client is ideally one of participant and authentic expresser of thoughts and feelings.

Goals

My overall goals in this work are to improve the self-esteem and autonomy of the student, to reestablish the natural hierarchy of the family with parents in charge, to put structure and limits around homework issues, to improve the overall communication in the family, to help the parents be a united team and to support each other, and to help the student understand and express his or her needs more directly so that underachievement is not a necessary mode of expression. My initial goal is to assess each child's situation so that reasonable alternatives can be explored. Usually one goal is to restore achievement and productivity so that opportunities are opened up and not cut off. An important step in reaching this goal is to help the student see that he or she is more hurt by underachieving behavior than are his or her parents or teachers.

My approach may appear to gloss over issues of genuine boredom (cf. Kanevsky & Keighley, 2003). However, my experience is that one must sort through a maze of claims about true boredom versus boredom reflecting long-term lack of engagement. At this juncture, intelligence and achievement testing can be useful. Students may need a way to demonstrate to teachers that they have indeed mastered material so that they can be allowed to accelerate to more challenging material, if that has been an issue. However, it does no service to students to be advanced to material ahead of their placement if they have not mastered the steps leading up to that level. Counselors need to help underachievers gain credibility with parents and teachers. If their scores on IQ and achievement tests are high, then overcoming behavioral blocks to making better grades is the next goal of counseling.

Although it is not my usual approach, I have occasionally recommended that a high school student drop out of school and pursue an alternative approach to learning, such as early admission to college, online courses, or specialized projects reflecting a student's specific interests (e.g., art, music, foreign language, or electronics). This kind of move must be done carefully and with the full support and cooperation of the parents, because the child will need a supportive environment, both at home and in whatever situation he or she chooses to pursue learning in. Some school districts are now supporting home-schooling through computerized instruction and making textbooks available.

Relationship

One goal of my relationship with students is to be someone different from their teacher, parent, or buddy. This means listening to them—more than talking "at" them. It means acknowledging their feelings without condoning self-defeating behaviors. This means supporting their dreams while keeping their feet on the ground. It means respecting them by being honest with them about my own feelings and reactions so that they experience an authentic relationship.

My relationship with parents is to be a mentor and guide so that they can regain confidence in their parenting abilities. A counselor's demonstration of consistency and reliability sets a powerful example for the parents and the child about how results are obtained, especially in the target behavior, which is studying and preparing for class. The outcome measure is grades achieved.

My relationship with the family as a whole is aimed at reestablishing the natural hierarchy with the parents in charge. This is accomplished by not siding with the child in power struggles (but rather guiding the family in negotiation skills) and by helping parents consider carefully the responses they make to the child's behaviors.

Assessment

My approach to assessing gifted students is to maximize my ability to treat them as individuals. Delisle (1992) stressed the importance of treating students as individuals so that they are not labeled merely as underachievers and so that the proper interventions can be made to correct learning disabilities, developmental problems, and emotional problems.

The assessment process actually encompasses at least the first month or so of contact, including parental interviews, standardized testing, feedback regarding test results, and designing interventions. Generally I follow the model for a diagnostic interview presented by Mandel and Marcus (1988) with both the parents and the child. However, the initial appointment is always conducted with only the parents in order to gather background information. I ask them during a telephone conversation to bring with them copies of grade reports, samples of work, and standardized test results.

If I can examine several years' worth of grade reports, I can see when and where the grades began to decline. This information, along with intake questions, such as whether the child has had any illnesses, injuries, family trauma, or geographical moves, can be correlated to see if these factors may have interfered with the child's intellectual and academic functioning. I can also examine patterns of behavior related to school and grades, such as absenteeism and tardiness, as well as the number and difficulty of courses (see Peterson & Colangelo, 1996).

Low grades often become a downward spiral because of a process of disengagement. It is not unusual for a child's report card to consist of straight A's initially and then to contain mostly D's and F's by the time the parents come for assistance. These D's and F's can exist in the presence of an intellect in the 98th percentile or above. There is also potential for the bouncing-ball effect: a high grade in algebra and a low grade in English one semester becoming reversed in a subsequent semester. The problem there is not a lack of intelligence or learning ability, but rather of motivation.

Underachieving gifted students can be described as engaging in self-defeating behavior, and their patterns begin to reinforce each other. As they avoid handing in work, their grades decline, which in turn affects their self-esteem, which then affects their belief in their ability to master knowledge. This ripple effect contributes to less desire to engage in learning activities, which diminishes their knowledge base relative to their peers, which affects performance on tests, further pushing down their grade.

Over long periods of time, the downward trend becomes more obvious: First, grades slide downward, and then achievement test scores decline. Finally, even verbal IQ test scores can be affected, especially in areas that test acquired skills such as general information, mathematics, and vocabulary. Comprehension and abstract reasoning skills tend to be less affected by under-achievement. Parents are usually surprised that IQ scores can be affected by underachievement. Most parents are well-enough informed to know that IQ scores are relatively stable over a life span. However, the fallacy of IQ tests is that, in large part, they can measure learning ability only by testing what the child has already learned. Few of the items are of a novel type, testing a person's ability to grasp and process new information.

The standardized tests given at school to evaluate students are usually group-administered paper-and-pencil intelligence tests and comprehensive achievement tests, such as the Iowa Tests of Basic Skills (ITBS). More recently these tests also have included statewide assessments, which I find less useful because of the way results are expressed. I believe they are more of an assessment of teaching methods and school performance than of an individual child's learning accomplishments.

Each achievement test report contributes to an overview of whether a child is learning at grade level in core subject areas such as reading and math, as well as of more specialized skills, such as punctuation and using maps and diagrams. It is useful to determine whether the child's skills are low generally or are low only in one or two subject areas. The latter lower scores are more indicative of learning problems than are the grade reports mentioned earlier. If I have an opportunity to see sequential results of the same test, the progression of their learning achievement can be traced over time. Long periods of doing very little homework and of being disengaged can eventually affect achievement test scores. However, in very bright youngsters, this effect may not occur because they can absorb most of the material just by listening.

On the Wechsler Intelligence Scale for Children (WISC-III), Performance scores, compared with Verbal scores, seem not to be as affected by under-achievement. Indeed, when Performance scores are significantly lower than Verbal scores, they may indicate a causal problem (e.g., difficulty with depth perception or with tracking right to left), rather than underachieving behavior (Kaufman, 1994). Especially when the discrepancy is statistically significant (20 points or more), there may be clues about factors interfering with achievement. For example, difficulty with visual processing and visual-motor coordination may affect reading, spelling, and handwriting. If these skills are deficient, output of written work may be laborious and of poor quality. The usual conception of a learning disorder, especially in reading skills, is a Verbal score that is lower than the Performance score. Verbal items, more than visual motor or performance items, test what the child has already learned and can express with verbal facility. It is reasonable to assume that if a child lags behind grade level in reading, then academic achievement will become much more difficult as he or she grows older because learning in our school system becomes increasingly more dependent on reading.

If I perceive a possible problem in visual-motor perception, I recommend eye exams, hearing tests, and complete physicals. These help to rule out physical factors as contributing to school and behavioral problems. If physical problems do emerge, treatment can begin for those issues with the appropriate professional.

Sometimes the level of family chaos is such that regular medical checkups such as eye exams have been neglected. Not being able to see the board in the classroom can affect one's achievement. Short-term illnesses and injuries may also have been glossed over. One 10-year-old girl that I had been seeing for about 2 months appeared not to feel well. When I asked her what was wrong, she said her stomach did not feel good. She also told me that she had fallen on the sidewalk the previous weekend, and that her arm was still hurting from the fall. After the session, I encouraged the parents to take her to have her arm checked. Examination revealed a "greenstick" fracture, and she wore a cast on her arm at her next appointment.

Although I may conceptualize a student's personality structure in terms of a *Diagnostic and Statistical Manual* (DSM) diagnosis as a guide in treatment, I am reluctant to identify a child with a label that will follow him or her throughout life. Although I write up a report interpreting scores on the IQ and achievement scores, I do not put DSM diagnoses in reports of test results because I know that these reports often are read by school personnel and parents who are not mental health professionals. I find it more helpful to characterize personality along developmental lines (e.g., Trust Seeking, Security Seeking, Dependent Seeking, and Independence Seeking [Pecaut, 1979]). Trust Seeking is the earliest stage of development and involves learning the trustworthiness and consistency of the physical and emotional world surrounding the child. Security Seeking is the second stage of development during which the child seeks reassurance from those around him or her to reduce anxiety by asking for clarification of expectations so as to maintain a "secure" position in the eyes of significant adults. Dependence Seeking is the third stage of development, during which the child seeks structure to depend on, because he or she is not yet ready to assume responsibility for choices and decisions. Independence Seeking is the final stage of development. The young person can be observed making decisions independent of peers and parental figures and being willing to experience the consequences of those choices.

Assessment of the family dynamics is conducted by listening and observing, mainly from the perspective of transactional analysis (Berne, 1964), to pinpoint interactions that contribute to conflict between the two parents and between the child and either parent. When a parent disagrees with the other parent, the resulting mixed message sets the stage for power struggles. When either parent communicates repeatedly from a Critical Parent position (characterized by behaviors such as negative statements about the child, labeling, put-downs, yelling, and finger pointing), the child often behaves from a rebellious position, which can be manifested by refusing to study or do homework. A boy said to me, "I really wanted my dad to come to my soccer games, but he wouldn't. So, I wouldn't give him what he wanted from me: good grades."

Process

In working with gifted young people, I meet with them separately from their parents for several months in order to establish a relationship with them. Trust in a relationship is established over time.

At the first session with children, I initially inquire if they know why they are coming to talk with me. The response is usually, "I don't know" or "My grades." As quickly as possible, I move toward finding out about their thoughts and feelings about the counseling situation. Some are angry, and I take some time to acknowledge their anger. When they acknowledge that the counseling has something to do with school performance, I ask if they want to make better grades. Invariably they do, and I ask them if they know what they need to do to make better grades. They usually respond, "Study harder." I then gather a great amount of factual information about how much time they spend on their homework, which classes are their favorite and least favorite, and how well they are performing in each class, as reflected in grades.

After setting out the limits of confidentiality, I expand on that by telling them that if they share something with me that is serious and may warrant a breach of confidentiality, I will say, "This is serious and we need to talk with mom and dad about it. Let's talk about how we will do that." There are three messages here:

- I am being up front with you about this.
- We will discuss these things with mom and dad.
- I will support you in communicating with them.

Sometimes young clients try to get me to act as their advocate for some special privilege. I handle this by saying, "I will help you talk with your parents about this." I ask about their extracurricular activities and jobs. Very frequently, these students are underinvolved and detached from the school. If they are involved in activities, I tell the clients that I will arrange their appointment times around their other commitments. My openness to accommodating them conveys respect for those aspects of their lives. From a pragmatic standpoint, I do not want to take away something that is going well. Jobs and activities can often teach kids a great deal about responsibility that cannot be taught in a counseling session or by their parents.

As stated earlier, I follow the model for the diagnostic interview as outlined by Mandel and Marcus (1988). This model provides some structure for the process. I find it useful because the questions are open-ended and nonjudgmental, and I can track progress. At the end of the first session, I encourage the students to make some commitment to a plan for some change. It may be a commitment to finish a specific long-term assignment, or it may be to talk with their parents about something that needs discussing.

At each subsequent session, I ask how things are going and what has happened since we last met. I frequently ask about exam scores and grades in classes. One way that underachievers maintain their disengagement is to remain unaware of how they are doing in class, sustaining their position of seeing no connection between behavior and results. When I ask them frequently what grades they are receiving (and have them bring in progress reports and grade reports), they can no longer sustain the avoidance. Sometimes at the beginning of a semester, I ask them to predict what they will achieve in each class. If they say they want to improve their grades, I ask them what they need to do each week to improve even a little. I also ask how things are going for them with their family, their friends, their jobs, and their extracurricular activities. As a result, they have opportunity to discuss other areas and to sort out their reactions and conflicts.

I typically meet with kids 3 weeks out of 4 and meet with the parents once a month. I avoid having kids sit in the waiting room during their parents' sessions because of the level of mistrust they develop while waiting.

Part of counseling with gifted underachieving children, particularly those in the stages of development below Independence Seeking, and their parents is simply to direct parents to require that children study for a specified amount of time each evening and that the study time be supervised by the parents. I recommend a study period of 45 minutes each evening for middle and high school students, less for younger students. Most parents tell me that this is not nearly enough and that 2 hours is closer to what is needed. My experience is that if I send the family home with a 2-hour expectation, they will never comply. Kids can tolerate 45 minutes, and they think they are getting off easier than they expected to. In fact, they have invariably been doing virtually no homework.

This is a somewhat paradoxical assignment for the family. The therapist is essentially telling the family *not* to have the child study for 2 hours. Although the parents believe 45 minutes is not sufficient, they are secretly relieved not to have a nightly battle that lasts most of the evening.

I prescribe 45 minutes of study time five times per week, regardless of whether a child has homework. This circumvents the question "Do you have homework?" (In fact, this question should not be asked.) The message is "It's time to study." I encourage the entire family to do something during this time that is oriented toward school-like activities, such as reading or balancing the checkbook. If kids say they "do not have any homework," then they are to be instructed to read a book, work on a long-term assignment, or, as a last resort, read the dictionary or encyclopedia. One parent or the other is to supervise the activity and answer questions, but they are not to become involved in the material being studied. The assignment is a contract between the student and the teacher. The child might insist that they are to do only every other problem or read only 10 pages. However, the parent should not become involved in what is essentially a power play.

Parents should take turns supervising the homework so that the child understands that both parents are jointly involved in this. Seeing both parents taking a clear, unified stand sends messages not only about the unity of the parents but also of the value they place on school (Rimm, 1986).

One key to the success of the homework plan is that there is no music, television, telephone time, or computer games until the 45 minutes of homework time has elapsed. Setting the clear time expectation prevents the child from rushing through the work (with resulting carelessness) to finish faster in order to be able to play. I coach the parents in the "When, then" instruction: "*When* you have worked on homework for 45 minutes, *then* you may watch TV." They are to avoid "If you don't, then you can't." If a child absolutely refuses to work on studies, parents are to specify a time by which the homework period should be completed, and at the end of that time, parents are to say, "I'm sorry you chose not to do any homework. There will be no TV (or computer games, etc.) this evening." End of discussion. I have never had a student as a client whose grades did not improve if he or she consistently did 45 minutes worth of homework five times a week.

Parents, in their frustration, may say in a session, "I took the TV away for the rest of the semester because the kids aren't studying." If parents return access to the TV at the end of each study session, then they have leverage tomorrow. If they put it in the closet for the next three months, what can they take away tomorrow? Kids learn to live around the deprivation (like a cast on a broken arm, it is very uncomfortable at first, but soon becomes unnoticeable), and the parents have lost control over the intended motivator. Putting privileges on a short time frame keeps the parent in charge.

If kids seem to be working effectively on homework, the next link in the chain is to find out if homework is being handed in. A surprising number of children do homework and do not submit it to their teachers. Why? Because it is not quite finished or it is not perfect or they lost it or "the dog ate it." One part of the process for the parents and the therapist is to find out from the teacher if the work is being turned in (sometimes teachers really do lose a paper, but not as often as kids would have parents believe). If work has not been turned in, it is important to help the child finish study time by gathering up study materials and putting books and papers into the book bag or backpack in preparation for leaving for school the next morning.

Several things begin to happen. First, the routine and habit of doing homework begins to be established. Then, self-esteem increases when students walk into class, hand in their homework, and experience the teacher beginning to react to them more positively. (One girl reported, "The teacher actually smiled

models of counseling gifted children, adolescents, and young adults at me today!"). Parents are more in charge, thus reestablishing the natural hierarchy. As students' grades begin to improve, and they begin to enjoy school, they become more engaged in the learning process and with school in general. When school is a more enjoyable, reinforcing experience, the students perform better and learn more.

Several months into the counseling, I recognize improvement because I have more difficulty finding times for their appointments. They are becoming more involved in activities and more attached to school in general. Kids will work for grades for a coach so that they can participate in a sport, but may not want to give their parents the same satisfaction.

Parents who are dysfunctional or especially needy require more of the therapist's time because they are insecure about losing to the therapist their role as the parental figure. One boy reported to me (somewhat fearfully) that his mother quizzed him intently on the way home from his counseling sessions about what we had discussed during his session. Sometimes parents fear that other information will come out, such as abuse or alcoholism. When these issues are present, the pressure on the child to keep the peace is enormous.

I recommend that the family meet each Sunday evening for 15 minutes so that family members can coordinate calendars (e.g., who needs rides when, what school activities are occurring, when one parent or the other is working late or going to be out of town). I find that many of these families are chaotic because of many commitments and lack of communication. Because they often do not share basic information, their lives cannot run smoothly. Just this small amount of organization and communication can dramatically improve accountability and involvement with each other.

I recommend to parents the book *How to Talk So Kids Will Listen and Listen So Kids Will Talk,* by Faber and Maizlish (1980). They teach by example the skill of reflective listening so that parents can respond to their children in helpful ways. The emphasis is on helping parents understand that they do not have to solve every problem that a child expresses, but rather that they are to support the child in working his or her own way to a resolution.

I also teach the basics of Transactional Analysis as a method of communicating (Parent-Adult-Child) so that there is less Critical Parent-to-Child talk and more Adult-to-Adult talk (see Figure 6.1). Adolescents especially do not want to cooperate with someone who talks to them from the Critical Parent ego state and treats them like a child.

Some parents have a value system that does not place a high priority on school. I gain information about this by observing (both from the grade reports and by verbal report) attendance patterns. Some parents allow children to miss school for many and trivial reasons. They may even think it acceptable to schedule vacations during school time. They do not make arrangements to have the children work on schoolwork during the trip so that all assignments are current when they return. Some parents allow kids to sleep in and not go to school if they are tired for any reason, or kids learn to manipulate the situation by saying, "I don't feel good."

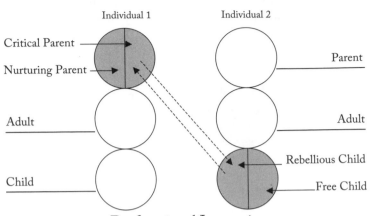

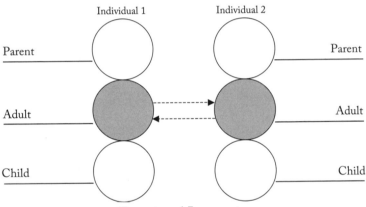

Figure 6.1. Transactional analysis models of interactions in families with achievement issues

Much of counseling is not elegant, but, rather, paying attention to basics. I make sure the family keeps their scheduled appointments. I make it clear that both parents are to come to the parent sessions. If one comes without the other, I schedule the next parent session with the parent who was absent. This reinforces the importance of balanced involvement. An individual session with each parent now and then can be used to check on each person's feelings and investment in the process without provoking defensiveness in front of the other parent. In situations where the parents are divorced, I have had success with

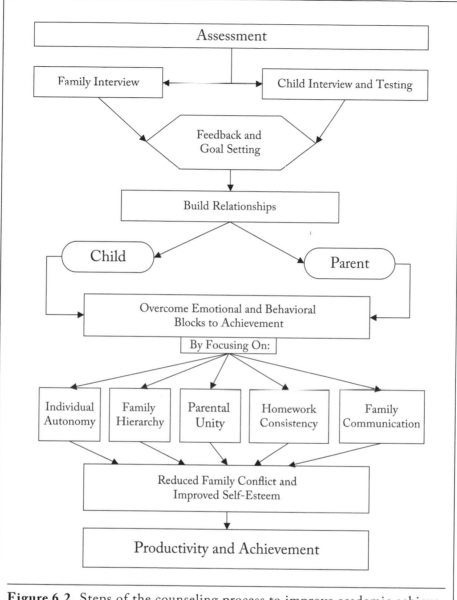

Figure 6.2. Steps of the counseling process to improve academic achievement and reduce family conflict

having both natural parents attend sessions—sometimes separately, sometimes together.

Graphic Illustration

The model I use, as illustrated (see Figure 6.2), involves a sequential process that starts with gathering information and establishing relationships with the parents and the child. This leads to making recommendations for change to the parents and allowing the child to explore consequences of his or her behaviors, both old and new. The information gathering process is ongoing, and the results are continually incorporated into interventions with both parents and child.

Application

Presenting Problems

I deal with almost anything that affects the identified client. Because we are dealing with personality issues and not just skills and behaviors, I think it is important to work with the whole person. I find that children and adolescents present their concerns differently than do adults who come for counseling. Kids present information in a way that to the untrained ear sounds like conversational commentary on the week's events. They usually do not identify emotional reactions. Often they jump from topic to topic. But the fact that they brought something up at all probably means that it is important to them. That is the time to say, "Tell me more about that" or "I wonder how you felt when the others left you behind." Such comments validate their feelings and experiences and help them differentiate themselves from others.

Underachievement

Academic underachievement is an issue I often encounter as a presenting problem because parents are anxious about its consequences. Each participant usually has a distinctly different perspective on the problem. The following are a few pertinent examples of problematic assumptions that are often presented in counseling:

- *Parents' position*: All kids should want to do well in school. Logic will convince them to do well in school: "You will need a good education to get a good job when you grow up. You don't want to be flipping hamburgers your whole life, do you?"
- *Kids*: All smart kids have it easy in school. I'm smart. Why isn't everything easy? Why do I have to work for grades?
- *Educators*: All kids should love school and accept the way content is taught. They should all be able to learn in the same way—that is, the way we teach it.

Usually, *underachievement* is a catchall term that parents and teachers use to indicate that a child is getting low grades. Most parents and students put grades under the umbrella of studying, without identifying the separate behaviors of completing the work, reviewing it for careless errors, handing it in, and preparing for tests. Classroom participation also enhances grades. When these components are in place, able students usually can achieve good grades. Many gifted children can make A's or B's on tests without doing homework. However, because the grade in many classes is a composite of assignments, test scores, and class participation, their grades are lower than their ability would predict. As children persist in failing to do homework, they may begin to fall behind in overall comprehension. As they fall behind in familiarity with the material, they become disengaged with the learning process and, finally, with school itself. This disengagement leads to negative feedback from teachers and parents and contributes to the low self-esteem referred to by Delisle (1992).

Early Testing. Contributing to underachievement is the increasing reluctance to test students for intellectual giftedness before they are in third grade. Schools justify this delay in testing by referring to the regression-toward-the-mean phenomenon of test scores and to the idea that some youngsters who test high early probably do so because of preschool learning and not because they are truly gifted. This delay in testing may increase the chances of underachievement because of some students' tendency to adapt to the slow rate of instruction and to detach from the educational process if it has little to offer them. In my opinion, if a child tests high at an early age, there is a responsibility to support and maintain that rate of learning. If the learning environment is appropriate, the child will continue to learn at a rapid pace.

School Issues. In my experience, most educators and parents believe students underachieve because they do not have adequate study skills ("They do not know how to study"), they have Attention Deficit/Hyperactivity Disorder, or they have some type of learning disability. These issues may indeed be contributing factors, but most parents report that their children do quite well in subjects they enjoy or in classes where they like the teacher. In addition, grades in certain classes may vary widely from semester to semester, dispelling the idea that the low grades are caused by a learning disability. Learning disabilities certainly can coexist with giftedness and underachievement, however, and therefore a thorough assessment should be part of the counseling process.

Verbal Talent as a Factor. The verbal facility of many young gifted children may set the stage for later underachievement. Baum, Owen, and Dixon (1991) reasoned that relying on verbal talent may enable them to slight their written work and in turn become careless and disorganized. As the demands for reading and long-term written assignments increase in middle or junior high school, these students, who have never had to study, find they are having difficulty. Subsequently, they may become depressed and confused about why making good grades has become difficult. I also believe that in elementary grades, because teachers have sustained contact with students, children can often get by on the charm factor. In middle or junior high, it is more difficult for a student to be recognized by, and receive credit for, subjective attributes because a teacher deals with 120 or more students each day.

Family Environment. In my practice, underachievement is due to psychological and developmental factors as often as intellectual factors. The psychological contributors are often rooted in family dynamics and usually are multiple.

For example, a child may be depressed due to a severe conflict between the parents. The child wants not only to please both parents, but also to keep the family in harmony and together. The depression itself (which may also have a genetic component) interferes with optimum functioning due to low energy, poor concentration, apathy, and social withdrawal, and the effort to keep the family intact may be an additional factor in underachievement.

Without necessarily being able to articulate it, children may realize that if they are misbehaving, the parents focus their energy and attention on them, thus diverting the parents from fighting with each other. One 12-year-old girl had figured it out. She said in therapy, "If I weren't so much trouble, my dad would leave my mom. He thinks she can't handle me by herself."

The emotional traits of giftedness intensify these behavior patterns because the child is often exquisitely sensitive to others' moods and feelings, thus heightening reactivity to stress and conflict. Coupled with that tendency is a heightened awareness of fairness. When children perceive situations as unfair, they become angry, vocal, and argumentative. With their skills of logic, they can often prevail in arguments with their parents.

Child's Specialness. Another aspect of being gifted that factors into the dynamics of underachievement is a child's rarity or, from the parents' point of view, their "specialness" (Rimm, 1986). There are many ways a child can be very special: being long awaited, having problems at birth, being first born, being last born, being the only girl or only boy, or being the first grandchild. Being a precocious learner, especially in verbal skills, is another way of being special. One possible consequence is that expectations are not consistently enforced. The child may say clever things and get off the hook, so to speak. There is also the issue of the parents' reasoning that because the children are so bright and talented, they should spend their time and talents in lessons and sporting activities (e.g., "I shouldn't expect them to waste their time with picking up their clothes and taking out the trash."). Being excused from the mundane extends to learning activities as well. "Why should they have to do homework that is material they already know?" Such reasoning puts the child on a pedestal and may contribute to the nonperformance discussed earlier.

Parenting Dynamics. I often observe a mismatch in parenting styles when underachievement is present. Usually one parent is the rescuer and the other the persecutor. The rescuer reasons that the child needs help and love because the other parent is strict and punitive. The persecutor believes that someone needs to hold the line because the other parent is easily manipulated and does not enforce limits and expectations. Many parents are aware of being played one against the other, with the child as the tail wagging the dog. These patterns can be intensified if one parent is absent, travels away from home a great deal, or is somehow unavailable, leaving one person to do most or all of the work of parenting. Even an absent parent sends powerful messages to the child. Each parent may expect the counselor to tell the other parent to change.

When parents are not living together, one parent may not reinforce homework time when the child is at his or her home. Sometimes this is a continuation of the parental conflict that led to the split, and sometimes it is a way to resist the wishes of the other parent.

Homework. Homework is particularly problematic because very bright children themselves complain that they already know the material. They do not believe they need to work examples of applications of the principles being taught. In reality they may understand principles quickly and easily, but do not know how to apply the principles to specific tasks because they do not do the homework. They miss the practice that would solidify the skills, and they miss the experience of learning finer points of application to special cases. My impression from clinical experience is that they seem to understand class material in broad terms but often do not master specific skills.

Problems Not Addressed

I do not deal directly with problems in the parental relationship. Setting this limit can create delicate situations, but I attempt to keep the therapy contract clear. If parents present a problem of their own, either individually or as a couple, I suggest that they consult with another therapist for those issues. Keeping clear boundaries in these families is difficult, and I feel it is important to keep the focus on the child not only for the sake of the child, but also in the interest of modeling for the family.

Case Illustration

Michael had just started his junior year at a Catholic high school when he came for counseling. His parents were interviewed first. They stated that his grades were not what he was capable of, and he was "not wild about school." He had been active in sports through eighth grade, including golf, soccer, and baseball, which was "everything" to him. However, he seemed to lose enthusiasm when he did not make the varsity golf team at the end of ninth grade. His father said, "Maybe he saw that I was disappointed in him." When asked about his other interests, they seemed at a loss except to say, "He likes rock bands. And art." When asked how the decision was made to seek counseling for him, they said he had actually stated he wanted to talk with someone after learning that a friend of his was seeing a therapist.

When Michael came for his interview, he appeared tired. He was casually dressed, and his hair was tousled. When asked to tell about himself, he said he did not like the kids at his school: "They're very opinionated." He was disappointed in high school because he thought he would meet new people with whom he would have more in common than in junior high. He said most of the friends he did have were like him: "left of center." They liked bands such as Pink Floyd and Phish. He played bass in a band, and that involvement gave him "a high." He was also interested in acting, but he had stage fright.

He also mentioned that he loved art, but there were not many opportunities at his high school for that. Although soft spoken, he talked freely and openly. His grades were, in his words, "average. I'm smart. I haven't tried to make good grades because I'm not that challenged. I don't have a strong enough work ethic to succeed in the harder classes." When asked which were his favorite classes, he readily named physics, psychology, and art. He said he like physics because it was interesting and he liked the teacher. His least favorite classes the previous year had been chemistry and geometry because, as he said, they were too easy.

He had quit sports (baseball, soccer) except golf. He had decided that he did not like team sports because he was uncomfortable when others pointed out his mistakes. He also said he felt pressured a lot by his parents. However, he did enjoy the satisfaction of playing well for himself. I asked him what his goals were, and he said he wanted to attend a local art institute, but couldn't because it was too expensive.

He spoke little about his parents except to say that when he tried to tell them he might want to go into art, they were concerned about whether he could make a living at it. He also had not said very much to them about how he felt about school, saying, "They just think I don't like school."

When asked if he felt depressed, he readily said, "Yes." He said he was bored, tired, uninterested in going out with friends, and not sleeping well. He was sleeping less than he previously had and said he could sleep 14 hours and not feel rested. He was 5 ft. 7 in. tall and weighed 115 pounds. He admitted to having lost a few pounds over the summer. He also admitted to thoughts of harming himself earlier in the summer, but he had not thought about how he would do it. I asked him to agree to a "no harm" contract, and he did. I also recommended daily physical activity.

"Is there a time when you feel good?" I asked him. He answered, "I feel *great* when I paint, but nobody seems to care." I asked him what he would like to work on in counseling, and he identified "feeling better" and having better communication with his parents. His parents, while generally supportive, did not recognize the depth of his passion for his art and music. His father was highly competitive, running marathons in his leisure time. He expected Michael to be similarly competitive. They did enjoy playing golf together.

Michael's demeanor, his fatigue, weight loss, difficulty sleeping, thoughts of self-harm, and his lack of interest in social activities pointed to a depressive disorder. If these symptoms persisted over the next few weeks, I was prepared to refer him to a psychiatrist for evaluation. At each subsequent session I asked Michael to rate his overall mood on a scale from 1 to 10. This scaling served to give me information and also gave him feedback so we could monitor progress and change. Based on his age (17) and his frequent references to wanting to be different from most of the students in his school, I categorized him as an "Independence Seeking" student. Tight structure for homework is less important for these students than younger types. What is important is approaching them in a collaborative way (Adult to Adult) to solve problems and encouraging them to pursue their interests so that they can find motivation from the passion they feel for a particular activity or subject area. I decided not to conduct formal IQ testing because whether he qualified for a gifted program was not a pertinent issue. Two weeks after the initial session with Michael, I met again with his parents.

At the session with his parents, they related that they had already done some thinking about his interests, about which he had begun to talk with them. I asked them if they had realized how strong his interest was. They admitted they had not. Their main concern was that he grow up to be a responsible, financially self-sufficient adult. His father worked for a Fortune 100 company, and his mother was a former English teacher. They saw him as "low-key and laid back." When I pointed out that he was keeping a lot inside himself and had been fairly depressed, they were surprised.

In the next few sessions with Michael, he said he was feeling a lot better, was writing more and drawing some. He said he was currently drawing something about his fear of flying. He still recalled being on an airplane when he was about 9 years old and hating it. He identified the feelings as having no control and being separated from people and things. When I asked about dating activities, he said October was a hard month because one year ago he had broken up with a girlfriend. They had subsequently reestablished a friendship, which he felt good about, but it had taken some time to reach the point of being able to talk frequently as friends.

I asked how things were going with his parents, and he said that his dad was backing off the competitiveness, and he was talking more with his mom. He said he felt equally close with both parents because he had interests in common with each of them: golf with his dad and English (reading and writing) with his mom. His mom had also found information about two art fairs for him to enter.

Capitalizing on his desires to pursue his art and make his life different (and less boring), I suggested he check into possibilities to take advanced art classes at a community college or art institute. He liked this idea, and, with the help of his high school art teacher, he set up plans to take studio art and photography at the community college.

I began to explore some of his feelings about his friends. They were complex. He admitted that when he got too close to someone, he sometimes did "something to mess things up." But, overall, he was very loyal to a select group.

He said his friends thought he had low self-esteem, and when I asked what *he* thought, he said the following:

> I feel so unintelligent and small. I haven't really done anything. When I walk into a bookstore, I feel bad because there is so much I don't know. How could I do something memorable? If I could publish a book of my poetry or paint a picture that people would see, I would feel better. Art is timeless.

Michael continued in counseling for about 12 months. His goals became more realistic: He decided he wanted a broader experience than what he would have at an art institute and decided to attend a state university with a good art department. He found a part-time job at a local restaurant and made friends there with coworkers, including a manager in his 20s. They both enjoyed attending concerts. Michael saved up enough money to follow a favorite band on a concert tour for several weeks the following summer.

References

American Psychological Association Task Force. (1995). *Stalking the wild taboo. Intelligence: Knowns and unknowns.* Washington, DC: Author.

Baker, J., Bridger, R., & Evans, K. (1998). Models of underachievement among gifted preadolescents: The role of personal, family, and school factors. *Gifted Child Quarterly, 42,* 5–15.

Baum, S. M., Owen, S. V., & Dixon, J. (1991). *To be gifted and learning disabled.* Mansfield Center, CT: Creative Learning Press.

Berne, E. (1964). *Games people play.* New York: Grove Press.

Carkhuff, R. R. (1984). *Helping and human relations* (Vols. 1 & 2). Amherst, MA: Human Resources Development Press.

Clark, B. (1983). *Growing up gifted: Developing the potential of children at home and at school* (2nd ed.). Columbus, OH: Charles E. Merrill.

Delisle, J. (1992). *Guiding the social and emotional development of gifted youth: A practical guide for educations and counselors.* New York: Longman.

Faber, A., & Maizlish, E. (1980). *How to talk so kids will listen and listen so kids will talk.* New York: Rawson, Wade.

Gardner, H. (1983). *Frames of mind: The theory of multiple intelligences.* New York: Basic Books.

Gear, G. H. (1978). Effects of training on teachers' accuracy in the identification of gifted children. *Gifted Child Quarterly, 22,* 90–97.

Harris, T. (1969). *I'm OK, you're OK.* New York: Harper & Row.

Jourard, S. M. (1964). *The transparent self.* New York: D. Van Nostrand.

Jourard, S. M. (1971). *Self-disclosure: An experimental analysis of the transparent self.* New York: John Wiley & Sons.

Kanevsky, L., & Keighley, T. (2003). To produce or not to produce? Understanding boredom and the honor in underachievement. *Roeper Review, 26,* 20–28.

Kaufman, A. S. (1994). *Intelligent testing with the WISC-III.* New York: John Wiley & Sons.

Mandel, H. P., & Marcus, S. I. (1988). *The psychology of underachievement.* New York: John Wiley and Sons.

Maslow, A. H. (1970). *Motivation and personality* (2nd ed.). New York: Harper & Row.

Montessori, M. (1964). *The Montessori method.* New York: Shocken.

Pecaut, L. S. (1979). *Understanding and influencing student motivation.* Lombard, IL: The Institute for Motivational Development.

Peterson, J. S., & Colangelo, N. (1996). Gifted achievers and underachievers: A comparison of patterns found in school files. *Journal of Counseling and Development, 74,* 399–407.

Pirozzo, R. (1982). Gifted underachievers. *Roeper Review, 4,* 18–21.

Rimm, S. (1986). *Underachievement syndrome: Causes and cures.* Watertown, WI: Apple Publishing Company.

Siegle, D., & McCoach, D. B. (2003). *Parenting strategies: Gifted underachievers— What's a parent to do?* Retrieved November 19, 2004, from http://www.ditd. org/Cybersource/Record

Stanley, J. (1979). Identifying and nurturing the intellectually gifted. In W. C. George, S. J. Cohn, & J. C. Stanley (Eds.), *Educating the gifted: Acceleration and enrichment* (pp. 172–180). Baltimore: Johns Hopkins University Press.

Sternberg, R. J. (1985). *Beyond IQ: A triarchic theory of human intelligence.* New York: Cambridge University Press.

Sternberg, R. J., & Detterman, D. K. (Eds.). (1986). *What is intelligence? Contemporary viewpoints on its nature and definition.* Norwood, NJ: Ablex.

Webb, J. T., Meckstroth, E. A., & Tolan S. S. (1982). *Guiding the gifted child: A practical source for parents and teachers.* Scottsdale, AZ: Gifted Psychology Press.

chapter 7

Counseling Highly Gifted Children and Adolescents

by Catherine M. Boland and Miraca U. M. Gross

Conception of Giftedness

The definition of giftedness or talent adopted by a school or education system will inevitably influence both the identification procedures that will be used and the curricula and programs that will be developed to respond to the academic and socioaffective needs of students who will be identified.

Equally, a counselor's view of the nature of giftedness and talent and the impact of social and emotional factors in the translation of high ability into high achievement will influence his or her perception of which elements of socioaffective development are most critical in facilitating talent development.

Influences

The conception of giftedness that underpins the model of counseling we will present here has been influenced by several sources and several considerations. We believe that the process of *talent development*—the translation of high potential into high performance—is mediated both by factors in an individual's environment, such as the support or lack of support provided by home and school, and by factors within the individual, such as his or her attitude toward his or her high ability, his or her levels and types of motivation, and his or her perceptions of self-efficacy. This belief has influenced our selection of the model of giftedness—Françoys Gagné's Differentiated Model of Giftedness and Talent (Gagné, 2000)—that underpins our center's programs of counseling. The influence of environment and personality on the translation of ability into achievement lies at the heart of the Gagné model.

Until the early 1980s, the definitions of giftedness and talent that influenced educators and psychologists in the United States, Canada, and Australia tended to be performance-based, and children or adolescents who were identified as gifted were generally successful, motivated students who were already achieving. The needs of gifted students who had not yet developed as high achievers were rarely discussed and, with a few notable exceptions, such as the work of Hollingworth (1926, 1931, 1936) in the first half of the 20th century and that of Kerr, Colangelo, and Zaffran in the second half (e.g., Colangelo & Zaffran, 1979; Kerr, 1986), the role of counseling in facilitating talent development was not well recognized.

However, during the 1980s, the dynamic models developed by Tannenbaum (1983) and Gagné (1985) drew attention to the developmental nature of high achievement and focused on the impact of environmental and personalogical variables in either facilitating or hampering the translation of high potential into high performance. These models placed high ability firmly within an environmental and personalogical context. Giftedness—superior aptitude or potential—could not by itself guarantee success; it had to be "scaffolded" by a "healthy" personality and a facilitative home and school environment. This set the scene for an enhanced consideration of family counseling, career counseling, and personal counseling in facilitating what came to be called "talent development" (Gagné, 2003)—the translation of ability into achievement.

Coincidental with the development of these two dynamic models, an intensified interest in the socioaffective development of intellectually talented children and adolescents arose. The work of Colangelo, Gross, Piechowski, Robinson, Silverman, and others, coupled with a renewed interest in the pioneering socioaffective research of Leta Hollingworth, set the scene for a new appreciation of ways in which intellectually gifted students differ from their age peers on a range of social and emotional variables. This led to a consideration of the role of counseling in assisting self-acceptance in gifted students—an understanding and acceptance of the ways in which they differ from age peers, as well as an appreciation of similarities with age peers that can assist assimilation into the child or adolescent culture.

As Hollingworth emphasized (1926, 1931) and as Gross (1999, 2004) and Robinson, Reis, Neihart, and Moon (2002) more recently restated, the emotional maturity of intellectually gifted students tends to be significantly advanced from that of age peers of average ability and seems to be more closely influenced by mental age than chronological age. Roedell (1984) noted that this *asynchrony* leaves the child vulnerable to a range of adjustment difficulties, including problems in relating to (and being understood by) age peers whose intellectual and emotional development are more congruent with their chronological age, the capacity to empathize with the feelings of other children or adults at unusually early ages, and expectations of themselves and others that do not usually develop until a child is much older. Roedell suggested that the social adjustment of gifted children in these situations is strongly dependent on the degree of environmental support.

This asynchrony, and the obligation of parents, schools, and the community to respond to it, is at the heart of the definition of *giftedness* coined by a group of psychologists known as the Columbus Group (1991):

> Giftedness is *asynchronous development* in which advanced cognitive abilities and heightened intensity combine to create inner experiences that are qualitatively different from the norm. This asynchrony increases with higher intellectual capacity. The uniqueness of the gifted renders them particularly vulnerable and requires modifications in parenting, teaching and counseling in order for them to develop optimally. . . . Cognitive complexity gives rise to emotional depths. Thus gifted children not only *think* differently from their peers; they also *feel* differently. (p. 1)

As we will discuss later in this chapter, the role of the counselor in providing an important element of Roedell's (1984) "environmental support" can be critical in facilitating self-acceptance in gifted students who may be intensely conscious of both their own asynchronous development and their difference from age peers.

Definition

The definition of *giftedness* that has most strongly influenced Australian educators in recent years is Gagné's Differentiated Model of Giftedness and Talent and, as indicated above, it is this definition that underpins our model of counseling. Gagné (2003) argues that we should not use the terms *giftedness* and *talent* synonymously. Rather, he suggests that we should use these terms selectively to identify two different stages in a highly able student's journey from high potential to high performance. He defines giftedness in childhood as possession of the aptitude or potential to perform at a level significantly beyond the average for one's age—specifically, a level of aptitude that would place the child in the top 10–15% of his or her chronological peer group— in any domain of human ability. A child might be gifted in any one of the cognitive, creative, socioaffective, or sensorimotor domains—or in several, or in all. However, the key to Gagné's view of giftedness is that it defines outstanding *potential* rather than outstanding performance.

By contrast, Gagné defines *talent* as performance or achievement that would place one within the top 10–15% of one's chronological peer group. Obviously, numerous fields of performance are associated with any ability domain and, again, a child may be talented in one or many fields of performance.

Within the Gagné definition a child can be gifted (possessing unusually high potential) without being talented (displaying unusually high performance). This model recognizes the existence, and the dilemma, of the under-achieving gifted child.

How does giftedness become talent? At the heart of his model, Gagné places the developmental process of learning, training, or practice. However, because learning occurs within environmental and personalogical contexts, he centers this developmental process between two clusters of catalysts that can either assist or hinder the learning process.

Personalogical Factors

Factors within the child's personality have impact on the quality and extent of her learning:

*   *Motivation.* Motivation, while not a necessary ingredient of giftedness, as in the Renzulli model, is essential if the child is to develop talent. She must have the motivation to start, apply herself, and persevere when facing obstacles. However, gifted students may never have the opportunity to practice perseverance in the face of challenge if the work they are given is so simplistic that they can master it without effort.
*   *Acknowledgement and acceptance of one's abilities.* The gifted child must have confidence in her abilities and she must accept and value her own gifts. Too often teachers confuse conceit, which they understandably want children to avoid, with a healthy pride in one's abilities, which is an essential constituent of self-esteem. The gifted child must learn to feel good about being gifted. This is unlikely to happen for children who are academically gifted if the school heaps justified praise on students with talent in sport or athletics but fails to acknowledge or reward academic talent.
*   *Realistic self-esteem.* When the gifted student is given only work that she can complete with little or no effort, academic self-esteem may become either unduly inflated through overconfidence ("I can do *anything* the teacher asks!") or depressed ("I'm never required to work hard—I don't know if I *can* work hard. I don't know what will happen if the work gets harder next year."). When the child has little or no access to other children of similar abilities or interests, she may not readily find congenial companionship, and social self-esteem may become significantly depressed (Gross, 2004).
*   *Organization.* Organization is likewise important. The capacity to become organized and stay organized is essential for success regardless of the domain in which the gift exists. Gagné described concentration as the

capacity to shut out external stimuli and keep working on essential tasks for as long as it takes to complete them. Students to whom learning has come easily in the early years may not have had to develop the skills of concentration.

Environmental Factors

A number of environmental variables also have an impact on the learning process. A supportive and facilitative environment can enhance not only the child's likelihood of academic success, but also the development of a strong and healthy personality.

Environmental factors that have a positive or negative impact on the learning process may include the following:

- The *milieu* in which the child lives and learns. This can include family issues such as family size, family economic circumstances, and family attitude toward education or toward the child's gifts.
- Significant *persons*—parents, siblings, teachers, other students, school leaders, community leaders—who encourage, discourage, or are neutral toward talent development. (Passivity—apathy or lack of interest in the student's talents—can sometimes be as negative as active opposition.)
- The *provisions* the school makes, or fails to make, to develop the student's gifts into talents, and even the social ethos of the community that can dictate which talents are valued and, therefore, which programs of talent development will be established or funded. A supportive school environment can enhance not only the child's likelihood of academic success, but also the development of a strong and healthy personality.
- *Significant events* in the family or community—for example, the death of a parent or a family breakup, winning a prize or award, suffering an accident or major illness, or finding the right teacher at the right time—can significantly influence the course of a student's journey from giftedness to talent.

Within the Gagné model, the school's and community's responsibility is to seek out students who are gifted but *not yet talented* and assist them to develop their abilities into achievements, as well as recognize and further assist those talented students who are already performing at high levels. For this to happen, the school must identify positive personal and environmental catalysts and harness them to assist the talent development process. Equally, however, the school must work to lessen or remove negative personal and environmental catalysts that may be hampering the gifted student's progress toward talent.

Gagné endorses Tannenbaum's caveat that *chance* can have a significant influence on talent development. Children have no control over the socioeconomic status of the family they are raised in, and usually they have little control over their school's attitude to gifted education. However, teachers and schools *can* enhance the student's "chance" of success. A gifted student is more likely to develop habits of motivation and perseverance if the work he is presented with is engaging, challenging, and at his ability level. There is less chance of a gifted student camouflaging his abilities for peer acceptance if the class and school climates encourage academic talent.

Characteristics

Levels of Giftedness

In special education—the education of children with special needs—each field employs specific terminologies that are used both to indicate the degree to which a child differs from the norm for his or her age peers, and, by association, to suggest techniques that educators might use to assist the child to attain his or her educational potential. Teachers working with children who have intellectual disabilities, for example, recognize mild, moderate, severe, and profound levels of intellectual disability. Similarly, teachers working with hearing impaired students acknowledge four levels of hearing impairment—again termed *mild*, *moderate*, *severe*, and *profound*. The use of these quantitative terminologies is not a matter of simplistically "labeling" the child; on the contrary, educators working with these young people are aware that the level and type of intervention that will be required are dictated by the degree of severity of the condition.

It would be simplistic to define intellectual giftedness solely in terms of IQ scores; nonetheless the intelligence quotient is a useful index of the relationship (and in the case of the gifted child, the discrepancy) between mental age and chronological age. A moderately gifted 9-year-old with a mental age of 12 and thus an IQ of approximately 133 is "out of synch" by a matter of 3 years before he has even passed through elementary school; however, his exceptionally gifted age-mate with a mental age of 15 and an IQ of approximately 167 looks across a chasm of 6 years from the age at which he is capable of reasoning to the grade level in which he is likely to be placed on the basis of his chronological age. The IQ can assist us in understanding the fundamental differences in mental processing between moderately and extremely gifted students.

Silverman (1989) defined the *highly gifted* as "those whose advancement is significantly beyond the norm of the gifted" (p. 71). By "advancement," she implies aptitude or potential rather than performance—giftedness in Gagné's terms rather than talent. Research on the school performance of highly gifted children suggests that the majority are required to work in the regular classroom at levels several years below their tested achievement (Gross, 2004; Silverman, 1993). Silverman suggests that any child who scores three standard deviations above the mean on a test of reasoning ability should be termed *highly gifted*; that is, children of IQ 145 or above.

However, even within this highly gifted group there are subsets classified by still increased levels of cognitive ability—and, by association, increased levels of scarcity. The classification *exceptionally gifted* refers to children who score in the IQ range of 160–179 (Kline & Meckstroth, 1985) while *profoundly gifted* refers to those very rare individuals who score at or above IQ 180 (Webb, Meckstroth, & Tolan, 1983).

Thus, levels of intellectual giftedness, as defined by IQ ranges, and the level of prevalence of such children in the general population, appear as follows:

Level	IQ range	Prevalence
Mildly (or basically) gifted	115–129	1:6–1:40
Moderately gifted	130–144	1:40–1:1000
Highly gifted	145–159	1:1000–1:10,000
Exceptionally gifted	160–179	1:10,000–1:1 million
Profoundly gifted	180+	Fewer than 1:1 million

Highly, exceptionally, and profoundly gifted children may differ from their moderately gifted age peers to an even greater degree than the latter differ from age peers of average ability. Benbow and Lubinski (1993) noted that the top 1% of students in almost any distribution of ability or achievement covers as broad a range as that encompassed by the 2nd to the 98th percentile. Goldstein, Stocking, and Godfrey (1999) translated this to IQ scores, showing that the range of scores of children in the top 1% on IQ—from 135 to more than 200—is as broad as the range of scores from the 2nd percentile (IQ 64) to the 98th (IQ 132).

Nor are these differences confined to the cognitive domain. As we discuss later in this chapter, research has identified socioaffective correlates of unusually high intellectual ability that can exacerbate these young people's awareness of their difference not only from classmates of average ability but even from more moderately gifted age peers.

Cognitive Characteristics

Some of the characteristics listed below appear in modified forms in moderately gifted students. Others are characteristics that essentially define the highly gifted.

- *The capacity to engage in intellectually demanding work at a level and complexity usually attained by students several years older.* When these young people are restricted to working with concepts and materials developed for age peers, they can experience quite severe levels of intellectual frustration.
- *The ability to ask reflective and probing, sometimes provocative, questions.* Academically gifted students thrive on work that requires them to engage in analytic, evaluative thinking. They enjoy complex topics that they can explore in depth. The level of their questioning can be remarkably sophisticated, and this can disconcert both their classmates, who may find their questions incomprehensible, and their teachers, who may find them threatening.
- *The capacity to see and create patterns and relationships in their field of special ability.* Mathematically gifted students are often keenly aware of patterns. Students with a special gift for language often compose writing rather like

musicians, with a special appreciation of sound and rhythm. Gifted students generally seem to be "systems" thinkers, who understand and appreciate the structure of their field.

- *Unusually fast rate of learning, particularly when the material is interesting, swift-paced, and challenging.* Highly gifted students taking math summer classes can telescope a year's math into 3 weeks (Colangelo, Assouline & Gross, 2004).
- *Extremely well-developed memory.* Highly gifted students need less review even than their moderately gifted age peers and much less review than age peers of average academic ability. Several studies (e.g., Flanders, 1987; Reis et al., 1993) have shown that even moderately gifted students may have mastered up to 80% of the math and English they will be presented during a school year—before the year has even started. Reis et al. commented that gifted students might well start their school year in January.
- *Dislike of slow-paced work.* It can be extremely frustrating for gifted students to be constantly held back to the pace of the group when they are already predicting, correctly, what the next stage will be.

Affective Characteristics
- *Emotional intensity.* Gifted children tend to experience emotional reactions at a deeper level than their age peers. They seem to have a heightened capacity to respond to intellectual or emotional stimuli. Finding a friend can be a truly joyful experience, particularly for a child who has been rejected by classmates for being "different." The breakup of a friendship or the death of a pet can cause deep distress.
- *Preference for the companionship of older children.* Their advanced intellectual development, their reading and play interests, and their relative emotional maturity may lead them to seek out older children who are at similar developmental stages as friends. It is important that teachers should facilitate, rather than discourage, these friendships. Often they are an indication that the gifted student would be a good candidate for some form of acceleration.
- *An unusually well-developed sense of justice and fairness.* Several studies (e.g., Gross, 2004; Kohlberg, 1963) have found that intellectually gifted children are able to make complex moral judgments much earlier than their age peers. They may become genuinely distressed if they feel that one child has been unfair to another or if they feel a teacher or other adult has been unfair to a classmate.
- *An unusual ability to empathize with the feelings of other children or adults.* The capacity to feel the emotions of others within themselves can make gifted children vulnerable to "infection" by other people's emotions or distress.
- *An unusually mature sense of humor.* They pass through the "stages" of humor significantly earlier and faster than their age peers. Visual humor leads on to verbal humor, which then progresses to humor based on incongruity of ideas. A gifted student who spends all of his school hours with age peers

can sometimes be "starved" of people who laugh at the things he finds humorous.

Assumptions

Education systems are based on a flawed assumption of synchronicity, in which age equates to grade. The students who are best served by the current age-grade structure of schools are those whose cognitive and affective development are most congruent with societal expectations for children of their chronological age: the students who fall happily in the middle of the curve, whatever that curve is measuring.

Differences on any variable are most pronounced at the extremes. Schools accept, tolerate, and, in general, respond effectively to students whose cognitive and socioaffective development lags significantly behind that of their age peers. However, students whose cognitive and socioaffective development are significantly ahead are less well served. They are not understood by their teachers—and in many cases barely tolerated by classmates.

Silverman (1993) has discussed the problems of external and internal asynchrony, which affect intellectually gifted students, and Gross (1999, 2004) has expanded on this with particular reference to the highly gifted. *External* asynchrony refers to the discrepancies we have already noted in intellectual and socioaffective development between the gifted child or adolescent and the classmates with whom she is expected to learn and socialize, often for the entirety of her school experience. *Internal* asynchrony refers to the disparate rates of intellectual, emotional, and physical development that may coexist within the gifted child herself. Emotional maturity is more closely linked to mental age than to chronological age, and the discrepancies between a child's chronological age and his or her intellectual/emotional maturity are most extreme in children who are intellectually delayed and in children who are intellectually advanced. Ironically, teachers note this easily in the child who is developmentally delayed, but are much less aware of it in children who are intellectually gifted.

Many of the difficulties experienced by intellectually gifted students derive from external and internal asynchrony. For example, a child is unlikely to be motivated to develop her abilities to the fullest if she is already aware of the intellectual and emotional asynchrony between herself and her classmates, and if she fears that academic success will set her even further apart from age peers than she is already. Additionally she may be aware of, and disconcerted by, the asynchrony between her physical and mental abilities. For example, she may have a handwriting speed that is typical of her age, but thoughts that race through her mind so swiftly that she cannot capture them on paper. The counselor of gifted students must work to increase the students' self-acceptance and acceptance of their gifts. This must include the restoration, when it has been quashed, of gifted students' motivation to achieve, without which their high abilities will not readily be translated into high achievement.

Conception of Personality

Personality

Personality research and theory is based on the assumption that an individual's behavior and experience can be traced to underlying causes within that person that comprise his or her "personality." A personality trait is a characteristic that distinguishes one person from another and that causes a person to behave more or less consistently. A related construct, "temperament," refers to consistent styles of behavior that are present from infancy onward.

However, personality research is rather fragmented (Cloninger, 1996) with a clear distinction between those who consider personality traits and temperament as a useful means of classifying individuals (e.g., the work of Cattell) and those who adopt a cognitive social learning theory (e.g., Mischel and Bandura) and assert that *situations* are more powerful determinants of behavior than fixed traits.

Personality of Gifted Students

There has been limited empirical evidence suggesting a specific personality profile intrinsic to highly gifted children and adolescents. Silverman (1993) suggests that there is some evidence of an overrepresentation of introversion in gifted people, although this is by no means a characteristic trait. However, there are a number of characteristic features of the typical social and educational experience of gifted children that may interact with preexisting personality features to provide similar behaviors, attitudes, and socioaffective responses in gifted children and adolescents.

We have discussed the asynchrony of chronological age, mental age, and emotional maturity that confronts many intellectually gifted children and adolescents. However, we should also consider the effects, on the gifted learner, of asynchrony of skill development. This refers both to the variability within the cognitive skills possessed by an individual and also to the discrepancy between that individual's abilities and those of his or her age-mates. For example, the abstract thinking and reasoning abilities of a gifted child are literally developed to a degree more typical of a child several years older; however, his processing speed or fine motor coordination is often commensurate with his chronological age. This asynchrony may lead to frustration for the child who may, for example, understand the abstract relationships between different constructs, have a superb vocabulary and expressive ability, and yet have extremely ill-developed handwriting. This can cause acute internal frustration for the child who has a heightened sense of the contrast between the maturity of his conceptions and literary style and the "childishness" of how it appears when he is required to commit it to paper in his own handwriting.

An added complication is that teachers often focus on the lesser, rather than the greater, skills of individual students, compounding the internal frustration experienced by the gifted child, who may feel that her identity in the eyes of the teacher lies in her relative weakness rather than her strengths.

As noted earlier, asynchrony can also occur between children's cognitive abilities and their emotional and social development. While it is evident that gifted children's social and emotional development is rather more akin to their cognitive abilities than to their chronological age, there is nevertheless the common experience of cognitive abilities eclipsing emotional *regulation* (Silverman, 1993). For example, a highly gifted 5-year-old may already have the capacity for metacognition and highly abstract thought, but limited exposure to negative social interactions. On the one hand, this child has the capacity to understand and empathize with others to a degree well beyond others in his class, and yet a limited capacity for emotional composure. This gifted child is also likely to have an enhanced capacity for introspection. Such asynchrony can lead to an apparent "oversensitivity" to perceived social slights. He may burst into tears at negative comments to which age peers would react with relative equanimity.

The Friendship Dilemma

Earlier we mentioned gifted children's tendency to gravitate toward older children or to age peers at similar levels of intellectual ability. This has been noted in several studies over many decades (e.g., Gross, 1998; Hollingworth, 1936; Janos, Marwood, & Robinson, 1985). Hollingworth made clear her conviction that the difficulties in peer relationships experienced by many highly gifted children did not arise from deficiencies within the children themselves as much as from differences *between* the individual and other members of the groups with whom he or she is required to learn, work, or socialize, and the consequent unlikelihood of their easily finding others who share their abilities and interests:

> This difficulty of the gifted child in forming friendships is largely a result of the infrequency of persons who are like-minded. The more intelligent a person is, regardless of age, the less often can he find a truly congenial companion. The average child finds playmates in plenty who can think and act on a level congenial to him, because there are so many average children. (p. 79)

Jung (1989) commented about loneliness in this regard:

Loneliness does not come from having no people about one, but from being unable to communicate to others the things that seem important to oneself, or from holding certain views which others find inadmissible . . . If a man knows more than others, he becomes lonely. (p. 356)

An Australian empirical study (Gross, 2000, 2002) found that children's conceptions of friendship form a developmental hierarchy of age-related stages, with expectations of and beliefs about friendship becoming more sophisticated and complex with age. The five stages appear in order as follows, from the lowest to the highest level in terms of age and conceptual complexity:

- *Stage 1: Play partner.* In the earliest stage of friendship conception, the relationship is based on "play-partnership." A friend is seen as someone who engages the child in play and permits the child to use or borrow her playthings.
- *Stage 2: People to chat with.* The sharing of interests becomes an important element in friendship choice. Conversations between "friends" are no longer related simply to the game or activity in which the children are directly engaged.
- *Stage 3: Help and encouragement.* At this stage the friend is seen as someone who will offer help, support, or encouragement. However, the advantages of friendship flow in one direction; the child does not yet see himself as having the obligation to provide help or support in return.
- *Stage 4: Intimacy/empathy.* The child now realizes that in friendship the need and obligation to give comfort and support flows both ways and, indeed, the giving and receiving of affection becomes an important element in the relationship. This stage sees a deepening of intimacy, an emotional sharing and bonding.
- *Stage 5: The sure shelter.* The title here comes from a passage in one of the apocryphal books of the Old Testament. "A faithful friend is a sure shelter: whoever finds one has found a rare treasure" (Ecclesiasticus 6:14). At this stage, friendship is perceived as a deep and lasting relationship of trust, fidelity, and unconditional acceptance.

The study found, however, that children of differing intellectual abilities pass through the five stages of friendship conception at different ages and at different rates. In general, intellectually gifted children were found to be substantially further along the hierarchy of stages of friendship than were their age peers of average ability, and exceptionally and profoundly gifted children were very much further advanced. At ages when their age peers of average ability were looking for play partners, these very highly gifted children were beginning to look for friends with whom they could develop close and trusting friendships. Their advanced intellectual development and their relative emotional maturity led them to seek out older children who were at similar developmental stages as friends.

We have described earlier the intellectual and emotional intensity that gifted and talented children bring to both learning and social relationships. The longing for friendship experienced by a gifted child who has experienced prolonged social isolation can become all-consuming. The gifted child who is intensely conscious of the developmental asynchrony that separates her from the age peers with whom the school has grouped her—ironically for the purposes of socialization—may be faced with a "forced-choice dilemma" (Gross, 1989) for which there is no easy solution. The need to develop her gifts into talents and feel a healthy pride in academic achievements may be at variance with the need for social acceptance and bonding. Even in the early years of school, young gifted children may feel the need to partly camouflage their abilities for peer acceptance (Silverman, 1993), and this behavior may be well established by the middle elementary years. Some may adopt the role of "class clowns" or even deride other gifted students in an attempt to curry favor with the class (Coleman & Cross, 1988).

Many gifted children and adolescents experience a strong sense of guilt at denying their high abilities in pursuit of peer acceptance. As Benbow and Stanley (1996) noted, they may begin to feel that they have entered into a Faustian bargain from which there is no easy escape and which will leave them with neither the warm glow of achievement nor the secure acceptance of intimacy. This, indeed, may be the central psychosocial dilemma of gifted youth.

Highly gifted students may be at serious risk for depression, ongoing underachievement, and social isolation if they are not given regular access to children or adolescents at similar stages of cognitive and socioaffective development (Gross, 2004; Hollingworth, 1926, 1942; Silverman, 1993).

Some gifted students can exhibit *perfectionist tendencies*. In its positive forms, perfectionism is a drive to achieve the standards the child knows he or she is capable of. However, this facilitative perfectionism may only appear when the child is enthusiastic about and challenged by the topic. Perfectionism can have its downsides, too. When a gifted child has never been presented with work commensurate with her ability, and has consequently never had to strive for success, she may develop a fear of failure. Students like this may settle for submitting work that is "correct," but substantially below their true ability level, rather than risking "failure" by attempting something that is more challenging, but slightly beyond their current level of achievement (Parker, 1997).

The *physical restlessness* of many gifted children, most frequently manifested in a classroom that offers inadequate intellectual challenge, is frequently misinterpreted by teachers as a sign of emotional immaturity. However, the research of a Polish psychiatrist, Kazimierz Dabrowski (1972), offers another explanation. His work focuses on a further aspect of asynchrony.

Dabrowski (1972), who developed a theory of the emotional development of intellectually gifted children and adults, investigated a commonly observed phenomenon—the *heightened awareness* of the gifted and the associated heightened capacity to respond to various stimuli. He called this tendency "overexcitability." This term is not used in any derogatory sense; it is a translation of a Polish word that means "superstimulatability," and it carries positive connotations, such as an insatiable love of learning, the capacity to care intensely for people and ideas, boundless energy, and a vivid imagination. Dabrowski identified five overexcitabilities: intellectual, emotional, imaginational, sensual, and psychomotor.

Piechowski (2003) calls *intellectual overexcitability* "intensified activity of the mind" (p. 299). Besides a passionate love of learning, it can be manifested as a delight in analytical or reflective thinking, introspection, tenacity in problem solving, and avid reading. It has been found to be particularly correlated with intellectual giftedness (Silverman, 1993)

Emotional overexcitability, which is also found in many gifted persons, is characterized by the capacity for emotional depth, an unusual sensitivity to and responsiveness to others, and a strong attachment to people, animals, or places. Often gifted children or adolescents are extremely self-critical, agonizing over their own faults or weaknesses. However, they may have a strong vision of what they could be if they were able to develop their talents fully.

Imaginational overexcitability may be displayed through a great facility for invention and fantasy, such as the creation of imaginary companions, an ability for vivid visual recall and detailed visualization, and a deep love for poetry and drama. Silverman (1993), in her study of highly gifted young children, reported that an unusual number expressed themselves in metaphor or in such great detail that adults begged them to get to the point. They had a need to describe the subtle nuances of a situation or interaction, rather than simply the factual details: "Sometimes it is difficult for them to express their thoughts in words, because they think in images" (p. 16). This phenomenon can place an almost insurmountable barrier between the gifted child and his or her age peers.

Sensual overexcitability may be displayed in a heightened awareness of the senses or a deep aesthetic appreciation of beautiful objects, phrases of music, or words. However, this may also be manifested in allergies to certain foods and physical sensations, and even in an oversensitivity to certain clothing materials. Silverman (1993) and her colleagues reported that parents of sensually overexcitable children had to cut labels off children's clothes and even had to be particularly careful about the placement of sock seams, because the children reacted so strongly. However, while sensual overexcitability seems to be moderately correlated with intellectual giftedness in adults, no significant correlation has been identified with giftedness in children (Silverman).

Psychomotor overexcitability can be manifested in the physical restlessness described earlier. The child's surplus energy may show itself in rapid speech, compulsive chattering, nervous habits such as tics or nail biting, a love of fast games and sports, and physical impulsiveness. The child or adult can seem to be a workaholic or a compulsive organizer.

Michael Piechowski (2003) suggested that the five overexcitabilities should be viewed as "channels through which flows information in the form of sensations, feelings, experiences, images [and] expectations" (p. 298). When any of these channels is stronger than those of a child's peers, the child may feel embarrassed, uncomfortable, or even guilty for being different from his classmates. Silverman (1993) commented that one of the greatest gifts a counselor can give gifted children or adolescents is an appreciation of their sensitivities and the intensity of their feelings. The need to be true to themselves can be in conflict with the desire to be accepted by others and the fear that the asynchrony between themselves and their age peers may be a gap too wide to be easily breached. The counselor can assist the gifted young person both with self-understanding and with techniques to facilitate peer relationships.

Model of Counseling

Influences

Research From Gifted Literature

For counselors and therapists working with gifted and talented children and adolescents, the need to balance empirical findings about giftedness with research that provides us with an understanding of the nature of psychopathology presents an ongoing challenge.

Specialists in the field of gifted education are rightly critical of the tendency of some in the helping professions to pathologize giftedness. However, this may present the clinician with a real dilemma. We rarely see happy, well-adjusted gifted children in a clinical setting: in general, a child is brought to us for assistance because "something is not going right." However, we must be careful not to label features of that child's presentation—for example, a gifted child empathizing so strongly with another's distress that she herself feels profound distress, or a child believing she is resented or even actively disliked by her classmates—as "pathological" when they may be, in fact, features of the child's giftedness.

On the other hand, giftedness and psychopathology are not mutually exclusive. We *do indeed* see gifted children who experience psychosis, depression, anxiety, social phobia, and a range of other problems. An informed practitioner with knowledge of giftedness does not want to dismiss these problems simply as correlates of high intellectual ability, yet neither does she want to confuse these problems with the unique patterns of thought and behavior that the child's giftedness entails.

Consider social isolation, an experience confronting many gifted children. The practitioner has to consider several possible rationales with respect to the origins of, and the appropriate treatment for, such a presentation. These could include social phobia, social anxiety, depression, an explicit lack of social skills, a deficit in empathic reasoning, inappropriate educational placement, lack of true peers, and vocabulary, play interests, and cognitive development that differ significantly from those of available playmates. Of course, the gifted child presenting for counseling may be experiencing a combination of these difficulties, and therapy needs to be tailored accordingly.

As outlined earlier, some socioaffective characteristics of gifted children and adolescents not only differentiate them from their age peers, but may also render them more vulnerable to particular types of psychological distress. The well-developed sense of justice and fairness of many intellectually gifted children may cause them to feel distress at situations that are perceived as unjust or unfair. Similarly, the emotional intensity of many gifted children may make them more susceptible to rumination about negative events and experiences, or indeed cause difficulties with emotional regulation.

This ongoing dilemma of definition and therapeutic response appears frequently in the research literature in gifted education. Is it indeed the case that gifted children are more at risk than others of psychological distress? The empirical evidence is mixed. There is little evidence that gifted children *as a group* are significantly more vulnerable than are other groups in terms of general psychosocial adjustment (Robinson et al., 2002). Rather, evidence suggests that social and emotional problems related to giftedness are often an artifact of a mismatch of educational and/or social environment with an individual's cognitive and/or socioaffective characteristics.

If this is indeed so, it would seem that modifying educational and social contexts can positively influence psychosocial outcomes. However, there are some important caveats to these findings. It seems that some variables (e.g., gender, age, ethnicity, language, income, level of giftedness, sexual orientation, disability, and asynchrony of skill level) may render certain types of gifted individuals liable to poor psychological outcomes. Colangelo (2003) argues that gifted children are, in fact, likely to have specific and recurring needs that are directly related to their giftedness, and advocates a position of preventative counseling—particularly focused on an educational, group, and family approach. Neihart (2002) has highlighted the specific characteristics and experiences of gifted children that make them more vulnerable to particular forms of social-emotional distress at particular developmental stages. In particular, asynchrony of skill development, difficulty finding friends with similar interests, and lack of educational challenge are all cited as vulnerability factors in a diathesis-stress model. Further research suggests that there are some specific cognitive patterns associated with social and emotional outcomes in gifted students. Social competence is one of the areas where gifted students who report "feeling different" from their peers are likely to have more negative appraisals of their own social adjustment (Cross, Coleman, & Stewart, 1995).

Influences From Psychological Literature

There are several theoretical and empirical influences from general psychological literature that can help guide assessment and intervention with gifted young people.

The movement of positive psychology, spearheaded by Martin Seligman and colleagues (Seligman & Csikszentmihalyi, 2000) attempts to reverse the traditional focus of psychologists from remediation to prevention; that is, identifying and capitalizing on individual strengths to initiate and maintain change. From the counselor's perspective, positive psychology poses the question "What unique strengths does this child bring and how can we harness these in the counseling process?"

A behavioral systems perspective combines the principles of cognitive behavior therapy and systems theory and remains a guiding influence in the assessment and intervention of highly gifted people. In brief, the goal of this treatment is to help children, adolescents, and their families change their behavior by becoming aware of, and realistically appraising, their thoughts and feelings. Cognitive behavioral techniques (commonly misunderstood as "positive thinking") encourage an individual first to recognize the relationship between thought and feeling and then to identify common cognitive distortions. The behavioral component of the model recognizes that contingency management is integral to many interventions. Positive reinforcement, negative reinforcement, and response cost are all examples of behavioral tools that can be utilized to facilitate change. Finally, a "systems perspective" refers to the notion that all members of a family provide mutual influence. While family interventions are beyond the scope of this chapter, a basic premise of this approach is that family and other significant adults must be involved in assessment and therapy. The child's family does not necessarily *cause* his or her problems but may exacerbate, maintain, or ameliorate them.

Much research, theory, and clinical intervention has failed to take account of contextual influences on children's development. Cognitive behavioral techniques have been identified as exemplary in treating a number of social and emotional difficulties in children and adolescents, from anxiety disorders (Dadds & Barrett, 2001; Dadds, Barrett, & Rapee, 1996; Kazdin & Weisz, 2003) to depression (Kazdin & Marciano, 1998). Developmental and educational models can also provide a salient perspective and inform counseling practice. The developmental approach proposes that children's development is dynamic and that a problem at one stage of development may not remain a problem at later stages. Similarly, a problem may present differently at different ages. For example, somatic complaints in younger children can often be the primary expression of depression, whereas in older children and adolescents, withdrawal, sadness, and loss of interest in activities are more likely to be typical presenting symptoms of the same problem.

Children of similar ages may have attained quite different stages of cognitive and emotional development and thus may respond differently to therapy at different times. The development and growth of cognitive abilities is particularly relevant when it comes to assessment and planning of counseling experiences for gifted young people. In fact, it is an awareness and understanding of the rather different developmental trajectory of gifted young people that differentiate this from a standard clinical intervention.

In general, it is not until the early years of school that children develop an awareness that they have their own individual thoughts and that these appear to them as an inward stream of consciousness (metacognition). Intellectually gifted children, however, may develop this sense of intellectual introspection well before their age peers. Similarly, an understanding of empathy, emotional response, and abstract thought may all appear earlier in gifted children. On the other hand, experience of reciprocal social relationships, adversity, or challenge may be age-typical. Any therapeutic intervention needs to be tailored to the complex asynchrony that such development entails.

The practice of motivational interviewing (Miller & Rollnick, 2002) is also a field that is influential in the counseling of gifted youth. Motivational interviewing represents an evidence-based approach to overcoming the ambivalence that inhibits many people from making change. Understanding the question "Why do people change?" is particularly relevant for those gifted children who have been referred to a counselor due to underachievement. In many cases, these gifted youth may feel that they have been coerced into counseling—not a particularly helpful start toward enhancing therapeutic rapport. The counselor of gifted children needs to consider what unique personal, environmental, and educational factors have led to underachievement and to work with them to explore future options in an objective and neutral manner. Motivational interviewing instructs the counselor to be attuned to ambivalence, which is integral to the process of change, and also cautions the counselor about engaging in arguments or advice-giving with the client. Gifted children are particularly likely to recognize the transparency of arguments to improve motivation or attitude. Instead, the motivational interviewing approach advocates examining the reasons for ambivalence, reflecting the discrepancies between self-determined goals and current behavior, and assisting clients to evaluate the cost of pursuing (or not pursuing) certain courses of action.

These models inform counseling practice with gifted children and adolescents. In essence, we advocate the scientist-practitioner model that brings a research orientation to clinical practice, utilizing empirically validated measures and treatments and a hypothesis-testing approach to each client and his or her presenting problem.

Definition of Counseling

Preventative group programs, career counseling, and educational programs are examples of counseling practice that have a useful place in providing information, mentoring, and support structures to assist gifted young people and the challenges they often face. In general, however, little attention has been afforded to those gifted young people who present to helping professionals because they are experiencing social and emotional difficulties for which they may require individual treatment. Psychiatrists and clinical psychologists who may be the "first port of call" generally have little, if any, training regarding gifted children and their social and emotional development.

Our focus of counseling, therefore, and how we define it within the parameters of practice at our center, is that it is an attempt to combine evidence-based practice in the treatment of psychological distress with knowledge of the unique cognitive and socioaffective characteristics of gifted children. Counseling for gifted and talented children and their families aims at facilitating independent problem solving and behavioral, cognitive, and emotional change. The guiding principle is that of an experimental-clinical approach to counseling, which implies that psychological distress is experienced as a result of behavioral, cognitive, social, and physiological processes. An examination of factors that may play causal and maintaining roles is crucial to the counseling process.

Several features differentiate this type of counseling from standard practices inherent to cognitive-behavioral therapy (CBT) with children and adolescents. Specifically, these include the pace of counseling, the degree of abstract content, the level of explanation of treatment rationale, the focus on existentialism, and the degree to which the practitioner engages in philosophical discussion. For example, when children present for therapy before age 8, the counselor typically anticipates *some* awareness of thoughts and labeling of emotion, but would expect that this would be relatively simple and concrete (e.g., "happy," "sad," "disappointed"). In standard practice, therefore, the clinician may use some simple cognitive techniques, but these are likely to be heavily supplemented with behavioral methods and parent involvement. However, in our modified use of CBT for gifted children, such assumptions may, in fact, be counter-therapeutic. The counselor must work on the premise that the gifted young child is capable of abstract thought, is capable of a reasonably high degree of introspection and is likely to have a preference for detailed explanations and discussions. The *passion* for detail embraced by many gifted children is discussed by Kline and Meckstroth (1985): "Nearly everything matters and it matters that it matters" (p. 25).

Attempts to simplify, gloss over, or trivialize the gifted child's need for detailed (and often abstract and existential) explanation are likely to result in the young person's feeling disinclined to engage therapeutically, and to feel misunderstood and patronized.

Role of Counselor

Rogers' (1961) seminal work on person-centered therapy had a profound influence on the role of the counselor, and the legacy of this work was the central obligation of helping professionals to provide "unconditional positive regard" toward their clients. Rogers' client-centered therapy emphasizes the need for the counselor to be able to experience "accurate empathy" (p. 63). Accurate empathy does not necessarily mean empathizing with the client through having experienced the same conflict or dilemmas; rather it emphasizes that reflective, active listening is at the core of the counselor's role.

Evidence-based practice informs us that the clinician is a significant determinant of treatment outcome, dropout, retention, and adherence. It is also clear that the most change in the client's behavior, affect, and responsiveness occurs in the first few sessions. An empathic counseling style facilitates change, and its absence seems to discourage change (Miller & Rollnick, 2002).

In practical terms, when counseling highly gifted young people, the counselor needs to display good interpersonal skills that contribute to trust, including warmth and accurate empathy. Establishing rapport and demonstrating accurate empathy begin with an understanding and accommodation of the gifted young person's perspective and unique qualities. For example, using vocabulary and concepts that are akin to the young person's intellectual capabilities (rather than to their chronological age) demonstrate that the counselor is sensitive to the unique qualities of the child.

A counselor who uses a dynamic approach is more likely to establish rapport and accurate empathy effectively with gifted people than one who adopts a passive or nondirective role. Restating and clarifying the child's response serves as a useful clinical tool promoting rapport and demonstrating empathy. Rather than nodding in agreement or using affirmative sounds, the active counselor attempts to check the content, significance, and meaning of the child's comments, using phrases such as "I am not sure I have quite understood what you mean there. Are you saying . . . ?" "Can I check that with you?" or "What does that mean to you?" Paraphrasing, checking, questioning, drawing conclusions, and synthesizing information are all techniques that the dynamic counselor employs to ensure that information is accurately conveyed and (just as importantly) to ensure that the client feels heard and understood. Such techniques not only establish rapport and therapeutic engagement, but also form an important part of the therapy itself.

Inherent to the dynamic counseling role is the assumption that the role of the counselor changes. At times, the counselor is involved in reflective listening and observing the client's verbal and nonverbal cues. At other times, the counselor may be involved in explicit instruction of a particular technique, and later in thought-challenging or role-playing. Typically, the counselor of highly gifted children and adolescents is most active in the early phases of assessment and treatment, with more explicit instruction, scaffolding, and active questioning than in the later parts of treatment, when gifted clients begin to question, challenge, and engage in active dialogue with the counselor. Later in the process the counselor fades out of the therapeutic relationship and may provide a reference point for future resources or mentoring opportunities.

Role of Client

The role of the gifted young person as a client should be that of an individual actively engaged in a joint process of problem solving. The format, pace, and design of counseling sessions necessitates that the client be an *active* participant in the change process. Home-tasks allow the client to practice the skills introduced in the session and apply them to real life scenarios. The "experimental" mode of counseling means that clients are often given in vivo experiments (exposure) both in session and to complete at home. Thought experiments, written exercises, and formulating questions are examples of tasks that the gifted young person is required to engage in as part of therapy.

Gifted young people as a client group need to be given latitude to engage in existential questioning, including, but not limited to, a need to question authority (including the counselor's). A counselor of gifted children needs to acknowledge that such questioning and arguing is an important phase in the change process and a characteristic feature of the type of thinking process that many gifted people engage in. If the counselor responds with defensiveness, sarcasm, or rigidity, the change process and counseling relationship are likely to suffer. Indeed, it is common for gifted clients to have the day-by-day experience of knowing more than most other students and many adults, which can result in a wariness of "authority" statements from adults.

Goals

The aim of treatment is to provide skills directly to the gifted young person, reduce risk factors, and promote protective factors in the child's environment. Both client and counselor work together to jointly determine goals and priorities and to set a therapeutic agenda. Problems are tackled according to how much distress they cause the young person and how amenable to change those problems are. For example, many gifted children present with problems causing some distress that are nonetheless difficult or impossible to change in the course of counseling, such as parental relationships, family dynamics, international terrorism, and socioeconomic status. On the other hand, managing overwhelming emotional reactions to such problems, low mood, anxiety, or stress are more amenable to therapeutic change and are therefore more likely to be the central focus of counseling.

Relationship

Intrinsic to the counseling of gifted children is a collaborative, active relationship between counselor and client. This involves jointly selecting problems to be worked on, providing regular feedback, and adopting a problem-solving therapeutic approach. Such an approach emphasizes the interpersonal skills of the therapist.

Of particular importance when working with highly gifted young people is the need to balance rapport within the professional relationship. A guiding principle of this practice is to attend to, converse with, and develop a relationship with the young client that would typically be reserved for a person several years older. It is often akin to an adult-to-adult therapeutic relationship with respect to concepts discussed, degree of abstraction in language, and examples given. It is preferable to err on the side of overestimating the child's vocabulary and understanding (which can later be remedied by further explanation and rephrasing) than to risk making the client feel patronized. Similarly, many highly gifted children and adolescents are extremely critical of forms of counseling that have involved "overly optimistic" presentation on the part of the counselor. For example, when asked to describe previous experiences of counseling, highly gifted children have reported on their perceptions of counselors as artificially positive: "She had this kind of fake smile on her face all the time"; "She always wanted me to think positive"; "He just wanted to pretend that everything was good." Simplistic, false, and overly positive demeanors do not sit well with this client group. The result is often that the gifted young person goes "through the motions" of participation without any real engagement and with limited change occurring.

As discussed earlier, humor has often been cited as a characteristic trait of gifted children (e.g., Gross, 2004; VanTassel-Baska, 1998) and one that many see as integral to the therapeutic relationship. When the counselor is responsive to cues from the client, and when the use of humor is appropriate, it can be an effective therapeutic tool that aids the rapport-building process (Silverman, 1993). However, the counselor of highly gifted young people should be cautious about being the initiator of humorous interactions that might be perceived as sarcasm or oversimplification. Subtle humor, black or dark humor, and puns or word play are often favored by the young gifted client, and the counselor facilitates the relationship by responding appropriately to these initiations.

Highly gifted adolescents who have been referred by a parent or third party, and who feel they have been coerced into treatment, may present a particular challenge to the therapeutic relationship. In these cases, the counselor should be especially sensitive and reserve giving advice. Rather, reflecting back the young person's ambivalence and allowing challenging questions may provide accurate empathy and allow the client choice, rather than compulsion, to work with the counselor.

Assessment

The authors provide clinical services for gifted children, adolescents, and their families within a referral service offered by the Gifted Education Research, Resource and Information Centre (GERRIC), a research, teaching, and service center for gifted education sited within a major university noted for its research and teaching in this field of education. The presenting problems of our clients are varied and include perfectionism, anxiety, depression, social-skills difficulties, underachievement, and interpersonal problems. Assessment at this clinic entails a thorough social and developmental history, together with formal measures of psychological functioning. Often, psychometric data is made available to us by the young person's school or family before consultation, and this is corroborated with other information collected at assessment. Formal diagnostic evaluation, using psychiatric criteria, also occurs when necessary.

The type of assessment conducted depends on the age of the child and the mode of referral. In cases where the child is young and has been referred by parents, an initial interview with the child's parents or caregivers is indicated. When the client is an adolescent or is self-referred, we are likely to initially assess the young person independently.

The emphasis of assessment is on gaining a thorough, multimodal understanding of the gifted young person and the frequency, severity, and duration of the presenting problem (see Wilson, Spence, & Kavanagh, 1989). In all instances, there is a focus on current functioning (e.g., "Let's start by discussing what is happening for you right now that has brought you here. What difficulties have you been having?").

Family Assessment

In the first meeting, we attempt to answer the question "Who is complaining?" Even a child who is fearful or depressed may not be willing to engage in counseling if brought to treatment by an adult. It could be that the adult's expectations are problematic, rather than the child's behavior. A further consideration in our assessment is to ascertain how ready the child and/or family is to embark on treatment.

The overarching aims of the initial interview with the family are to develop a shared perception of the child's difficulties and to create a sense of collaborative partnership with the parents (Sanders, Turner, & Markie-Dadds, 1996). The general areas covered include these:

- parents' main concern about the child (including specific situational contexts, durations, and parental perceptions of and reactions to the problem);
- other difficulties the child has;
- understanding how the child's giftedness has an impact on the problem;
- history of the presenting problem, including a full functional analysis (frequency, severity and duration);
- ascertaining whether the family has sought help elsewhere and what they have found useful;
- an outline of family relationships and interactions (e.g., relationship between parents, parent/child interactions, parental expectations and family rules);
- developmental history (pregnancy, delivery, neonatal period, toddlerhood, preschool, middle childhood);
- educational history (including any acceleration, ability or achievement grouping, or modifications to curriculum);
- medical history and general health;
- the child's strengths (cognitive, psychological, interpersonal); and
- the family's expectations for counseling.

Assessment of Gifted Children

The objectives of assessment of children and adolescents presenting for counseling are to provide an in-depth understanding of a child's functioning, degree of psychological distress, and world (Ginsburg, 1997). Assessment of children can also actively engage the child in therapy. After general introduction and rapport-building, the following areas are covered in the initial assessment:

- Establish the child's own perception of the reason for attendance and clarify any misperceptions (especially if the child feels coerced into attendance or that counseling is an attempt to "get them to comply").

- Gain an understanding of the presenting problem from the child's perspective. For example, "When I met you with your family last week, mom said that you have some worries about school. Do you remember that? What are your biggest worries about school?" (Depending on child's response, ask for a specific occasion: "Tell me about a time when your teacher told you off and you thought it wasn't fair.")

- Clarify other problems and check for comorbid conditions. For example, "Are there other things that are bothering you?" "Sometimes when children are getting into trouble, they feel pretty worried (sad, angry) about that. Is that how it is for you?" "When do you worry about school? Is it while you are at school or do you worry at night time as well?"

- Gain insight into the child's view of the family and significant others. For example, "What are the things that you do with your family that you really like?" "Who in your family do you have the most fun with?" "What do you do?" "Who in your family do you tell when you have worries?" "Who's the person who gets most angry about things in your family?"

- Clarify the child's view of his or her social network. For example, "How do you get along with the other kids?" Gifted children commonly experience social isolation or lack of true peers. It is important to gauge the degree to which the child has an intimate connection with a friend or friendship group. For example, "Are there any friends who you can talk to about these things?" "Who is it that you are closest to?" Some gifted children who display a high capability in social analysis might be asked to comment more specifically on their social relationships, "How do you view your friendships?"

Assessment of Gifted Adolescents

Assessment of highly gifted adolescents mirrors the objectives of the assessment of gifted children and their families. It is an opportunity to establish accurate empathy and to initiate a collaborative understanding of the adolescent and his or her world. Areas to be covered include the following:

- a thorough description of the presenting problem—frequency, duration, severity, nature of onset, and development;

- establishment of features associated with presenting problem—physiological, cognitive and behavioral features, antecedents, consequences, and current precipitants;
- maintaining factors—positive reinforcers for occurrence, avoidance, social context;
- developmental information;
- health;
- history and summary of previous treatment; and
- an understanding of the adolescent's motivation and expectation of treatment outcome.

Other aspects of the young person's behavior are observed during the assessment session, including affect (e.g., emotional expressiveness and range; laughs, smiles, sadness, tearfulness, irritability, anger, tension, anxiety); motor activity (e.g., restlessness, fidgeting, coordination, involuntary movements, tics, mannerisms, rituals, hyperventilation); language (e.g., speech, vocalization, gesture, hearing, comprehension); and social responses to the interview (e.g., social use of language and gesture, responsiveness, eye contact, cooperation and compliance, social style). (See Sattler, 1998, for further details.)

The *problem formulation* is a parsimonious way of summarizing and reframing the client's presenting problem from a cognitive-behavioral perspective and is a useful tool in guiding treatment. The client is an active participant in creating this problem formulation, which becomes a reference point for the active phases of therapy. The case presented at the end of this chapter is an example of problem formulation.

Process

The process of counseling can be broadly understood as comprising several phases, each with its own concomitant goal:
- *Phase 1: Assessment.* In the assessment process described above, the client is actively involved in monitoring *symptoms*—frequency, severity, and duration.
- *Phase 2: Cognitive and behavioral learning phase.* The next stage of therapy involves explicit instruction and appropriate behavioral and cognitive interventions to promote change. The counselor is initially involved in explicit instruction of behavioral techniques, such as progressive muscle relaxation, reward contingencies, and pleasant-event scheduling. The "cognitive model" is introduced, and the client is taught how to identify thought patterns and is introduced to thought challenging.
- *Phase 3: Putting it into practice.* The more active phase of counseling involves the client putting into practice the skills learned, developed, and planned in session. This phase may involve behavioral experiments and exposure (if indicated).

- *Phase 4: Relapse prevention and therapy termination.* The final phase of therapy involves preparing the young person for treatment termination and focusing on future goals and individual strengths to prevent relapse. This phase is comprised of planning future goals, appropriate educational interventions, and problem-solving "high risk" situations. It may involve further collaboration with the family, school, and community. For many highly gifted youth, referral to a mentoring program occurs at this point.

Techniques

Specific techniques from cognitive-behavioral therapy have been modified for use with highly gifted children and adolescents.

- *Socratic questioning.* This fundamental technique used by cognitive-behavioral practitioners involves active listening and framing open-ended questions that necessitate further explanation and thought, as in this example:

Co: So when you walked past them, no one said anything?
Cl: That's right.
Co: And what was it about no one saying anything that made you so upset?
Cl: I was completely ignored.
Co: What made that so bad?
Cl: I am always ignored.

- *Explicit instruction.* This technique involves detailed, complex, and accurate rationales for phases of treatment, and, at times, explicit instruction. For example, for progressive muscle relaxation, the counselor provides a scientifically detailed and accurate explanation of the fight-or-flight response, using appropriate biological terminology. We also encourage our gifted clients to extrapolate and to refer to similar processes (a process that often occurs spontaneously), to ask questions, and to restate main points back to us.
- *Eliciting automatic thoughts and schemas.* The capacity of both counselor and client to elicit automatic thoughts and schemas, and to differentiate these from emotional reactions, is intrinsic to the success of cognitive-behavioral techniques. As a client group, gifted young people tend to demonstrate considerable capability in this regard, possibly due to their excellent analytical abilities and their capacity for introspection. Clients are instructed to record key events, emotional reactions, and associated thoughts using a standard monitoring form (see Beck, Rush, Shaw, & Emery, 1979, or Burns, 1999, for examples).

The authors have found an overrepresentation of particular patterns of negative automatic thoughts in gifted clients, such as the following:

- *Black–or–white thinking.* Rigid thinking that polarizes situations and people as dichotomous (e.g., "for me or against me"; a great job or a hopeless job; bright or stupid).
- *Absolutistic thinking.* Thinking in absolutes or extremes, identified by the use of "everyone," "always," "never" (e.g., "You always pick on me"; "Everyone thinks I'm weird.")
- *The "impostor" phenomenon.* A belief that one's ability level is not as high as others assume and will one day be "found out," a thinking style that is surprisingly common in gifted students, particularly girls, and involves external and temporary attributions for success ("It was a fluke"; "It was an easy exam"; "They were only being kind."); internal and stable attributions for failure ("I don't belong in this class."); and possibly guilt for "unwarranted" praise for ability and achievements.
- *Catastrophic thinking.* Thinking that catastrophizes minor difficulties and imagines and predicts worst outcomes (e.g., "Everyone laughed at me. I will never be able to show my face again"; "I completely messed up my exam, and I will definitely drop out of school").
- *Perfectionistic thinking.* A specific form of absolutistic thinking related to achievement and performance, involving rigid and inflexible (and unrealistically high) standards, which lead inevitably to disappointment (e.g., "I must get High Distinctions in all areas"; a nagging "It's not good enough" on any achievement).
- *Effortlessness of others:* A thinking pattern involving the fallacy that other people achieve things with minimal effort, perhaps the result, for highly gifted children, of having had few experiences demanding commitment to effortful study (e.g., "I am actually stupid"; "I used to be good at math, and now I can't do it anymore"; "Matthew can do these without even trying.").
- *Embarrassment about explicit learning.* Embarrassment about not automatically achieving a basic learning outcome and needing explicit instruction, rehearsal, or assistance (e.g., learning study skills, organizing time, learning material by rote) and about asking for help (e.g., "I should know this"; "People will think I'm an idiot.").
- *Thought-challenging.* A variety of techniques to encourage reevaluation of automatic thoughts, with counselors needing to be aware when modifying these techniques that gifted young people may be reluctant to adopt a simplistic and overly positive view of the world.

The counselor of gifted students should allow the negative thought to be one of many possibilities, rather than immediately negating it or offering a positive alternative. Consider the gifted child or adolescent who thinks, "I'm different." For many gifted young people who are experiencing psychological distress, ruminating on their perceived difference (in a negative sense) and wishing to eliminate this difference can contribute to social isolation and negative affect. However, the counselor of the gifted needs to acknowledge that, in many ways, the thought "I'm different" *is* an accurate reflection of reality. The skilled counselor encourages the gifted young person to consider both the ways in which this thought is true and the ways in which it is an exaggerated explanation of reality.

We assist clients to evaluate their thinking by having them ask themselves how helpful a thought is and the positive and negative effects of it. They consider whether the feared outcome is really as bad as they imagine, what someone else would say about this thought, what advice they would give someone else with this thought, what a more reasonable and helpful way of looking at this situation would be, and what they can tell themselves the next time they have this thought.

When this process has been completed, the client is then encouraged to elaborate on the more reasonable and helpful way of appraising the situation at hand. For example, in the example given earlier ("I'm different"), our clients have imaginatively captured more reasonable ways to acknowledge their differences from age-mates in a way that is less likely to exacerbate social isolation and negative affect. These have included statements such as "I am different in many ways from the kids in my class, but I am also similar to other people who *are* like me"; "Sometimes being different gives me a unique perspective, and I am more reflective and less likely to simply follow the crowd"; and "I am not like other people, but I'm interesting and can be an interesting friend and conversationalist."

- *Point-counterpoint.* Point-counterpoint is a useful technique when counseling gifted young people, particularly verbally gifted students, because they usually appreciate that it requires logical and lateral thinking. The technique is usually used as a step in cognitive challenging, especially for those thoughts that occur repeatedly and for those schemas that underpin the client's current functioning. The counselor can assume the position of client or devil's advocate (providing verbalizations of the client's negative thinking), and the client practices rational responses to his own negative thinking. Following is a demonstration of this technique with a 13-year-old girl who was prone to perfectionistic thinking:

Co: I am going to be like an investigative journalist interviewing you about this and really get to the bottom of things. OK? (Pause) So, I understand that you got a credit rather than a distinction on your science exam. Is that correct?

Cl: Yes.

Co: Well, it sounds like you are not as smart as you pretend to be (deliberately exaggerating the client's own negative thinking—"the impostor phenomenon").

Cl: Well, everyone has a bad day every now and then.

Co: Oh, right. So, now you are telling me that you've stuffed up. I thought smart people like you could easily manage that kind of thing.

Cl: Well, I have done really well in all my other exams. I was really nervous and didn't answer the question properly in the amount of time I had left.

Co: It doesn't seem right to me that smart kids stuff up exams in that way.

Cl: Well, lots of bright people don't do well in exams, but do really well in other ways.

Co: What do you mean, lots of bright people don't do well in exams? Where on earth did you get that idea?

Cl: But, it's true!

Co: Do you really think so?

Cl: Yes.

- *Confrontation.* When used sparingly and appropriately, confrontation may be helpful, particularly when the client appears to be avoiding particular topics, thoughts, or behaviors. If used before initial trust and rapport have been firmly established, the gifted client is likely to become defensive and to avoid elaboration. Confrontation involves reflecting back to the client his or her avoidance, hesitation, or emotional reaction and requires the client to comment (e.g., "I get the feeling that discussing this is uncomfortable for you"; "I noticed some hesitation—you looked away and paused when I asked that. Can you tell me what you were thinking?").

- *Exaggeration.* Exaggeration involves suggesting to clients that they are worried about a situation—but in a far more exaggerated way than they articulated. Often, when working with gifted and talented children and adolescents, directly challenging their thinking merely serves to strengthen their position. Consider the comment "I am stupid" from a gifted child. Teachers, parents, and counselors often fall into the trap of directly challenging such thinking with retorts such as, "Of course you are not, look at how you. . . ." This challenge invites the gifted young person to elaborate on the position and paradoxically strengthens the initial thought. With exaggeration, on the other hand, the counselor may suggest, "So, you really are stupid"; "It sounds as if it's been a big mistake, putting you in the gifted program"; or "Gifted people should be able to do everything perfectly, on first attempt." The client may laugh at the absurdity of the exaggerated proposition and argue against his or her initial thought.

Model of Counseling Process

Figure 7.1 provides a summary of the trajectory of a typical CBT intervention. The three primary phases of counseling (assessment, cognitive and behavioral learning, and practice) are detailed. The final phase of counseling in this model (relapse prevention and therapy termination), involving less active components, is also outlined.

Phase 1: Assessment
Therapy may involve referral to more appropriate practitioner. Counselor and client collaborate to produce problem formulation.
Interview with parent(s) Interview with child Collated psychometric data Self-report measures
Phase 2: Cognitive & Behavioral Learning Phase
Behavioral Techniques Progressive muscle relaxation Reward contingencies Pleasant-events scheduling Cognitive Techniques Introduction to the Cognitive Model Identifying thoughts Thought Challenging Point-counterpoint Confrontation Exaggeration
Phase 3: Putting It Into Practice
Behavioral experiments Systematic exposure Systematic risk-taking Cognitive reappraisal
Phase 4: Relapse Prevention and Therapy Termination
High-risk situations planning Summary of cognitive counter-statements Referral to outside agency

Figure 7.1. Cognitive-behavioral therapy with highly gifted children and adolescents

Application

Presenting Problems

Gifted children present to our service, GERRIC, with a range of difficulties. According to information collected at intake, the most common problems are perfectionism, anxiety, social difficulties, depression, and managing extreme sensitivities. We also see a number of gifted children with other comorbid conditions, including Attention Deficit Disorder (ADD), Attention Deficit/ Hyperactivity Disorder (ADHD), and Asperger's syndrome, all of these commonly labeled "twice-exceptional" children (e.g., Moon, 2003).

In a number of cases, referral to an outside agency is indicated. For children and adolescents presenting with difficulties that are best assessed and treated by a multidisciplinary team or for those children who need medical supervision, an appropriate referral is provided. We also refer and consult with other professionals (e.g., teachers, school counselors, speech pathologists, occupational therapists, medical practitioners) to provide adjunct assessment and treatment.

For young children whose parents request counseling, the primary mode of intervention involves working with parents and family. Indeed, parent-management training, emphasizing the unique socioaffective and behavioral characteristics of young gifted children, appears to be an efficacious means of treating "oversensitive" young gifted children.

For older children and adolescents, we primarily adopt a cognitive-behavioral approach to assessment and treatment of problems such as perfectionism, anxiety, and depression. We also provide group programs to assist those gifted children who require social skills training.

For each of these presenting problems, diathesis-stress models provide a useful framework for understanding the etiology of social, emotional, and behavioral problems and for guiding assessment and treatment of gifted children. A diathesis is a predisposition toward developing a disorder, which can have its origin in biological, psychosocial or sociocultural factors. These models of disorders (e.g., Metalsky, Abramson, Seligman, Semmel, & Peterson, 1982) hold that a predisposition is a necessary, but not sufficient, cause of disorder. In addition to the diathesis, there must also be a stressor or a series of stressors that also contribute to the development of social and emotional distress. In addition to considering the role of risk factors, such models accommodate the role of protective factors in ameliorating social and emotional problems.

Gifted children who present with depression, for example, may have inherited a biological vulnerability to the disorder, had poor early parenting, and experienced a learning environment that predisposed them toward dysfunctional thinking. The asynchronous development of a gifted child may also act as a vulnerability factor because the social, emotional, and cognitive discrepancy between a child and his peers may contribute to negative self-appraisal (e.g., "I'm weird.). Educational and social environments that are not responsive to academic, social, and emotional needs of the gifted learner become stressors that may provide a catalyst to "turn" the predisposition to an expression of the disorder. Other acute and chronic life experiences (e.g., social ostracism, family breakdown) may act as subsequent psychosocial stressors that contribute to the development and maintenance of a mood disorder such as depression.

Case Illustration

Rachel (pseudonym) was an 11-year-old girl who was referred to the GERRIC Clinic by her classroom teacher, who was worried about her negative affect, social isolation, and tendency for angry outbursts in the classroom.

An only child who lived with her mother in an inner-city suburb, Rachel was a highly gifted child. A psychometric assessment conducted when she was 7 years of age revealed an overall ability in the Very Superior range on the then-extant version of a standardized test of cognitive functioning (Wechsler Intelligence Scale for Children–Third Edition; WISC–III), with a Full Scale Score of 148. Rachel had been a high achiever in the early years of her schooling—winning prizes, producing excellent classroom work, and displaying considerable strength in the area of language and literature. She was in an "Opportunity Class"—a full time, self-contained sixth-grade class of academically gifted students within a state elementary school. Students gain highly competitive entry to these classes on the basis of results on tests of general ability and academic achievement.

Rachel's parents had been separated since she was a young child, and she had had ongoing contact with both parents, although she resided with her mother. Approximately 2 years prior to presentation, Rachel's father had died from an illness of short duration. At the time, Rachel appeared to have suffered the usual grieving process, but did not seem overly debilitated by her grief. She was reported to have had close friends and to have continued enjoying everyday activities with good interpersonal skills. However, 6 months prior to referral, Rachel's academic performance deteriorated, primarily due to the fact that she had "stopped handing anything in." Rachel's mother and teacher also reported that she was experiencing "anger outbursts" and was becoming increasingly socially withdrawn.

Phase 1: Assessment (Sessions 1–2)

When Rachel's mother was seen for an initial interview, she reiterated the concerns of the teacher and also expressed her own concern about "not really being there" for Rachel over the last few years as she had been busy with her own work and study commitments. Rachel's mother completed a Child Behavior Checklist–Parent Report Form (Achenbach & Rescorla, 2001).

Rachel then met with the counselor for an interview. After some initial discussion and a briefing about confidentiality, the counselor presented an introduction to the client-counselor assessment process, including a frank acknowledgement that there was no guarantee that treatment would continue at the University Clinic and absolutely no compulsion for her to continue participation. Such caveats are particularly important when gifted young people feel that they have been coerced into treatment. The counselor adopted the active-listening and rephrasing approach in this early session.

Co: Today is going to be a chance for us to have a talk about what is going on for you and to see whether there is anything that we think I would be able to help you with. It's also an opportunity to see how we work together and whether that is a good thing or whether either one of us feels that we might not work so well together. If that's the case, then it will be my job to try and find you someone who would be better suited.

Cl: OK.

Co: Last week I met with Mum and she outlined a few things that were going on with you that she was worried about. In particular she said that she was worried about how you were going at school and thought that things might be a bit rough for you. Is that how you see things?

Cl: Well, not exactly, I know that she is pissed off [*sic*] at me for not doing much work, and I don't feel very motivated, but that's not the main problem.

Co: Uh-huh.

Cl: Well, um, mostly I have been feeling lonely and worried about what is happening next year, and I can't stop wishing that Louise was in my class.

Co: So, it sounds like a few things are on your mind. The main worries are that you have been feeling lonely and really wish your friend was with you on a day-to-day basis and also there are lingering thoughts about what will happen next year.

Cl: Exactly.

Co: Well, I am quite interested in hearing more about what you're worried about in terms of next year.

The remaining section of the assessment session focused on Rachel's feeling of "being different to everyone" and her perceived social incompetence.

Rachel completed the Child Behavior Checklist—Youth Self Report form (Achenbach & Rescorla, 2001) and the Children's Depression Inventory (CDI; Kovacs, 1981), which assesses cognitive, affective, and behavioral signs of depression.

In the second assessment session, Rachel revealed that she had become preoccupied with recent world events (including the siege by terrorists of a school in Russia, which resulted in the deaths of many children) to the exclusion of all other things. Her language and degree of introspection and analysis are typical of many highly gifted children.

Cl: I just can't stop thinking about it [school siege]. There seems to be no justice and no explanation for it, and yet on the other hand I can see that it just seems to have incited hatred on our behalf as well.

Rachel became preoccupied with a story of a family whose three children were killed in the siege. The counselor and Rachel continued with detailed, adult-level conversation about the implications of international terrorism, religious fervor, and ideological differences between countries. However, Rachel tended to refer back to her difference from her peers:

Cl: No one else seems to worry about this. None of my friends seem to care; people are more worried about who wins "Idol" [referring to an Australian television pop-star competition].

Further assessment revealed that Rachel had begun following international events on Web sites, while purporting to be "researching" school assignments.

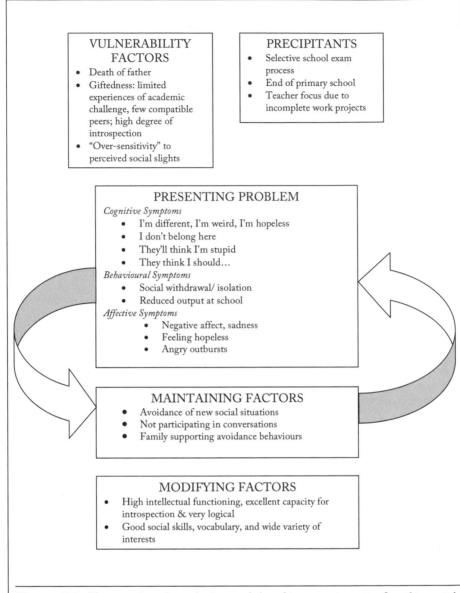

Figure 7.2. Transactional analysis models of interactions in families with achievement issues

At the conclusion of the second assessment session, Rachel and the counselor compiled the problem formulation, summarizing the areas that Rachel had identified as problematic and their associated cognitive, behavioral, and affective components (see Figure 7.2).

Phase 2: Cognitive and Behavioral Learning Phase (Sessions 3–6)

Because Rachel and the counselor identified that "getting work in" was an immediate goal due to the negative consequences for her schooling, much of the third and fourth sessions were spent problem solving. Despite her outstanding capacities for problem solving and abstract reasoning, Rachel had few, if any, organizational skills. She had explained that she had felt embarrassed about needing help: "I should be able to work this out for myself." A simple daily timetable was devised and an action plan for completing outstanding work was implemented.

Like many highly gifted children, Rachel was quick to grasp the cognitive model and could extrapolate from given examples to her own experiences of cognition and emotional response. The explanation given by the counselor was pitched as though to an adult. Rachel's capacity for introspection was remarkable and a great asset to cognitive therapy. However, this advanced capacity for introspection also exacerbated her feelings of "difference" and often translated to excessive rumination and worry about perceived competence.

The counselor typically gave an explanation or rationale for thought identification and asked Rachel to provide further examples:

Co: One of the things that we know about human experience is that as a result of both genetics and learned experience, we tend to habitually think and respond in certain ways, even if these habits of thought aren't all that helpful. Can you think of any examples of that?

Cl: That's easy. "I'm stupid": that's an unhelpful thought and yet one I can't seem to get rid of.

Co: That's right, "I'm stupid" is an example of a thought that we often habitually have, often despite lots of evidence to the contrary. Can you think of examples of other thoughts that might be linked to that?

Cl: Well, yes. "*He's* an idiot." That's a thought I have a lot as well. I think I am really, really judgmental about other people and I hate myself for it.

Co: Good, you have caught on to this quickly. It's interesting that people who apply one principle to themselves often apply the same standard to their appraisals of others.

Cl: Like "the beautifuls."

Co: What do you mean?

Cl: Well, you know, those girls at school that are super-conscious of how they look. They spend so much time on grooming, clothes, hair, make-up and everything. It's really important to them and they wouldn't be seen dead stepping out without looking perfect. But on the other hand, they are really judgmental and totally ostracize other people who don't fit the mould—wrong hair, too fat, bad clothes.

Co: Exactly.

Rachel was quickly able to extrapolate from the succinct explanation to other examples.

The next phase of the cognitive model involved getting Rachel to identify her thoughts. The counselor used an example that Rachel had cited about schoolyard dynamics and her concern that she was being excluded from a friendship group of two girls. The girls were not interested in discussing the Russian siege or international politics with Rachel.

Cl: They were rolling their eyes at me, I know. Casey and Melissa are just like that. They say, "Oh, here she goes again" and then swivel around to find something else to talk about. So, they just ignored me.

Co: What kind of thoughts were you having when that happened?

Cl: Well, on the one hand, I don't care, because I think that is an unbelievable act of stupidity, and then I was thinking this is just like everyone else: They hate me and we used to be really good friends.

Co: So, one of the thoughts is "everyone hates me."

Cl: I guess so, but I've never put it that way.

Rachel was quickly able to identify thoughts and differentiate these from emotional reactions to situations. However, she acknowledged that, at times, it was difficult for her to "catch" these thoughts, which occurred quickly and "with great fury." This was particularly salient at times when she felt overwhelmed by anger. The counselor was able to use this as a preface for a discussion of the automatic nature of such thoughts and the necessity of slowing down at times when she felt that her thoughts were racing.

Rachel participated well in thought monitoring and within 1 week presented the counselor with a "list" of her thinking errors:

- The impostor phenomenon
- Exaggeration of difference
- Mind reading—other people will think I am stupid
- Belief that schoolwork should always be easy and effortless; otherwise I am stupid. Other people achieve things effortlessly.

Rachel quickly progressed to the cognitive-challenging phase of therapy. Cognitive therapy with highly gifted youth needs to be differentiated from regular cognitive therapy by allowing philosophical questions and arguments to be part of the therapy process. Rachel engaged in some philosophical discussion of the difference between an accurate perception of events and the relative helpfulness of thinking. At the outset of counseling, Rachel had presented as a rather angry and defiant child, and it was interesting that this behavior reappeared at this stage of therapy. Indeed, the counselor needed to practice considerable restraint to avoid "arguing back" and to allow Rachel's processing to incorporate appropriate challenging. In the following vignette, the counselor had been summarizing the session and the need to consider "how helpful is this thought?" when feeling anxious. Rachel, however, was not prepared to accept this principle on a superficial level:

Cl: The thing that I don't like about what you are saying is that it can absolve people from personal responsibility. I think it's crap.

Co: I think you might be right about that. Tell me a little bit more about what you mean, specifically.

Cl: Well, if you mean that it's more helpful for me to be thinking, "Well, I did the best I could, we all have bad days from time to time," OK, but I had actually done something really careless that had hurt Mum or a friend or something.

Then you are actually giving me permission to not accept any responsibility for what I've done and I just don't think that's fair.

Co: Yes, it's true that people can let themselves off the hook in that way. Is nonacceptance of responsibility something that you think that you are likely to do?

Cl: No, I guess not, actually I think I am probably *on* the hook a bit too often.

Co: So, I wonder if you could consider a kind of compromise position. We are not trying to say, "Don't worry about anything; nothing is your fault"; but on the other hand we don't want you overcompensating and feeling personally responsible for a lot of things that actually aren't in your control.

Cl: Yeah.

Discussion then ensued about the research that reveals that people engaging in negative appraisals may, in fact, be viewing the world more accurately (Seligman, 1995).

Rachel's reactions and thoughts continued to return to the theme of "being different" in tandem with a "hypervigilance" toward negative appraisals by others. She described this happening with her mother, friends, and teacher. In the following session transcript, Rachel was describing the conflict she had had with her teacher about not completing compulsory book-review assignment work:

Co: Tell me a little bit about what happened when you got so angry.

Cl: Well, Mrs. J is always picking on me. She never notices anything good that I do and I am really sick of it.

Co: I can hear that this really upsets you. Why don't you tell me about how she picks on you?

Cl: Well, yesterday we had project time and I was trying to write the book review. Actually, I had been working really hard on it, because I knew that I had to get as much done as I could. Everyone else was pretty well working, but lots of people were making noise and talking. Phoebe and Melissa were not doing their work at all and were really mucking up. Anyway, I was writing, and I just looked up and was kind of staring off into space, only because I was thinking about what I was writing—it's something that I always do. Anyway, I caught Mrs. J's eye. She was staring at me with this kind of questioning look on her face, like she was saying, "What exactly are you doing with your head up? You should be working furiously." So, I just got really pissed off [*sic*] and stared right back at her.

Co: And what was going on in your head?

Cl: Not much, just pure rage. Well, I guess I was thinking, "Why are you picking on me? Look at all the other kids for once." And I was thinking about the fact that she always focuses on me and notices my shortcomings and the way I am different to others.

Co: Hmm, I can see why, with those thoughts going on, that you got really mad. I wonder if we can have a look at those thoughts in more detail and really put them to the test.

In Australia, secondary schools, serving students in grades 7–12, are called high schools. The state of New South Wales, in which Rachel lives, has 19 selective high schools enrolling only academically gifted and talented students. These are not private schools; they are run by the state and are cost-free. The only requirement is that students must meet the academically demanding entrance criteria. Entry to these schools, which are highly selective academically, is through a sequence of ability and off-level achievement tests, as well as ranked nominations by the principal and teachers of the student's primary school. Entry is highly competitive, with an average of five applicants for every available place.

Rachel had a number of significant concerns about the results of the selective schools' entry tests that she had recently sat. Her mother had decided that Rachel needed some assistance with managing exams and working to time limits and had therefore enrolled her in a coaching college. In the following transcript, the counselor uses reflection and questioning to encourage Rachel to consider what the underlying thought was that was contributing to her sense of anxiety about this exam. Such ruminations are common for many gifted students.

Cl: I just can't think of any way that it [getting into a selective high school] is going to happen. It's definitely my maths marks that are letting me down. There is only one other boy [at coaching] who gets a lower score than me. And I just don't know what I am going to do if I don't get in.

Co: So, it sounds like you are worried about what will happen if you don't get into the selective school, and you are thinking that your chances are pretty low at this stage.

Cl: Exactly. I think I just have to face the fact that I am not getting into [school].

Co: What would that mean for you, if you didn't get into that school?

Cl: Well, it's just that that's where everyone expects that I'll go. From the time I was little, that's where I thought I would go, and that's where most of the kids in my class are going.

Co: And what would be so bad about not getting into that school?

Cl: Well, I wouldn't know anyone.

Co: You're worried about not getting into the school, and you think that you definitely won't. Everyone is depending on you getting into the school and that's where all your classmates are going. If you have to go to [a different] school, you won't know anyone at all.

Cl: Well, it's not that they are depending on it; it's just that I know that is what Mum expects.

Co: How do you know that?

Cl: It's just a tone of voice she adopts. Although she says, "It doesn't matter. Just do your best, I just want you to be happy," I can tell that she would be really upset if I didn't.

Co: Hmm, you could be right about that, but as you know, one of the things we have been working on is not necessarily accepting our initial thoughts on face value. It's true that Mum could be really upset if you don't go well on this exam. What evidence do you have that supports this proposition?

models of counseling gifted children, adolescents, and young adults

Cl: Well, she wants me to be happy.

Co: True. How does that support the idea that she will be really upset if you don't go well in this exam?

Cl: Well, she gets upset with me if I haven't been putting in much effort.

Co: So, if you don't put in much effort, Mum might get upset?

Cl: Exactly.

Note that, on "reflecting back," the counselor changed the semantics of Rachel's original summation to include qualifiers such as "could" and "might." The interaction continued in this manner, and Rachel suggested that her mother had previously "got upset" when Rachel performed poorly due to her minimal effort. On the other hand, she was able to generate considerable counter evidence that contradicted this notion. Rachel was able to conclude that she was "mind reading" and that it was unlikely that her mother would be angry or upset, but concluded that she might be disappointed. Cognitive challenging continued in this manner, and Rachel extrapolated that on many occasions she had the thought "everyone expects me to _____". After applying the same principle (generating evidence for and against this thought), Rachel concluded that this underlying theme was contributing to her anxiety and anger. The counselor summarized the cognitive challenging process and reminded Rachel of ways to deal with this type of anxious thinking in the future:

Co: So, when you are feeling panicky and stressed out about things, one of the things you can do for yourself to calm down is to try to catch this thought, "Everyone expects me to ____" and remind yourself of this conversation and decide for yourself whether "everyone expects you" to do whatever it is—if it's true that every time you have that thought, "everyone expects me to," you are going to feel anxious and likely to feel compelled to do something based on what you think others think.

A similar strategy was used to appraise the thought "I won't know anyone at all":

Co: So, one of the other worries is this idea that you might get to [the less preferred school] and you wouldn't know anyone.

Cl: Yes, I wouldn't.

Co: Well, OK then. Tell me what would be bad about that?

Cl: What do you mean? It would really suck.

Co: Why?

Cl: Well, it's awful, not knowing anyone. You stress out about every little thing, like what you look like, where you sit, what you do at lunchtime. It's really lonely and unknown.

Co: So, you think that it's awful, not knowing anyone.

Cl: [Laughing] Don't start. I know it's an exaggeration and it's fortune telling. You're right, but it's not exactly my preferred option.

Co: I am sure that it's not. Can you think of some counterevidence?

Cl: Well, actually I met Melissa on a languages camp where I didn't know anyone and we became really, really close friends.

The session continued with examining counterevidence for the "not knowing anyone" thought. Rachel came to the conclusion that she tended to catastrophize in her thinking about situations where she did not know anyone. The counselor concluded the session by prompting Rachel to consider how she was going to transfer this knowledge into future experiences.

Co: When you are thinking back about our conversation today, I wonder what it is that you can do to remind yourself that this habitual way of thinking about school next year has been a bit exaggerated.
Cl: I don't know.
Co: [Silence]
Cl: I think I am starting to do it automatically now, I really think I have been a catastrophizer. I guess I can say to myself, "It's probably not that bad. Think about all sides of it" and "I have met some nice people that I didn't know before at other times."

Phase 3: Putting It Into Practice (Sessions 7–8)

The next stage of therapy involved Rachel participating in several prenegotiated exposure experiences. These were designed to reduce anxiety around new social situations and reduce her fears for the following year, as well as provide social risk-taking experiences. Rachel and the counselor devised the following list of exposure experiences:

*   Attending open days at two different schools.
*   Introducing myself to a new person at coaching.
*   Initiating and sustaining a conversation of interest for at least 5 minutes. (Rachel had previously aborted conversations she enjoyed due to perceived lack of interest from the other party.)

In preparation for each exposure experience, Rachel was trained to rate her anxiety using a scale of 0–100, where 0 = no anxiety and 100 = maximum anxiety possible. She rated her anxiety before, during, and after each exposure. Rachel was also briefed about the nature of anxiety and its physical, behavioral, and cognitive correlates (see Barlow, 2001, for review). She was instructed to expect an initial increase in anxiety prior to each exposure experience.

A transcript of the counseling session following one of the exposures (continuing a conversation of interest) is given here. Of note, when planning social exposures, the counselor (and often the client) has very little control over the outcome. All possible care must be taken to facilitate an optimal outcome (e.g., the choice of conversation partner in this exposure was carefully planned). However, both counselor and client need to keep in mind that the object of the exercise is to reduce social anxiety and to practice appropriate risk-taking, not to guarantee a particular outcome:

Co: I am really keen to hear how things went.

Cl: Yeah, it was actually really good. I was really happy with it. I felt incredibly stupid the whole day beforehand [the planned exposure was during school lunch hour] as if I was doing something really wrong. My ratings were really high—like around 80 all morning.

Co: What were you able to do to keep yourself calm?

Cl: I just tried deep breathing and saying what we agreed, "What is the worst that can happen?"

Co: How did that work?

Cl: It was OK, but I was still worried and I did keep on thinking, "She'll think I'm an idiot," and then I would kind of switch over to thinking, "So what? Is that the worst that can happen?"

Co: OK. That sounds good. It's a good sign that you're not automatically reacting to the first thought that jumps into your head. What happened then?

Cl: Well, Melissa and I were leaving the library, and I started my conversation [about the forthcoming Federal election], and I asked her what she thought about it. She wasn't that thrilled or anything, and I guess in the past I would definitely have slunk away. Anyway, she kind of looked weirdly at me, but then said that her parents are really into it and so she had been watching a bit of it on TV. So, I kept going a bit and said that I thought it really sucked about the war [in Iraq] and that I really hoped that this country would consider what is happening with children in detention. She said she thought so, too, but I wasn't really sure if she was just saying that to shut me up. But it was better than I thought. Anyway, she kind of changed the topic and asked me about the news review we were meant to do for homework.

Co: What was your anxiety like throughout?

Cl: It was hard to catch exactly, but you were right. It definitely went down and then by the time we got to where we were going to eat lunch, it was just nothing.

Co: So, what did you get from the experience?

Cl: Well, I definitely think that I have kind of forced myself to stop conversations in the past because I've been mind reading and thinking, "They'll think I'm an idiot," and maybe I have been the one to miss out on some things. But I still don't think that many people are interested in the things that I am.

Co: Well, probably not many people your age

Cl: [laughing] Yeah, I'm just in the wrong age-zone!

Phase 4: Relapse Prevention and Therapy Termination (Session 9)

The final treatment session was spent reviewing treatment and encouraging Rachel to problem solve future high-risk situations.

Co: So, let's try to project you forward in time and imagine your first day at a new school. What are you going to do to help yourself manage your anxiety?

Cl: Not mind read.

Co: That's good, and I quite agree. The trouble is that sometimes when you say *don't* do something, it sometimes becomes quite hard. Like when you say, "Don't eat chocolate" and then all you can think about . . .

Cl: . . . is chocolate!

Co: Exactly. So, what are the specific things you can do or say to yourself that might help you out?

Cl: Well, I know that I can use the "What is the worst thing about that?" question, because usually I have found myself worrying and stressing about something that is ultimately not that important anyway, like what some stranger might think about me.

Co: That's good. What else have you done that you've found helpful?

Cl: I think sometimes distraction still works well for me or else thinking about it the next day. It often makes things a little clearer, and I just have to keep practicing.

Rachel and the counselor prepared summary cards of the key cognitive challenges and more helpful appraisals. These comprised a statement of common automatic thoughts (e.g., "I won't know anyone"), through challenging questions (e.g., "What would be the worst thing about that?") and rephrasing the original thought (e.g., "I might meet new friends. I don't have to know everyone.").

Rachel was feeling optimistic about finishing treatment and reported decreased anxiety and anger. Indeed her self-report measures and her mother's self-report revealed significant reductions in anxiety, depression, and anger. The counselor also referred Rachel to a "Big Sister" peer-mentoring program.

Rachel contacted the clinic several months following cessation of therapy to let us know that she had "made it" into her preferred selective high school. She had also received a scholarship to a prestigious private secondary school with an emphasis on music, literature, and the arts. She had not yet decided which school she would select.

References

Achenbach, T. M., & Rescorla, L. A. (2001). *Manual for the ASEBA School Age Forms and Profiles.* Burlington, VT: University of Vermont, Research Center for Children, Youth, & Families.

Barlow, D. H. (Ed.). (2001). *Clinical handbook of psychological disorders* (3rd ed.). New York: Guilford Press.

Beck, A. T., Rush, A. J., Shaw, B. F., & Emery, G. (1979). *Cognitive therapy of depression.* New York: Guilford Press.

Benbow, C. P., & Lubinski, D. (1993). Psychological profiles of the mathematically talented: Some sex differences and evidence supporting their biological basis. In G. R. Bock & K. Ackrill (Eds.), *The origin and development of high ability* (pp. 44–66). New York: John Wiley and Sons.

Benbow, C. P., & Stanley, J. S. (1996). Inequity in equity: How "equity" can lead to inequity for high-potential students. *Psychology, Public Policy and Law, 2,* 249–292.

Burns, D. D. (1999). *The feeling good handbook.* New York: Plume.

Cloninger, S. C. (1996). *Theories of personality: Understanding persons.* Englewood Cliffs, NJ: Prentice Hall.

Colangelo, N. (2003). Counseling gifted students. In N. Colangelo & G. A. Davis (Eds.), *Handbook of gifted education* (3rd ed., pp. 373–387). Boston: Allyn & Bacon.

Colangelo, N., & Zaffran, R. T. (Eds.). (1979). *New voices in counseling the gifted.* Dubuque, IA: Kendall Hunt.

Colangelo, N., Assouline, S. G., & Gross, M. U. M. (2004). *A nation deceived: How schools hold back America's brightest students* (Vol. 1). Iowa City, IA: The Connie Belin & Jacqueline N. Blank International Center for Gifted Education and Talent Development.

Coleman, L. J., & Cross, T. L. (1988). Is being gifted a social handicap? *Journal for the Education of the Gifted, 11,* 41–56.

Columbus Group. (1991). *Unpublished transcript of the meeting of the Columbus Group.* Columbus, OH.

Cross, T. L., Coleman, L. J., & Stewart, R. A. (1995). Psychosocial diversity among gifted adolescents: An exploratory study of two groups. *Roeper Review, 17,* 181–185.

Dabrowski, K. (1972). *Psychoneurosis is not an illness.* London: Gryf.

Dadds, M. R., & Barrett, P. M. (2001). Psychological management of anxiety disorders in childhood. *Journal of Child Psychology & Psychiatry & Allied Disciplines, 42,* 999–1011.

Dadds, M. R., Barrett, P. M., & Rapee, R. M. (1996). Family process and child anxiety and aggression: An observational analysis. *Journal of Abnormal Child Psychology, 24,* 715–734.

Flanders, J. R. (1987). How much of the content of mathematics textbooks is new? *Arithmetic Teacher, 35,* 18–23.

Gagné, F. (1985). Giftedness and talent: Reexamining a reexamination of the definitions. *Gifted Child Quarterly, 29,* 103–112.

Gagné, F. (2000). Understanding the complex choreography of talent development through DMGT-based analysis. In K. A. Heller, F. J. Mönks, R. J. Sternberg, & R. Subotnik (Eds.), *International handbook of giftedness and talent* (pp. 67–79). Oxford, England: Pergamon Press.

Gagné, F. (2003). Transforming gifts into talents: The DMGT as a developmental theory. In N. Colangelo & G. A. Davis (Eds.), *Handbook of gifted education* (3rd ed., pp. 60–73). Boston: Allyn & Bacon.

Ginsburg, H. P. (1997). *Entering the child's mind: The clinical interview in psychological research and practice.* Cambridge, NY: Cambridge University Press.

Goldstein, D., Stocking V. B., & Godfrey, J. J. (1999). What we've learned from talent search research. In N. Colangelo & S. G. Assouline (Eds.), *Talent development 3: Proceedings from the 1995 Henry B. and Jocelyn Wallace National Research Symposium on Talent Development* (pp. 143–152). Scottsdale, AZ: Gifted Psychology Press.

Gross, M. U. M. (1989). The pursuit of excellence or the search for intimacy? The forced-choice dilemma of gifted youth. *Roeper Review, 11,* 189–194.

Gross, M. U. M. (1998). The "me" behind the mask: Intellectually gifted children and the search for identity. *Roeper Review, 20,* 167–174.

Gross, M. U. M. (1999). Small poppies: Highly gifted children in the early years. *Roeper Review, 21,* 207–214.

Gross, M. U. M. (2000, May). *From "play partner" to "sure shelter": A comparison of conceptions of friendship between children of average ability, moderately gifted and highly gifted children.* Paper presented at the Fifth Wallace International Research

Symposium on Gifted Education and Talent Development, Iowa City, University of Iowa.

Gross, M. U. M. (2002). Gifted children and the gift of friendship. *Understanding Our Gifted, 14*(3), 27–29.

Gross, M. U. M. (2004). *Exceptionally gifted children* (2nd ed.). London: RoutledgeFalmer.

Hollingworth, L. S. (1926). *Gifted children: Their nature and nurture.* New York: Macmillan.

Hollingworth, L. S. (1931). The child of superior intelligence as a special problem in social adjustment. *Mental Hygiene, 15*(1), 3–16.

Hollingworth, L. S. (1936). The development of personality in highly intelligent children. *National Elementary Principal, 15*, 272–281.

Hollingworth, L. S. (1942). *Children above IQ 180.* New York: World Books.

Janos, P. M., Marwood, K. A., & Robinson, N. M. (1985). Friendship patterns in highly intelligent children. *Roeper Review, 8*, 46–49.

Jung, C. G. (1989). *Memories, dreams, recollections* (Rev. ed., R. Wilson & C. Wilson, Trans.). New York: Vintage Books.

Kazdin, A. E., & Marciano, P. L. (1998). Childhood and adolescent depression. In E. J. Mash & R. A. Barkley (Eds.), *Treatment of childhood disorders* (2nd ed., pp. 211–248). New York: Guilford Press.

Kazdin, A. E., & Weisz, J. R. (Eds.). (2003). *Evidence-based psychotherapies for children and adolescents.* New York: Guilford Press.

Kerr, B. A. (1986). Career counseling for the gifted: Assessments and interventions. *Journal of Counseling and Development, 64*, 602–604

Kline, B. E., & Meckstroth, E. A. (1985). Understanding and encouraging the exceptionally gifted. *Roeper Review, 8*, 24–30.

Kohlberg, L. (1963). The development of children's orientations towards a moral order. I: Sequence in the development of moral thought. *Vita Humana, 6*, 11–33.

Kovacs, M. (1981). Rating scales to assess depression in school aged children. *Acta Paedopsychiatrica, 46*, 305–315.

Metalsky, G. I., Abramson, L. Y., Seligman, M. E. P., Semmel, A., & Peterson, C. R. (1982). Attributional styles and life events in the classroom: Vulnerability and invulnerability to depressive mood reactions. *Journal of Personality and Social Psychology, 43*, 612–617.

Miller, W. R., & Rollnick, S. (2002). *Motivational interviewing: Preparing people for change* (2nd ed.). New York: Guilford Press.

Moon, S. M. (2003). Counseling families. In N. Colangelo & G. A. Davis (Eds.), *Handbook of gifted education* (3rd ed., pp. 388–402). Boston: Allyn & Bacon.

Neihart, M. (2002). Gifted children and depression. In M. Neihart, S. M. Reis, N. M. Robinson, & S. M. Moon (Eds.), *The social and emotional development of gifted children. What do we know?* (pp. 103–112). Waco, TX: Prufrock Press.

Parker, W. D. (1997). An empirical typology of perfectionism in academically talented children. *American Educational Research Journal, 34*, 545–562.

Piechowski, M. M. (2003). From William James to Maslow and Dabrowski: Excitability of character and self-actualization. In D. Ambrose, L. M. Cohen, & A. J. Tannenbaum (Eds.), *Creative intelligence: Towards theoretic integration* (pp. 283–322). Cresskill, NJ: Hampton Press.

Reis, S. M., Westberg, K. L., Kulikowich, J., Caillard, F., Hébert, T., Plucker, J., et al. (1993). *Why not let high ability students start school in January? The curriculum compacting study.* Storrs: National Research Center on the Gifted and Talented, University of Connecticut.

Robinson, N. M., Reis, S. M., Neihart, M., & Moon, S. M. (2002). Social and emotional issues: What have we learned and what should we do now? In M. Neihart, S. M. Reis, N. M. Robinson, & S. M. Moon (Eds.), *The social and emotional development of gifted children: What do we know?* (pp. 267–288). Waco, TX: Prufrock Press.

Roedell, W. (1984). Vulnerabilities of highly gifted children. *Roeper Review, 6,* 127–130.

Rogers, C. R. (1961). *On becoming a person: A therapist's view of psychotherapy.* Boston: Houghton Mifflin.

Sanders, M., Turner, K., & Markie-Dadds, C. (1996). The treatment of childhood disorders. In P. Martin & J. Birnbrauer (Eds.), *Clinical psychology: Profession and practice in Australia* (pp. 287–314). Melbourne, Australia: Macmillan Education.

Sattler, J. (1998). *Clinical and forensic interviewing of children and families.* San Diego, CA: Author.

Seligman, M. E. (1995). *The optimistic child.* New York: HarperPerennial.

Seligman, M. E., & Csikszentmihalyi, M. (2000). Positive psychology: An introduction. *American Psychologist, 56,* 216–217.

Silverman, L. K. (1989). The highly gifted. In J. F. Feldhusen, J. VanTassel-Baska, & K. R. Seeley (Eds.), *Excellence in educating the gifted* (pp. 71–83). Denver, CO: Love.

Silverman, L. K. (1993). *Counseling the gifted and talented.* Denver, CO: Love.

Tannenbaum, A. J. (1983). *Gifted children: Psychological and educational perspectives.* New York: Macmillan.

VanTassel-Baska, J. (1998). Characteristics and needs of gifted learners. In J. VanTassel-Baska (Ed.), *Excellence in educating gifted and talented learners* (3rd ed., pp. 173–191). Denver, CO: Love.

Webb, J. T., Meckstroth, E. A., & Tolan, S. S. (1983). *Guiding the gifted child.* Columbus, OH: Ohio Psychology Publishing Company.

Wilson, P. H., Spence, S. H., & Kavanagh, D. J. (1989). *Cognitive behavioral interviewing for adult disorders.* Baltimore: Johns Hopkins University Press.

chapter 8

Gifted Identity Formation: A Therapeutic Model for Counseling Gifted Children and Adolescents

by Andrew Mahoney, Don Martin, and Magy Martin

Conception of Giftedness

In our model, giftedness and holistic identity development are intertwined and inseparable. Understanding and acknowledging this partnership provides a key to helping gifted youth. Nearly a decade ago, Sternberg (1996) labeled the problems of gifted children as "the sounds of silence" while clearly, yet paradoxically, indicating that gifted children are our most valuable natural resource. Yet there are few research-based counseling models available to assist counselors and therapists in identifying and helping gifted individuals (Gallagher, 2003; Winner, 1996). Because giftedness is an abstract concept, it is a challenge to bridge identification of giftedness to pragmatic application of the concept in effective practice. We believe our model helps to fill this void.

Gifted individuals often experience isolation and separateness, which are driven by a lack of self-acceptance and self-appreciation. The Gifted

Identity Formation model is a powerful tool that helps counselors identify and understand giftedness and be able to use this identification as the baseline for counseling intervention. This model helps gifted individuals explore and strengthen their identity while enhancing wellness and embracing their potential.

In developing The Gifted Identity Formation model, we explored the complex issues related to identity formation in the gifted. Influenced by renowned researchers such as Erikson (1968) and Hollingworth (1926), we explored identity relative to developmental stages (Fiedler, 1998). Erikson's views have been particularly helpful, because he was one of the first to identify individuals who deviate from their true identities (Clark, 1997). He was able to describe the process whereby gifted individuals retreat to an inner world and separate themselves for safety. Paradoxically, this safety is an illusion, because healthy self-development requires successful integration of the inner self and the internal interplay of the self with the outside world. Our model describes how therapists can help gifted individuals break out from this isolation and become integrated human beings who can contribute to the lives of others and the world at large. The Gifted Identify Formation model travels well beyond helping the gifted individual identify "Who am I?" It asks the more important question about the core of the gifted individual, "What is my purpose?"

Influences

The pioneers of gifted education have been discussed in many textbooks and articles, which have detailed basic influences, definitions, characteristics, and assumptions related to working with the gifted (Rimm, 1990). Our review will be brief, because our intent is to describe our counseling model rather than reiterate information that is easily accessible.

Hollingworth (1926) began inventing strategies to help identify and counsel gifted children. She understood that these children were highly vulnerable and were often detached from their peers. Noticing how gifted children often became apathetic in school, Hollingworth believed that these children needed to be taught differently both for their own good and for the good of society. She observed that gifted children may become negative toward authority figures and eventually become troubled youth, if they do not receive appropriate instruction.

A clinician's interest in giftedness often begins when he or she is faced with clients with advanced cognitive abilities and heightened self-awareness (Klein, 2000). Scholars have noted that gifted individuals often feel isolated and behave as if they are in psychosocial crisis (Gross, 2000; Tolan, 1990), suggesting that the lifespan development of gifted individuals involves an atypical course of emotional and physical maturation. Development may follow unusual patterns and vary chronologically or simply be out of normal sequence. Yet, it has only been in recent years that emotional dimensions of giftedness have been given a defined research focus (Csikszentmihalyi, 1999).

Our clinical work emphasizes the interrelationship of cognitive complexity and emotional intensity (Gardner, 1983, 1999; Sternberg, 1988a, 1988b, 1997). We have been influenced by a number of researchers who believe in the paradox that emotional instability is evidence of a rich inner life that is expressed through intense emotions. According to both Hollingworth (1926) and Lovecky (1992), in order to help the gifted individual a clinician needs to understand giftedness across the lifespan. Lovecky (1986) believed that gifted individuals must learn to value themselves and find support. If gifted individuals do not have this guidance, conflicts ensue and recurrent depression is a likely result (Brody, 1999).

Self-growth and awareness are critical to the development of gifted individuals (Lovecky, 1992). Knowing and accepting oneself leads to the discovery of personal power. Through nurturing and supportive relationships, gifted individuals can flourish and grow. By identifying and fully integrating giftedness, the individuals are then prepared to have purpose, meaning, and direction in their lives. The need for differentiated and specialized counseling services for the gifted is evident throughout the literature (Alverado, 1989; Colangelo & Ogburn, 1989; Feldman, 1995; Rocamora, 1992; Treffinger & Feldhusen, 1996). The task of integrating an intricate and complex concept such as giftedness or the development of a gifted identity into workable counseling applications offers a multifaceted challenge.

Definition

Our definition of *giftedness* combines the conscious and unconscious; genetic and chemical make-up; and a myriad of learning experiences that influence lives (Gross, 2000). We believe the search for identity is the core component of any definition of giftedness, and this journey is the foundation of our model. This often-confusing journey is marked by separation from peer groups and from significant relationships. If identity formation according to Erikson (1968) and others is the integration of the inner self and the outer world, the question remains unanswered why the gifted individual who is continually rejected by the outside world can comprehend and be aware of this rejection and yet want to be a contributor to this same environment (Bloom, 1985).

Robinson and Noble (1991) commented as follows:

> There is no more varied group of young people than the diverse group known as gifted children and adolescents. Not only do they come from every walk of life, every ethnic and socioeconomic group, and every nation, but they also exhibit an almost unlimited range of personal characteristics in temperament, risk-taking, conservatism, introversion and extroversion, reticence and assertiveness, and degree of effort invested in reaching goals. (p. 14)

A definition of gifted identity may be as complex as developing one's identity. Even Erikson (1968) was hesitant to offer a definitive explanation of the unity and integration of all aspects of self, including the conscious and unconscious.

Most definitions of giftedness refer to a divergent thinking ability characterized by traits and behaviors such as sensitivity; perceptiveness; excitability; moral, creative, or academic aptitude; and the need for self-determination (Feldman, 1995). We believe that gifted individuals experience an intense need to define themselves and find their place in the world. The search lasts throughout a lifespan and includes a search for both meaning in life and meaning of interpersonal interactions. In her infamous article entitled "Is It a Cheetah?" Tolan (1995) used the cheetah as a metaphor for identification of gifted children. Because the cheetah is the fastest animal on earth and runs nearly 70 miles an hour, it is easily identified, especially when it is chasing prey, which is often the antelope. But the cheetah is also an odd cat. It is hyperactive, compared to most cats, has no bulk, cannot retract its claws, and catches rather than overpowers its prey. Among its colleagues in the wild, the cheetah is considered a strange animal. When it runs 70 miles an hour, it is doing what is natural for the cheetah. It is not hard to identify a cheetah in those situations.

More importantly, Tolan asks whether it is still a cheetah when it is in a zoo. How can one know if this animal is a cheetah if it eats only zoo chow, runs 5 miles an hour, and sits in a 10 x 12 enclosure? The zoo will never provide antelope for the cheetah to chase, and therefore, in the zoo, the cheetah is never really a cheetah. When we attempt to define the nature of gifted children in the therapeutic relationship, we are often looking at the cheetah in the zoo that has forgotten its natural abilities. Every organism has a desire to fulfill its biological design (Davis & Rimm, 1998). If the gifted individual loses purpose, the results are often devastating.

Thus, for the purposes of our model, we simply define giftedness as an exceptional ability in one or more of a variety of areas, such as intellect, the arts, or personal creativity. Our hope is that any definition of giftedness illuminates the complexity, process, and nuances of identity formation related to giftedness. Inherent in our definition is the belief that the lack of an appropriate developmental process can seriously inhibit the attribute of giftedness in some individuals (Silverman, 1998). For example, a young man may have fine and gross motor delay until his freshman year in high school, when he begins a developmental growth spurt. Suddenly, he is able to produce art far superior to other students in his high school. This gifted child exemplifies asynchrony—in this case occurring between his internal artistic desire and a level of output that did not qualify him as gifted in that domain until later in adolescence.

Characteristics

Most researchers define giftedness as performing exceptionally in academic or other arenas (Tolan, 1989, 1990). If only life for these individuals were as simple as applying the gifted label. Paradoxically, gifted individuals in the therapeutic encounter are often defined by their lack of self-understanding and lack of success, and they often have experienced a developmental trajectory that seems to have a life of its own. For example, the development of cognitive skills at an early age predisposes an individual to higher level thought processes that make life different from normal for the individual. Depending on a myriad of circumstances, including a child's teachers or school environment, achievement level can vary. However, the giftedness remains, whether the child achieves or not. Researchers or clinicians often attempt to define giftedness by external achievements, but we believe, as do others (Burks, Jensen, & Terman, 1930), that it is defined by internal reality. Gifted individuals who have external achievements are not nearly as difficult to help in schools and therapy as children who have few or no extrinsic rewards and whose gifts are rarely explored or demonstrated.

The Gifted Identity Formation model serves to enhance and complement existing models. It defines giftedness beyond the tangible outcomes that others see as requisite. For example, the child who is able to write exceptional prose at a young age or attain extraordinary grades is not only gifted but is situated within a potentiating environment. Many children are not so fortunate and, for this reason, giftedness is not dependent on performance or product, according to our definition. We believe that extenuating circumstances may seriously interfere with the output or fluency of an individual's general, specific, or relative gift. These circumstances might include the absence of opportunity to develop that ability, the presence of an undiagnosed and unaccommodated learning problem, or a developmental delay in the demonstration of giftedness. This absence of conscious will or intent in the gifted individual may occur for a host of reasons. Lovecky (1986) called this *conation*, or the will to do. In reference to the gifted, conation is the critical motivation, desire, effort, or will that drives all productive work. Without conation, gifted abilities cannot come to fruition. Thus, giftedness has to include a "will to do."

The lack of conation as a defining element of giftedness can limit one's perceptions of and capability of identifying the gifted. Individuals can be overlooked and inappropriately labeled (Lovecky, 1992). The Gifted Identity Formation model defines conation as affinity, or a drive to find meaning, and notes that conation must be accounted for in the process of both identifying and counseling gifted individuals. The difference for therapists is whether or not that drive has been cultivated in the gifted individual. If one were to use only conation as an identifying variable without looking at what impedes development, giftedness might go unrecognized in that individual. The Gifted Identity Formation model assesses for the construct of affinity in all systems that may be impacting the individual's identity.

If identity encompasses the complexity of all aspects of "who I am," then identity formation is the process of integrating and shaping discrete pieces of the self into a unique being. Erikson (1968) spoke of identity formation as "a process located in the core of the individual and yet also in the core of his communal culture" (p. 22). Erikson referred to the integrative and complex relationship between the inner self (all inner aspects and the internal interplay of the self) and the outer world (self as it relates and contends with the external world). He described a "few minimum characteristics" to consider when contending with the complex process of identity formation. The Gifted Identity Formation model utilizes these characteristics as the working underpinnings of the model:

- identity formation employs a process of simultaneous reflection and observations;
- identity formation takes place on all levels of mental functioning; and
- individuals perceive themselves as others view them.

According to the Gifted Identity Formation model, gifted children have unlimited potential and unlimited characteristics, rather than defined characteristics. Thus, characteristics are actually broad descriptions of the complex interaction of extremes in the potential of human beings and the variances associated with the asynchronous development of the gifted individual. In light of these limitations, some of these characteristics may include the following:

- creative, theoretical, and abstract thinker;
- independent, inventive, and nonconforming processors;
- instinctive sensitivity;
- alertness and eagerness;
- intuitiveness, often without sequential thoughts;
- intensity, with concentrated periods of thinking; often defined as a daydreamer;
- aesthetical orientation;
- preferences for democratically oriented authority;
- compassion, with fear of loss of others; and
- exploratory learning within preferred styles (Winner, 1996).

Unfortunately, these characteristics cannot be all that defines the nature of giftedness. The goal of the Gifted Identity Formation model is to help the counselor examine the uniqueness of or variance within each individual. This model allows for a more flexible approach than using only characteristics when considering meaning in context and is more appropriate for counseling regarding individual identity development. It is interesting that even after decades of research there is still a lack of consensus among professionals about who should be identified as gifted. Thus, the notion of a noncharacteristic view of giftedness seems to make sense, allows for a more flexible approach to exploring context of meaning, and is more valid within the individual's identity (Rogers, 2002). We believe that clinicians need to see giftedness as a potentially unlimited deviance from the norm, with this deviance paradoxically enabling a view of the endless potential of human nature and ability (Hollingworth, 1942).

Two aspects of the general concept of asynchrony relate to a noncharacteristic view of giftedness. One premise is that disparity exists between and among intellectual ability, chronological age, and physical ability (Sternberg, 1988a). The second notion is that asynchrony intensifies as IQ increases (Sternberg, 1988b). These complex concepts are difficult to quantify and make giftedness a unique variation of the human condition. One of the major underpinnings of the Gifted Identity Formation model is this intricate view of giftedness. The model rests heavily on a noncharacteristic view of giftedness, but does not exclude the use of characteristic descriptors to understand the gifted population. In our model, characteristics are defined, used at pertinent interludes for general understanding, and then carefully discussed in a manner tailored to each individual in therapy.

Clinicians are likely to utilize descriptive traits when identifying characteristics of the gifted individual, because they are fluid and allow for a range in qualitative descriptive analysis. Traits have been used as descriptors by others in the field (Kearney, 1992) in a manner that reflects the depth and complexity of gifted identity. By identifying the characteristics of giftedness, clinicians can evaluate the perceptions of an individual struggling with complex and varying degrees of giftedness. Characteristics related to giftedness become evident when gifted clients articulate their experiences of being gifted. These characteristics reflect the unique development of each gifted individual's identity. The Gifted Identity Formation model uses these characteristics to move clinicians from a simplistic psychoeducational approach to a more descriptive methodology that is enriching and reflexive in nature. Therefore, in this model, development and integration of a client's characteristics of giftedness must be accounted for as variables in the development of self-identity across the lifespan (Mahoney, 1998).

Assumptions

In the Gifted Identify Formation model, assumptions regarding giftedness have been developed across four basic constructs (see Figure 8.1). These constructs represent some of the forces or underpinnings that shape and influence the formation of gifted identity. There is no distinct order for the four constructs, although they may in fact be sequential. These four constructs—validation, affirmation, affiliation, and affinity—represent important building blocks in the development of self (Mahoney, 1998).

Validation
Validation is an acknowledgement of a deviation of human behaviors, emotions, cognitions, and sensitivities. Dabrowski's Theory of Positive Disintegration (Davis & Rimm, 1998) refers to these as overexcitabilities that reflect developmental potential. Validation is an acknowledgement that one's giftedness exists, as corroborated by others or by oneself. It originates from acknowledgement from significant relationships, such as with the self, parents, teachers, institutions, and persons in positions of authority. Gifted individuals

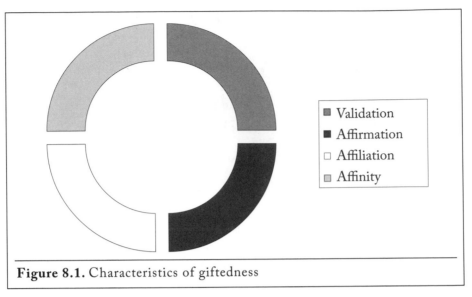

Figure 8.1. Characteristics of giftedness

are dependent on these relationships as sources of validation. Although giftedness can be validated through academic evaluation, the acknowledgment of giftedness by significant others and/or exceptional personal accomplishments facilitates personal growth. Individuals who are not validated for their giftedness are likely to suffer from low motivation and define their giftedness in a limited manner.

Affirmation

Affirmation assumes giftedness is integrated internally (intrapersonal) and externally (interpersonal) during a gifted individual's identity development. It focuses on the whole individual, but does not diminish isolation. Giftedness is a complex and varied aspect of a gifted individual's nature, and nurture has an impact on it. Affirmation means acknowledgment and reinforcement of giftedness by many significant individuals or processes, including enriched learning experiences, environment, and ongoing interaction with the world.

Affiliation

Affiliation means associating with individuals with similar interests while being integrated into a group without loss of identity. It refers to opportunities for gifted individuals to connect with a community that is supportive of their giftedness.

Affinity

Each individual needs to connect with the world to fulfill life goals, and affinity refers to this connection. The lack of affinity creates anguish, makes life tenuous, and inhibits the process of gifted-identity development. Affinity provides appropriate challenge and stimulation for developing gifted attributes. Without an awareness of affinity needs, and if affinity needs are not met, a gifted individual may feel powerless and alienated. Affinity can drive affiliation and development of the giftedness, and it can relieve the existential angst associated with being gifted. Without affinity, there is no shelter from the harsh, nonspiritual aspects of the world.

Conception of Personality

Personality

Varied personality development can frequently be evident in the life of a single child (Davis & Rimm, 1998). Personality traits are fluid and not fixed. Development of a personality is cumulative and changes within the context of social contacts, new experiences, and sociohistorical changes. When working with children, we believe that trust, sense of self, and independence are the most important characteristics of personality. Children develop trust when they have a feeling of physical comfort and a minimal amount of fear and apprehension about the future. Such status allows children to view their world as a good and pleasant place to live. If, for some reason, their parents are separated or divorced under conflicting circumstances and there is no longer a caring, warm, and consistent environment, mistrust develops. However, children can again change, once they experience a trustworthy environment.

After gaining trust in their caregivers, children discover that their behavior is their own, and they then begin to assert themselves. They realize their will and develop a sense of self and independence. At an early age, they identify who they are and what makes them different from everyone else. They cling to this identity and, as they continue to construct themselves and their personality, they begin to feel secure in the knowledge that their identity is becoming more stable. Real or imagined, the sense of self is a strong motivating force in life. Children are motivated to do, at their own pace, what they are capable of doing. However, when caregivers are impatient and do for children what they are capable of doing themselves, excessive fear and apprehension develop about their ability to control themselves and their world. Nevertheless, as these children develop their personality and move into adolescence, they may have the courage to be independent individuals who can choose and guide their own future. Their personality can change again if the environment changes, of course.

Personality of Gifted Individuals

Early personality development of gifted children is often affected by changes in interest and opportunity. Precocious language skills probably affect relationships with peers, and it is critical that the gifted child's abilities be recognized and acknowledged. It is difficult for the personality to develop positively when there is a negative focus on differences in vocabulary and modes of expression (Roedell, 1984). Similarly, some gifted children may possess advanced social cognitive skills, but not demonstrate these skills in their social interactions. For example, a gifted child may understand how to solve social conflicts and interact cooperatively, but not know how to translate this cognitive understanding into concrete socially acceptable behaviors. Adults are confused when observing a young child who is discussing the meaning of death and at the same time fighting with a peer over a toy or hitting a peer because a pencil was stolen.

Gifted children's personality development reflects the complex nature of giftedness. These individuals have widely varying interests, skill levels, social development, and physical abilities. Their uneven development can be frustrating and unpleasant for them and others, and they may lack coping skills. Gifted children often have high internal expectations and enter school ready to learn concepts that are beyond the understanding of their peer group. These gifted children require nurturing appropriate to their unusual abilities. Like other children, gifted children want friends, but they discover that a developmentally equivalent peer is hard to find. Their best friends may not be in the neighborhood, but instead far across town, with parents unable to arrange convenient visits. Being restricted from appropriate opportunities and encounters may actually stunt the personality development of gifted children. Significant adults need to understand them and become their advocates so that they may be socially and emotionally successful.

Gifted children's needs for differentiation are often clearly evident, but ignored by adults (Rogers, 1992). Gifted children have significant needs for stimulation, which today's busy parents can perceive as excessively demanding. For example, most of the parents of our gifted adolescent clients describe their world as a constant frenzy, running from activity to activity while juggling a chaotic marriage and demanding jobs. Having a gifted child who seeks constant stimulation is often seen as an inconvenience or hindrance, especially if the child disturbs this chaotic existence further.

Gifted children often "do not fit" with their age peers in personality development. In peer relationships they may constantly monitor their own thoughts, words, and behavior. It is difficult for them to find kindred spirits. It is an interesting fact of American life that children are forced to associate largely with individuals who are of their same age. For gifted children, these peer associations are often devoid of love and acceptance. Therefore, nurture, commitment of time, and love in the home environment are critical for personality development.

Early personality development in gifted children is different from the typical personality development of other children. Gifted children may have enhanced intellectual development and perceptual skills, but may lack in social and personality development (Schultz, 2000). A gifted child is most vulnerable during the early development of personality, and primary caregivers can be confused or unaware of the child's giftedness. Parents of gifted children often do

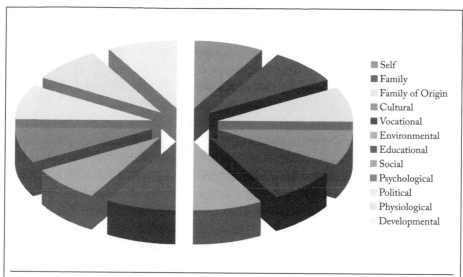

Figure 8.2. Self-exploration constructs

not understand giftedness. The child may face being different from a peer group and at the same time experience a lack of understanding and support from parents and other significant adults. This situation is not optimal for personality development. However, gifted children are often resilient and can overcome these early challenges and develop a strong ego. The child who is identified as gifted in the early years and nurtured accordingly has an opportunity to develop a personality characterized by creativity, good social skills, and enthusiasm.

We have identified 12 systems that influence the personality development of gifted students. These systems represent the internal and external forces that impact identity formation and the development of individual giftedness. The Gifted Identity Formation model requires the clinician to explore each system in order to understand how the gifted personality has developed. The model challenges the gifted individual to apply these systems in self-exploration (Mahoney, 1998; see Figure 8.2):

1. *Self System*: This system refers to the individual's values and beliefs. It includes the perception of how the gifted individual is viewed by others.
2. *Family System*: This system includes the immediate family, spouse, parents, siblings, children, and partners.
3. *Family of Origin System*: This system refers to the values, beliefs, and traditions held by past generations of the extended family.
4. *Cultural System*: This system includes the definition of giftedness in the context of heritage, gender, race, religion and ethnicity.
5. *Vocational System*: This system refers to career choice, career development, occupation, and the type of vocational exposure of the gifted individual.
6. *Environmental System*: This system refers to the environment of the gifted individual and the impact of that environment on personality formation.

7. *Educational System*: This system refers to the gifted individual's formal or informal education.
8. *Social System*: This system involves significant relationships with peers, family, and community.
9. *Psychological System*: This system refers to personality development and to the psychological impact of being gifted.
10. *Political System:* This system refers to political agendas that impact the gifted individual.
11. *Organic Physiological System*: This system explores areas where there is a behavioral or physiological relationship with one's giftedness.
12. *Developmental System*: This system represents the life-cycle development of the gifted individual.

The 12 systems are the forces that have impact on the development of the gifted identity.

Many of these systems simultaneously interface and overlap. It is the exploration of these complex variables that contribute to the understanding of personality development.

Model of Counseling

Influences

A delicate interplay occurs in the development of a gifted person's identity. How an individual integrates and develops giftedness has ramifications for his entire lifespan and quality of life. Counseling offers an appropriate context for understanding identity formation so that needs may be met.

Training of counselors, regardless of whether the approach is Rogerian, cognitive behavioral, or systemic, generally emphasizes the nature of the relationship (Gladding, 2004). The context in which therapy is most effective includes a caring and competent provider. The skills associated with these models are often enhanced by a thorough knowledge of assessment, including projective and personality measures. The key to successful treatment is proper assessment and diagnosis.

The Gifted Identity Formation model is influenced by systemic concepts including family-of-origin work by James Framo (1982), the affective focus of Virginia Satir (1985), change strategies of both structural and systemic therapies, and the resilience theory of the Wolins (1993). These systemic concepts help identify, explain, and frame the vulnerability and isolation of the gifted individual. By having vulnerability identified, the gifted individual is able to listen to a message of hope. In our view, gifted individuals are often socially deficient and strive for intimacy. Much of the therapeutic encounter is a demonstration of intimacy, with intimacy needs simultaneously identified.

Definition of Counseling

Counselors of gifted individuals should be aware of the variance of the deviation that giftedness represents and the complexity of identity formation. The Gifted Identity Formation model accommodates, adjusts for, and accounts for the variance among gifted clients. Counseling involves a multitude of roles, processes, interventions, and options based on a variety of theoretical orientations (Gladding, 2002). Counseling gifted individuals must involve a variety of modes of intervention and process in response to the complexity of gifted persons and the needs they bring to the counseling process. The Gifted Identify Formation model allows counselors to utilize the following extended roles and approaches:

* consultation,
* formalized counseling/psychotherapeutic process,
* mentoring,
* teaching,
* advocacy, and
* alternative therapies.

Role of Counselor

A collaborative and expansive role for the counselor is appropriate for addressing the complexity of the gifted client. Our model requires the counselor to use a more fluid and flexible approach to counseling than that used with typical clients. The multiplicity of complex needs of gifted clients often requires multiple, complex interventions. For example, in the case of a gifted underachieving client, Sternberg (1988b) states clearly that no one intervention is sufficient. A multitude of interventions and approaches are required to reverse patterns of underachievement. In a case involving a gifted child with a learning disability, the role of the counselor may expand to consultant, teacher, and advocate. In addition, the understated nature of the child's situation may enlarge the role of the counselor into areas such as academic tutoring or mentoring.

The counselor has a crucial role in the validation of the gifted individual's self-perception and perception of giftedness. When gifted clients come to counseling, they often see themselves as disenfranchised. Many have been unable to perform at a level that matches how they view their ability. Such gifted clients may question whether they are gifted, and these doubts have impact on self-esteem, self-concept, and performance at many levels.

Because counselors play a crucial role in the validation process, and because giftedness is viewed as variations of extremes in human nature, they need to assess their own value structures as they relate to deviance in human nature. It is a common human experience to struggle with others' deviant behavior and make negative judgments. The intense alienation and isolation that are commonly experienced by gifted clients are directly related to being different from the norm in many ways. If the counselor has not examined his or her attitudes toward deviance, then those biases will likely be projected onto the client in the counseling process. Counselors may deny their negative views about the deviance of giftedness. Gifted individuals are able, in most cases, to recognize when they are being judged negatively for their deviant nature. When these judgments and unexplored values emerge, the counselor must openly acknowledge them in order to help facilitate change. If judgments are addressed openly and as being related to the client's struggle, then trust may develop.

Counselors who utilize only one orientation may not be effective when working with giftedness, due to its complex nature. If counselors rigidly adhere to a specific theoretical approach in counseling the gifted population, they may find that the population they serve will become limited to a specific type of gifted individual. We encourage counselors to expand their repertoire of available theoretical approaches. Having a variety available may help to address the complexity of clients. The Gifted Identity Formation model helps counselors adjust various theoretical approaches to gifted clients.

Role of Client

The gifted clients need to identify aspects of their development that have caused difficulties and confusion in the identify formation. They also need to be willing to do the following:
*   identify their goals for counseling,
*   share the roadblocks to these goals and their strengths to defeat these roadblocks,
*   believe they can be more effective and in control of their personal lives,
*   change their defeating behaviors, and
*   be truthful and communicate openly (Mahoney, 1998).

Goals

The following questions were the impetus for the evolution of the Gifted Identity Formation model:
*   How do we adjust models of counseling for the variance associated with giftedness so that these methodologies are appropriate for the complexity of gifted individuals and so that these clients embrace it?
*   How do we provide counseling in a manner that systematically manages the magnitude of variables and complexities associated with giftedness without compromising the counseling process?

The primary goals of this model are as follows:
*   assist the client in the process of identity formation;

- work toward fulfilling and aligning the four constructs of identity formation (validation, affirmation, affiliation, affinity) within a framework that is congruent with the client's identity and gifted attributes;
- support and respect the client in a manner that reflects the individual's gifted identity;
- provide the client with an opportunity to utilize gifts when and if possible, based on an informed decision to do so;
- move counselors, teachers, parents, and other professionals from a simplistic or traditional linear view of working with the gifted to a complex model that reflects the diversity of the gifted population; and
- provide the counselor with a framework that accounts for the variance associated with giftedness for assessing, guiding, and intervening in the counseling process.

Relationship

The Gifted Identity Formation model examines people's strengths and affirms them in the initial stages of the first interview. Within the counseling relationship, the counselor challenges the client to move away from the role of victim and interact in a functional manner with external environments. This counseling process helps the client to develop resiliency and to recognize that his or her life is full of opportunity. At the same time, it is important to help the client identify the pain and loneliness of being gifted and develop skills necessary to connect with a community. This desire to have emotional connections is also the core of counselor-client interaction. Self-disclosure by the client helps to develop a trust that is based on willingness to be vulnerable. It is important that gifted clients feel free to share their greatest fears. The counseling relationship ideally provides a safe and trusted environment for sharing.

Assessment

The Gifted Identity Formation model uses available forms of assessment and evaluation information. The counselor provides a gifted client profile based on school and family demographics, achievement test scores, intelligence test scores, and artifacts such as drawings, software, poems, or songs. The Gifted Identify Formation model is applied after an individual's giftedness is confirmed. The model then provides a guide for interventions and facilitates the counseling process. Giftedness is assessed on a continuum of human behavior. The four constructs (validation, affirmation, affiliation, and affinity) provide a framework for assessing identity development. Each construct is assessed according to 12 systems: self, family, family of origin, cultural, vocational, environmental, educational, social, psychological, political, physiological, and developmental. As gifted identity is deconstructed and enhanced, areas of strength are noted.

Process

The initial phase of the counseling process involves understanding how the gifted individual perceives and conceptualizes self in relation to gifted attributes. This involves an assessment of how a client is gifted and what role that giftedness played in the motivation to seek counseling. The Gifted Identity Formation model provides a framework for examining basic perceptions on a continuum of struggles that may seriously exacerbate psychological symptoms and/or neurophysiologic distress (e.g., disturbances such as depression)—in short, how their giftedness impacts overall well-being and development. We believe that most gifted clients seek counseling because they are experiencing distress related to their giftedness. One of the underlying assumptions of The Gifted Identity Formation model is that when giftedness is not validated, affirmed, affiliated, and met with affinity, lack of gifted identity development can result in a form of disturbance to self.

Techniques

It is the counselor's task to begin the process of helping the gifted individual understand giftedness and integrate it into the view of self. The counselor focuses on the immediate family, taking into consideration the variances within cultures and cultural differences regarding how giftedness is constructed. Collaboratively, the client and counselor explore how the family interfaces with the giftedness of its members. The values, beliefs, and traditions held by the family of origin play a large role in how people experience and contend with giftedness. Each of these variables reflects how giftedness is perceived.

Through the relationship, an integral part of counseling, the clinician nurtures the client's gifts. The therapy focuses on discussions about environmental systems that include, for example, a child's room at home, the cubicle at work, geographic considerations, and the raw materials available to be creative. The counselor explores both traditional and nontraditional educational environments. It is important for the clinician to examine the educational system as it relates to the identity of the gifted client, because the educational system often tends to define giftedness in only an academic context.

Later, when appropriate and feasible, group work can offer a context for socialization in which the clinician facilitates a connection to others and, potentially, to raised self-esteem, which in turn can impact future social interactions and coping ability. This socialization within a group includes complex defenses, ego, and individual character. The group eventually begins to communicate attitudes regarding giftedness. The purpose of the group is to help the gifted individual assess and understand how giftedness is related to his or her identity.

Group members may help each other to answer questions and concerns related to how their physiology is connected to their sense of self. Benbow

(1986) has shown that some physiological traits occur more frequently in extremely able students than in others. She found the traits of left or mixed handedness, myopia, and symptomatic atopic disease (asthma and other allergies) among extremely mathematically and verbally precocious students. Often, changes such as entering adolescence, the birth of a child, and individuation and separation from the family are discussed in the group. Learning to understand other group members' developmental process can help gifted individuals understand their own asynchronous development (Silverman, 1998).

As the group matures and healthy relationships develop, the change process begins. Through this extensive journey of self-discovery, gifted individuals begin to develop appropriate social skills. Understanding one's self is critical to understanding others' behavior.

Graphic Representation of Model

The graphic representation of the model helps the therapist to document the extent to which the identity development constructs (validation, affirmation, affiliation, and affinity) interact with the 12 basic systems that impact the gifted individual. The chart helps identify these connections and provides critical information for development of the treatment plan (see Figure 8.3).

Application

Presenting Problems

We have a combined history of more than 80 years in the fields of psychology and counseling. Beyond developing successful private practices, the authors have had experiences with gifted individuals in roles such as school principal, curriculum director/associate superintendent, director of four university clinics, evaluator of large inner-city grant projects, supervisors of hundreds of graduate students, and presenters at both national and international conventions. The types of issues that gifted individuals have presented during our clinical work are many, but most of our child and adolescent gifted clients have displayed problems such as school underachievement, isolation, aggression, sexual promiscuity, stealing or conduct disorder, truancy, drug abuse, drug selling, relationship difficulties, sexual identity issues, anxiety, depression, thought disorders, and adjustment disorders. Although elaboration on these problems is beyond the scope of this chapter, it is important to note that giftedness affects treatment regardless of issue and that gifted individuals are rarely exempt from any disorder that affects the rest of humankind. In fact, we might argue that the gifted are more miserable than most others in this world, because of their sense of differentness.

GIFM GRID	VALIDATION	AFFIRMATION	AFFILIATION	AFFINITY
SELF				
FAMILY				
FAMILY OF ORIGIN				
CULTURAL				
VOCATIONAL				
ENVIRONMENTAL				
EDUCATIONAL				
SOCIAL				
PSYCHOLOGICAL				
POLITICAL				
PHYSIOLOGICAL				
DEVELOPMENTAL				

Figure 8.3. Gifted Identity Formation Model (Mahoney, 1998)

Criteria for being accepted as clients in our practice have varied through the years. When beginning a practice, if making a living is a prime concern, clinicians often accept almost any client. In addition, supervisors often place with interns difficult cases that other clinicians have long abandoned, labeling the situation as a learning experience. In recent years, we have become more stringent in our criteria for accepting someone for counseling, recognizing that aggressive children and those with conduct disorders are difficult for anyone to treat, particularly if they are gifted. The gifted sociopath has likely been brutalized and sexually assaulted by family members and relatives and is not a candidate for our practice. In addition, we rarely treat sexual offenders because they are a unique population more appropriate for a practice devoted entirely to abused children. However, we have provided consultation to fellow clinicians who have sought guidance regarding the role of giftedness in the aberrant behavior of clients with conduct disorder and clients who are sexual predators.

Case Illustration

The client in this case is a 17-year-old gifted male adolescent who is considered to be experiencing an adjustment disorder with depressive symptoms. He is a senior in high school and has done well academically. However, he is lonely and has always lacked a social group of peers. He rarely has participated in extracurricular activities until this year, when he began involvement in the drama department. His parents are divorced, but highly supportive. He is the second child of several siblings and stepsiblings. Like many gifted children, he suppresses many of his thoughts, feelings, and behaviors with his peer group in order to be socially accepted. This is the fourth session, and it begins with the client unable to understand how his abilities are factors in his struggle for affiliation. We begin with the client's feelings of abandonment.

Co: This idea of what you're calling "a sense of abandonment." There are two things going on. You have some awareness that your beliefs are changing. Secondly, you've got some realization that you're talking a lot in school to fill space. You're saying you're doing this out of a sense of abandonment.

Cl: That's not the cause. It's more what I feel when I think about it. I think I can put it better. It's more out of a sense of loneliness and isolation, but if I sit there and I don't talk, I feel like just another person. But when I do talk, it's not any better because I feel that people are just thinking of me as a set of behaviors that aren't even me.

The client is beginning to clarify the way he is behaving in school. Talking a lot is a manifestation of his deeper feelings of loneliness and isolation, which he had formerly identified as abandonment. He also is angry, and it is possible that when he talks in class, he also wants to get back at classmates and his teachers. His pain is evident.

Co: It sounds then that you're invalidated.
Cl: Uh huh. Stabbing myself at every turn.

The client demonstrates here how deeply he internalizes the pain of not being able to affiliate with others. He is stabbing at himself and others.

Co: So you're expecting these people to understand and relate to you on the level that you're relating to them.

The therapist is helping the client clarify his expectations that people should understand him before he understands others. That expectation is another way the client externalizes responsibility for his struggle and defends against facing its complexity as it relates to his high level of giftedness. In some ways he is not being honest with his peers because he is angry with them.

Cl: I'm not really expecting them to. I'm just feeling disappointed if they don't even know I've set it up so they couldn't possibly—well, I guess they could, possibly. I've set up an unreal situation to keep undermining myself, I think.

The client is beginning to struggle with the reality that he has actually set up a dynamic where he is placing unrealistic expectations on others. He starts by blaming himself for a lack of understanding of why he is doing this, which relates to his earlier comment about "stabbing myself at every turn." He is vacillating between blaming others for not understanding him to, now, blaming himself for creating the dynamic.

Co: I hear you, but there's something missing in the equation.
Cl: Fear? Anger? Happiness?
Co: No. It's none of those things. It has to do with the audience or the classmates or the set of people or the individuals you're trying to relate to [*all fall under the category of affiliates*] and whether or not you're assuming they could actually relate with you. You're assuming they have the same level of interests, same level of desire, same level of intellectual precocity, same level of understanding of material. When they don't reciprocate, that sets off your feelings of abandonment and loneliness. Then you go back and attribute it to—what?
Cl: Fears of loneliness and abandonment I attribute to loss. I go in a full circle of—Yeah, I see what you mean. My mind has liked to ignore that fact, hasn't it, that maybe it's not that they don't want to relate to me or communicate to me; it's just that they can't. Or even if they did have the mental capability to, they'd be afraid to or wouldn't be ready to.

Most therapists might interpret what the client just described as arrogant or elitist. It is not. The client clearly has to get to a point where he can distinguish a distinct difference in the way gifted people relate. He attaches negative emotions and a negative view of self to a situation where peers are not malicious but simply without the skills to understand him.

Cl: I'm using my different level or trend of thinking, which is so different than theirs, I guess. Most people wouldn't be able to relate to me, and then I feel disappointed when everybody can't. I expect everybody to be able to understand me.

Co: Which speaks to what about your self-awareness?

This is the client's first clear realization in regard to loneliness as related to giftedness and why he is struggling so intensely. He is beginning to formulate a new concept. He is beginning to gain a perspective about himself as it pertains to affiliation with others in a social system. This is actually the point in the therapy when change may occur.

Cl: It makes it seem that I try to use other people to define my self-aware-ness. I try to go through other people to understand myself, [and I] let their reactions to the things I'm saying dictate the way I think about if the things I'm saying matter.

This statement is indicative of self-validation and affirmation as it pertains to the self and social system. Everyone needs to feel accepted and understood.

Co: It sounds like that process doesn't work for you.

Cl: No, it doesn't. Because they're not really in a position to invalidate what I'm saying, and yet I let them. I'm giving them too much power over me. I'm giving everybody too much power over me because I don't really want it myself. Then I would really have to deal with myself instead of trying to make other people deal with me.

The client has come to an understanding of self and validation.

Co: Dealing with you would include—?

Cl: Recognizing how I feel.

Co: If I asked you how you feel, my sense is we'd go back into that cycle, and again you wouldn't talk about what the issues are around why you feel that way, even though you can identify how you feel quite readily.

Cl: I'm doing it again.

Co: What is "it" that you're doing?

Cl: I'm using understanding to shield myself again.

Co: From what? Shield?

Cl: What do you mean, "shield"? I'm using my shield to avoid understand-ing my shield?

Co: You said you're shielding yourself again.

The client is the teacher here—the therapist is not the expert. The therapist needs to understand the term the client is using. The therapist is asking the client to define his defensive posture—his "shield." The client wanted the therapist to define the term, and the therapist turned the question/challenge back to the client. This all occurred very subtly when the client responded to the therapist, "What do you mean, 'shield'?" as if the therapist used the word first. If the therapist had "taken the bait," the client would have been rescued from exploring his defensive posture.

Cl: Uh huh. Stop using that word. Well, abusing that word.

Co: Sounds like some aspect of yourself that you're not acknowledging. You started to talk about it, and you acknowledged that on some level people couldn't relate to whatever words you used. And then you moved away from saying more about that, and you went back into your feelings around isolation, loneliness, and feeling less worthy.

Cl: Yeah, OK. I see what you mean now. I think what I'm doing is I'm avoiding thinking about how I have trouble interacting with people instead of focusing on these feelings that I can't just by themselves do anything about. Ignoring why I'm really feeling these things—trying to explain why I feel.

Co: Talk about your feelings of isolation.

The therapist is challenging the client to move further into exploring his feelings. The counselor is trying to hold the client accountable, not to just identify his feelings, but also to express them and to explore them on a deeper level, so that the client can begin to understand how they relate to his struggle with being gifted and, in turn, affect his ability to form affiliations with both gifted and nongifted people.

Cl: I see what you mean now. I think what I'm doing is avoiding thinking about how I have trouble interacting with people instead of focusing on these feelings that, just by them, I can't do anything about. Ignoring why I really feel these things. I've been trying to explain why I have these feelings. Which isn't possible.

The client is admitting here that he has not really explored the depth of his trouble interacting with people, and the therapist is moving him toward discovering the function of his avoidance. He is still avoiding his anger and hurt, and with those feelings comes a large amount of negative thinking, which negates his gifts and himself.

Co: What function does that behavior serve for you?

Cl: It makes me not have to face that there are going to be very few people who can relate to me the way I need to be related to, and I don't want to face that. Instead I try to focus on the way I feel so I don't have to do anything about it.

For the first time, the client admits that his isolation and loneliness have something to do with his gifted identity. This is a crucial awareness. Prior to this point, the client's belief system was that the trouble he was having with social affiliations was not related to any aspect of his being gifted. What is important for the counselor to know, and what makes this type of counseling session different from working with conventional problems with affiliation and socialization, is the client's level of awareness regarding the root of why he is not able to experience affiliation. Once he can identify that being gifted creates unique challenges concerning affiliation, the process differs from conventional counseling. The client will not be able to progress to the next phase without this understanding. In actuality, if this part of the counseling did not reconcile the client with his giftedness, the counseling would inevitably hit an impasse and possibly produce more feelings of isolation and loneliness. Not only would the client think his peers couldn't affiliate and understand him; he would also believe that the therapist could not. This approach moves him out of victim status, and he can begin to realize that he is in control of his life, mood, thoughts, and behavior. He can find friends, but it will require hard work.

Co: So you can express how you feel, but it's not connected to the real reason you're feeling that way. So you don't have to deal with the fact that you can't find people that can really relate to you.

Cl: So probably people that can relate to me, I assume that, well, I don't know if this is true, but it could be that I am seeking out people that won't be able to understand me. Well, actually, I don't think it's true.

Co: I don't think it's true either. And I'm glad that you acknowledge that it isn't true.

Cl: Yeah. It didn't seem right to me. I think it's just a way of me . . .

Co: Well, I think you're judging your quest for seeking people, and I think it's totally appropriate for you to seek out people.

Cl: Yeah, I was contradicting it by focusing on something else again.

Co: Rather than starting to realize that this process of seeking out like minds is quite a challenge for you. It brings up all these issues around your loneliness and isolation that have been relevant to your life up to this point. It's a lack of awareness as to why you've been so lonely and isolated.

Cl: Yeah, I'm skittering away from the issue every single way I can.

Co: And the issue is . . .

Cl: OK. The issue is that I cannot find people that I can relate to fully and who I feel can understand and accept me for who I am.

Co: And who are you?

The client has progressed considerably since the session began. The fact that so early in the session he has been able to take on and integrate this issue clearly reflects the giftedness of the client. The therapist can now delve even further into issues surrounding the client's identity.

Cl: I don't know.

Co: You've just shut down.

In actuality, the client didn't "shut down." He actually became introspective, as is evident in his next statement.

Cl: Yes. I'm a very bright person who is very sensitive to a lot of things and who feels a deep need to help people and to be understood.

Co: What's it like for you to say that?

The therapist is asking the client to explore his feelings around professing his identity—to discuss what it is like to validate his own identity as a gifted person. The qualities he described are characteristics of giftedness. He has obviously experienced this sensitivity and need. Therefore, much of this session is not really new to this client. It may be seen as an unveiling of his gifted self that he knew to be there. It is important that I affirm him and that he realizes he is special. It is appropriate and good to have pride.

Cl: It's kind of frightening because not only am I realizing that's true; I'm realizing that I don't want to admit that it's true. I don't want to admit that I'm unique and that it's going to be hard for people to relate to me because I'm different from them in a lot of ways.

Co: And that's frightening.

The therapist is simply reflecting the client's fright. However, this therapeutic "event" is of great magnitude in assisting the client in his struggle with social affiliation. Reflecting feelings, without interpretation, oftentimes is the key to unlocking even more awareness. This simple use of reflection of feelings, when done appropriately, can move the client forward significantly. It is a rare event when someone reflects feelings, instead of reflecting content, advising, interpreting, fixing, rescuing, or preventing feelings.

Cl: Yes, it is. I think what I've been doing in response to feeling that way is instead of realizing that I am different and I have different thoughts and trying to find people who can understand me for who I am, I've been trying to change myself or hide myself in order to be accepted by people who I don't feel could really accept who I am, whether that is true or not.

The client is realizing how deeply engrained his defenses are against, and his feelings are about, being different, and how those defenses are functioning in his relationships with others.

Co: Can you say more about this process of hiding yourself?

Cl: Yes. I feel a lot of negativity when I talk about the way I feel and the way I think. I get a lot of negative reinforcement. Like people are going to say that some of it is true and some of it is imaginary and created by me. But for whatever reason, I don't often talk about things that really matter to me. I don't try to relate to people on my own level. I try to relate on theirs. I spend very little time focusing on myself in conversations—well, no time, almost. I try to relate to everybody by focusing on who they are, their needs, their desires, thus ignoring myself and creating a very bad relationship which is dependent on them.

Here the client is acknowledging his own compensation strategies. He is also indirectly acknowledging how much he is giving up in relationships, particularly with other gifted people.

> **Co:** It sounds like a lot of that evolves out of your desire to be understood. And yet it leads you to be totally misunderstood, because you won't express your real self, and the things that are really important to you. This is the paradox of when people desperately need others and change who they are to be accepted. Quickly, they become resentful.
>
> **Cl:** Or when I do try to express them occasionally, I quickly back down and allow myself to be completely diverted. Because it's so hard for me to talk about things, about myself, because I think the other person wouldn't understand. So I give up and I run away.
>
> **Co:** What are you thinking?
>
> **Cl:** I'm thinking a few things. That I have quite a bit more self-awareness now, and I'm realizing how much this has been impacting my actions and how it will impact my actions now.

The client has made a major breakthrough. He is now able to conceptualize his struggle in relationship to his social system and affiliation.

> **Cl:** I'm also kind of uneasy because this is a lot for me to face, for me to deal with, because it is a very frightening thing that I've never dealt with before. That there will not be very many people that I will be able to relate to and who can relate to me and understand me and I understand them. And the other thing is . . .

He is beginning to strategize how he is going to implement this new awareness—and integrate it—without any direct intervention or advice from the therapist. In the next statement, the therapist's language reflects basic tenets of counseling: recognizing the client's strengths and calling attention to positive movement.

> **Co:** You talk about it, though, as though it's in the future. And yet it's happening already.
>
> **Cl:** Yes.
>
> **Co:** I want to go back to the part where you were frightened about facing this awareness.
>
> **Cl:** Yeah. I think that what really is scaring me is feeling that in most of my relationships with other people I have right now and have had in the past, I've been not actually able to relate to a person on the level that I need. That's a really frightening thought. It doesn't really make me feel alone. Yeah, it makes me feel alone.
>
> **Co:** Sounds like there is more that it does to you.

Typically I change the word *make* to *choose* to enable client responsibility. I did not do that here because I did not want to divert attention away from his new awareness.

CI: I guess it makes me feel like the relationships that I've had with people are less real or less meaningful, in a way. Because almost all my relationships, I've just had them on a distant, superficial level. A great example of that is my cousin Steve, who is one of my best friends. Until about two months ago, I had never talked to him at all about anything real. Ever.

The client refers to benefits to the relationship with his cousin in response to earlier work in sessions.

Co: It sounds like about two months ago you talked to him about something more real, then?

CI: Yeah. On the phone I got this intense . . . like a prelude to the realization of what I'm realizing now.

The therapist knows that good therapy is a client learning what he already knows, but the function of the therapist is to help bring this knowledge to a greater awareness, integration, and availability for the client's later reference.

CI: I've realized how dysfunctional, in a way, our relationship was, and how, although we'd done lots and lots of stuff together, we didn't really understand each other more than a vague kind of companionship. So I talked about it and then after I chiseled through 30,000 tons of ice and humor and such, I finally kind of got through to him. Now, although we kind of avoid it off and on, now we kind of realize it, and we're a lot closer to each other. We have some kind of mutual, real understanding relationship. Now it makes me realize how little of that I've done in my life and how few relationships I have that are like that. Most of the relationships that I've had I've tried to change myself for the other person. I've tried to change myself into what I thought the person I was talking to or relating to could understand. Putting it on a level that I thought they could understand, but not even that, not even explaining myself, just going into topics that I thought I could relate to them with while remaining distant.

Not only does the client clarify his defenses, he is able to grasp a fundamental core truth that he can access later. The client indicates that he is one step ahead of the therapist. A key ingredient to working with gifted individuals is recognizing their ability, because they may be, in many ways, more intellectually nimble than the therapist. However, the therapist—or teacher or counselor— must be able to affirm his or her own professional expertise and life experience and not be intimidated by them or in awe of them. Those adults must recognize that gifted clients/students are also developing, and that they need assistance, like anyone, maybe more so, in the process of development.

Co: So far, you sound like you're getting a bit of an overview or understanding of what is happening to you. But you've not yet said anything about future possibilities of having more connectedness or mutual affinity with people.

CI: Ah. What a coincidence.

Co: You don't talk about that as a possibility yet.

Cl: Yeah, you're right. I have been talking about all this as though I was kind of trapped in it. I guess what I need to do is analyze how I relate to people and figure out all these little ways of changing myself to fit the mold of what I think they would accept of me. I'm going to try to stop doing that and allow myself to be who I am without putting up all these shields of trying to assimilate. Now that I've said that, which makes me think that it was bothering me, I feel much, much better. I feel kind of free, released and not shoved into a little box that I've created for myself. It's still very confusing and very frightening, since I'm still very much getting used to it, but it's making me feel very optimistic.

The client is realizing that he is not limited in terms of how he affiliates with others—differing from his earlier statements that it was going to be with very few people. Even though he is still highly gifted, and the number of people he can relate with may be limited at some level, he is realizing that it is not an impossible task for him to find social affiliation.

Co: What is it that is making you feel optimistic?
Cl: Realizing that I don't have to change myself to be accepted or that I can't change myself to try to be accepted allows me to be free not to try to undermine my self-confidence based on other people's opinions of me—or what I perceive other people's opinions of me [to be].

Even if this client regresses from this powerful acknowledgement of some sort of change here, the fact that during this session he has been able to come to this level of awareness—that he does not have to change himself to be acceptable for affiliation—shows the potential for him to integrate and continue this growth. The fact that he has been able to come to this point so quickly may in some ways be deceiving because it is so rapid. With the gifted client, the change might be even more deceiving than with an average-range client. In actuality, the gifted client may be able to integrate this change as rapidly as it appears to have been integrated in this session. For an average-ability client, a counselor would have to be concerned that the change occurring in this session would not be thoroughly integrated so immediately.

Co: Now that you're acknowledging this or are more aware of this dynamic process that you've been involved in, why aren't you falling back right at this moment into your feelings of abandonment and isolation and helplessness that you were expressing at the beginning?
Cl: Because I've realized that I don't need those things and I need to be hugging those things into me like some evil teddy bear? Those feelings are just things I'm creating to hurt myself. They're not real things that serve any purpose. They're just me undermining myself and hurting myself. Now that I realize what I've been using them for, I have no desire to feel them any more, and therefore I don't.

This transcript session with a highly gifted client illustrates a therapeutic process that results in raised client awareness regarding the function of giftedness in his problems with social affiliation. The therapist's interspersed comments illuminate various aspects of the session, including the intent of the therapist's questions and comments, the significance of the client's insights, and the extent of the client's remarkable, rapid integration of his new understanding of the social impact of his giftedness. The result of the efforts by both client and therapist in the session is that the client will have access to his new awareness and be able to relate to others without "shields" of anger, pain, and resentment.

Until now, the client's identity as a gifted individual has been affected by feelings of isolation and loneliness in his social context. He has sought out people who are unable to communicate with him and fundamentally has denied his gifted identity. He has attempted to adjust his behavior to fit their expectations, "hiding" himself in order to be accepted and understood and focusing on the needs of others, while ignoring his own needs. However, his inauthentic behavior, unreal self, and the accompanying superficial level of communication has left him feeling limited, insecure, lonely, unsatisfied, disappointed, unworthy, and disconnected. He has blamed others for not understanding him, and he has blamed himself for ineffective communication. He has become a victim of his own created world rather than recognizing that he can create a much better world.

The therapist helps the client explore significant feelings of loneliness and isolation early in the session, using comments and open-ended questions to encourage expression and examination of feelings and elaboration. As a result, the client is able to acknowledge that few people can relate to him easily, a reality he has attempted to deny in the past. In addition, through examining his need for affiliation and the feelings that result from his lack of connection, he is finally able to affirm his differences, essentially validating himself as a gifted person. Ironically, by embracing his differences, the client feels "released" and optimistic. In his future relationships he will likely be able to be more authentic and consequently more affiliated.

The therapist is faithful to basic counseling tenets in his work with this highly gifted individual. The focus is on client strengths, not limitations. The therapist reflects the client's feelings, thereby validating them as real and important. The therapist also pays attention to the positive movement the client is already experiencing. The emphasis is not on pathology, but on the complex reality of the client's giftedness and the problems in communication to which his differences contribute. These are problems in living, not pathology. The therapist, respectfully and collaboratively, helps the client to be released from an ineffective and unsatisfying pattern of behavior. Most important, the therapist recognizes the high ability of the client, encourages client self-direction, and affirms and challenges client growth.

Also important to note is the application of fundamental concepts related to The Gifted Identity Formation model (Mahoney, 1998). Recognizing the cross-matrix intersection of the construct "affiliation" and the system "social," as well as the client's frustrations and intense feelings surrounding social contact, helps the therapist to maintain focus on these two elements as they relate to gifted identity. The therapist does not need to identify these, per se, in the session. However, the sustained attention to these areas, including the feelings related to them, eventually moves the client to embrace an identity that includes being gifted. Integration of his new awareness into a sense of self will likely help him to relate authentically to others and find the affiliation he desires and needs.

This differentiated counseling model is offered as a starting point, a place of reflection as the field of gifted counseling embarks on new ways to view the development of gifted individuals. The model is open for review, to be challenged and potentially enhanced. This case illustration is an example of actual clinical work that utilizes the construct of giftedness in working with clients as they develop their self-identity.

References

Alverado, N. (1989). Adjustment of gifted adults. *Advanced Development, 1,* 77–86.

Benbow, C. P. (1986). Physiological correlates of extreme intellectual precocity. *Neuropsychologia, 24,* 719–725.

Bloom, B. S. (1985). *Developing talent in young people.* New York: Ballantine Books.

Brody, L. (1999). The talent searches: Counseling and mentoring activities. In N. Colangelo & S. Assouline (Eds.), *Talent development III: Proceedings from the Henry B. & Jocelyn Wallace National Research Symposium on Talent Development* (pp. 153–157). Scottsdale, AZ: Gifted Psychology Press.

Burks, B. S., Jensen, D. W., & Terman, L. M. (1930). *Genetic studies of genius, Vol. 3: The promise of youth: Follow-up of 1000 gifted children.* Stanford, CA: Stanford University Press.

Clark, B. (1997). *Growing up gifted: Developing the potential of children at home and at school.* Upper Saddle River, NJ: Merrill.

Colangelo, N., & Ogburn, K. M. (1989). Giftedness as multilevel potential. *Advanced Development, 1,* 87–100.

Csikszentmihalyi, M. (1999). Creativity across the life-span: A systems view. In N. Colangelo & S. Assouline (Eds.), *Talent development III: Proceedings from the Henry B. & Jocelyn Wallace National Research Symposium on Talent Development* (pp. 9–18). Scottsdale, AZ: Gifted Psychology Press.

Davis, G. A., & Rimm, S. B. (1998). *Education of the gifted and talented.* Boston: Allyn & Bacon.

Erikson, E. H. (1968). *Identity youth and crisis.* New York: W. W. Norton & Company.

Feldman, D. H. (1995). Parenting talented children. In M. Bornstein (Ed.), *Handbook of parenting* (pp. 285–304). New York: Longman.

Fiedler, E. (1998). Foundations for understanding the social-emotional needs of the highly gifted. *Highly Gifted Children, 12*(1), 25–30.

Framo, J. L. (1982). *Explorations in marital and family therapy: Selected papers of James L. Framo.* New York: Springer.

Gallagher, J. J. (2003). Issues and challenges in the education of gifted students. In N. Colangelo & G. A. Davis (Eds.), *Handbook of gifted education* (3rd ed., pp. 11–24). Boston: Allyn & Bacon.

Gardner, H. (1983). *Frames of mind: The theory of multiple intelligences.* New York: Basic Books.

Gardner, H. (1999). *Intelligence reframed: Multiple intelligences for the 21st century.* New York: Basic Books.

Gladding, S. (2002). *Family therapy: History, theory, and practice* (3rd ed.). Upper Saddle River, NJ: Prentice-Hall.

Gladding, S. (2004). *Introduction to family therapy.* Princeton, NJ: Pearson Publications.

Gross, M. U. M. (2000). Exceptionally and profoundly gifted students: An underserved population. *Understanding Our Gifted, 12*(2), 45–53

Hollingworth, L. S. (1926). *Gifted children: Their nature and nurture.* New York: Macmillan.

Hollingworth, L. S. (1942). *Children above 180 IQ Stanford-Binet: Origin and development.* New York: World Book.

Kearney, K. (1992). Life in the asynchronous family. *Understanding our Gifted, 4*(6), 1, 8–12.

Klein, A. G. (2000). Fitting the school to the child: The mission of Leta Stetter Hollingworth, founder of gifted education. *Roeper Review, 23,* 7–103.

Lovecky, D. V. (1986). Can you hear the flowers singing? Issues for gifted adults. *Journal of Counseling and Development, 64,* 590–592.

Lovecky, D. V. (1992). Exceptionally gifted children: Different minds. *Roeper Review, 15,* 3–4.

Mahoney, A. (1998). In search of the gifted identity. *Roeper Review, 20,* 1–13.

Rimm, S. B. (1990). *How to parent so children will learn.* Watertown, WI: Apple.

Rocamora, M. (1992). Counseling issues with recognized and unrecognized creatively gifted adults. *Advanced Development, 4,* 75–89.

Robinson, N., & Noble, K. (1991). Social-emotional development and adjustment of gifted children. In M. Wang, M. Reynolds, & H. Walberg (Eds.), *Handbook for special education: Research and practice: Vol. 4: Emerging programs* (pp. 57–76). New York: Pergamon Press.

Roedell, W. (1984). Vulnerabilities of highly gifted children. *Roeper Review, 6,* 127–130.

Rogers, K. B. (1992). A best-evidence synthesis of research on acceleration options for gifted students. In N. Colangelo, S. Assouline, & D. Ambroson (Eds.), *Talent development: Proceedings from the 1991 Henry B. and Jocelyn Wallace National Symposium on Talent Development* (pp. 406–409). Unionville, NY: Trillium Press.

Rogers, K. B. (2002). *Re-forming gifted education: Matching the program to the child.* Scottsdale, AZ: Great Potential Press.

Satir, V. (1985). *Conjoint family therapy.* New York: Science and Behavior Books.

Schultz, R. (2000). Flirting with underachievement. *Highly Gifted Children, 13*(2) 12–20.

Silverman, L. K. (1998). Developmental stages of giftedness: Infancy through adulthood. In J. VanTassel-Baska (Ed.), *Excellence in educating gifted & talented learners* (pp. 37–46). Denver, CO: Love.

Sternberg, R. J. (1988a). Beyond IQ testing. *National Forum, 68*(2), 8–11.

Sternberg, R .J. (Ed.). (1988b). *The nature of creativity*. New York: Cambridge University Press.

Sternberg, R. J. (1996). The sound of silence: A nation responds to its gifted. *Roeper Review, 18*, 168–172.

Sternberg, R. J. (1997). *Successful intelligence*. New York: Plume.

Tolan, S. (1989). Discovering the gifted ex-child. *Advanced Development, 1*, 7–10.

Tolan, S. (1990). *Helping your highly gifted child*. Reston, VA: ERIC Clearinghouse on Handicapped and Gifted Children. (ERIC Document Reproduction Service No. ED321482)

Tolan, S. (1995). *Is it a cheetah?* Retrieved June 5, 2006, from http://www.sengifted. org/articles_learning/Tolan/IsitACheetah.shtml

Treffinger, D. J., & Feldhusen, J. D. (1996). Talent recognition and development: Successor to gifted education. *Journal for the Education of the Gifted, 19*, 181–193.

Winner, E. (1996). *Gifted children: Myths and realities*. New York: Basic Books.

Wolin, S. J., & Wolin, S. (1993). *The resilient self: How survivors of troubled families rise above adversity*. New York: Random House.

chapter 9

Science, Spirit, and Talent Development

by Barbara Kerr

Conception of Giftedness

My introduction to giftedness came not through a textbook, but through my experience as a gifted child in the St. Louis public schools. We were told on our first day of school that we had been given a "gift from God." Our teachers said that giftedness meant that we had an IQ over 140, and that an IQ was a measure of intelligence. Intelligence, we heard, was the ability to learn rapidly and well. My school's curricula was based on a general acceleration model; that is, we were all advanced from fourth- to sixth-grade work in math, science, social studies, and English. Our education was enriched with daily French lessons, "choral reading," an abacus system of calculation, art, drama, and music. The purpose of gifted education, we were told, was to prepare "leaders of tomorrow." We were told in no uncertain terms that we were expected to work much harder than other students, to aspire to high goals, and to seek leadership positions in our fields when we were grown.

Therefore, my earliest notions about giftedness were steeped in the faith that our abilities were unearned gifts bestowed by nature, that our gifts were accompanied by awesome responsibilities, and that giftedness must be nurtured by challenge and hard work. Like trust-fund babies, some of us squandered our inheritance, some of us lost our way because of having too many choices, and a few of us were fortunate enough to be able to find work that we loved. Because my story and that of my classmates has been told before, in *Smart Girls: A New Psychology of Girls, Women, and Giftedness* (Kerr, 1997), and in *Smart Boys: Talent, Manhood, and the Search for Meaning* (Kerr & Cohn, 2001), I will not go into detail here. I will say only that after 25 years as a scholar of giftedness, my ideas about giftedness have changed only a little.

In college, I read *Genetic Studies of Genius* by Lewis Terman and Melita Oden (1935) and found myself full of ambivalence. On one hand, I recognized myself in their every description; on the other hand, Terman's obsession with the strength, virility, and eliteness of this group gave me the creeps. I could see then, even at the dawn of the multicultural and gender revolution, that there was something very dangerous about these attitudes toward giftedness. If these were gifts given by some unseen, random forces of heredity, I reasoned, then how could we feel as if they lent us any special privilege? Remembering well the vocabulary items on the intelligence test, I imagined how difficult it would be for my Italian-, Spanish-, and Chinese-speaking friends to do well on it. Furthermore, recalling the tall, stern, gray-haired White lady who gave the individual intelligence test, I wondered how the shy Black kids in my all-city choir could possibly have had the courage to speak up in the testing session. The intelligence test seemed to be about words and pictures; so I wondered how the kids who played guitar around the summer bonfire, or who figured out the best hockey strategies on our frozen pond in winter, or who created the wildest and most daring games through our city streets would ever be recognized for their special abilities.

As a psychology major, my suspicions were confirmed that all psychological instruments were flawed. Later, as I explored the cultures and languages of people other than my own, I learned that sexism, ethnocentricity, and cultural bias run deep throughout science, psychology, and education. In addition, I learned that there was another prejudice that ran deep through American culture: anti-intellectualism. All of these together, I realized, were forces that could prevent the identification, the cultivation, and the blossoming of talent. This was the realization that would lead eventually to my commitment to a career as an advocate and psychologist for gifted students.

Influences

My work as a scholar of giftedness has been most influenced by the works of Leta Hollingworth (1926); James Webb, Betty Meckstroth, and Stephanie Tolan (1989); Howard Gardner (1983); Mihaly Csikszentmihalyi (1996);

Nicholas Colangelo (Colangelo & Davis, 2002); Sanford Cohn (Kerr & Cohn, 2001); John McAlister (Kerr & McAlister, 2000, 2001); and Kathleen Noble (1999; Noble, Subotnik, & Arnold, 1999). From Leta Hollingworth, whose work I discovered when I was a young professor at the University of Nebraska, I learned a kinder and gentler approach to gifted children than that advocated by Lewis Terman (Terman & Oden, 1935). His insistence on the psychological adjustment of gifted children and inevitable blossoming of talent was cast in doubt by her case studies of highly gifted children who struggled against the rejection of other children and who hungered for intellectual nourishment. Leta Hollingworth was the first scholar to call for a compassionate, child-centered approach to the guidance of gifted children. James Webb (Webb et al.), like Leta Hollingworth, showed in *Guiding the Gifted Child* that gifted children have difficulty at home, in peer groups, and at school. He helped me to feel the outrage at the loss of their gifts. I remember that when he gave me a newly printed copy of his book at an American Psychological Association convention, I read it from cover to cover in one night. I realized there were a few other psychologists who cared about bright kids.

Howard Gardner's (1983) *Frames of Mind: The Theory of Multiple Intelligences* gave voice to my intuition that specific, extraordinary talents were often ignored and misunderstood. Csikszentmihalyi's (1996) wonderful book *Creativity* first opened my eyes to the role of expertise in a domain, the importance of challenge, and the means of engaging that intriguing consciousness state, *flow*.

Nicholas Colangelo (Colangelo & Davis, 2002), a pioneer in counseling gifted individuals, was an extraordinary colleague and mentor. He recruited me to The University of Iowa in 1985. The years I spent there as Associate Director of the Belin-Blank Center for Gifted and Talented were the most productive years of my life. Nick taught me an entrepreneurial approach to research and practice. *Just do it* was his philosophy; no question about genius need go unanswered and no project was too great to undertake. In that heady atmosphere of intellectual freedom and creativity, I thrived and learned more each day. We had a beautiful onsite counseling laboratory and more graduate assistants than I knew what to do with. Nick's habitual morning greeting spurred me on: "Hey, Barb, what are we going to learn about today?" We studied inventors, writers, artists, musicians, kids who scored perfectly on the ACT, kids who were brilliant and managed to flunk out of school, and minority gifted students who had something to prove (Colangelo & Kerr, 1990, 1993; Kerr & Colangelo, 1988, 1994). We wrote grants, ran workshops, and taught many cohorts of gifted education classes. When my book *Smart Girls* became successful, Nick urged me to travel the world with my ideas about gender and genius.

It was ironic, then, that the thesis of *Smart Girls*, that gifted women often compromise their dreams in order to maintain relationships, should become precisely my own narrative. I was forced to move from the extraordinarily nurturing environment of The University of Iowa to Arizona State University, because it was my spouse's turn to be happy. He had given up his career at University of Nebraska for me; now it was my turn to sacrifice for him. It was riches to rags for me. I left abundant resources, a strong reputation, and a thriving research mission to go to an institution where I had none of these. Giftedness was viewed by most of my colleagues with suspicion or distaste, and my initiatives for bright students got lost in the rigid chain of command. I was miserable—except when working and chatting with my best friend and colleague, Sanford Cohn. Sandy had helped implement what was to become one of the most successful research and service programs for gifted children in the United States: the Study for Mathematically Precocious Youth. He had founded the Center for Academic Precocity at Arizona State University and taught most of the gifted education courses. His knowledge of the cultures of Arizona was helpful to me in developing a National Science Foundation project for counseling Hispanic and Native American gifted girls (Kerr, Kurpius, & Harkins, 2005; Kurpius Kerr, & Harkins, 2005). His knowledge of men's issues was central to our creation of the book *Smart Boys* (Kerr & Cohn, 2001). Our friendship, however, was based not only upon our shared interest in giftedness, but upon a dialogue about science and spirit that began in 1992, and has continued, every night on the phone, in an unbroken thread to this day. Sandy's therapeutic approach was highly influenced by his experiences with Jungian analysis. The fact that a person as intellectually hardheaded as Sandy freely used references to symbol and metaphor, and synchronicity and Shadow, was fascinating to me. Here was a man who was a study in himself not only of intelligence and creativity, but also of wisdom. I came to understand that there were mysteries of giftedness that I had never dared to explore, as well as mysteries of the Self.

By the early 1990s, I had a good understanding of many domains of human ability. I had studied firsthand the lives of linguistically gifted people as a counselor for the Iowa Writers Workshop; I had interviewed scores of inventors; I had surveyed and counseled musicians and artists; and I had identified and guided many future scientists. I thought I knew just about everything there was to know about intelligence—until I fell serendipitously into a Native American sweat lodge. Here, in a hot, dark, crowded hut in the middle of a sacred ceremony, I witnessed an intelligence I had never seen before. The leader, Ten White Bears, seemed to be able to orchestrate consciousness itself. He guided the young participants in the sweat lodge ceremony through dream states, imagery, and trance. He led them on a journey of self-understanding and mutual compassion—while in a trance state himself. His exquisitely timed interpretations seemed to go far beyond the domains of interpersonal or emotional intelligence, and his ability to intuit the hidden joys and fears in each person tapped some capacity alien to my understanding.

It was Kathleen Noble (1999; Noble et al., 1999), a scholar of giftedness, gender, and spirituality, who gave me the words I needed to understand this phenomenon: spiritual intelligence. And it was Kate who gave me the courage to explore it. So it was that I came to study the abilities of shamans, curanderos, and natural healers, the most challenging work I had ever attempted. To learn about spiritual intelligence, I apprenticed myself to Ten White Bears,

I learned basic Navajo and Apache languages, and I engaged in a harrowing personal journey into a new worldview and new way of being. *Letters to the Medicine Man* (Kerr & McAlister, 2001), written with Ten White Bears (under his Christian name, John McAlister), was the book that resulted from this experience. Recently, I developed a grant proposal to the National Institutes of Health to investigate the phenomenon of extraordinary healing abilities. It is this work that I will continue to pursue in the coming years, even as I continue as a therapist and trainer of therapists for gifted people.

Definition

I believe, with Linda Gottfredson (2002), that intelligence is the ability to catch on, to make sense of things, and to know what to do about it. Gifted people are those who have these qualities in abundance. General intelligence, or *g*, seems to be the power behind specific abilities such as linguistic, musical, and mathematical capacities or spiritual abilities. At moderate levels of *g*, abilities cluster together. Verbal and mathematical ability, in particular, are highly correlated for most of the population. Moderately gifted people, from the 90th to the 97th percentile, seem able to learn and become skillful in almost everything they try (Colangelo & Assouline, 2000; Kerr & Erb, 1991). At the highest levels of *g*, however, intelligence manifests itself in highly specific ways, so that the people we call geniuses usually have just one extraordinary area of expertise (Colangelo & Kerr, 1990; Feldman & Goldsmith, 1986; Morelock & Feldman, 1991). My definition of giftedness, therefore, is as follows: Giftedness is the potential for extraordinary performance in a valued domain, as evidenced by high intelligence and capacity to channel that intelligence into expertise in a discipline or practice.

I believe that intelligence emerges evolutionarily out of the "seeking" behaviors observed even in the lowest life forms (Mobus, 1994); therefore, intelligence drives behaviors that will satiate the seeking urge. Neuroscientists Ikemoto and Panksepp (1999) provided a unifying interpretation that can account for the functions of dopamine in the brain's nucleus accumbens septi (NAS). From primitive mammalian brains to human brains, NAS dopaminergic processes in the basal ganglia seem to play key roles in behavioral arousal; in the facilitation, as well as an induction, of reward processes; and in the avoidance of negative stimuli. Dopamine processes govern not only the high energy and elevated mood of the very gifted person at work on a valued task, but also the enhanced capacity to learn and remember. What this means is that intelligence and motivation may not necessarily be separate processes.

In addition, Antonio Damasio's (1995) groundbreaking brain imaging and neurochemistry studies have shown that learning, thinking, and emotion are inextricably intertwined. The relatively new sciences of neurochemistry, brain imaging, and behavioral genetics seem to be revealing that the words such as *intelligence*, *motivation*, and *emotion* are linguistic conventions for talking about complex sets of behavior that were once obscured in the "black box" of the human brain. Therefore, I try to think of intelligence—and giftedness—holistically. In my most recent research, I have begun to investigate combining measures of intelligence with motivational, emotional, and behavioral descriptions to create "profiles" of gifted adolescents who seem to match the abilities, motives, feelings, and behaviors of eminent individuals when they were adolescents (Kerr & McKay, 2006). In this way, I hope to better understand what giftedness is, and how it might predict extraordinary accomplishment in a domain.

Characteristics

Certain commonly observed characteristics of gifted individuals seem to arise not only from the inherent press of the intelligence (the urge to "seek"), but also from the interactions of intelligence with personality, brain-body chemistry, and arousal capacities. In addition, what are called characteristics of the gifted may also be the result of interactions of their intelligent behavior with the environment. Intelligent behaviors elicit some predictable responses from adults and peers in any particular culture ranging from admiration to rejection. I do not believe there is any one set of characteristics that can help us to identify or understand all gifted children. When gifted children are grouped by ability in a domain, certain personality characteristics do seem to emerge in clusters matching fairly well those of the results of Holland's (1985) factor analyses of vocational interests (e.g., mathematically gifted people tend to have "investigative" vocational interests, introverted personalities, and theoretical values).

My assumptions about giftedness are reflections of my own personal ethical and moral orientation. I believe giftedness is important. I believe that the development of giftedness is a responsibility shared by the individual and society. I believe that intelligence "will out"—that gifts have a life of their own. And, I believe that gifts are blind to sex and race, although societies, unfortunately, are not. I believe in research.

Conception of Personality

Personality

Conventional conceptualizations of personality seem to me inadequate for predicting and explaining the variety and complexity of human performance. My evolving theory of personality involves inherited tendencies, energy level, hormonal levels, and capacities for altering consciousness.

Certain tendencies seem to be inborn (Rothbart & Bates, 1998; Thomas, Chess, & Birch, 1968). One of the most robust is the tendency to go toward or away from people, usually called extraversion and introversion. Another is the tendency to dominate or submit, and an additional one is the attraction to new experience or the avoidance of new experiences. The tendency to become easily aroused or slow to become aroused seems to be present at birth. The Big Five, or five-factor theory of personality (Costa & McCrae, 1992) closely parallels my own conceptualization of tendencies. Costa and McCrae factor-analyzed the data from all major personality inventories to yield five factors of human personalities that seemed to emerge out of personality tests across many ages and cultural groups.

Another source of variability in human behavior is energy level, ranging from little sleep/high activity level to a lot of sleep/low activity level. Combinations of neurotransmitters, particularly dopamine and serotonin, seem to contribute to these different kinds of energy levels. Some people just seem to be born without an "Off" switch. Others are hard to get moving. However, I believe that energy levels, more than basic tendencies, are subject to a vast array of environmental influences, including daylight; the presence of natural, nutritional, or pharmacological stimulants; and the presence of other people.

Differing hormonal levels affect behavior in complex ways (Rosenzweig, Breedlove, & Watson, 2005). Sex hormones affect both sexual orientation and sensual excitement levels. Other regulatory hormones affect everything from appetite and temperature sensitivity to the capacity to adjust to stress. People are not born with one level of hormonal activity; interaction with the environment can increase or decrease available hormones. For example, a very active little boy with high testosterone levels will often seek opportunities for the kind of competitive play that will in turn raise those levels of testosterone even higher (Kerr & Cohn, 2001).

Finally, the capacity to alter arousal levels and consciousness states at will, an area much neglected by researchers of human behavior, seems critical to predicting and explaining gifted behavior. I am curious about our culture's ignorance of both the abilities and the human technologies for altering consciousness deliberately without drugs. Some people seem very prone to trance states and other alterations of consciousness, learning to meditate easily, entering hypnotic states easily, and having vivid, meaningful dreams (Wilson & Barber, 1983). Gifted children who have these abilities may be more likely to be creative, empathetic, and drawn to spiritual activities, but they may also be more at risk in a culture that ignores or fails to value these abilities (Noble, 1999).

Combinations of these characteristics give rise to what we call personalities. If a person is introverted; submissive; avoidant of new experience; slow to arouse; low energy; unmoved by sex, food, or sensations; and stuck in a narrow band of consciousness, that person is deemed to be depressive. If a person is extraverted, high energy, easily aroused to action, highly sexual, and permanently in a state of excited consciousness, that person is said to have attention deficits with hyperactivity. At higher levels of arousal, gross perceptual and cognitive changes occur, and we call that person manic and psychotic. If a person is extraverted, dominant, difficult to arouse to anxiety or fear, sexually aggressive, and unable to alter consciousness states without extraordinary stimulation or powerful drugs, we call that person a sociopath. These clusters of characteristics are seen often enough, and disturb people enough, to motivate psychologists to give personality labels to the people who manifest them.

Personality of Gifted Individuals

Similarly, there are clusters of characteristics that we like to believe are characteristics of gifted persons. Usually these include extraversion, curiosity, moderate dominance, moderate impulsiveness, high energy, alertness, and sensitivity. This phenomenon, I believe, is simply the tendency to confuse giftedness with conventional desirability. People with these characteristics are productive people who are good leaders but also cooperative followers—the perfect students. As I said before, there do seem to be personality characteristics associated with talents in particular domains, and I believe it is more productive to understand how gifted people's personalities compare to those who are accomplished and happy in particular disciplines.

I think it is interesting that experts in giftedness (including me) often develop lists of characteristics that reflect their own sort of intelligence. Enterprising, widely knowledgeable, verbally gifted Lewis Terman identified enterprising, widely knowledgeable, verbally gifted children; Julian Stanley was a mathematician who saw mathematical precocity as giftedness; Robert Sternberg seems like a guy with a chip on his shoulder concerning Terman-type smart people, so he developed a theory of giftedness for all the guys with street smarts like himself. Joseph Renzulli seems to have the right amount of intelligence, creativity, and task commitment to persuade an entire nation that this is what giftedness is.

Therefore, I believe that these lists of characteristics tell us more about the authors of the lists than about extraordinary children and adults. Giftedness is socially constructed; however, the ability to perform in an outstanding manner in one or more domains of talent is real. For personality characteristics of people in the six major vocational interest areas see Holland (1985) and my attempt to integrate the literature of personality and vocational interests with domains of talent (Kerr, 1991).

Model of Counseling

Influences

The major influence on my counseling approach is common factors theory, pioneered by Jerome Frank in his book *Persuasion and Healing* (Frank & Frank,

1993). Since the publication of that groundbreaking book, many studies and meta-analyses have supported the notion that all therapeutic approaches share common factors that serve to persuade the patient to change his or her behavior. A repeated finding is that all psychotherapies are about equally effective in producing positive outcomes (Smith & Glass, 1977). It is the skillful use of common therapeutic factors, not adherence to a particular theory, that defines a therapist's ability to effect change in a client. Wampold's (2001) meta-analyses of all bona fide therapy outcome studies showed convincingly that all modes of therapy are more effective than no therapy (yes, even primal scream therapy), and that common aspects of clients, counselors, interactions, and environments determine efficacy. Shamanic modalities of treatment also may share common factors (Winkelman, 2000). Psychologists and anthropologists have long theorized that common factors in shamanic treatments center around the capacities of the healer to establish a healing environment; to build a therapeutic relationship based on trust, caring, and credibility; to provide ritualized procedures to focus attention and alter psychophysiological arousal states; and to give prescriptive suggestions that change behavior in the direction of wellness.

Definition of Counseling

Counseling is a relationship in which one person, the counselor, persuades another person, the client, toward changes in behavior that will help the client to fulfill his or her intellectual, social, physical, and spiritual potential in such a way as to contribute toward the client's well-being and the common good.

Role of Counselor

My role as a counselor is to persuade the client to achieve his or her own goals and to guide the client's own self-healing. My counseling approach is an attempt to maximize all possible therapeutic common factors, while developing creative specific techniques tailored to each client's needs. My combination of research-based strategies and shamanic creativity helps me to bridge the chasm that has existed too long between science and spirit.

Role of Client

If we are here to help others, then what are the others here for? I assume that my client is not with me to be a passive recipient of my counseling skills. Instead, the role of the client is to *engage* with me; to display those behaviors in the present that are working or not working; to resist me or to oppose me as he or she sees fit; to struggle with his or her demons in my presence; and to try out all reasonable suggestions for changes as much as possible in daily life. I prefer that my client show up for scheduled sessions, but I do not take "no-shows" personally; it may be part of the client's repertoire not to show up or to have emergencies, and that is material for counseling when we are together again. My only ground rules have to do with safety. Clients cannot hurt themselves or me, and if they threaten to do so, or to hurt someone else, I act in the interests of everyone who needs to be safe from harm.

Goals

The goal of counseling is change. Counseling is not conversation, or paid friendship, or simple comfort. I am not there to collaborate with clients in self-destruction or to help them adjust to abuse or oppression. I am there to help them change—in the direction of psychological health and beyond health to self-actualization. Although I seldom quote Freudians, I am solidly with them in their opinion of what constitutes psychological health: the ability to love and the ability to work. To this I would add the ability to connect with something greater than oneself, whether that is an intellectual idea, a cause, a deity, or simply a sense of the majesty of the universe, because this capacity seems to be a prerequisite for true self-actualization (Maslow, 1999).

Relationship

To build a relationship that can bring about change and self-actualization, I must bring all of the general knowledge, goodwill, wisdom, and humility that I can muster up to the session. I am always aware that success rides on my ability to build a persuasive, authentic relationship and the client's ability to overcome resistance to change. A persuasive, authentic relationship develops when the client sees me as an expert who has the resources to help him or her; when the client sees me as a person who is likable, similar in worldview, and trustworthy. Expertness, attractiveness, and trustworthiness are the characteristics of people who are able to influence others to change attitudes and behaviors. Watch any commercial, or read any editorial, and you will see the same persuasive and rhetorical skills in action. Like any persuader, the counselor must find ways to overcome people's natural resistance to a new communicator and natural opposition to new ideas and ways of behaving. With most clients, the expertness that reputation, titles, degrees, and diplomas provide is enough to make the counselor a persuasive person. If a counselor adds a little kindness and attentiveness, most clients will readily accept the new ideas presented.

Working with gifted people, however, is a true test of one's expertness, attractiveness, and trustworthiness. Gifted individuals are used to authorities who are not as bright as they are, and they often despair of ever finding a helper who can speak their language and match their enthusiasm measure for measure. They become cynical and resistant to helpers, having too much experience with teachers and counselors who just do not or will not understand them.

Therefore, one of the ways in which counseling gifted people is different from ordinary counseling is in the need to "treat the gift first." I have said that gifts have a life of their own, and this is nowhere more apparent than in my work with artists, writers, musicians, and architects. To attempt to create a relationship with these creatively gifted people without intelligently exploring the gift is futile. Without the music, there is no musician; without the art, no artist. Therefore, I fully explore how the client's giftedness has shaped his or her life and dreams. I like to experience the art, the writing, or the music, and to provide my honest and carefully considered reactions. I explore the barriers to the expression of the client's gifts and the ways in which the client is coping with those barriers. In doing this, I not only honor the gift, but also show that I am truly interested in the ideas that drive that person's sense of meaning and purpose.

Another way of building a relationship with gifted individuals is showing curiosity rather than ignorance in discussing the client's most precious ideas. Too many counselors lose all credibility with gifted individuals when they say, "Wow, you lost me there" or "I don't know *anything* about quantum physics!" One does not have to be an expert in everything the client is an expert in, but it is important to be genuinely intrigued by all things under the earth and sky. Therefore, I ask, "What is it about quantum physics that has recently engaged you?" or "Tell me how it is you came to love Herman Melville's works." And, then I read a book like *Quantum Physics for Dummies* and pick up a copy of *Billy Budd*.

There are also special gender issues in building the relationship. I am aware when I am building the relationship with a gifted woman that she may have learned to carefully camouflage her gifts and to be too well adjusted for her own good. I might frustrate her attempts to deny her abilities to me and challenge her to show me her true self. In working with gifted women, my credo is the same as feminist Lucy Stone's (Lewis, 2005):

> In education, in marriage, in religion, in everything, disappointment is the lot of women. It shall be the work of my life to deepen that disappointment in the heart of every woman until she bows down to it no longer. (¶ 7)

When a gifted woman knows that I see through her camouflage, and that I am allied with her hidden hopes and dreams, she perceives me as someone who can truly help.

I know that if I am building a relationship with a gifted man, he may have spent a lot of his life attempting to be "aggressively ordinary"; this too I will challenge, by treating him as the extraordinary person that he is.

Assessment

Although I do not administer intellectual assessment tests, I am often interested in the results of intelligence tests, achievement tests, and tests of specific abilities. I find intelligence tests to be useful in two kinds of cases. I often find myself reinterpreting intelligence tests that have been insufficiently studied by school psychologists or decision-makers. For many years, psychologists were trained to interpret only full-scale scores of intelligence tests. Many times this practice led to misunderstandings about the behavior of gifted children. For example, when full-scale scores on the WISC-R were the primary means of entry into gifted programs, I frequently saw young people—often boys—whose combined verbal and performance scores allowed them entry into gifted programs. When verbal scores and performance scores were quite different, particularly in cases where the verbal score was 110 and the performance score was 150, the students began promptly to "underachieve" in gifted programs. Because gifted programs rely heavily on verbal productivity, it should be no mystery that high-performance scorers with average verbal ability fail to achieve. Nevertheless, I often found myself explaining to parents and teachers why boys with these scores tended to be very interested and achieving in spatial visual tasks and only average in achieving on all other tasks. Another common situation I found was that schools placed undue emphasis on "task commitment" and failed to admit students who scored as "highly gifted" into gifted programs. I was often told that these students did not "deserve" to be placed in gifted programs—as if appropriate, challenging education was a privilege! Therefore, I have not been above using the results of intelligence tests to bludgeon schools into providing the appropriate challenge to bright students who may have been so bored that they showed little interest in the tasks that were set for them.

My favorite use of assessment instruments, however, has been personality assessment. For 20 years, I have used Jackson's (1987) Personality Research Form (PRF), combined with Holland's (1985) Vocational Preference Inventory (VPI), to yield fascinating and complex profiles of adolescent and adult personalities. With the results of these tests, I have been able to create profiles for my clients that sometimes astound them with new information that is so right and so clear that they at last understand the personal and vocational dreams that they have only begun to desire. The beauty of these tests is that they show how the client compares to happy, normal, successful people on a wide variety of scales. From the VPI, my clients can discover the three-letter vocational code that describes the kind of work environment in which they are likely to be happiest. For example, by learning that one's Artistic-Investigative-Social code is the most common one for literary editors, a client can understand why the business classes that she is taking are such a bore for her. By learning that one's profile is the very pragmatic Realistic-Enterprising-Investigative combination, a client can understand why her parents' desire for her to become a teacher seems so wrong.

From the PRF (Jackson, 1987), my clients gain an extraordinary array of data about how their needs compare to others. By examining such scales as Autonomy, Affiliation, Dominance, Endurance, Play, Nurturance, and 14 other scales, clients have an opportunity to discover how their needs are met or unmet by the situations in which they find themselves. Even more important, when these results are combined with the Holland Codes, clients have the opportunity to pinpoint not only the careers but also the life situations in which they are most likely to feel happy and fulfilled. To create a thorough description of how these assessments are used in career counseling of bright females, my colleagues Sharon Kurpius and Amy Harkins and I put all of this information into our book *Counseling Girls and Women: Talent Development* (Kerr et al., 2005), a publication sponsored by the National Science Foundation.

In addition, I use the results of neuropsychological assessments, as well as my own observations, to develop a picture of my clients' general cognitive functioning, general arousal level, adaptiveness, and judgment. I use medical records to assess how various medications and medical conditions may be affecting the client's intellectual capacities, personality, mood, and activity level.

Process

I try to put goodwill in my heart before entering the room, and to welcome the client with caring and compassion. I engage almost entirely in open-ended questions and verbal tracking in the first stage of counseling. I reinforce the client's self-exploration with nods and smiles and statements of support; I reinforce emotion and discourage intellectualizing. My reflections tend to be simple, Anglo-Saxon statements rather than Latinate expressions: *work* instead of *occupation*; *love* instead of *affection*; *sad* instead of *depressed*; *mad* instead of *annoyed*. I try to keep my client in the present, in the here and now, rather than narrating in the there and then. I am sometimes outrageously honest: If I'm bored I say so (and things become less boring immediately). I engage in standard, mutual goal-setting, guiding the client in establishing clear, attainable goals and clearly stating the purpose of counseling and my role as a counselor.

I give suggestions for next steps (but I never call it "homework," because that term sounds patronizing) and help the client to establish in his or her mind the support system, or community, that will help maintain the changes that have been made. As a feminist and multiculturalist, I understand that there are structures of oppression that contribute to clients' feelings of helplessness and despair. Therefore, I also attempt to mobilize the client not only to seek community, but also to seek opportunities to join with others to overcome sexism, racism, heterosexism, or any other prejudices that limit peoples' opportunities for self-actualization.

I like brief counseling, even one-session counseling when possible, because I do not like to encourage dependency or the belief that I am necessary to the person's healing process. I am a change agent, and once change has been accomplished, I want to empower the individual and the community to carry out the rest of the process. Most of my counseling relationships last one to five sessions, with occasional "tune ups" when requested.

Techniques

I like techniques that are powerful enough to provoke action quickly. I have no patience with long, psychodynamic examinations of the past; I am most interested in what is happening right now in the client's life and the impact of recent events and conditions on his or her behavior. I also have no patience with techniques that are so nondirective that it takes many sessions for the client to discover the insights that will provoke change. And finally, I become bored with techniques that do not create the necessary excitement, frustration, and challenge to motivate the client to change.

Despite the fact that shamanic-based counseling sounds exotic, I tend to use very ordinary, tried-and-true techniques for most of the counseling process. Therefore, I use active listening to focus quickly on what the problem is, and then move quickly into here-and-now statements that surprise the client into manifesting the problem, rather than just talking about the problem. I do not want to hear the client talk about his frustration; I want to see the frustration, right in the session, so that I can understand what elicits it, what sustains it, and what reduces it.

I use mind/body techniques to help the client to verbalize what his or her body is clearly expressing. I say, "Where are you feeling your sadness? What would your tight shoulders say? What's beneath the tightness in your shoulders?" I often "peel" the layers of the client's feelings, going further and further below each feeling until the genuine, basic fight or flight responses are apparent.

I use well-known Gestalt techniques to encounter the client and to build the client's awareness of how his or her emotions are informing every gesture and word. I also use many experiments to help the client to enact and resolve conflicts. These experiments can involve an "empty chair" or a visioning experience.

I try to make interpretations that are surprising in their accuracy and honesty; that are carefully timed to be delivered right before or after peak arousal (crying out, weeping, or rapid breathing); and that create an opening for changed ideas and behaviors. In the session, if the client is having difficulty with accepting a new idea, I deliberately reduce the client's level of physiological arousal through breathing and relaxation or increase arousal with experiential activities in order to enhance the capacity to change.

Where I diverge from ordinary counseling is in my willingness to use ceremonial elements and the client's own spirituality to assist the client in healing. I might build a small medicine wheel to help the client focus upon the cycles and seasons of his or her life; I might help the client to put stresses into small medicine bundles and return them to the Earth; I might encourage a client to meditate upon a sacred text from his or her own religion.

Not only sacred texts, but great works of literature and philosophy may be a part of our counseling. Gifted clients respond particularly well to bibliotherapy. Therefore, reading books in between sessions is almost always part of my treatment.

Graphic Illustration

In the graphic illustration (see Figure 9.1), I have shown the way in which I use the metaphor of the seasons to describe the stages of the counseling. The Native American medicine wheel is a powerful symbol of the cycles of human life, the seasons, and the circle of life on earth. I use this symbol to organize my thinking about counseling as a cycle of birth, growth, flowering, ending, and rebirth.

Preparation

The "spring" of counseling is a time of preparation, when the environment is created to marshal all of the forces of physical architecture, design, and symbol to enhance safety, trust, warmth, comfort, and a sense of hope. The healing environment also establishes a "passage between the worlds" (Frank & Frank, 1991), where the client enters a place apart from the ordinary world. I also prepare myself by cleansing myself symbolically or literally, and centering myself through reflection and meditation.

I use opening words or ceremony to invoke counselor, client, and community strengths and willingness to enter the healing process; this can be a simple ritual of lighting a candle, offering a cup of tea to share, and saying a few words of welcome.

Relationship Building

As the "summer" of counseling approaches, I engage in active listening and reflection to reveal the person's worldview and the nature of the problem. Here, it is also important for me to use expert, referent, and genuine statements to create the credibility I will need to be a powerful agent of influence. An important part of the relationship building is mutual goal setting to create therapeutic alliance. This alliance will carry us through the difficult parts of counseling.

Assessment

I use tests and interpretation to establish client strengths, needs, and goals. I ask the client to engage in self-observation and to reflect upon those observations in the session. Now begins the most crucial part of counseling: the interpretations of words and behavior. Together, the client and I must create new words to describe his or her inner world, and a whole new narrative of the client's life. I use here-and-now, encounter, and awareness techniques to make the problem manifest in the counseling session itself so that we can work

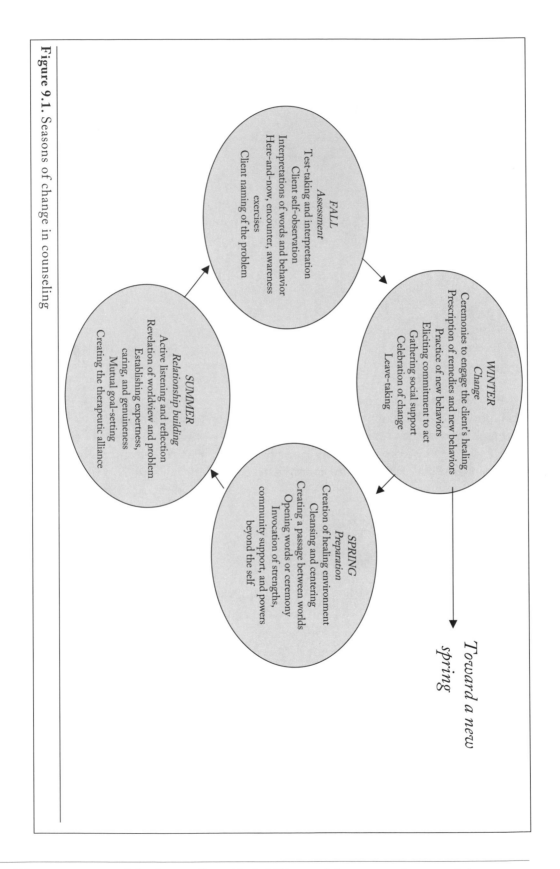

Figure 9.1. Seasons of change in counseling

FALL
Assessment
Test-taking and interpretation
Client self-observation
Interpretations of words and behavior
Here-and-now, encounter, awareness
exercises
Client naming of the problem

WINTER
Change
Ceremonies to engage the client's healing
Prescription of remedies and new behaviors
Practice of new behaviors
Eliciting commitment to act
Gathering social support
Celebration of change
Leave-taking

SUMMER
Relationship building
Active listening and reflection
Revelation of worldview and problem
Establishing expertness,
caring, and genuineness
Mutual goal-setting
Creating the therapeutic alliance

SPRING
Preparation
Creation of healing environment
Cleansing and centering
Creating a passage between worlds
Opening words or ceremony
Invocation of strengths,
community support, and powers
beyond the self

*Toward a new
spring*

together to understand how the client's emotions and behaviors affect not only me, but probably others in his or her life.

Change

In this stage come ceremonies or symbolic actions to engage the client's healing capacities; these can be the reading of the "new story" of the client's life, painting a picture or imagining a vision of the future, or even making a small fire and burning little papers with the roles, emotions, or behaviors that the client now puts behind him- or herself. I then prescribe activities, remedies, and new behaviors that will consolidate the learning that has happened in counseling. As "fall" approaches, the client is now practicing new behaviors, establishing the necessary support from friends and family, and committing to future action.

Engaging Community Support

I like to bring in the support system in real time, in virtual space, or symbolically to provide encouragement to client in change process. This displays publicly that the client wishes to sustain the changes and wants help doing so.

Leave-Taking

During the "winter" of counseling, we begin reviewing the events of the healing process. Winter is not just a time of closing, but also a time of giving thanks to one another. We may create a ceremony together to symbolize the end of the healing process: a new candle is lit, a blank book is given as a gift to the client, or a circle is closed as we say goodbye. Just as the winter yields to spring, I hope that my client goes on to a new life.

Application

Connor, a 26-year-old male writer and composer who had won several national awards for his poetry and prose, came to me for help with writer's block and depression. He was referred by the dean of his college because he had noticed that Connor was increasingly disengaged from his interdisciplinary team of teachers and missing some of his classes. The dean believed that my expertise with writers, as well as the Native American elements that I integrate into my work, would be appealing to this client, who had both literary and personal involvement in Native American spirituality.

I prepared our counseling space in a beautiful shelter at the Frank Lloyd Wright School of Architecture, a small, open-air circular building with a fireplace and a magnificent view of the open desert and the McDowell Mountains. Because it was chilly, I lit a fire, laid blankets over the chairs for warmth, and made herbal tea. Upon arrival, I greeted Connor with a handshake and introduction and led him to the shelter with my hand lightly placed on his back to guide him down the slope. He was attractive and fit, but thin and unkempt in appearance. He spoke quietly and slowly and was extremely courteous.

I opened the session with a short ceremony, lighting a candle, while I explained that we were in a place apart and a time apart in which we could dedicate ourselves to the healing process. I explained my role in helping him to change and asked for his commitment to this process, which he affirmed. In the first session, I asked open-ended questions and engaged in verbal following and reflection while he told me the precipitating incident (his academic advisor had noticed his absences and delays in his thesis work and referred him to me); his typical day (he was sleeping late, eating little, drinking a lot of coffee and smoking heavily, trying to write and failing, drinking alcohol at night to get to sleep); and his concerns and goals (he wanted to "clean up his act," to stop feeling as if he was a "poser," and to start writing again). We clarified those goals. I asked him to visualize a "movie" of what he would be like when he was well and whole, and he did that for me, somewhat haltingly. His description of his future self was of a man who had regained his zest for living, who wrote with passion, who took care of himself, and who was able to attract a happy and caring partner. I administered the PRF (Jackson, 1987) and the VPI (Holland, 1985), joking that it was better than Tarot cards for divination, and that these instruments might help us understand more about how he had lost his direction and what strengths might guide him back.

In the second session, I repeated the opening ritual and suggested that we build a small medicine wheel of colored pebbles on the trunk I use as a table. I asked him to touch each of the 12 rocks in a clockwise fashion, beginning in the East, and describe the seasons of his life. At several points, I asked him to elaborate or drew out a theme. In this way, I was able take a rapid "history" of my client without the cold, clinical tone of a typical history interview. His childhood had been a terrifying one, with a musician father who disappeared and a frustrated artist mother who was usually drinking and depressed, but who sometimes flew into wild fits of rage, in which she punished her child ruthlessly for small infractions, holding his head in the toilet or burning his favorite toys in the fireplace. He learned to be quiet, polite, and disengaged. Connor developed a secret world in his crawl space under the house, where he wrote stories and played softly on his harmonica. School extended his unhappiness; he felt as if he were a visitor from another planet. He made few friends until he was 13, when he developed a friendship with a girl who was as much of an outsider as he was.

This period was the "summer" of his life. All through high school, they explored the city together, finding coffee houses and groups of college students and musicians, where they were accepted. They spent lazy summer days lying on the roof, drinking beer and dreaming of places they would visit and people they would meet. Connor was also noticed by an English teacher, who encouraged him to write for the school literary magazine. Although Connor had no money for college, an English teacher recommended him for a scholarship to her own alma mater, a small liberal arts college renowned for its writing program. To his amazement, he received the scholarship. The hardest part of going to college was leaving his best friend Allie behind.

College could not have been more different from his previous schooling. Suddenly his courses were challenging, his teachers "clued in," and his writing "extravagant and brilliant," according to a review of his set of poems. He had not one mentor, but two. One English professor helped him hone his writing and publish; his professor of music took him to the frontiers of composition, where music, theater, and virtual space came together. His dual majors in music and creative writing, with a minor in mediated instruction, made it possible for him to be courted by Arts and Technology and Mediated Arts programs throughout the world. Now at one of the leading programs, he had arrived at the pinnacle of his profession, only to feel depressed and hopeless about his future.

I listened intently and ended the session with a few tentative interpretations and prescriptive suggestions. My scientific interpretation, I said, was that, like almost 30% of writers, he had been born with tendencies such as mood instability, introversion, expressiveness, and fluid consciousness that are sometimes called bipolar disorder. His mother showed clear symptoms, and he may have inherited a milder, mid-range form of hypomania/moderate depression. It is both a blessing and a curse to be "touched with fire," I said. The gift is prodigious creativity; the curse is the shadow of depression. My spiritual explanation was that he had been in a dark night of the soul, a time in which he was experiencing the wisdom of depression: a chance to slow down and integrate his past as an outsider with his future as an insider and leader in the new field he was co-inventing with others. My prescriptive suggestions were a referral to a psychiatrist for some mild medication to take the edge off of his depression and allow him sleep; a recommendation with tips for reducing alcohol, tobacco, and caffeine; and a recommendation to drink water, eat lightly, and sleep long to complete the cleansing process his body had already begun. In addition, he must read *Touched With Fire* by Kay Jamison so that he would understand his inherited condition and how to contain and channel it into creativity rather than illness.

In our third session, we discussed the book, which he said had "nailed" his mother and father, and he said that he saw a lot of himself there, too. He discussed what his 2 weeks on the drug Effexor had been like. He felt more balanced, he said, and was sleeping more and drinking less. I interpreted the results of his personality tests, which showed him to be a clear Artistic-Investigative-Realistic on the Holland Code (Holland, 1985), a classic code for people who combine aesthetic, scientific, and technical interests, and a perfect profile for a writer/composer on the frontier of mediated arts. "You are not a poser," I said. "You are the genuine article, a person whose profile matches out of thousands of possibilities the precise career to which you have wisely been led." His PRF (Jackson, 1987) confirmed his mild bipolar tendencies, but, even more important, showed extraordinary scores in endurance and autonomy, the hallmarks of successful artists, and, intriguingly, nurturance, the need to care for others and to be sympathetic and kind. "How beautiful," I said. "Out of the sadness of your childhood, you are in the process of transforming that suffering into a capacity for loving, nurturing, and caring for another." This result, I suggested, was an intimation of his next phase, in which he made peace with the "angry mother" and "abandoning father" within himself and created out of that peace a new, internalized parent who could nourish himself and others with love and caring.

Connor wept when I made this interpretation, and said that he hoped this was so, and that he wanted to explore and work on this part of himself. I asked him to stand and speak his intentions aloud to the mountains and sky before us. He said, "I will heal myself as this new soul grows within me; and I will heal others through my art. I am not a phony or an impostor or a charlatan. I came here on earth to do this work, and I choose it."

The next week was a surprise. Connor was not coming to our session. I had a message on my phone that he had flown to Maine, where his mother was buried, and then was going on to the town where he had grown up in Ohio.

He returned 2 weeks later, smiling and full of more surprises. He had gone to his mother's grave and had forgiven her for being ill and unable to love him or do her art. He felt free and somehow uplifted by the experience. Even more surprising, he had found Allie, and they had spent a wonderful 2 days together and had committed to frequent visits. Finally, he was writing again. It had begun on the plane trip, and now the work was "unfolding" within him, he said, with a sense of inevitability and rightness.

"Then you're done," I said. "And you will be well."

"Yes," he said. "I will."

I asked him to call upon the spirits of all of those who had cared for and mentored him, those who were new friends and old. "Pretend you are in your Lodge of Elders," I said. "Who is there? Who will support you in your new changes?"

He visualized this, and asked for their support quietly. He opened his eyes, and I said, "And I will be here, too, thinking of you, and ready to help you if you need a tune-up!" We closed by burning the sage one last time, and sprinkling the ashes of the sage to the wind, and wished each other well.

I saw him occasionally on campus, and sometimes I read about his work. I knew he would have ups and downs, like all artists. However, I was present at the birth of his new spirit, and I know that it will endure.

References

Colangelo, N., & Assouline, S. G. (2000). Counseling gifted students. In K. A. Heller, F. J. Mönks, R. J. Sternberg, & R. F. Subotnik (Eds.), *International handbook of giftedness and talent* (2nd ed., pp. 595–607). Amsterdam: Elsevier

Colangelo, N., & Davis, G. (2002). *Handbook of gifted education* (3rd ed.). Boston: Allyn & Bacon.

Colangelo, N., & Kerr, B. A. (1990). Extreme academic talent: Profiles of perfect scorers. *Journal of Educational Psychology, 82*, 404–410.

Colangelo, N., & Kerr, B. A. (1993). A comparison of gifted underachievers and gifted high achievers. *Gifted Child Quarterly, 37*, 155–160.

Costa, P. T., Jr., & McCrae, R. R. (1992). Normal personality assessment in clinical practice: The NEO Personality Inventory. *Psychological Assessment, 4*, 5–13.

Csikszentmihalyi, M. (1996). *Creativity: Flow and the psychology of discovery and invention.* New York: HarperCollins.

Damasio, A. (1995). *Descartes error: Emotion, reason, and the human brain.* San Francisco: Harper.

Feldman, D. H., & Goldsmith, L. T. (1986). *Nature's gambit.* New York: Basic Books

Frank, J. D., & Frank, J. B. (1991). *Persuasion and healing: A comparative study of psychotherapy.* Baltimore: Johns Hopkins University Press.

Frank, J., & Frank J. B. (1993). *Persuasion and healing: Comparative studies.* Baltimore: Johns Hopkins University Press.

Gardner, H. (1983). *Frames of mind: The theory of multiple intelligences.* New York: Basic Books.

Holland, J. L. (1985). *Vocational Preference Inventory (VPI).* Odessa, FL: Psychological Assessment Resources.

Gottfredson, L. S. (2002). *Scientific American: The general intelligence factor.* New York: ibooks.

Hollingworth, L. S. (1926). *Gifted children: Their nature and nurture.* New York: Macmillan.

Ikemoto, S., & Panksepp, J. (1999). The role of nucleus accumbens dopamine in motivated behavior: A unifying interpretation with special reference to reward-seeking. *Brain Research Reviews, 31*, 6–41.

Jackson, D. N. (1987). *Personality Research Form—Form E. Manual.* Port Huron, MI: Sigma Assessment Systems.

Kerr, B. A. (1991). *A handbook of counseling the gifted and talented.* Alexandria, VA: American Association for Counseling and Development.

Kerr, B. A. (1997). *Smart girls: A new psychology of girls, women, and giftedness.* Scottsdale, AZ: Gifted Psychology Press.

Kerr, B. A., & Cohn, S. J. (2001). *Smart boys: Talent, manhood, and the search for meaning.* Scottsdale, AZ: Great Potential Press.

Kerr, B. A., & Colangelo, N. (1988). The college plans of academically talented students. *Journal of Counseling and Development, 67,* 42–49.

Kerr, B. A., & Colangelo, N. (1994). Something to prove: Academically talented minority students. In N. Colangelo & S. Assouline (Eds.), *Talent development* (pp. 352–375). Columbus, OH: Ohio Psychology Press.

Kerr, B. A., & Erb, C. (1991). Career counseling with academically talented students: Effects of a value-based intervention. *Journal of Counseling Psychology.* 38, 309–314.

Kerr, B. A., Kurpius, S., & Harkins, A. (2005). *Counseling girls and women: Talent development.* Mesa, AZ: MTR/Nueva Science/NSF.

Kerr, B. A., & McAlister, J. (2000). Shamanic journey: An apprenticeship in spiritual intelligence. *Advanced Development Journal, 9,* 45–55.

Kerr, B. A., & McAlister, J. (2001). *Letters to the medicine man: The shaping of spiritual intelligence.* Cresskill, NJ: Hampton Press.

Kerr, B. A. & McKay, R. (2006, July). *Profiling creative students: The CLEOS Project.* Paper presented at the CREA International Creativity Conference, Paris, France.

Kurpius, S., Kerr, B. A., & Harkins, A. (2005). *Counseling girls and women: Talent, risk, and resiliency.* Mesa, AZ: MTR/Nueva Science/NSF.

Lewis, J. J. (2005). *Women's voices: Quotations by women.* Retrieved July 16, 2005, from http://womenshistory.about.com/library/qu/blquston.htm

Maslow, A. H. (1999). *Toward a psychology of being.* New York: Wiley and Sons.

Mobus, G. E (1994). *Toward a theory of learning and representing causal inferences in neural networks.* Retrieved June 15, 2006, from http://faculty.washington.edu/gmobus/Adaptrode/causal_representation.html

Morelock, M. J., & Feldman, D. H. (1991). Extreme precocity. In N. Colangelo & G. Davis (Eds.), *The handbook of gifted education* (pp. 347–364). Boston: Allyn & Bacon.

Noble, K. D. (1999). *Riding the windhorse: Spiritual intelligence and the growth of the self.* Cresskill, NJ: Hampton Press.

Noble, K. D., Subotnik, R. F., & Arnold, K. D. (1999). To thine own self be true: A new model of female talent development. *Gifted Child Quarterly, 43,* 140–149.

Rosenzweig, M. R, Breedlove, S. M., & Watson, N. V. (2005). *Biological psychology: An introduction to behavioral and cognitive neuroscience* (4th ed.). Sunderland, MA: Sinauer Associates.

Rothbart, M. K., & Bates, J. E. (1998). Temperament. In W. Damon (Series Ed.) & N. Eisenberg (Vol. Ed.), *Handbook of child psychology: Vol. 3. Social, emotional, and personality development* (5th ed., pp. 105–176). New York: Wiley.

Smith, M. L., & Glass, G. V. (1977). Meta-analysis of psychotherapy outcome studies. *American Psychologist, 32,* 752–760.

Terman, L. M., & Oden, M. H. (1935). *Genetic studies of genius: Vol. 3. The promise of youth.* Stanford, CA: Stanford University Press.

Thomas, A., Chess, S., & Birch, H. G. (1968). *Temperament and behavior disorders in children.* New York: New York University Press.

Wampold, B. (2001). *The great psychotherapy debate.* London: Erlbaum.

Webb, J. T., Meckstroth, B. A., & Tolan, S. S. (1989). *Guiding the gifted child: A practical guide for parents.* Scottsdale, AZ: Great Potential Press.

Wilson, L., & Barber, T. X. (1983). The fantasy prone personality. In A. A. Sheikh (Ed.), *Imagery, current theory, research, and application* (pp. 340–347). New York: Wiley.

Winkelman, M. (2000). *Shamanism: The neural ecology of consciousness.* New York: Bergin & Garvey.

chapter 10

The Role of Counseling in the Development of Gifted Students' Actiotopes: Theoretical Background and Exemplary Application of the 11-SCC

by Albert Ziegler and Heidrun Stoeger

Conception of Giftedness

When we assert that an individual is gifted, in essence we are saying that this individual can eventually display excellence in one or more areas. However, how can we substantiate this allegation? First, we must consider which excellent actions an individual may be able to execute at some point in time. For instance, this could be the publication of a successful novel, running 100 meters in less than 10 seconds, or being able to play a difficult musical composition on the violin. Each of these actions demands the command of unique competencies. If giftedness researchers are able to recognize that, with optimal encouragement, such a high level of proficiency can be reached, then we can maintain that we were able to identify a *learning path* for an individual. Put another way, a learning path bridges the distance between the current state of performance and a state that can be referred to as excellent performance (Ziegler & Stoeger, 2004a). Of course, a research scientist cannot merely rely on his or her intuition here; rather, an assessment of this type should be made based on theories of expertise acquisition in a specific domain and a judgment made on a well-founded diagnosis of the *actiotope* (to be defined later) of this person.

This view of giftedness is, in the first place, rooted in learning theory (Ericsson, 2002). It is supported by evidence gained from biographical research (Simonton, 2003; Weisberg, 2003) and expertise research (Ericsson, 2003; Howe, Davidson, & Sloboda, 1998). Indeed, there exists ample documentation of the finding that the time needed to attain the state of excellence is exceptionally long, generally a minimum of 10 years. Allegations of cases in which persons have been able to realize extraordinary achievements in shorter periods of time have proven either to be unfounded or are based on findings attained with methodological practices that are somewhat questionable (e.g., Simonton, 2000). Characteristic of this 10-year interval is intensive practice and training governed by the permanent goal to improve one's own performance. This constant expansion of one's own achievement boundaries can be perceived as being rather arduous and in some cases is found to be aversive, a finding that refutes the cliché that learning is nothing but child's play for the gifted (Howe et al.).

Our conception of giftedness is, in the second place, characterized by a rejection of the customary focus of giftedness research that concentrates on traits—for the most part intelligence—and a shift of interest onto the *actions* of a person. This perspective, at first seemingly unusual, is supported by common intuition. For example, in 1903 Marie Curie was awarded the Nobel Prize for Physics not on the basis of her outstanding talents, but rather on the basis of her actions: "In recognition of the extraordinary services they [Mme Curie and her colleagues] have rendered by their joint researches on the radiation phenomena discovered by Professor Henri Becquerel" (Nobelprize.org, n.d., ¶ 2). In 1911 she was awarded the Nobel Prize for Chemistry "in recognition of her services to the advancement of chemistry by the discovery of the elements radium and polonium, by the isolation of radium and the study of the nature and compounds of this remarkable element" (Fröman, n.d., ¶ 31). At the core of our approach are, so to speak, excellent actions. Therefore, if we ask ourselves, "What was it that put the scientist Marie Curie into the position of making these discoveries?" the answer is not simply her IQ. Her IQ presumably did not change much between the age of 6 and adulthood, and she did not make her discoveries at the age of 6. The answer is rather to be found in a closer examination of her learning path, over which she was able to cultivate a unique action repertoire, which is the competence to execute excellent actions. These actions were recognized with the bestowal of the highest distinctions possible for scientific works.

The third feature of our approach is that it is based on systems theory. In contrast to the dominant focus on individual personality characteristics such as intelligence or creativity, we exercise a holistic perspective and consider the systemic interaction among several components. In our Actiotope Model of Giftedness (Ziegler, 2005) we draw direct analogies to terminology used in biology (biotope) and sociology (sociotope). The term *biotope* refers literally to a living space or place of life. It is largely characterized by abiotic factors such as a brook or a valley. The spatial criterion defining the boundaries is reflected by the ecosystem of the various species that inhabit a specific biotope. Thus, a biotope is the place where a specific biological community is found. The term *sociotope* refers literally to a living space of social entities. Sociotopes also demonstrate a close relationship between the space that is being inhabited (e.g., apartment house, factory, neighborhood) and the social entities that occupy them (e.g., family, employees, neighbors). Thus, a sociotope is the place where a specific social community is found.

An *actiotope*, in contrast, is defined by the actions taken by an individual. In order to ensure that these actions are successful, the individual has access to genetically fixed information, which has been accumulated over the long period of adaptation experienced by the species in the biotope (e.g., breathing, use of speech organs). The individual also has access to information about successful actions, which have been amassed through the generations of social communities, and which have been preserved, developed further, and passed on to individuals in the community (e.g., moral norms, cultural techniques, traditions). In addition to this social and biological knowledge, an individual must acquire a wide variety of further behavioral competencies through learning, in order to be able to function successfully in his or her actiotope. This functioning cannot be enabled by either the wisdom contained in the genes of our species or the wisdom contained in the memes of a social community. In principle, each person seeks out a mix of completely individual niches, in which, over the course of a lifetime, the execution of increasingly more successful actions can be learned. Some of these "niches" are of particular interest for giftedness research when they have at least four things in common: (1) We perceive them as domains that belong together, (2) they appear to be of value in a specific context, (3) a uniform standard of excellence exists that can be used to compare the quality of actions executed in these niches, and (4) excellent actions in these niches are rare. Examples of such talent domains, as they can be designated, are music, athletics, or mathematics. Similar to how we can understand the development of a species or a social entity as the result of a progressive adaptation to the conditions of a biotope or sociotope, in our model we consider excellence to be the result of a progressive adaptation of the actiotopes of an individual to the structures in a talent domain. In the next section we will examine the actiotope of an individual from three perspectives: (1) the component perspective; (2) the dynamic perspective, that is, the (successful) adaptation to a talent domain; and (3) the systems perspective.

The Component Perspective

Conceptually, an actiotope can be reduced to four components: the action repertoire, goals, the subjective action space, and the environment. In the following section we offer a short description of each of these four components, as well as a few descriptive illustrations. The *action repertoire* consists of all actions an individual is essentially in the position to execute at a specific point in time. Of course, a person does not have to execute all of these actions. For example, after one has mastered the task of multiplication, one is in the position to calculate innumerable multiplications. However, over the course of a lifetime, one will have to compute only a small fraction of all of the potential multiplications one can possibly compute.

We know many individuals whom we consider to be gifted who do not, however, execute the actions we think a gifted person is capable of. For example, in the media coverage of German sport events, it is not uncommon to come across the declaration that an athlete "seine Leistung nicht abrufen konnte [did not call up his potential]." A possible explanation could be that these actions were not available to him at this point in time, because the action repertoire is subject to several determinants. An example of this would be fatigue, and another would be that the time difference between his last nutritional intake and the sporting event may have been miscalculated.

In order for an individual to execute an action, he must set a *goal*. Let us use the example of test anxiety here for illustrative purposes. Students with test anxiety, when faced with performance situations, are not only pursuing the goal of executing the actions called for (e.g., the solution of multiplication exercises), they are also pursuing self-related goals (Ziegler & Stoeger, 2004b): They do not want to embarrass themselves, and they do not want to disappoint their parents. For example, it may well be the case that while they were preparing for the examination, the mere thought of embarrassing themselves on the test was so aversive that they were no longer in a condition to formulate the goal of preparing for the examination, and rather procrastinated with the entire process.

An individual has a potentially infinite number of actions at his disposal. Therefore, a *subjective action space* must be constructed out of those actions that represent the most appropriate ways of attaining the goal at hand. In many cases, an individual may have actions in his action repertoire that are "overlooked" and subsequently not chosen for inclusion in the subjective action space. An example of such behavior is illustrated by the number of girls talented in mathematics and the natural sciences (Stoeger, 2004), who, despite objectively high talent levels, do not have the self-confidence to see themselves as being able to act successfully in these subjects.

Another reason that an effective action may not be chosen from the action repertoire can possibly be found in the *environment*. This nonselection can also be examined from several points of view, for example, from the perspective of the biotope (if a test is being taken in a loud environment, the student will not be able to concentrate properly; if the weather is damp or rainy, the track being used by a sprinter will be wet and his or her speed will be reduced) or the perspective of the sociotope (a student may not feel confident enough to contribute during class if the teacher is seen as too stringent; parents who do not support the mathematical engagement displayed by their daughter exercise an influence on her decision to enroll in advanced mathematics courses).

Of particular importance is that sector of the environment we refer to as the *talent domain*, that is, the area in which the individual, following a long learning process, is eventually able to execute excellent actions. The progressive adaptation to the talent domain and the development of an effective action repertoire are the central objects of counseling.

Dynamic Perspective

So far, we have made a static examination of the four components of an actiotope. As already illustrated in the example of Marie Curie, her action repertoire at the age of 6 was by no means sufficient to execute the excellent scientific actions associated with remarkable discoveries in the fields of physics and chemistry. Her actiotope had to be progressively developed. In the Actiotope Model of Giftedness, five aspects of successful adaptation have been specified. By the same token, they can be understood as the prerequisites for successful learning, as well as the conditions forming the foundation for effective interactions with the talent domain, which permit increasingly more efficient actions in the talent domain.

In order for an individual to be able to act in a talent domain effectively, he or she must first be in the position to determine which action will lead to success. Such actions can be retained in reserve or even used as a springboard for the development of further, more successful, actions. In many cases, individuals are not always able to determine whether an action was successful or not. A violin student, who is not playing cleanly and is not able to recognize this fact, will never be able to become a great violinist. When a gifted student does not utilize appropriate learning strategies, and never notices that he is learning inefficiently, he will never attain excellence.

Second, in any situation, an individual must be able to recognize the characteristics that will lead to attaining a specific goal. A basketball player who wants to dribble around an opponent must be able to decide which maneuver will be more effective. When a student is preparing for an oral examination, she should know not to use the techniques that help only in the preparation for a multiple-choice test.

Third, for progressive adaptation to an actiotope, it is also important to be able to engage continual action variations. For example, after 40–50 hours of being occupied in a specific domain, we may reach a satisfactory level of competence, and the phenomenon of arrested performance sets in (Ericsson, 2003). We are now in the position to play chess rather well, or are capable of effectively using a data-processing application on our computer for normal daily practices. Similarly, we often have standard solutions for problems that come up again and again. If an individual wants to improve herself and expands her action repertoire, action variations must be found that will allow for even more effective actions. While most chess players are satisfied with their action repertoires rather early in the course of their association with the game, chess experts are constantly expanding their repertoire of opening moves and are continually searching for better moves for specific positions. In other words, they actively want to find better actions in their talent domain. Similarly, programming experts are not satisfied with standard algorithms, but rather are always on the lookout for newer, better algorithms. Even when stronger chess moves or better algorithms have been found, the attempts at adaptation are by no means ended: Neither the game of chess nor the field of computer science ends with the next best solution. Experts in these areas will always be propelled to search for better action variations.

During the long course of developing an actiotope, unexpected barriers can come to light, such as performance limitations or critical events. Fourthly, an actiotope must therefore also be anticipative in order to be able to overcome the various types of barriers that can crop up. When, for example, we suggest that a student should transfer to a boarding school for gifted children, we must also be sure that the student has the social competencies at his or her disposal to cope with a prolonged separation from his or her family. When a theoretical physicist is not able to make progress with a specific problem, this may be due to the fact that she erred in anticipating future math challenges while attending college and did not take the appropriate mathematics courses.

In many talent domains the achievement standard is extraordinarily high. Feedback on the success of an individual action is by no means sufficient. Throughout, to the attainment of excellence, adaptations of the actiotope necessitate effective feedback and feed-forward loops. A good example here is the specific trainings developed to improve self-regulated learning. Although students usually have access only to test results to determine whether their learning was successful, the students attending our training (Stoeger & Ziegler, 2005) in the subject of scholastic mathematics were to complete small tests/quizzes on a daily basis over a period of several weeks, on which they could attain a maximum of 10 points. These tests were conceptualized to correlate with the usual difficulty and learning progress experienced by average students in their corresponding grades. The students in our study were able to try out several types of learning strategies over the course of the training and were then able to perfect them. Furthermore, they had access to a feedback loop: They could determine how effective a specific learning strategy was (or was not) by the test associated with this strategy. If the test results declined, they knew that the learning strategy either needed to be improved or was inefficient. In effect, these feedback loops permitted a constant adaptation of the learning behavior of the students, which led to better and better performances. Exceptional feedback loops can be found, for example, in the interactions cultivated with mentors, or in interactions with trainers who have often spent years filing away at the small imperfections of their trainees.

System Perspective

Over the course of the long learning process leading to the attainment of excellence, not just one single ability is developed. The most prominent characteristic of this lengthy process is how the components of the actiotope coadapt to one another as a result of successful dynamic interaction with the environment.

Indeed, it is by no means accidental how the action repertoire, subjective action space, goals, and environment of the former World Chess Champion Bobby Fischer interacted at the peak of his career. At the age of 8, Fischer's adaptation to the domain of chess was characterized by studies he was making of reigning chess greats, becoming acquainted with their solutions. The solutions they developed provided him with the first effective expansions of his action repertoire. Each additional expansion of his action repertoire also led to coadaptations. For example, he was able to realize which chess-related goals were linked to specific moves and was able to assimilate them. Many of the moves used by the chess masters, which he was then certainly also in the position to execute, had not yet, however, been incorporated into his subjective action space, because he did not assess them as being very efficient. In his environment at that point, he was not being adequately challenged by suitable chess opponents, and for this reason his mother placed an advertisement in the newspaper and tried to find appropriate chess rivals for him.

When Fischer attained the title of world champion, his environment revolved almost totally around chess, and his daily training partners were among the strongest players in the world. Coadaptations were obvious at several points. When, for example, an effective action to counter a unique opening was missing in his action repertoire and he wanted to be able to execute it in his next tournament, his goal was to expand his action repertoire. He was then able to consider how appropriate specific action variations were for inclusion in his subjective action space and was able to discuss and develop potential action variations for this opening with the numerous chess masters who were now a staple of his environment. Furthermore, from another perspective, his actiotope as world champion allowed for a rather remarkable coadaptation. The fact that he was a professional chess player and was able to make a living from the proceeds of this sport enabled him to devote time to improving this opening instead of having to work in more conventional employment, such as in a factory.

In order for an actiotope to undergo an adaptation, it must, of course, be subject to modification. Fischer was a trailblazer in the struggle to secure better payment for professional chess players. The actiotope of a so-called "state amateur" in the Soviet Union would have been much easier to modify, because these individuals received payment for 8 hours of chess training per day. However, this status was not possible in the United States at that time. Therefore, when a learning path has been identified for an individual, we need to determine whether a coevolution among the individual components of the actiotope, necessitated by the learning path, can occur. For example, would an individual, in response to a successful learning phase, be able to formulate new goals so that the next learning phase would also be appropriate and productive? Are better trainers, mentors, training partners, or even a better school available, should the current environment not be able to guarantee the optimal conditions required to nurture the individual? The degree to which an actiotope can be modified is in this sense an important area to address in counseling.

One also needs to address the question of whether these often time consuming modifications in an actiotope pose a threat to the stability of the actiotope. The actiotope of an individual on a learning path is not in a state of equilibrium, but rather operates in an unbalanced state. In the field of systems theory, it has been shown that in physical or biological systems this state of unbalance can function only when a form of energy is constantly being fed into it. An application of this aspect into the theory of the actiotope is, however, beyond the scope of this chapter. Instead, we would like to offer two points as examples.

In almost all cases, a strong motivation is necessary to support and maintain the adaptation of an actiotope and the lack of equilibrium associated with this process over long periods of time. Sometimes the environment of the gifted individual is organized in such a manner that alternative actions other than adaptations in the talent domain are more or less unavailable. Recently, we inspected a boarding school for highly gifted students. Extracurricular activities organized by the school were primarily associated with learning activities, such as a well-stocked and inviting library, or special interest groups, which were devoted to learning topics. The students attending this boarding school could and should learn. Common chores (e.g., shopping for groceries) or minor social conflicts were removed from their daily experiences and executed or resolved by attentive, specially trained educational specialists. Social conflicts, for example, were discussed in group meetings and, when they appeared to threaten learning progress, professional countermeasures were undertaken. The entire environment was completely focused on making optimal learning progress and success possible over a long period of time, as well as ensuring the stability of an actiotope in the academic area, which was in a constant state of adaptation.

In many of the cases we encounter as counselors, developing an actiotope is met with resistance, and the stability of the actiotope is thereby endangered. Envious peers of a student who is able to expand his or her action repertoire quickly, teachers whose self-confidence is threatened by intelligent pupils, or parents who do not want to contribute their share in enabling the development of an actiotope (e.g., purchase of proper learning material, fees for better schools, transportation to training camps) are all examples of how coadaptations can fail and thereby endanger the stability of an actiotope in a developmental state to the point that further adaptations may no longer be possible.

Conception of Personality

The Actiotope Model of Giftedness differentiates itself from other models of giftedness through its emphasis on actions and its systemic approach. Accordingly, traits are theoretically replaced here by the components of the actiotope and their dynamic interaction. We would like to illustrate this model with two examples.

Traditionally, intelligence has been considered to be a central attribute in the personality profile of a gifted individual (Gagné, 2004; Sternberg, 2003). Typically the quantitative magnitude of this characteristic is determined on the basis of IQ: Persons are considered to be gifted when their IQ surpasses a specific cut-off point. In the Actiotope Model of Giftedness, in contrast, it is the actions an individual can execute that are of prime interest. When a student with a high IQ sits in a mathematics class bored to distraction and begins to daydream, although this student may have attained a high score on an IQ test, in this very situation the student, metaphorically speaking, makes no use of any of his many IQ points. In other words, in this situation he is not engaging in any of the mental actions in the action repertoire that would be relevant for the improvement of his mathematical abilities. In some ways, this action perspective is related to the differentiation made by Ackerman and Heggestad (1997), who distinguished between intelligence as maximal performance and intelligence as typical performance. The IQ may be a good indicator of the richness and effectiveness of an action repertoire, but is in no way a guarantee that effective actions will be executed. The phenomenon of underachievement teaches us a different lesson. To make full use of the action repertoire, the individual must pursue the appropriate goals, be able to represent appropriate actions in the subjective action space, and be in position to execute these actions in the surrounding environment.

Our second example deals with the theme of perfectionism, a construct that several researchers in the field of giftedness view as a personality trait, and which seems to be more prominent among gifted students than among those with average abilities (Dixon, Lapsley, & Hanchon, 2004; Flett & Hewitt, 2002; Speirs Neumeister, 2004). Usually, perfectionism is defined as a meticulous pursuit to reach excellence, which is often linked to maladaptive consequences (Blatt, 1995; Hewitt & Flett, 1991). From the perspective of the Actiotope Model of Giftedness, perfectionism is once again not considered to be a personal trait, but is rather seen as an aggregation of frequently demonstrated behavioral patterns. In this case, it is clear that the goals a person is pursuing lead to the frequent selection of "perfectionist" actions located in the individual's subjective action space. Because the actiotope at a specific point in time can be seen as the result of an adaptation to a specific environment, one would obviously want to find out how a preference for such perfectionist actions is generated in the first place. Simply to call an individual a perfectionist does not really help much in understanding such actions and is no more than a reification, that is, treating a common attribute of actions as if it were a real, concrete thing, namely a trait.

Instead of personality, the components of the actiotope move, as a *system*, into the middle point of counseling. In order to fully understand this shift, one must keep in mind that the actiotope is not to be seen as a static entity, but must rather be considered within its dynamic adaptation to a talent domain. The question as to whether there is a distinct personality associated with being gifted does not make much sense from the perspective of the Actiotope Model of Giftedness. A better formulation would be to assert that distinct actiotopes are associated with being gifted: those for which an extreme adaptation to a talent domain is possible and for which a learning path, which leads to excellence, exists.

Model of Counseling

Systemic approaches have proven to be extremely fruitful in the fields of psychological counseling (e.g., Mikesell, Lusterman, & McDaniel, 1995) and coaching (e.g., Kilburg, 2000). One point they have in common is that they consider human behavior to be the result of complex interactions between persons and their environment (Doherty, 2000). Actions cannot be isolated from stabilization and self-reorganization of many components, among them, for example, goals, entities from the environment, and other actors, such as teachers, parents, and peers, who are in turn part of larger systems (e.g. classrooms, families). Similar to Csikszentmihalyi (1998), we commence with the premise that the mind is not the place where genius can be found. The location of genius is not in any particular individual's mind, but in a system where an individual interacts with a cultural domain and with a social field. Counseling does not concern itself with persons, but rather with *systems*, in our case the actiotope of a person. Accordingly, our definition of counseling of the gifted reads as follows: Counseling of gifted individuals refers to a conversation in a supportive atmosphere, the goal of which is to stabilize and/or modify an actiotope, for which a learning path to excellence has been identified, with the objective of establishing more effective actions in a talent domain.

Two points are worthy of emphasis in this definition of counseling gifted individuals. First, it is *not* the gifted person who is the focus of the counseling, but rather, in accord with our system-based approach, the complex system between a person and the environment in which this person functions. Second, the identified learning path, on which this person is already moving or intends to move, builds the framework for the counseling. Counseling gifted individuals is, in this respect, not statically fixed to a single moment in the life of a

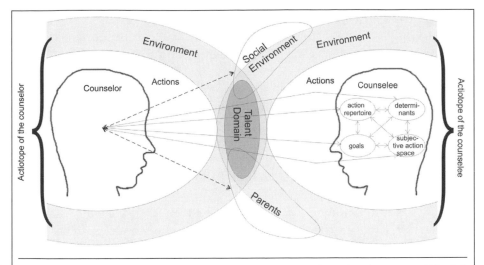

Figure 10.1. Model of a counseling situation based on the Actiotope Model of Giftedness

gifted person, but rather corresponds to the dynamic of the development of this person's actiotope in the talent domain.

A counseling session does not have to address only the person whose actiotope is to be further developed to ensure that excellent actions will be enabled. In either private sessions or group sessions, counselors meet with parents, teachers, or trainers who can offer advice or suggestions. These persons are often capable of serving in the role of counselor. The following will, however, be directed at the practice of professional counseling, which is conducted by qualified and trained persons.

The Basic Model of a Counseling Situation

Our basic model of a counseling situation is depicted in Figure 10.1. It illustrates that at least two actiotopes are in interaction with one another, that of the counselor and that of a counselee. The counselee is a person for whom a learning path to excellence needs to be identified. The contact point of the two actiotopes is located in the talent domain. Here a connection develops between the competence of the counselor in fostering the evolution of actiotopes toward excellence and the interest the counselee, who wishes to develop his or her actiotope toward excellence, has in counseling. During this developmental process, the counselor pays close attention to all components of the actiotope (i.e., the action repertoire and its determinants, the subjective action space, goals being pursued, and the environment). The ultimate goal of the counseling is the coevolution of these components to a point in the developmental process at which excellent actions can be executed.

The 11-SCC Within ENTER

The quality of a counseling program depends on the quality of the diagnosis to which it is responding. We have elsewhere (Ziegler & Stoeger, 2004a) presented a model for the identification of giftedness. Here we would like to reiterate the characteristics on which this model is based. Our ENTER Model differentiates itself from other identification models in that the intention of the model is not to classify a *person* as being gifted. The aim is much more concerned with locating a *learning path*, which allows the actiotope of this person to evolve to excellence. Counseling gifted clients should be integrated in ENTER.

ENTER is an acronym made up of the first letters of the words Explore, Narrow, Test, Evaluate, and Review, which refer to the five phases of the diagnosis. In the Explore phase, a general inquiry regarding the actiotope of a person is conducted. In the next diagnostic phase, Narrow, the analysis of the actiotope is limited to potential possibilities for development to excellence in concrete talent domains. In the Test phase, attempts are made to specify a learning path (i.e., a concrete plan is drafted with the counselee, and solid behavioral steps are specified).

Should the learning path successfully arise, the next two phases of ENTER serve as quality checks. The aim of Evaluate is to determine whether the learning path proposed had been successfully implemented. Review takes a critical survey of the learning path itself and compares it to possible alternative learning paths. Although a suggested learning path could lead to success (e.g., a talent program could be successfully completed), it is entirely possible that, in hindsight, an alternative promotional measure may have become even more promising (e.g., an alternative talent program that the diagnostician only later became aware of). This final step of ENTER serves primarily to improve the action repertoire of the diagnostician.

We would at this point like to illustrate briefly the five phases of ENTER with a problem that often arises in our counseling center, Landesweite Beratungs und Forschungsstelle an der Universität Ulm (State-wide Center for Counseling Gifted Clients and Research at the University of Ulm). For many parents, the decision as to whether their child should skip a school grade is extremely serious and difficult. In order to be able to answer this question, we first examine the actiotope of the child in the Explore phase, that is, (a) the four components of the actiotope, (b) the aspects of dynamic adaptation, and (c) the related stability and inclination to modification. In the next phase, Narrow, the diagnosis concentrates on the academic area for which counseling regarding skipping a grade has been requested. In particular, we examine various learning paths that might be able to help the pupil to compile a more effective academic action repertoire. Therefore, the investigation seeks to determine not only whether grade skipping would be possible in this case, but also whether skipping this grade would be the most effective and appropriate form of encouragement available. Let us assume the following. In the Test phase, we

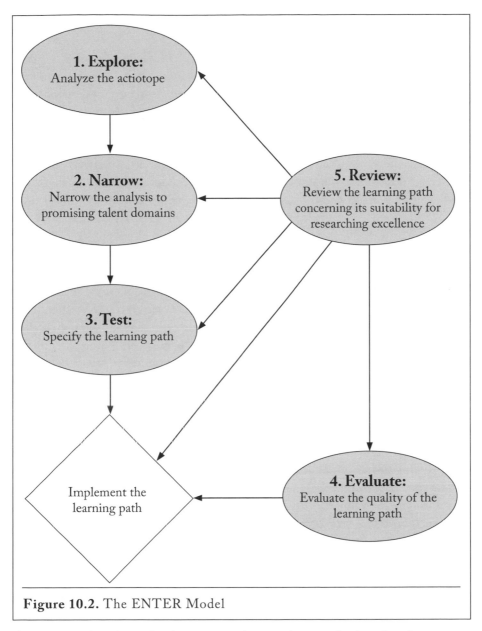

Figure 10.2. The ENTER Model

determine what form this learning path must have and what the chances are for realization. These conclusions are integrated into the counseling, a process that will be described in greater detail below. In the Evaluate phase, a judgment is made as to whether the grade skipping was successful or not. In instances where this is actually the case, in the last diagnostic step, Review, it may be evident that in retrospect a different learning path may have been able to promise even more success. ENTER, therefore, proposes a process in which not only the counselees, but also the counselors, can further develop an actiotope. An overview of this process is depicted in Figure 10.2.

The 11-Step Counseling Cycle (11-SCC)

In ENTER, counseling is conducted during the Test phase, that is, after potential learning paths have been disclosed. Counseling is at the heart of the Test phase. The goal of this phase is characterized by the mutual development of potential implementations of a learning path by the counselor and the counselee. In our counseling center we orient ourselves on a process that consists of 11 steps, which, if need be, can be cyclically repeated. We named this process 11-SCC, which stands for the 11-Step Counseling Cycle. An overview of the 11 steps is depicted in Figure 10.3. In the following descriptions we will always speak of the counselor in the singular and of the counselees in the plural. This can, in practice, be somewhat different, of course: There may be several counselors and/or only one counselee participating in counseling.

Step 1: Mediation of the Potential Learning Path

The first step is the presentation of the results of the diagnosis. It is important to stay in touch with the original intentions of the counselees. The counselor must always consider the significance of the original counseling goals for all concerned, what the original expectations were, what problems had already been defined, and above all, what differences in opinion came to light.

In the first step of the counseling cycle, as for all of the following steps, as well, the principles of systemic counseling are to be observed, such as establishing a cooperative climate. Because we presume that these principles are known by our readers, we will not address them in the following.

Step 2: Assessment of the Learning Paths by the Counselees

In the second step, the counselees' perceptions of the learning path must be examined carefully. The suggested learning path demands their full cooperation, and potential reservations must therefore be made clear. At this point, counselors often find themselves tempted to minimize or even refute differences in opinion. This is, however, counterproductive. Differences in opinion should certainly be addressed and resolved. Furthermore, it is important to ask the counselees to assess the consequences they could personally experience should the learning path be pursued.

Step 3: Importance of Alternative Goals

Even when a consensus can be reached in Step 2, one should inquire as to whether alternative goals exist, because the existence of such goals could represent an ongoing enticement to abandon the learning path or to pursue it with dampened enthusiasm. Also important here is paying attention to points of both agreement and disagreement. If an alternative goal is identified, and the counselor has reason not to support it, she now has the opportunity to present her arguments. If a consensus still cannot be reached, one is to proceed to Step 11 of the counseling cycle.

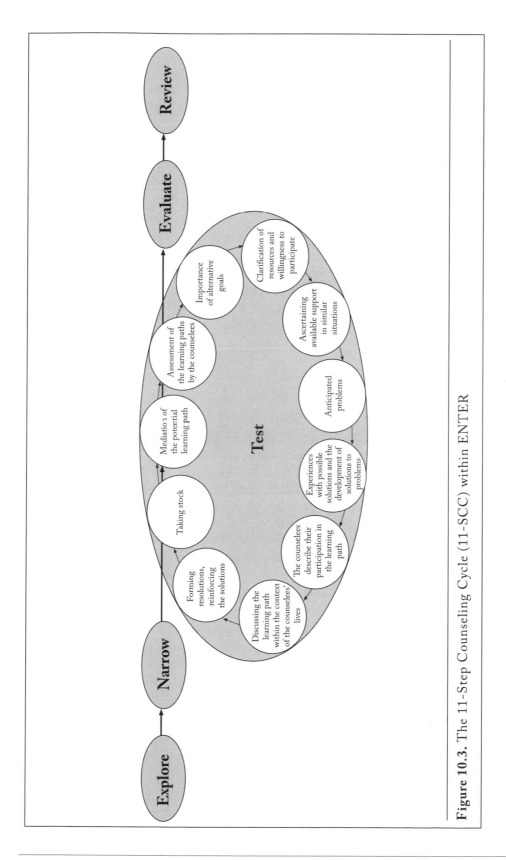

Figure 10.3. The 11-Step Counseling Cycle (11-SCC) within ENTER

Step 4: Clarification of Resources and Willingness to Participate

When the counselor and counselees agree on the merit of the learning path, a detailed survey of the resources available to the counselees, as well as their willingness to participate, must be made. Furthermore, it is absolutely necessary to ask the counselees to identify other people's expectations of them and the significance they ascribe to these expectations.

It is also helpful to find out which steps they are planning to take. It is not uncommon to observe counselees acting unilaterally, whereby they undertake steps that are less than functional. For example, counselees often set extra goals for themselves that are extremely high and next to impossible to attain, which in turn can only lead to disappointment. Finding out their plans can help prevent inappropriate or counterproductive behaviors.

Step 5: Ascertaining Available Support in Similar Situations

Usually, the counselor takes pains to develop learning paths that can best be integrated into the actiotopes of the counselees. Typically, counselors have already had experiences with similar actions. Being aware of such actions can help the counselor to have insight about the chances for success of this learning path. When, for example, parents in similar situations have demonstrated little or no support for their child, or were not able to come to terms with similar situations involving their child in the past, it is important to determine whether solutions for these problems were sought and to find out why they did not work.

Step 6: Anticipated Problems

A new learning path almost always calls for significant adjustments in the actiotope. For this reason, counselees are asked to anticipate what types of problems they might face on the intended learning path. It is also important to know who might become involved, should a problem actually arise; how the involved persons might react; and what types of effects the problem might have on those involved and others.

Step 7: Experiences With Possible Solutions and the Development of Solutions to Problems

It may well be that the counselees already have encountered problems similar to the anticipated problems and have already generated plausible solutions. Discussing these topics is often a useful starting point for developing a repertoire of suitable reactions, which itself is the aim of this step.

Step 8: The Counselees Describe Their Participation in the Learning Path

It is vital that the participants formulate a concrete description of their participation in the learning path. Here the counselor must ensure that this description includes concrete action: Who does what, where, when, and how needs to be specified. This step serves to help the counselees recognize unrealistic plans and to remove any possibility of internalizing them into the actiotope. If this process is not successful, one must return to Step 4. When repeated attempts to work through Steps 4–8 are not able to produce a promising solution, one must move on to Step 11.

Step 9: Discussing the Learning Path Within the Context of the Counselees' Lives

The counselor must be completely sure that he is merely presenting a potential learning path: Counselees must decide to pursue this path themselves, based on information gathered and processed during sessions without being influenced by others, including the counselor. Yet consideration must be given to the effects generated by the decision to follow this learning path on all those involved. For example, if changing schools is appropriate, old friendships may no longer be maintained. Are the counselees willing to pay this price? What could help them manage this transition? It is extremely important, in the interest of serious counseling, that the counselor exert no pressure on the counselees at this point.

Step 10: Forming Resolutions, Reinforcing the Solutions

If a decision is made in favor of the learning path, the counselor should then require the counselees to formulate resolutions (Gollwitzer, 1999). The counselor reinforces these resolutions, and in some cases she may need to insist that the counselees further develop their resolutions if she finds them to be flawed. In certain circumstances, a return to Step 9 may be warranted.

Step 11: Taking Stock

To conclude, the counselor takes stock of the counseling sessions as a whole. Specifically, she reiterates all parties' intentions or explains why a consensus regarding a learning path could not be reached. All who are involved agree as to how the process will proceed. Steps 1–10 of the counseling cycle may have to be repeated—and in extreme cases, a return to the Explore or Narrow phases of ENTER is needed.

The 11-SCC must be completed in full at least once before a learning path can be entered. Counseling, however, should be a continuing process in which an individual receives help and support in either stabilizing his or her actiotope or, in the case of attaining excellence, altering it. After the learning path has been implemented, there is no reason that the counseling cycle cannot be reaccessed if needed. Counseling should come to an end only when the counselor determines that he or she is not able to contribute further or that the counselor's capacity role can be delegated.

Application

With a case that surfaced in our counseling center, we demonstrate the application of the 11-SCC in the framework of ENTER. Clients contact our counseling center either by telephone or electronically by e-mail, upon which we return the call. The first encounters are fairly standard. In addition to personal data, we make an initial appraisal to see whether the case is appropriate for the services our counseling center provides. Furthermore, we set a preliminary goal (Ziegler & Stoeger, 2004a). A case to be undertaken by our center must fulfill two requirements, which we address as counselee criterion and issue criterion.

- *Counselee criterion.* Indicators of giftedness must be present, or, in the framework of our approach, there must be indications that excellent performance in an area is possible.

- *Issue criterion.* The situation that precipitated counseling and the ultimate counseling goal must have either the stability or the modification of the actiotope (or both) in the talent domain as its objective.

The second criterion is rather broad, because in a systemic understanding of an individual, all psychic dynamics bordering on the talent domain will be affected. Many occasions for counseling, such as problems with siblings, peers, or teachers, although they do not appear to be directly linked to the talent domain, can, however, exercise an influence on the stability of or the ability to modify the actiotope in the talent domain. However, for a case to be accepted by our counseling center, it is crucial that the client does not see the solution to such problems as an end in itself, but rather in terms of a development within a talent domain. If this is not the case, then the case is transferred to a counseling center specializing in child or juvenile issues.

In the case we selected to discuss here, the mother contacted our counseling center by telephone. She related that she was a member of a support group for parents of gifted children. Her son was 16 years old and had already been tested for ability at a counseling center for gifted children at the age of 11. The results had been positive enough that he was advised to skip a grade. Later, he skipped a second grade and was attending the 12th grade of a German public college-preparatory high school (Gymnasium). He was scheduled to take his college-entry examinations in 17 months. As a general counseling goal, the mother expressed a desire to receive general information about how to best support and develop her son's talents.

The information supplied by the mother met the two criteria of our counseling center for accepting a case: (1) In light of the prior testing results and exceptional academic performance, we thought it feasible to find a learning path for the son that would lead to excellence in a talent domain; and (2) The mother's expressed intention was a modification of her son's actiotope with respect to excellence.

Because our counseling cycle is tightly integrated within the ENTER Model, we will first summarize the most important results of the Explore and Narrow phases of the diagnosis. Diagnostic sources were as follows:

- Two 16-page standardized questionnaires, which contained both multiple-choice questions and open-ended questions and an initial screening. The questionnaires were mailed to the parents and to one of the son's teachers (identified by the parents). The parents filled out their questionnaire together. Addressed in the questionnaires were state of health, general development, achievement development and current state of performance, indicators of giftedness, learning behavior, learning environment both at home and at school, indicators of instability in the actiotope, interests, social relationships (family, peers, school), and extracurricular activities. In addition, we asked the parents and their son to detail the course of a typical week both when school was in session and during school holidays in one-hour units, on prepared forms.
- Two cognitive-ability tests: Cognitive Abilities Test 4-13, (CAT 4-13; Kognitiver Fähigkeitstest 4-13, German adapted version by Heller & Perleth, 2000); and Standard Progressive Matrices (SPM; German adapted version by Heller, Kratzmeier, & Lengfelder, 1998).
- Ulmer Motivation Test Battery
- Ulmer Learning Style and Learning Strategy Test
- School records (e.g., scholastic)
- Interview with the son
- Interview with the mother
- Telephone interview with the math teacher
- Telephone interview with the expert adviser to the selection committee for the team representing Germany in the Mathematics Olympics

The results of the ability testing, performed at age 11, were unfortunately no longer available.

The results of the first two phases of ENTER, Explore and Narrow, which cannot be related here in detail, led to the conclusion that a learning path to excellence in the domain of mathematics existed. The most important grounds for this conclusion were as follows:

- The son's action repertoire contained a broad base of effective actions in the academic area. His scholastic achievements were exceptional and, despite having skipped two grades, well above his classmates. Further indicators of an effective action repertoire in the academic area were his performances on the SPM and the CAT 4-13, where he scored far above the above-average ranges in both cases. On the SPM he correctly solved all tasks, and on the CAT 4-13 he scored more than three standard deviations above the class means.
- The action repertoire in the area of mathematics was exceptional. The scholastic demands in his mathematics courses were child's play for him; he was able to solve all of the tasks on the quantitative subscales of the

CAT 4-13. The mathematics advisor to the selection committee for the German Mathematics Olympics Team confirmed that the mathematical abilities demonstrated by the son were extraordinary. He demonstrated, both during interviews and on questionnaires to assess learning strategies, that he was in command of several very effective learning strategies and that he set appropriate learning goals when studying mathematics.

- The results of the Motivation Test Battery confirmed that the son was highly motivated and pursued ambitious academic goals. The interviews also confirmed that this was particularly true in mathematics. Concurrent goals existed primarily in the area of music. He played the cello and the piano, sang in a choir, and was involved with the school orchestra. Social goals were less prominent; he was less interested in socializing with friends.

- The action repertoire was well represented in the subjective action space (e.g., with respect to how goal oriented the actions were). The regulatory skills (e.g., affect regulation, action regulation) were well cultivated, especially with respect to learning in the area of mathematics. The attributional style was functional.

- The social environment had a positive influence on learning. The son had access to a wide range of learning opportunities. His parents were in a position to supply motivational, attentional, and material resources necessary to support his learning.

- The actiotope was characterized by ample stability, and all components of the actiotope appeared to be well coadapted. We could not detect problems or conflict fields that may have posed a threat to the stability of the actiotope.

- Various factors indicated favorable conditions for modifying the actiotope with respect to excellence in mathematics: the good coadaptive qualities among the components of the actiotope, the motivation demonstrated by the son for mathematics, the engagement of the parents, and the access to existing resources.

- The five adaptive functions needed to successfully realize a learning path, however, were not guaranteed. Although several beneficial skills had been developed (e.g., good computer programming skills, indispensable in anticipating an actiotope for a career in mathematics), they were not sufficient for the extended processes that were imminent. We made a decision to work together with the parents to determine how the five adaptive functions could be best installed.

The promotional goals we suggested were brought up over the course of the 11-SCC. However, because the entire five-session counseling process lasted almost 22 hours, we will offer only a summary here. Participants were the son, the mother, the father, and, at various points, the authors. These sessions were conducted in part as group sessions and in part as individual sessions.

Furthermore, we made telephone contact with a professor in mathematics who had previously demonstrated interest in mentoring. He was also given access to the results of the earlier diagnosis and a description of the learning path. In response, he reiterated his interest in acting as a mentor.

Step 1: Mediation of the Potential Learning Path

First, we revealed the results of the diagnosis and discussed them in detail. During sessions and discussions with the counselees, we avoided technical terminology as much as possible, except when it became absolutely necessary to use it (e.g., when reviewing the results of the IQ tests). In particular, we completely avoided unfamiliar terms from the Actiotope Model of Giftedness. When these terms are mentioned in the following summary, it is only to justify suggestions that we made to the counselees. In fact, in discussions with the parents, these terms were paraphrased with language understandable to counselees.

The counselees had several questions that were clarified at this time. For example, they were not sure what attributions were and what types of attributions were functional. In conclusion, we indicated to the parents that we believed it plausible that their son could attain excellence in the field of mathematics. We outlined a potential learning path. The main elements of this path were the following:

1. striving toward a career in the field of mathematics;
2. developing a learning plan for mathematics that included, among other things, reducing the engagement associated with preparations for the Mathematics Olympic Team;
3. increasing the amount of time spent with mathematics;
4. attending university courses before finishing high school;
5. constructing a social network in the domain of mathematics;
6. improving the abilities associated with self-regulated learning; and
7. flanking these measures.

All measures were presented in tandem, with detailed explanations, which will be sketched out below, along with other background information.

1. Because excellence in mathematics appears to be an attainable goal for the son, it made sense for him to choose a career in this domain. Learning could be framed as preparation for this occupation. Our counseling center would assist in planning the learning path and support the candidate until doctoral studies, which would begin in 5.5 years. The learning path would be devised so that excellence should have been attained by that time. Afterward, the doctoral advisor would assume further support, or the son himself would be in a position to further develop his actiotope.

2. It has been pointed out that developing achievement excellence requires goal-oriented, well-planned, systematic learning. In this case, the parents benefited from an illustrated explanation of the concept of deliberate practice

(Ericsson, 2003) and were made aware that deliberate practice does not refer to the time spent dealing with the domain of mathematics, but rather simply to systematic expansion of one's own boundaries. In these explanations, we emphasized that the daily amount of deliberate practice a person is capable of executing is limited to a few hours. In this regard, it is important that when planning daily learning activities, one must not only choose the best possible learning methods, but also the subject matter with the most potential to ensure optimal movement toward excellence in the area of mathematics.

We related the outcomes of the two telephone calls with the expert advisor to the selection committee of the Mathematics Olympics and the mathematics professor, who both verified that solving mathematic problems for the Olympics Team involves a special type of expertise. However, this expertise is only slightly similar to what a mathematician who has attained a state of excellence has. For example, the mathematical content of the Olympics tasks are not representative of the types of problems a mathematician must grapple with, because one prerequisite for the problems used in the Olympics is that they be grounded in the curriculum being covered in corresponding mathematics courses at school. In addition, the approaches used to solve these problems, for each of which a solution can always be generated, are little like the usual day-to-day work of mathematicians. The recommendation here was, therefore, to reduce the focus on participation in the Mathematics Olympics and to direct it instead toward systematically developing competencies associated with the tasks of a mathematician.

3. We presented a brief overview of research regarding the amount of practice individuals need to be able to execute excellent actions. (According to Simonton [2003] approximately 10 years, that is, about 10,000 hours of deliberate practice is needed.) According to our estimations, in addition to the amount of the son's prior deliberate practice in mathematics, at least 7,000 hours were necessary to be able to generate excellent achievements on an international level. These hours could be accrued before beginning doctoral studies in approximately 5.5 years (assuming an average of approximately 3.5 hours of deliberate practice daily during the next 1.5 years at school and 4 years of undergraduate studies).

4. As a measure that could be implemented immediately, we suggested that he begin attending university courses before finishing high school. These courses did not need to be mathematics courses and could include courses mediating secondary competencies in line with an anticipative actiotope, such as in computer science or English-language courses, because mathematics is an international science with English as the common means of communication.

5. We suggested forming a social network in the field of mathematics. It seemed particularly important to us that a mentor be made available. This mentor could help to plan learning steps with appropriate subject matter and to integrate the counselee into the scientific community surrounding mathematics (e.g., by pointing out potentially interesting lectures and introducing the student to the culture of journal publication). Above all, he would benefit from the feedback loop pertaining to individual learning growth. The counselees were informed that a mathematics professor had showed interest in becoming a mentor in this case.

Furthermore, we suggested that a network be formed with age peers who also had the goal of improving their competencies in mathematics. Potential members could be identified from preparation courses for the Mathematics Olympics, but could also include other university students with whom both learning and social circles could be established.

6. We offered to have the coworkers of the counseling center assist the son in improving his self-regulated learning skills so that the son would be able to control many of the learning processes in mathematics for himself in the future. In order to be able to do this, he would need to have competencies such as self-evaluation of strengths and weaknesses, goal-setting, self-monitoring, and goal-oriented selection of learning strategies, for example (see Stoeger & Ziegler, 2005). We offered to accompany the son during the first 8 weeks of the new learning path and to conduct regular counseling sessions following this period.

7. In conclusion, we pointed out that the measures undertaken could be effectively supported by a series of additional measures (e.g., optimal nutritional intake and sleep patterns). Steps 4–9 of the 11-SCC explain what could be efficiently integrated into the daily routine.

Step 2: Assessment of the Learning Paths by the Counselees

The counselees were able to follow the report of the diagnostic assessment and expressed that it was in alignment with the expectations they had had. We had become aware, in the diagnostic discussions, that a career in the field of mathematics was a goal of both son and parents. They basically assented to the learning path without hesitation (see Steps 3 and 6 for caveats).

The parents expressed reservations only in connection with the mentor and how cooperative he might be. We asked them to put this question aside, as this point would be concretely addressed after reaching consensus regarding the goals of the learning path and the most important measures to be used in attaining these goals. The parents declared that a basic consensus had been reached.

Step 3: Importance of Alternative Goals

In response to the question of alternative goals, the father asked if it was completely necessary for his son to renounce his goal of participating in the Mathematics Olympics. After the counselor asked for his opinion, the son answered that he thought it would be "a great thing" to be able to qualify and participate. However, it was more important to him, in the long run, to be able to reach the highest level of competence. The mother also said that her top priority was to ensure the best support possible for him. For her, the significance of short-term goals was not as high as a potentially long-term and lasting promotion. The counselor repeated that time-consuming efforts to qualify for the Mathematics Olympics would contribute little to the goal of attaining excellence. In addition, he indicated that this activity could also cause time conflicts with university class schedules. He did, however, offer to discuss the matter with the mathematics professor to see whether a solution could be found. In response to these explanations, however, all counselees expressed their preference to stick to the original learning path.

Step 4: Clarification of Resources and Willingness to Participate

We clarified resources and ascertained the willingness of each counselee to participate in individual sessions. We prefer to conduct individual sessions in our counseling center when a consensus appears to be tenuous or when extensive changes in the actiotope need to be made. The latter was likely to occur in this case. Because the father had also indicated brief support for an alternative goal, individual sessions appeared to be appropriate. Steps 4–8 were conducted at first with each of the counselees in individual sessions and later in a group session. In the group session, the counselor reiterated conclusions from each of the three individual sessions and discussed them with the group.

The counselees all demonstrated high levels of willingness to participate and, in response to concrete inquiries, stated that they had ample resources available to them (in particular, time). Using the weekly time planners filled out by the parents, we held individual discussions as to what types of changes would need to take place in daily activities when additional learning time needed to be integrated into these plans. Weekends and holidays received intense focus here.

Of a number of topics addressed, two have been selected to illustrate the detail that was given to planning at this point. We asked all three counselees how the nutritional and sleeping behaviors of the son could be improved, and who would undertake that responsibility for these elements. It was extremely fortunate that not only with respect to these two examples, but also in general, the contributions offered individually and the expectations voiced by the others with respect to these points were in harmony.

Step 5: Ascertaining Available Support in Similar Situations

Earlier explanations here have already made clear that the choice to pursue a particular learning path is related to changes in the actiotopes of the counselees. It is therefore of the utmost importance that none of the modifications will endanger the stability of the actiotopes. For example, we asked the son if he had already had experiences working intensively over a long period of time toward a learning goal, which indeed had been the case for each of the grades he had skipped. The parents were asked to describe how they had supported him during these phases and what the consequences had been for them. These effects were also discussed, when pertinent, with regard to other types of support. Here the points established in the first two phases of ENTER could be observed again, namely (a) that the parents demonstrated a large amount of support and (b) that the son was extremely motivated regarding pursuing learning goals, even when goals called for significant modifications of his actiotope.

How failures had been dealt with during the learning process and how the parents had reacted in such situations were given considerable attention. Although these areas had already been addressed briefly in the first two phases of ENTER, here the topic was covered in greater detail. Here again, as we focused on concrete situations, the parents' high degree of support was clearly evident. Fortunately, in response to failures related to the learning process, the son typically had responded with increased effort.

Step 6: Anticipated Problems

The modifications needed in the learning path could pose a threat not only to the individual actiotopes of the counselees but also to the family system. Although both the father and the son were optimistic that no major problems would arise, the mother reported having reservations. Particularly important to her was to discuss what effect the learning path would have on family life: Would the son still have adequate free time and would he be motivated to spend enough free time with his family? Because the entire family was affected by this problem, during her individual session we asked the mother what her intentions were and which specific problems were causing her concern. We agreed to bring up this point again later in the group meeting and to clarify it at that time (see Step 7 of the 11-SCC below).

The counselor himself brought up some potential problems. Because the father had previously voiced concern as to whether they would be able to find a suitable mentor, but did not actively address this topic in Step 6, he was asked what he expected of a mentor. Because the mathematics professor, in the opinion of the counselor who knew the professor personally, was likely to fulfill these expectations, all agreed to discuss this topic once again in the group meeting. In case further reservations were then raised, the discussion would be postponed to a time when all parties, including the mathematics professor, could meet and clarify details.

Another problem the counselor addressed was a possible move away from the family for university studies, a phenomenon that is not at all uncommon in Germany. Because the son would be only 22 years old when the learning path being implemented would end, and the university was in the same city as the family home, all counselees assumed in their individual sessions that the son would not move out.

Step 7: Experiences With Possible Solutions and the Development of Solutions to Problems

The most important topic of Step 7 was the fears raised by the mother that the learning path could have a negative effect on the family in general. Both of the weekly time plans constructed by the parents were discussed together in session and altered according to the learning path suggested by the counselor. The father and son both saw the potential for detrimental effects on the family life, but declared that they would be willing to take this risk. The counselor noted, however, that the concerns expressed by the mother were justified, because all involved parties agreed that a "risk" potentially existed. If a solution for this potential problem were possible, it should be sought out together before the fact. Because a repetition of the approximately 90-minute clarification of this point is not advisable here, we will limit ourselves to a reiteration of the seven-step solution co-constructed by the family and the counselor:

- The learning path should be implemented as planned.
- During the first 8 weeks of the learning path, the son would receive support from the counseling center to develop self-regulated learning skills, among which are time-management skills, so that the son would also learn how to protect enough free time to maintain family life as it was.
- After 8 weeks (i.e., after the son had improved self-regulating activities through interactions at the counseling center), each member of the family would compile lists of personally negative and positive effects of the learning path. In addition, they would determine whether, in their opinion, the learning path generated an improvement, deterioration, or no change in the quality of their family life.
- After the 8-week period had been completed, all family members would hold individual discussions with an associate of the counseling center, as well as a group meeting, to discuss the lists and to make a final assessment.
- For the group meeting, insofar as this was related to individual counseling issues, the counselor would bring in the mentor.
- If a solution could not be established for a specific problem, the learning path would be altered, if needed.
- The family would conduct discussions on a regular basis, or in response to problems that arose, and, if necessary, a member of the counseling team or the mentor would be called on to participate.

Step 8: The Counselees Describe Their Participation in the Learning Path

The counselees were then asked to describe how they were to participate in the learning path. As previously mentioned, Steps 4–8 of the 11-SCC were first covered in individual sessions, with individual participation roles almost fully clarified. The seven main points of the learning path were discussed concretely with each of the counselees (i.e., what each was to do where, when, and how). The degrees of specificity and accuracy built into the time schedules were very high for the first few weeks so that all parties could draw a clear picture of exactly what kinds of changes were expected.

In the group sessions, all aspects that were anticipated to have consequences for the other counselees were discussed. Each counselee was requested to repeat the resolutions he or she had made and to give the other two family members the opportunity to articulate their reactions to these points.

Step 9: Discussing the Learning Path Within the Context of the Counselees' Lives

In Step 9, the counselor emphasized the effects the learning path would potentially have on each of the participants. Afterward he pointed out that a learning path to excellence was *one* possible option for support. Alternatives were certainly possible, and it was up to the counselees to make the final decision for the suggested learning path to excellence. At this point, counselees almost always inquire as to what alternatives may be open to them, although if they do not, the counselor explicitly points out alternative goals. In this case, a wide range of possibilities existed, for example, a different university major (concrete references were made here to music, as the son had demonstrated a high degree of interest in this direction) or a later entry onto the learning path. At the same time, the counselor made clear that the duty of our counseling center was to supply gifted individuals with competent assistance for developing their gifts to a state of excellence on a learning path. The counselees, after being informed of all aspects of the learning path, which they had forged together, did decide to begin this developmental process.

After the counselor had named the alternative of a university major in music, the mother related that she could also imagine her son pursuing such a path. Although the father rejected this immediately, the son confessed to his mother that he would be open to considering such a move. At this point, the counselor suggested postponing the remainder of the session, recommending that the three counselees give thought to whether they wanted to commit themselves to the proposed learning path. At the same time, they were advised to initiate contact with other counseling centers or with the school guidance counselor. Should they resolve to go ahead with the learning path, they could make an appointment with the counseling center. After only 4 days, the son called the counseling center and stated that the family had decided to work with the learning path. The mother then arranged for a session in which the son, mother, father, and counselor again took part.

Step 10: Forming Resolutions, Reinforcing the Solutions

The counselor requested that each member reveal why he or she had decided in favor of the learning path and repeat their individual goals. The other counselees were asked to express their opinions as to whether these goals were sufficient. Because this was the case, the process moved on to Step 11.

Step 11: Taking Stock

The counselor then summarized all resolutions. The next steps were agreed upon, which, among others, included making an appointment to meet the mentor. It was agreed that the counselor should first meet with the mentor and jointly plan out the learning steps to be taken over the next 2 months. Furthermore, they were to gather information pertaining to suitable university courses.

The counselees stated that they were willing to make immediate contact with the son's scholastic counselor. The aim here was to make an appointment to meet with school officials (those the counselor considered to be appropriate) and both discuss the results of the counseling and determine how they could enable the son to combine continued regular school attendance with university courses. After it was clarified what information was to be supplied to the school officials, the parents were requested to relate the results of this meeting to the counselor as quickly as possible. The counselor agreed to contact the parents immediately following his meeting with the mentor, inform them about what had been accomplished, and plan further steps jointly.

Finally, the evaluation points (i.e., the fourth diagnostic phase of ENTER), were drawn up. These included the meeting after 2 months (already agreed to), at which an analysis would be made as to whether the family life of the counselees was being negatively influenced and if the measures undertaken by the counseling center to improve self-regulated learning had been effective. Further benchmarks of the evaluation were current scholastic records and a good start in university studies, the latter to be determined following the first eight classes. In addition, the family was assured that the counseling center would establish regular contact (approximately every 2 months) with the mentor, in order to alter the learning path if necessary. If alterations had the potential to affect the family, they would be contacted immediately for permission.

Conclusion

The authors invite the readers to compare the first three steps of ENTER and the 11-SCC contained in the text outlined here with the selection and promotion of talented athletes. The idea that a child at age 8, determined to be a gifted soccer player, and offered a 2-hour counseling session, even with the best soccer trainer in the world, would then go on to attain athletic excellence without having experienced further supportive measures, appears to be absurd. However, this is unfortunately exactly what is common practice in counseling centers that advise the academically talented. For young soccer talents, close attention is paid to proper nourishment, regular rest and breaks, adequate sleep, exceptional training facilities, the best trainers, opportunities to play on the best teams, and continuing support over a period of years. In contrast, most counseling centers are content to supply inquirers with only a brief (in most cases only 1 or 2 hours) explanation of possible general interactions. Excellence can hardly be attained when a complete learning path is not carefully planned, down to the minutest of details, and closely monitored.

In the case presented here, the fears expressed by the parents that the learning path would have detrimental effects on family life proved to be unfounded. After a period of 11 months, no signs of this had surfaced. Evaluations indicated that the chosen learning path appeared to be successful. Collaboration with the mentor went extremely well.

However, despite all the planning and investment, learning paths do not offer a guarantee of attaining excellence. Some counselees will grasp opportunities because those opportunities fit with one of their life goals, not because the learning path can lead to excellence.

We sincerely hope that the case study depicted here is also a good illustration of Csikszentmihalyi's (1998) idea, which we referred to earlier, that the mind is not the place where genius and creativity can be found. The location of genius is not in any particular individual's mind, but in a system. Counseling of the gifted is thereby a process, the center of which is not a single characteristic of a person. The ultimate aim of counseling the gifted is the development of an actiotope to the point at which a person is in the position to execute excellent actions in a talent domain.

References

Ackerman, P. L., & Heggestad, E. D. (1997). Intelligence, personality, and interests: Evidence for overlapping traits. *Psychological Bulletin, 121*, 219–245.

Blatt, S. (1995). The destructiveness of perfectionism: Implications for the treatment of depression. *American Psychologist, 50*, 1003–1020.

Csikszentmihalyi, M. (1998). Creativity and genius: A systems perspective. In A. Steptoe (Ed.), *Genius and mind: Studies of creativity and temperament* (pp. 39–64). London: Oxford University Press.

Dixon, F. A., Lapsley, D. K., & Hanchon, T. A. (2004). An empirical typology of perfectionism in gifted adolescents. *Gifted Child Quarterly, 48*, 95–106.

Doherty, W. J. (2000). Systems theory. In A. E. Kazdin (Ed.), *Encyclopedia of psychology* (pp. 536–537). London: Oxford University Press.

Ericsson, K. A. (2002). Attaining excellence through deliberate practice: Insights from the study of expert performance. In M. Ferrari (Ed.), *The pursuit of excellence in education* (pp. 21–55). Hillsdale, NJ: Erlbaum.

Ericsson, K. A. (2003). The acquisition of expert performance as problem solving: Construction and modification of mediating mechanisms through deliberate practice. In J. E. Davidson & R. J. Sternberg (Eds.), *Problem solving* (pp. 31–83). New York: Cambridge University Press.

Flett, G. L., & Hewitt, P. L. (2002). *Perfectionism: Theory, research, and treatment.* Washington, DC: American Psychological Association.

Fröman, N. (n.d.). *Marie and Pierre Curie and the discover of polonium and radium.* Retrieved June 2, 2006, from http://nobelprize.org/physics/articles/curie

Gagné, F. (2004). Transforming gifts into talents: The DMGT as a developmental theory. *High Ability Studies, 15,* 119–149.

Gollwitzer, P. M. (1999). Implementation intentions: Strong effects of simple plans. *American Psychologist, 54,* 493–503.

Heller, K. A., Kratzmeier, H., & Lengfelder, A. (1998). *Standard Progressive Matrices.* Göttingen, Germany: Beltz.

Heller, K. A., & Perleth, C. (2000). *Kognitiver Fähigkeits-Test für 4. bis 12. Klassen, Revision* [Cognitive Abilities Test]. Göttingen, Germany: Beltz.

Hewitt, P. L., & Flett G. L. (1991). Perfectionism in the self and social contexts: Conceptualization, assessment, and association with psychopathology. *Journal of Personality and Social Psychology, 60,* 456–470.

Howe, J. A., Davidson, J. W., & Sloboda, J. A. (1998). Innate talents: Reality or myth? *Behavioural and Brain Sciences, 21,* 299–442.

Kilburg, R. (2000). *Executive coaching: Developing managerial wisdom in a world of chaos.* Washington, DC: American Psychological Association.

Mikesell, R., Lusterman, D., & McDaniel, S. H. (1995). *Integrating family therapy: Handbook of family psychology and systems theory.* Washington, DC: American Psychological Association.

Nobelprize.org. (n.d.). *The Nobel Prize in physics 1903.* Retrieved June 2, 2006, from http://nobelprize.org/physics/laureates/1903

Simonton, D. K. (2000). Genius and giftedness: Same or different? In K. A. Heller, F. J. Mönks, R. J. Sternberg, & R. F. Subotnik (Eds.), *International handbook of giftedness and talent* (2nd ed., pp. 111–121). Tarrytown, NY: Pergamon.

Simonton, D. K. (2003). Exceptional creativity across the life span: The emergence and manifestation of creative genius. In L. V. Shavinina (Ed.), *International handbook of innovation* (pp. 293–308). Oxford, England: Elsevier Science.

Speirs Neumeister, K. L. (2004). Factors influencing the development of perfectionism in gifted college students. *Gifted Child Quarterly, 48,* 259–274.

Sternberg, R. J. (2003). WICS as a model of giftedness. *High Ability Studies, 14,* 109–139.

Stoeger, H. (Ed.). (2004). Gifted females in mathematics, the natural sciences and technology [Special issue]. *High Ability Studies, 15.*

Stoeger, H., & Ziegler, A. (2005). Evaluation of an elementary classroom self-regulated learning program for gifted math underachievers. *International Education Journal, 20,* 261–271.

Weisberg, R. W. (2003). Case studies of innovation. In L. Shavinina (Ed.), *International handbook of innovation* (pp. 204–247). New York: Elsevier Science.

Ziegler, A. (2005). The Actiotope Model of Giftedness. In R. J. Sternberg & J. Davidson (Eds.), *Conceptions of giftedness* (2nd ed., pp. 411–436). New York: Cambridge University Press.

Ziegler, A., & Stoeger, H. (2004a). Identification based on ENTER within the conceptual frame of the Actiotope Model of Giftedness. *Psychology Science, 46*, 324–342.

Ziegler, A., & Stoeger, H. (2004b). Test anxiety among gifted students: Causes, indications, and educational interventions for teachers and parents. *Journal of the Gifted and Talented Education Council, 19*, 29–42.

PART III
Conclusion

chapter 11

Conclusion

by Jean Sunde Peterson

The models chapters in this volume present the perspectives of individuals representing various professional affiliations: school and mental health counseling, counselor education, marriage and family therapy, clinical and counseling psychology, and educational psychology. Given the variety of professional areas, it should not be surprising that influences, definitions, assumptions, goals, and processes vary from chapter to chapter. Yet, in almost every chapter section (see Table 11.1 on pp. 295–299), one might not expect the wide range of perspectives that, in fact, the authors collectively articulate. How giftedness is conceptualized and how counselors, therapists, and psychologists respond to gifted individuals in practice probably reflect varied sources of relevant knowledge: general academic preparation and professional journals; clinical practice; literature, coursework, and conference presentations related specifically to giftedness; and authors' own research.

Conception of Giftedness

Influences

Well-known, foundational figures in the field of gifted education are acknowledged as being influential in forming most authors' conception of giftedness. Besides Lewis Terman and Leta Hollingworth, with the longest history, highly respected individuals in the field who are noted are Joseph Renzulli, Robert Sternberg, Linda Silverman, James Webb, Michael Piechowski, Lawrence Coleman, Barbara Kerr, Nicholas Colangelo, and Françoys Gagné. Kathleen Noble, Roger Taylor, Deirdre Lovecky, Susan Jackson, Jean Peterson, and Sanford Cohn are other influencers mentioned, much of their work specifically related to affective concerns of gifted individuals. Important and influential voices from outside of gifted education are Howard Gardner, Mihaly Csikszentmihalyi, John McAlister, and Volker Thomas. Individuals mentioned in connection with underachievement are Harvey Mandel and Sander Marcus, Sylvia Rimm, Jean Baker, Robert Bridger and Karen Evans, Lannie Kanevsky and Tacey Keighley, Del Siegle and Betsy McCoach, and Linn Pecaut. In addition, learning theory, biographical research, biological and social concepts, and systems theory are identified as influential.

Definition

Authors' definitions of giftedness all emphasize exceptionality and fall generally into two categories: demonstrated behavior and evidence of potential. Boland and Gross focus exclusively on potential in their definition, as does Mendaglio, who also notes that some manifestations of superior intellectual potential are socially acceptable (implying that some are not). Kerr, Peterson, and Mahoney, Martin, and Martin refer to ability; Kerr and Thomas, Ray, and Moon note *levels* of giftedness; Boland and Gross emphasize that giftedness and talent are not synonymous; Saunders refers to qualitative and Thomas et al. refer to holistic definitions; and Ziegler and Stoeger define giftedness in terms of behavioral display. Kerr; Peterson; Mahoney et al.; and Ziegler and Stoeger make giftedness domain specific; and Mendaglio similarly mentions superior intellectual potential with many possible manifestations. Peterson notes that giftedness may be defined differently from culture to culture.

Characteristics

Characteristics of giftedness are generally positive, as presented. Kerr views characteristics as reflecting interaction of individual with environment, and, for Ziegler and Stoeger, characteristics are a dynamic interaction among components of actiotopes. Some characteristics are not routinely found in the literature about giftedness—for example, an "urge to seek," provocative questioning, reflectiveness, ability to conceptualize higher order relationships, nonconforming processing, aesthetic orientation, acute observation, preference for democratically oriented authority, and compassion. Others are more commonly noted, such as sensitivity, perfectionism, mature sense of humor, rapid learning, exceptional memory, well-developed sense of justice, abstract thinking, intuitiveness, alertness, and eagerness.

Assumptions

Authors' assumptions are more related to the enterprise of counseling and are less uniformly positive than the characteristics noted above. Social and emotional complexity, including sensitivities and asynchrony, are seen as playing a role in difficulties. Differentness in terms of ability is potentially related to isolation and poor fit in the educational system, especially at extreme levels of intellectual ability.

Peterson notes that gifted youth are not exempt from personal difficulties, but are not inclined to seek counseling when distressed. Saunders views counseling as potentially helpful for fostering self-acceptance and the ability to communicate feelings. Mahoney et al. focus almost entirely on identity development, offering four pertinent constructs as a framework for counseling. Peterson acknowledges that giftedness is often seen by others in terms of performance. In that regard, Ziegler and Stoeger assert that more than IQ is involved in excellence. They view giftedness as progressive adaptation of actiotopes to a particular talent domain.

Several authors emphasize what gifted persons share with others developmentally, albeit sometimes in "heightened" forms—for example, in regard to dealing with developmental challenges. Peterson and Thomas et al. specifically note that gifted individuals are part of multiple systems and that expression of giftedness is influenced by environmental factors. Saunders views underachievement as rooted in family dynamics. For Kerr, the individual and society share responsibility for the development of gifts.

Conception of Personality

Personality

The authors generally see personality as being distinguished by consistent patterns of relating to one's environment: The patterns reflect an interaction between hard-wired temperament and socialization, with self-concept the result of reflected appraisals and social comparisons and personality affected by life events and circumstances. Mendaglio mentions Dabrowski's perspective as influential on his conception of personality.

Personality of Gifted

The discussions of personality as related to giftedness range from Thomas et al.'s assertion that there is no distinct "personality of gifted" and Ziegler and Stoeger's statement that personality has no relevance to their model, to Peterson's statement that giftedness is an overlay on basic temperament, potentially exacerbating or constraining basic tendencies. Peterson and Boland and Gross note that commonly cited characteristics such as asynchronous development, excellent memory, novel problem-solving abilities, introspection, keen awareness, introversion, perfectionism, overexcitabilities, and cognitive abilities eclipsing emotional development all have impact on personality development and are part of the personality of gifted individuals. Mahoney et al.'s model acknowledges the impact of 12 systems on personality development in gifted individuals, and Ziegler and Stoeger view personality related to giftedness as a high level of adaptation within a talent domain. Finally, Kerr offers a reminder that "giftedness" is socially constructed.

Model of Counseling

Influences

Some authors were influenced largely by major theorists who focused on clinical conceptualization and practice, such as psychologists Carl Rogers, Alfred Adler, Eric Berne, Fritz Perls, James Framo, Harry Stack Sullivan, and, in general, cognitive-behavioral theorists. From the field of marriage and family therapy, Virginia Satir, Michael White and David Epston, and Douglas Breunlin, Richard Schwartz, and Betty MacKune-Karrer are cited as influential. Social scientist Robert Carkhuff is also cited. Of all of these, Rogers, Perls, cognitive-behaviorists, Satir, and White and Epston are mentioned by more than one chapter author in this text. Two authors were influenced by brief, solution-focused, and prevention-oriented approaches.

Authors also note the influence of developmental psychologists, such as Jean Piaget, Erik Erikson, Abraham Maslow, and Kazimierz Dabrowski. Kerr was influenced by shamanic creativity, combined with research-based strategies in psychotherapy. Mahoney et al. were influenced by Stephen and Sybil Wolin's work related to resilience.

Definition of Counseling

Chapter authors define *counseling* with terms and phrases reflecting an interactive, dynamic process; a conversation; a supportive atmosphere; psychological assistance; an exploration; a unique relationship between counselor and client; and skillful use of common therapeutic factors. For Thomas et al., counseling is a process involving experts—clients, who are experts on their own lives, and counselors, with expertise in various areas and techniques. The counseling focus ranges across developmental problems, more effective living, problem prevention, problem containment, and establishing more effective actions in a talent domain.

Counselor Role

The role of the counselor is described along a continuum including educator and model, observer and researcher, relater and reactor, persuader and cheerleader, and guide. Fundamentally, according to Kerr, the counselor is an agent of change—an empowering influence—with the counselor not seen as necessary to the healing process. Peterson notes that being nonjudgmental, empathic, respectful, and validating are important counselor attributes. Mendaglio sees the role of the counselor as progressing from nondirective to directive-didactic. Peterson and Mahoney et al. both note that counselor self-reflection is important, particularly when working with gifted individuals.

Client Role

The role of the client is to be an actively engaged, collaborative participant in the process, according to all authors. The client's role, for Peterson, is to complete homework, reflect and apply insights and new skills, and take initiative. Saunders and Mendaglio emphasize authentic expression of thoughts and feelings, and Mendaglio also notes the value of applying client expertise.

Goals

Goals noted by chapter authors tend to fit into three categories: self-actualization, problem solving, and performance. Several of the mentioned goals fit into the self-actualization category: improved psychological health, increased self-awareness, enhanced skills, enhanced expression of needs, and personal growth. The problem-solving category, in addition to reduction of risk factors and an increase of protective factors, includes improving family communication, unifying parents, developing homework structure, and accepting situations that cannot be changed. Excellence in a talent domain and productivity in the form of academic achievement fit into the performance category.

Relationship

The counseling relationship is discussed as crucial to the process by several authors. In addition, the uniqueness of this relationship is implicit in some comments—for instance, that it is different from other relationships in the client's life in being focused entirely on meeting the client's needs, with regular feedback and potential emphasis on problem solving. It is a collaborative relationship. Boland and Gross note that in the counseling relationship with gifted children, counselors should err on the side of overestimating vocabulary and understanding.

Assessment

Some of the authors employ a variety of assessments in their practice—of family cohesion, adaptability, and environment; of cognitive ability; of personality; of vocational interests. Mahoney and colleagues use his model as an ongoing framework and guide for counseling. Clinical interviews (including of parents), observation, genogram construction, and data obtained from school and clinical records are also components of assessment, collectively. Peterson applies a developmental template on presenting issues, including underachievement, and Boland and Gross use assessment to engage the child.

Process

Four of the authors mention working within a limited number of sessions—ranging in length from Kerr's 1–5 to Mendaglio's 6–12 sessions. In contrast, Saunders uses several sessions to establish trust and generate commitment to the plan. Generally, exploration, including assessment, constitutes the initial 1–2 sessions. However, thereafter, the models vary considerably, including being concerned about not giving excessive attention to presenting issues, sharing perspectives and analyzing situations, initiating a cognitive and behavioral learning phase, focusing on establishing trust, examining the impact of giftedness, beginning construction of a conceptual framework, and narrowing the focus of counseling.

Subsequently, Mendaglio co-constructs a conceptual framework, focuses on goal setting, and moves to an action stage, ending with evaluation and termination. Kerr uses experiential activities to increase arousal, times interpretations to occur before or after peak arousal, and uses breathing and relaxation to reduce arousal. Boland and Gross focus on putting new learning into practice, followed by relapse prevention. Saunders involves both parents in the process, generates predictions, and notes accomplishments. Mahoney et al. focus on the four constructs related to gifted identity, and Thomas et al. stay open to what grows out of the counseling relationship with family members. Ziegler and Stoeger's model consists of 11 stages within the "Test" stage of their process.

Techniques

There are few commonalities among the authors related to techniques. Kerr's here-and-now statements, mind-body techniques, experiments (e.g., visioning), bibliotherapy, and healing ceremonies offer the most varied techniques. Peterson employs a brief, solution-focused approach, externalizing the problem when appropriate, employing semistructured activities, and intentionally focusing on resilience. Boland and Gross employ Socratic questioning, explicit instruction, thought-challenging, confrontation, and exaggeration. With gifted underachievers, Saunders offers instruction in transactional analysis as related to family communication and works collaboratively to establish study routines. Mahoney et al. focus on integrating giftedness into the view of self in various contexts and on nurturing clients' gifts. Thomas et al. employ one of three models, including an imaginative-postmodern approach, which incorporates changing family narratives after generating "thick description." Mendaglio uses confrontation, didactic informing regarding characteristics of giftedness and Dabrowskian concepts, and homework assignments and focuses on enhancing awareness and expression of emotion. Besides individual sessions, Ziegler and Stoeger incorporate group sessions with counselees and significant others in their lives when appropriate.

Application

Presenting Problems

Apparently, for counselors working with gifted individuals, presenting problems are potentially wide-ranging. Depression, anxiety, underachievement, social difficulties, and behavioral problems are mentioned most often by chapter authors here, with drug abuse and adjustment to life events next in frequency. Developmental issues, perfectionism, twice-exceptionality, extreme sensitivity, sexual promiscuity, truancy, Asperger's syndrome, problems with ADHD, thought disorders, school-related problems, and abuse are also noted.

Conclusion

Eight chapters in this volume are a rare compilation of clinical models for counseling gifted individuals. The authors represent a variety of professionals who are involved in some way and in some venue with responding to counseling needs related to giftedness. Their professional backgrounds likely had an impact on who influenced them in regard to both clinical practice and conceptualization of giftedness. They offer a variety of perspectives and approaches to clinicians in various settings, including schools. Collectively, they attest to the importance of being knowledgeable about characteristics associated with giftedness when working with clients with exceptional ability. Giftedness may be an asset, and it may also be a burden—a risk factor in itself.

Highly able children and adolescents often are enjoyable clients to work with (Thompson & Rudolph, 1996). When counselors, therapists, and psychologists are comfortable with gifted individuals, free of biases and stereotypical thinking related to giftedness, and open to entering the complex inner world of young gifted clients, they can likely build a trusting, productive counseling relationship that edifies both professional and client.

References

Thompson, C. L., & Rudolph, L. B. (1996). *Counseling children* (4th ed.). Pacific Grove, CA: Brooks/Cole.

Summary of Author Perspectives

	Mendaglio	Thomas, Ray, & Moon	Peterson	Saunders	Boland & Gross	Mahoney, Martin, & Martin	Kerr	Ziegler & Stoeger
Influences	Terman; Marland; Renzulli; Roeper	Stanley; Feldhusen; Kerr; Jackson; Peterson; Silverman; Colangelo	Taylor; Thomas; Lovecky; Coleman; Piechowski; constructivist teaching; ethnographic research methods	Clark; Stanley; Gardner; Sternberg; Montessori	Gagné; Hollingsworth; Tannenbaum	Hollingworth; Lovecky	Hollingworth; Webb; Gardner; Csikszentmihalyi; Colangelo; Cohn; McAlister; Noble	learning theory; biographical research; systems theory; concepts borrowed from biology and sociology
Definition	superior intellectual potential with many possible manifestations, some of which are socially acceptable	(holistic) various definitions currently available; a family's conception; includes different levels of giftedness	top 2–3% in general or domain-specific ability or talent valued by one's culture; in education, exceptionality warranting differentiated curriculum	(qualitative) precocious understanding and creative application of concepts; underachievement as not producing up to capacity	Gagné's Differentiated Model of Giftedness and Talent: giftedness as outstanding potential, not outstanding performance; giftedness and talent not synonymous	exceptional ability in a variety of areas (e.g., intellect, arts, personal creativity)	the ability to catch on, make sense of things, know what to do about it (Gottfredson); intelligence as a type of motivation; 10% in any domain are bright, 5% moderately gifted, 1% highly gifted	behavioral display of excellence in one or more talent domains
Characteristics	advanced comprehension; rapid information processing; excellent memory; heightened multifaceted sensitivity; self-criticism; emotional intensity	need for complexity and precision; early abstract reasoning; can see complex patterns rapidly; memory; large, complex knowledge bases; different processing; idiosyncratic strategies shape environment	Lovecky's five characteristics (divergent thinking, excitability, sensitivity, perceptiveness, and entelechy)	intense reactions; depth of feeling; acute observations; perfectionism	(highly gifted) reflective, probing, provocative questioning; rapid learning; pattern-perception; memory; dislike of slow-paced work; emotional intensity; older companions; sense of justice; empathy; mature sense of humor	creative, abstract thinker; alert; eager; intuitive; compassionate; independent; sensitive; intense; inventive; nonconforming processor; aesthetic; exploratory learner within preferred styles	the urge to "seek"; interaction of intelligence with personality, brain-body chemistry, arousal capacities; may be the result of interactions of intelligent behavior with the environment	dynamic interaction among the components of actiotopes

	Mendaglio	Thomas, Ray, & Moon	Peterson	Saunders	Boland & Gross	Mahoney, Martin, & Martin	Kerr	Ziegler & Stoeger
Assumptions	possess traits in a heightened form; use of "individual who is gifted" indicates commonalities with others; adjustment problems rarely the result of a lack of knowledge of what is expected	embedded in systems—family, school, and society; genetic-brain foundation; expression of giftedness influenced by environment	complex socially, emotionally; sensitivities may be related to problems; protect image; face same developmental tasks as others; reluctant to seek counsel; counselor biases may interfere	need a reliable relationship to support emotional development and communication of needs; feelings of differentness; no sense of mastery; underachievement rooted in family dynamics	poor fit in educational system; differences most pronounced at extreme levels; internal, external asynchrony; need counseling to increase self-acceptance	gifted identity formation involves four constructs: validation, affirmation, affiliation, and affinity	giftedness is important; development of giftedness is a responsibility shared by the individual and society; gifts "will out"	IQ not sufficient to explain excellence; excellence results from progressive adaptation of individuals' actiotopes to talent domains
Personality	the result of an interaction of temperament and socialization; self-concept from reflected appraisal, social comparison and attribution; personality also from perspective of Dabrowski	enduring patterns of perceiving, relating to, and thinking about self in context; systems approach focuses on perceptions of family members, patterns of interactions rather than personality	Costa and McCrae's inter-related elements; significant fluctuations during adolescence, stabilizing during the 20s	Maslow's (1970) hierarchy of needs applies; personality affected by asynchronous development, life events, life circumstances	trait or characteristic that distinguishes one person from another, and that causes someone to behave more or less consistently	fluid, not fixed; personality cumulative, changes within context of experiences, sociohistorical changes	inherited tendencies, energy and hormonal levels, capacities for altering consciousness; combinations give rise to personalities; hard-wired but not immutable	the concept of personality is replaced by a concept of complex interaction among individuals' actiotopes, biotopes, and sociotopes
Personality of Gifted	tendency to have greater awareness; tendency to resist socialization practices; for some gifted individuals, potential for advanced development in Dabrowskian sense	no distinct personality	giftedness as overlay on basic temperament with ability/talent, hypersensitivity, perfectionism, and drivenness potentially exacerbating or constraining basic tendencies	idiosyncratic; reflects traits such as ability to grasp concepts quickly, excellent memory, novel problem-solving abilities	frustration from asynchrony; enhanced introspection; friendship dilemmas; perfectionism; overexcitabilities; overrepresentation of introversion; cognitive abilities eclipse emotional regulation	12 systems influence personality: self, family, family-of-origin, culture, vocational, environmental, educational, social, psychological, political, organic physiological, and developmental	giftedness sometimes confused with conventional desirability; giftedness is socially constructed, the ability to perform in an outstanding manner in one or more domains of talent	not relevant to the model; replaced with distinct actiotopes with high levels of adaptation to a talent domain

Influences	Rogers; Perls; Ellis; Sullivan; Piaget; Lewis; Dabrowski	family systems; client-centered; cognitive-behavioral; humanistic; solution-focused; narrative; Gestalt	Adler; Erikson; Minuchin, Breunlin, Schwartz, & MacKune-Karrer; Rogers; Satir; White & Epston; Littrell	Carkhuff; Jourard; Maslow; Berne; Harris; Mandel & Marcus; Rimm; Baker, Bridger & Evans; Kanevsky & Keighley; Siegle & McCoach; Pecaut	giftedness and psychological literatures; Miller & Rollnick; Seligman & Csikszentmihalyi; Colangelo; Neihart	Framo; Satir; the Wolins; systems; prevention; client-centered; Gestalt; narrative; solution-focused; cognitive-behavioral; humanistic	Frank; Smith & Glass; Wampold; Winkelman; shamanic creativity combined with research-based strategies	systemic approaches; Csikszentmihalyi
Definition	an interactive process directed by a counselor to provide psychological assistance to clients in areas that they present; counseling is rooted in a unique relationship between counselor and client	a dynamic process between people who are experts about their life and a counselor who has expertise in system, human development, wellness, pathology, diversity, and therapeutic techniques	a process focusing on developmental problems; helping people live more effectively, not feel stuck, make changes, make sense of things, solve their own problems, prevent problems, prevent problems from becoming worse	a unique relationship in which the counselor creates an atmosphere for exploring thoughts, feelings, reactions, and motivation	an attempt to combine evidence-based practice in the treatment of psychological distress with knowledge of the unique cognitive and socioaffective characteristics of gifted children.	a multitude of roles, processes, interventions, and options, based on various theoretical orientations; must account for the variance of the deviation that giftedness represents and the complexity of identity formation	skillful use of common therapeutic factors, not adherence to a particular theory	a conversation in a supportive atmosphere, with the goal of stabilizing and/or modifying an actiotope and establishing more effective actions in a talent domain
Counselor Role	a progression from a nondirective to directive didactic; director of the process; problem solver; educator; encourager of stories; establisher of conceptual framework to view client concerns	changes throughout the process: educator, persuader, negotiator, ally, cheerleader, chairperson (e.g., family, school personnel), observer	self-reflection; entering the world of the client; a developmental focus; being a safe, respectful, nonjudgmental, empathic harbor during difficult times	researcher; reactor; relater; model for parents; supporter during personal exploration	examine factors that may play causal and maintaining roles	self-reflection regarding attitudes toward deviance; a more flexible approach than used with typical clients; validator of client's self-perception and perception of giftedness	change agent, empowering the individual and community to carry out the rest of the process; de-emphasis on counselor as being necessary to the person's healing process	guide counselee through counseling process
Client Role	be an active, motivated participant, an expert on self; provide honest feedback to conceptual framework and assignments	be active, goal oriented, apply own expertise to the process	engage in collaborative work; complete homework; reflect; apply insights and new skills; take initiative to move toward more effective living	participate and authentically express thoughts and feelings	actively engage in problem solving, home-tasks, existential questioning	identify goals, roadblocks, strengths; be truthful; believe in ability to change; change behaviors	engage; display behaviors in the present that are working or not working; resist; struggle; try out reasonable suggestions for changes	participate actively in the process; co-create learning path

	Mendaglio	Thomas, Ray, & Moon	Peterson	Saunders	Boland & Gross	Mahoney, Martin, & Martin	Kerr	Ziegler & Stoeger
Goals	clients solve problems, accept situations that cannot be changed	improve relationships among family members and between family and other systems; change *context* of the problem	increase self-awareness; enhance skills and personal growth	improved self-esteem, autonomy, homework structure, family hierarchy and communication; parents united, mutually supportive; student able to express, understand needs; productivity	independent problem solving and behavioral, cognitive, and emotional change; improved skills; reduced risk and increased protective factors; managed reactions to problems in environment	fulfilling and aligning the four constructs of identity formation; opportunities to utilize gifts; adults working with the gifted from a complex model that reflects the diversity of the gifted population	change in the direction of psychological health and eventual self-actualization; the ability to love, work, and connect with something greater than oneself	co-creation of a learning path to assist a counselee to attain excellence in a talent domain
Relationship	an essential ingredient for effective counseling; uniquely focuses only on meeting client needs; Rogerian conditions used to establish, maintain relationship	a crucial component of family treatment; built with each family member; counselor enters the family system for the duration of counseling	collaborative; built initially through focus on development, pertinent information, and appropriate small talk and humor	different from relationships with teachers, parents, peers	collaborative, active, feedback, problem solving; use of humor; likely to be akin to an adult-to-adult therapeutic relationship; erring on the side of overestimating vocabulary and understanding	a safe and trusted environment for sharing	depends on counselor's ability to build a persuasive, authentic relationship, and client's ability to overcome resistance to change	importance of a good relationship between counselor and counselee implicitly acknowledged
Assessment	interviews, observation, empirical assessment of conceptual framework in client's daily experience	specific to each of 3 models: Belin-Blank Center (family scales); structural-strategic (information gathering); imaginative-postmodern (stories, interviews); other: observation, genogram, personality and vocational tests	developmental template; degree of differentness as related to giftedness; informal, developmental assessment of underachievement	parental and child interviews, feedback on testing, following Mandel and Marcus's (1988) model; developmental terms, not diagnostic label put into report; family dynamics assessed through transactional analysis lens	used to engage the child in therapy; social and developmental history; family assessment; corroboration of psychometric data; diagnostic when necessary; focused on current functioning; goal: a multimodal understanding of client, problem	Gifted Identity Formation (GIF) model	refer to results of intelligence and neuropsychological assessments; reinterpret intelligence tests; conduct personality and career assessment	cognitive ability tests; various personality measures; documents; interviews

Process	6–12 sessions; Conceptual, Action, Evaluation, Termination; initial exploration of problem; then co-construction of conceptual framework; process continues until client objectives met	6–10 sessions; first few sessions similar across clients: sharing perspectives, analyzing situations, being open to what develops; subsequent sessions depend on clients	1–10 sessions; adequate but not extensive attention to presenting issues, frequent punctuating of client narrative; giving all members present a chance to speak; solution-focused mode; early attention to termination	several sessions to establish trust; commitment to plan; generating predictions and noting accomplishments of achievement; involvement of both parents	examining how giftedness impacts overall well-being and development; helping clients feel valued regarding the four constructs in Gifted Identity Formation model	1–5 sessions, with occasional tune-ups; traditional techniques, in addition to ceremonial elements; interpretations timed to occur before, after peak arousal; techniques to reduce, increase arousal	model with five phases: Explore, Narrow, Test, Evaluate, Review; counseling process consists of 11 stages within the Test phase
Techniques	empathy; congruence; nonjudgment; confrontation; didactic concerning affective characteristics of giftedness and Dabrowskian concepts; cognitive restructuring; homework; enhancing emotion awareness, regulation, expression	empathy; Belin-Blank: role-play, consultation with teachers; structural-strategic; joining, working in the present, reframing, boundaries, and alliances; imaginative-postmodern: restructuring stories from thin to thick description; solution-focused techniques; scaling	brief, solution-focused approach; externalizing the problem; focus on strengths, resilience; activities; semistructured small group work	establishing routines for study time, unified parental support, family meetings; suggestions for reading; instruction regarding communication (transactional analysis)	Socratic questioning; explicit instruction; eliciting automatic thoughts and schemas; thought-challenging; point-counterpoint; confrontation; exaggeration; cognitive-behavioral approach	collaboration; focus on integrating giftedness into view of self; on family (in the cultural context) and impact of values, beliefs, traditions; on nurturing client gifts; on exploring the educational environment; group process as vehicle for change	powerful techniques to generate motivation for rapid change; active listening, here-and-now focus, mind/body techniques, experiments (e.g., empty chair or visioning); bibliotherapy; healing ceremonies
Presenting Problems	academic underachievement; social, emotional, and behavioral disturbances (e.g., depression, anxiety, ADHD, Asperger's, oppositional defiance)	children's school-related problems; depression; anxiety; abuse; chemical dependency	developmental issues for both high and low achievers; depression; adjustment in response to life events; underachievement	underachievement; issues presented by young clients indirectly	perfectionism; anxiety; social difficulties; depression; twice-exceptionality; problems related to managing extreme sensitivities	isolation; sexual promiscuity; sexual aggression; stealing or conduct disorder; truancy; drug abuse; drug-selling; anxiety; sexual identity issues; relationship difficulties; depression; thought disorders; adjustment disorders; underachievement	potential counselees need to meet two criteria: evidence of giftedness; precipitating situation relates to dealing with actiotope in a talent domain

About the Authors

About the Editors

Sal Mendaglio is associate professor in the Division of Teacher Preparation and the Graduate Division of Educational Research, and research associate in the Centre for Gifted Education at the University of Calgary, Alberta, Canada. Prior to his current involvement in teacher education, Sal taught counseling psychology in a graduate program for more than 20 years at the same institution. His primary interests are related to counseling gifted individuals of all ages. Current projects include gifted individuals' perceptions of counseling, influence of congregated settings on self-concept of gifted students, and Dabrowski's theory of positive disintegration. Sal is a licensed psychologist with 30 years experience of counseling gifted individuals. He is chair of the Counseling and Guidance Division, National Association for Gifted Children.

Jean Sunde Peterson is associate professor and coordinator of the school counseling program at Purdue University. Before entering the counseling field as a licensed counselor and counselor educator, she was a long-time classroom and gifted education teacher. She is a past chair of the Counseling and Guidance Division of the National Association for Gifted Children (NAGC) and has been a regular presenter at NAGC conventions for 20 years. Her workshops, convention and symposia presentations, and award-winning qualitative and longitudinal research reflect her interest in the social and emotional development and counseling concerns of gifted youth, particularly those populations that otherwise receive little scholarly attention. She is a national award winner in group work, and her books on group work with teens are used internationally.

About the Authors

Catherine Boland is a clinical psychologist who specializes in child and adolescent mental health. Catherine has a background in educational psychology, and she has worked in education, health, and private sectors. Catherine was the clinical psychologist at the Gifted Education Research, Resource and Information Centre (GERRIC) at the University of New South Wales in Sidney, Australia, where she was involved in assessment and counseling of gifted children and adolescents.

Miraca U. M. Gross is director of the Gifted Education Research, Resource and Information Centre (GERRIC) at the University of New South Wales in Sidney, Australia. Miraca is a leading authority on the education of gifted and talented children, particularly in areas of ability grouping, acceleration, socio-affective development, and underachievement. She has won six international research awards in the education and psychology of the gifted, the most recent being the 2005 Distinguished Scholar Award from the National Association for Gifted Children. She is a regular keynote and invited presenter at international educational conferences. She served on the executive council of the World Council for Gifted Education from 1995–1999. Recently, she coauthored a major international report on acceleration titled *A Nation Deceived: How Schools Hold Back America's Brightest Students.* In 2003, she was awarded the Sir Harold Wyndham Medal for service to Australian Education.

Barbara Kerr is Distinguished Professor of Counseling Psychology at the University of Kansas. She received her master's degree from The Ohio State University and her Ph.D. from the University of Missouri, both in counseling psychology. Her research has focused on the development of talent, particularly in women. She has served as the founder of the Guidance Laboratory for Gifted and Talented at the University of Nebraska, associate director of the Belin-Blank National Center for Gifted and Talented at the University of Iowa, and as a faculty member in counseling psychology at Arizona State University, where she was also president of the faculty. She is author of *Smart Girls, Smart Boys, Counseling Gifted and Talented, Letters to the Medicine Man, Counseling Girls and Women,* and more than 100 articles and chapters in the area of talent and creativity.

Andrew S. Mahoney is a licensed professional counselor, marriage and family therapist, and director of Andrew S. Mahoney and Associates, a counseling center for the gifted and talented in Pittsburgh, PA. He is known as a pioneer in the field of counseling and psychotherapy of the gifted and talented. For more than 20 years, he has taught, researched, and developed frameworks for the counseling, psychotherapy, and identity formation of gifted and talented individuals. He is a nationally recognized presenter and practitioner in this specialty area. He has delivered many keynote addresses and conference, seminar, and symposium presentations and has published on the topic. In addition, he has been a long-standing executive board member of the Counseling and Guidance Division of the National Association for Gifted Children and past chair of that division. His work offers new and original perspectives for serving this unique population.

Don Martin is director of the school counseling program at Youngstown State University. He is the author of more than 60 research articles, as well as 4 books. As a licensed neuropsychologist, Don recently directed a large federal 21st-century grant with children of poverty in alternative schools. He has worked with gifted children for more than 30 years.

Magy Martin is director of counseling services at Thiel College and a member of the doctoral psychology faculty at Walden University. She has published more than 35 research articles and 4 books. In her present work, she has developed workshops for faculty in helping gifted college students, and she teaches doctoral psychology students methods in counseling the gifted.

Sidney M. Moon is director of the Gifted Education Resource Institute and associate dean for learning and engagement in the College of Education at Purdue University. She has been active in the field of gifted education for almost 25 years. In that time, she has contributed more than 60 books, articles, and chapters to the field. Her most recent book is *The Handbook of Secondary Gifted Education*. Sidney is active in the National Association for Gifted Children, where she has served as chair of the Research and Evaluation Division and a member of the Board of Directors. Her research interests include talent development in the STEM disciplines (science, technology, engineering, and mathematics), underserved populations of gifted students, and personal talent development.

Karen E. Ray is a doctoral candidate in counseling psychology at Purdue University and completing her clinical psychology internship with the Rappahannock Community Services Board in Virginia. She has been a school counselor and outpatient therapist at a community mental health center in addition to teaching. Her research interests are in social and emotional development, career development, giftedness, spirituality, and attachment theory.

Caryln L. Saunders has maintained a private practice in the Kansas City area for more than 30 years, specializing in evaluating and counseling gifted students and their families. She has taught counseling practicum courses at the University of Missouri–Kansas City and has supervised counseling and psychology interns. She has also taught gerontology courses at Kansas City Kansas Community College. She is a licensed psychologist and a licensed professional counselor. After attending Park University, she completed her B.A. at the University of Kansas. Her master's and doctoral degrees were completed at the University of Missouri–Kansas City.

Heidrun Stoeger is assistant professor at the University of Ulm. She studied psychology and mathematics at the University of Munich (Germany). In 2002, she wrote her doctoral dissertation on motivational orientations, and in 2006, she finished her privatdozent (PD) on giftedness. She is head of the research department at the State-wide Counseling and Research Center for the Gifted at the University of Ulm.

Volker Thomas is associate professor of marriage and family therapy (MFT) in the Department of Child Development and Family Studies at Purdue University, and former director of the doctoral MFT program. He has studied family relationships and interventions in families with gifted children from preschool to high school.

Albert Ziegler is professor of psychology and a director in the Centre of Educational Sciences at the University of Ulm. He has published approximately 200 books, chapters, and articles in the fields of educational and cognitive psychology. He is director of the State-wide Counseling and Research Center for the Gifted. He is also the editor-in-chief of *High-Ability Studies*, one of the most highly regarded journals in the field of gifted education. His main research interests are the development of exceptional performances, motivational training programs, and knowledge acquisition.